A PERFECT MEDIUM?
ORACULAR DIVINATION IN THE THOUGHT OF PLUTARCH

PLUTARCHEA HYPOMNEMATA

A PERFECT MEDIUM?

ORACULAR DIVINATION IN
THE THOUGHT OF PLUTARCH

by

ELSA GIOVANNA SIMONETTI

Leuven University Press

© 2017 by Leuven University Press / Presses Universitaires de Louvain / Universitaire
Pers Leuven
Minderbroedersstraat 4, B-3000 Leuven (Belgium)

ISBN 978 94 6270 111 3
D/2017/1869/29
NUR 735-732

Cover design: Joke Klaassen

A Filippo

Ἐλθὼν οὖν Φίλιππος λοιπὸν ἐκ τῆς ἀποδημίας
ἀπῆλθε τάχος εἰς Δελφοὺς τοῦ χρησμοδοτηθῆναι,
τίς βασιλεύσει μετ' αὐτόν, τίς Μακεδόνων ἄρξει.
Ἡ δὲ Πυθία τῶν Δελφῶν νάματος Κασταλίου
προσγευσαμένη τὸν χρησμὸν φωνεῖ διὰ χθονίου·
«Ἑλλάδος ἄναξ Φίλιππε, καὶ γῆς ἐκείνης ἄρξει
καὶ βασιλεὺς γενήσεται πάσης τῆς οἰκουμένης
καὶ δόρατι τροπώσεται πάντας τοὺς ἐναντίους,
ὅστις αὐτὸν Βουκέφαλον τὸν ἵππον διοδεύσει,
ἐπάνω προσκαθήμενος χωρὶς τῶν χαλινίων.»

*Historia Alexandri Magni, Recensio Byzantina
poetica,* 692-701

Contents

Acknowledgements

If my dissertation, discussed in 2016, has now become a book, this is also due to the encouragement of many people.

My first and deepest thanks go to my home university, Università degli Studi di Padova, and particularly to my co-supervisor Maria Grazia Crepaldi, for having promoted and supported my doctoral research, while constantly pushing me beyond my limits.

Jan Opsomer, despite knowing very little of me, accepted to act as my co-supervisor and allowed me to spend a long research stay at KU Leuven. My gratitude to him is immense. I will always treasure everything that he has generously taught to me, and be thankful for the trust that he has placed in me and in my project – also against my own many doubts!

In 2014, Fritz Graf welcomed me as a Visiting Student at the Department of Classics of Ohio State University; I am very grateful to him, especially for his suggestions on the historical-religious aspects of my research.

My very special thanks go to Franco Ferrari and Geert Roskam, whom I was lucky to have as members of my defence committee; they shared with me a number of thoughtful comments and challenging observations that helped me to improve my work greatly, and then assisted me with incredible dedication throughout all the stages of the revision. This book has also been enhanced by the efforts of the two referees for Leuven University Press. Naturally, I alone am responsible for every possible shortcoming.

I am sincerely grateful to Paolo Scarpi and Marco Zambon, whose wise advice, particularly in the first phases of my work, has been crucial. I am also indebted to Frederick Brenk, Pier Franco Beatrice and Crystal Addey, who have all provided me with essential insights. I am glad to extend my warmest thanks to Bram Demulder and Michiel Meeusen, two wonderful Plutarchist companions, from whom I learned a lot, and with whom I spent some refreshing, hilarious conference days.

During these last years, my dearest friends Irene, Alessia, Anna, Antonella, Elena, Federica and Felice were always there, with their patience and heartwarming sweetness. The optimism of my parents, Margherita and Giovanni, and the sparkling affection of my little sister Maria Francesca have been a vital source of joy and inspiration. My soulmate Filippo, radiating energy and cheerfulness, made this hard task considerably easier: this book is dedicated to him, with love.

Introduction

Delphic divination, given its crucial importance in the life and works of Plutarch, constitutes a privileged position from which to observe his philosophical reflection and understand its profoundly original character. As the present research will attempt to show, the Delphic oracle is ideally located at the very core of Plutarch's thinking, and at the crossroad of its main theoretical lines, bounding together his ontology and metaphysics, his view of the soul (individual and cosmic), his idea of god and his epistemological stance. This study is guided by the captivating contrast, which is present in Plutarch's works, between the idea of Delphi as a 'privileged medium' between the transcendent and the immanent realm, from both a practical-communicative and metaphysical-ontological perspective, and its constitutive fallibility and imperfection.

During the Imperial age, the Delphic shrine is a crucial place of interaction between Greece and Rome, by virtue of the important role that it plays within the formation of Greek political identity and for its diplomatic-religious function. The central geographical position of the temple, marked by the 'navel' (ὀμφαλός) there enshrined, makes it a privileged place of worship and a special means of communication between humankind and the god – a function also confirmed by the standard vocabulary of the oracular consultation[1]. The Delphic oracle has the task of supervising and regulating the prophetic expression, while dictating the standard mode, and the socially most acceptable form, of inspired divination (ἄτεχνος μαντική). In this time, religious and cultic customs are influenced precisely by oracular utterances, while the question of the authenticity of prophecy will soon become central in the debate between paganism and Christianity.

Despite its immortal fame and its extraordinary status, the 'medium' of the Delphic oracle, as a closer look at Plutarch's Delphic dialogues clearly reveals, presents some objective limits. Nevertheless, they are precisely its flaws and crises that stimulate Plutarch's relentless reflection, aimed at founding oracular divination on philosophical grounds, and at explaining

---

[1] Cf.: μάντις ('diviner', which apparently comes from μαίνομαι, to rant, rage); χρησμός (which means both 'oracular shrine' and 'oracular utterance', and comes from χράω, to proclaim, declare) with its derivatives χρηστήριον, χρησμολόγος and πυθόχρηστον; θεσφατίζω (from ὁ θεός φημί, the god says); προφήτης (from πρόφημι, to predict); λόγιον ('prediction'). All these terms emphasise the prerogative of oral communication within the practice of oracular divination.

it with authentically rational and scientific arguments. The gap between the centrality of the Delphic oracle as the only place on earth where some telluric exhalations can inspire the prophetess to speak on behalf of Apollo, and the fallible and uncertain nature of its activity, encourages Plutarch's theoretical endeavour.

The way in which Plutarch deals with the complex issue of divination is emblematic of his method of philosophical inquiry as an aporetic process founded on epistemic caution (ἀσφάλεια) and suspension of judgement (ἐποχή), and enacted within a dialogical set. Plutarch's consideration of oracular mantic fully reveals the consonance between his aporetic-zetetic spirit and his sincere religious feeling (εὐλάβεια πρὸς τὸ θεῖον): he believes that exactly these features give shape to the whole Platonic tradition, of which he declares to be a committed adherent. Jan Opsomer's seminal contribution devoted to Plutarch's conception of "divination and academic 'scepticism'" is extremely precious for our understanding of these prerogatives, and proves the historiographical and theoretical relevance of this topic[2].

Many scholars have employed Plutarch's precious testimonies and arguments with the aim of reconstructing and analysing ancient divination, but few specialist studies have explored Plutarch's own conception of divination. One notable exception is Xavier Brouillet's recent work on the Delphic dialogues, which clearly displays their internal unity and connections, while shedding light on the intertwining between Platonic tradition and Delphic wisdom[3]. Looking at the history of Plutarchan scholarship, the book by Hans von Arnim on the notions of 'demon' and 'mantic' focuses on the mythical-eschatological sections of De genio Socratis and De facie in orbe Lunae[4]. Frederick Brenk's monographical work devoted to "Religious Themes in Plutarch's Moralia and Lives" is more concerned with oracular divination, while providing a comprehensive overview of religious themes in Plutarch's oeuvre[5]. The classical and fundamental contributions by Guy Soury, Robert Flacelière and Yvonne Vernière have pointed out many distinct aspects of Plutarch's conception of divination[6], while the crucial research of Paul Veyne and, especially, Daniel Babut has greatly emphasised its theoretical importance and originality[7]. Geert Roskam, Philip Stadter and Paolo Desideri have effectively contextualised the activity of Plutarch as a philosopher and

---

[2] Cf. Opsomer (1996); see also Opsomer (1997).
[3] Cf. Brouillette (2014).
[4] Cf. Arnim (1921).
[5] Cf. Brenk (1977).
[6] Cf. Soury (1942a); (1942b); Flacelière (1938); (1943); Vernière (1990).
[7] Cf. Veyne (1999); Babut (1992); (1993).

Delphic priest within his cultural-historical environment[8], while Franco Ferrari has examined Plutarch's metaphysics also in the light of the Delphic set[9].

The present research, which has greatly benefited from the works just mentioned and has been encouraged by an ever increasing scholarly interest in divination, will try to provide an original and comprehensive view of Delphic divination in Plutarch. First, and more generally, this study will attempt to assess the value of oracular divination as a link between the visible-temporal and the intelligible-atemporal realms. Its ontological-mediatory role between immanence and transcendence will be combined with its gnoseological function of mediating between human fallible knowledge and divine truth. This analysis will also explore the possible connections between Plutarch's psychology of prophetic enthusiasm on the one hand, and his anthropology and demonology on the other. Attention will be paid to the influence of divination in Plutarch's controversies against other philosophical schools (primarily, Stoicism and Epicureanism), as well as in his attempt to trace a wise 'middle path' between two opposite world-views, halfway from superstition and atheism, and to find an acceptable ethical-religious standard for individual and collective life. The inquiry will finally consider the role of Delphi in Plutarch's idea of a harmony between religious faith and philosophical reflection, and will attempt to bring to light the relation between divination and cosmology in his thought.

The methodology adopted consists of two stages: first, providing a thorough analysis of each of the Delphic dialogues, which Plutarch devotes to the prophetic dynamics and foundation of the Delphic shrine; second, developing a personal interpretation of divination in Plutarch, based on the results acquired. The order of the dialogues taken into account intends to trace an ascending path, which starts from the medium of the Pythia and her words (*De Pythiae oraculis*), passes through to the more complex dynamics of divination, based on the interaction between material and spiritual agents (*De defectu oracularorum*), and finally reaches Plutarch's theological view of Apollo as a supreme beneficent god, and of the Delphic temple as a symbol of the interaction between the material and the transcendent (*De E apud Delphos*). In particular, *De Pythiae* and *De defectu* appear in the beginning of the present study since they effectively show the intrinsically doubtful and questionable perfection (as expressed in the interrogative form of my title) of the Delphic temple as a human means of interaction with the divine. Indeed, both dialogues are animated by an apologetic aim: dispelling the fear of divine abandonment and

---

[8] Cf. Roskam (1999); (2001); (2010); Stadter (2004); (2005); Desideri (1996); (2012).

[9] Cf. Ferrari (1996a); (2010).

preserving the faith in god and his providence, despite the (qualitative and quantitative) crisis of the oracular medium. Based on the results obtained through the preliminary philosophical-conceptual analysis, an original account of Plutarch's explanation of divination will be provided, which will attempt to consider his cosmic and individual psychology, as well as his ontological and epistemological stance.

This research will constantly resort to literary and philosophical sources useful to reconstruct the philosophical-religious context of the first centuries AD. References will include other works of Plutarch that are relevant for the topic investigated, such as those devoted to eschatology and demonology (*De facie in orbe Lunae, De sera numinis vindicta*), and individual mantic (*De genio Socratis*). *De Iside ed Osiride*, fundamental for an understanding of Plutarch's theological conception and hermeneutical method, will be considered in its key passages. Some exegetical (*Quaestiones Platonicae, De animae procreatione in Timaeo*) and moral (*De virtute morali*) treatises are also essential for this research, since, differently from the dialogues, they convey Plutarch's doctrine and reflections directly from his own voice.

My research is articulated as follows: Chapter 1 focuses on *De Pythiae oraculis*. First, it will explain that the character of Diogenianus, with his enthusiastic thirst for knowledge and intelligent and cautious curiosity, exemplifies the dialogical, zetetic nature of Plutarch's philosophy. The divinatory practice, centred on the interaction between the material and the immaterial, will be connected to the function of symbols, scattered in the world as well as within the suggestive Delphic set, and working as possible vehicles of knowledge acquisition. The extraordinary role of the temple as a chosen medium will be tested through the prodigies there occurred, and considered in the light of the key-notion of mixture (κρᾶσις). The analysis will also include the relationship between poetry and prose, given the literary nature of the topic debated in the dialogue (the formal-expressive decline of Delphic utterances). The second part of the chapter, devoted to the dynamics of enthusiasm, will reach the heart of the interaction between human and divine at the Delphic shrine: the god employs the soul of the Pythia as a living medium and instrument. The final section will stress the extraordinary role of the Delphic oracle by recalling its glorious history and exploring the symbolic connections between Apollo and the sun.

Chapter 2 concentrates on *De defectu oraculorum*. While *De Pythiae oraculis* deals with the gnoseological function of symbols and prodigies, *De defectu* attests to the usefulness of narratives and inquiries as sources of knowledge. The character of the Cynic philosopher Didymus Planetiades soon emerges as the perfect antithetical *exemplum* of the way in which an authentic, balanced philosophical discussion should be held. The (mediated) relation between god and the world will be explored considering the notion of 'divine responsibility' and Plutarch's application of the 'double causation theory' on the mantic phenomenon. The key elements and agents of oracular prophecy here investigated will be: the Pythia, the pnuematic stream, the demons, the animals employed in preliminary sacrifices, the concept of '*kairos*' (perfect moment).

Chapter 3 is devoted to *De E apud Delphos*. After stressing the valuable role of 'symbols and riddles' in philosophy, the analysis will dwell on the multifaceted image of Apollo, the oracular god who transmits his thoughts to mortals through the exceptional means of the Delphic shrine. The tentative explanations of the mysterious 'E' proposed by the speakers will be regarded as descriptions of the multiple aspects of the god, aimed at capturing his elusive essence. Apollo, firstly celebrated for his traditional, popular prestige, and exalted for his 'luminous' power (in line with solar symbolism), is praised for the support that he gives to humankind through his wise advice, as well as for his logical-dialectical character. Numerology stresses the sublime correspondences between god's majesty and the cosmos at large, and Ammonius' conclusive speech defines him as the supreme principle of being, while acknowledging the ontological and cognitive limits of humans. Finally, the chapter will focus on Plutarch's dualistic conception and on his encounters and relations with foreign wisdom.

Chapter 4 builds upon the results achieved in the previous chapters, by proposing an overall, tentative explanation of Plutarch's conception of divination – especially in light of his theory of the soul (human and cosmic). *De virtute morali* will be employed to reconstruct his moral psychology; the consideration of the different roles, proportions and functions of the psychic parts involved in divination will prove useful to distinguish oracular-institutional mantic from demonic-individual forms of inspiration present in *De genio Socratis*. Plutarch's idea of divination will be put in connection with his cosmology and gnoseology by relying on *De animae procreatione in Timaeo*. A comparative section will take into account Plato's *Timaeus* in order to better explore the material and cosmic aspects of Plutarch's idea of oracular mantic, and its ontological and epistemological references.[10]

---

[10] The critical edition employed for the analysis of Delphic dialogues is Sieveking, W. (1997), *Plutarchi Moralia*, vol. III, editionem correctiorem curavit H. Gärtner, Lipsiae (BT). Critical editions and translations of other sources are listed in the general bibliography.

Chapter 1
An analysis of *De Pythiae oraculis*

1. Introduction

De Pythiae oraculis is a relevant source for our knowledge of the Delphic oracle, its functioning, its physical appearance and its landscape[1]. Philinus, an expert guide of the temple, reports a challenging dialectical exchange that once occurred at the shrine: the accurately chosen succession of monuments, locations and works of art guides the sometimes technical and philosophical, but always engaging and animated discussion, while accompanying the readers through a complex path towards Theon's extensive closing speech. Along the way of a captivating itinerary, the readers encounter a series of significant Delphic artistic, cultic and architectural elements, introduced by the protagonists of the dialogue, who analyse their history and hidden meaning.

The present chapter, by taking inspiration from the monuments encountered in *De Pythiae* and from the complex phenomena discussed by the participants, aims to emphasize the function of the Delphic oracle as a unique place of worship; it will also prove that the fundamental role of the shrine, as attested by its peculiar and sometimes mysterious appearance, is to act as a special means of communication between the human and the divine. My analysis, while following the ideal itinerary traced in the dialogue, will dwell on some selected passages in order to explore: the history, role and ritual framework of the Delphic oracle, the function of symbols and prodigies, and the notion and dynamics of enthusiasm in connection with the psychical constitution and anthropological status of the Pythia. I intend to demonstrate that all these elements attest to the *mediated interaction* that Plutarch envisions between the transcendent god and the material realm – which lies right at the core of his metaphysical conception as well as of his philosophical reflection at large.

Daniel Babut has stressed how, from a compositional perspective, it is the succession of the arguments that in *De Pythiae oraculis* determines the order of the places encountered along the way[2]: in other words, the Delphic

---

[1] Robert Flacelière hypothesises that this dialogue belongs to the mature period of Plutarch's production and fixes its *terminus post quem* at 117 AD – cf. Flacelière (1974). Christopher Jones, instead, suggests 95 AD as the *terminus post quem* for this dialogue – cf. Jones (1966) 72. Frederick Brenk antedates its composition and believes that the three Delphic dialogues were all written at a short time distance – cf. Brenk (1977) 87.

[2] Cf. Babut (1992).

periegesis is to be intended as a mere *'prétexte'* for the expression of some philosophical concepts and ideas at the core of Plutarch's reflection[3]. The overall framework is that of a confrontation between two main parts that express contrary views and explanations: Philinus and the pious Sarapion (who incarnates the Stoic religious spirit) on the one side[4], and Boethus on the other[5], who impersonates instead the Epicurean anti-religious rational spirit and is depicted as a hateful, arrogant discussant. Plutarch, by employing the moderate character of Theon as his 'spokesperson', apparently intends to draw a middle path between these two opposite world-views.

Nevertheless, from a general standpoint, the Chaeronean seems to conceive the Stoic perspective as more acceptable than the Epicurean one, and somehow closer to his own ideas. For instance, the Stoic poet Sarapion stresses the key prerogative of the whole discussion as follows: not to fight (μάχεσθαι) against the god, and not to destroy (ἀναιρεῖν), along with the mantic activity (μαντική), his providence (πρόνοια) and divinity (τὸ θεῖον). He also focuses on the necessity of analysing the topic in rigorous, rational terms, and to investigate (ἐπιζητεῖν) and solve the arguments proposed with the greatest respect for traditional faith (εὐσέβεια) and the religion of the fathers (πάτριος πίστις)[6]. This stance, as Daniel Babut points out[7], seals a kind of agreement among the participants of the dialogue, marking at the same time the exclusion of Boethus – a theoretical operation that implicitly identifies the Epicurean point of view as the most dangerous, irreverent and threatening with regard to oracles and their cognitive claim.

1.1. The character of Diogenianus and the style of philosophy

One of the characters taking part in the dialogue is a 'stranger' from Pergamon, named Diogenianus[8], who fosters the discussion by advancing stimulating questions and presenting original arguments. He is praised for his cleverly curious and inquisitive attitude, his enthusiastic spirit, noble character and sincere desire to learn. Rather than being simply willing to contemplate (φιλοθεάμων), or to listen passively (φιλήκοος) to the guides' instructions, he is anxious to receive profound knowledge (φιλόλογος) and to engage in active comprehension (φιλομαθής)[9]. His greatest quality is his

---

[3] Cf. *ibid.* 207.

[4] For a reconstruction of the character of Sarapion, cf. Babut (1969) 246; Bowersock (1969) 67-68; Jones (1978) 228-231.

[5] For an account of the character of Boethus, cf. Boulogne (2003) 22 *et passim*.

[6] Cf. *De Pyth. or.* 402E.

[7] Cf. Babut (1993) 211.

[8] Diogenianus also appears in *Quaest. conv.* – cf. Flacelière (1974) 173, n. 1.

[9] Diogenianus' attitude recalls a renown passage of Plato's *Republic* (Plato, *Resp.*

mildness (πραότης), full of kindness and grace (χάρις), which he shows by fighting (μάχιμος) gently against inadequate arguments, and by questioning (διαπορητικός) the other participants, with an open and kind spirit[10].

In the context of *De Pythiae oraculis*, Diogenianus' delicateness and 'good-spirit', proved as some of the most fundamental and highly esteemed human qualities according to Plutarch's thought and sensibility[11], positively influence and balance the discussion. On closer inspection, the presence of the wisely-inquiring 'stranger', who spurs the dialogical exchange with his educated interventions, constitutes a precious hint to what Plutarch believes the authentic philosophical and ideal ethical attitude should be, thus confirming the genre of the dialogue as the principal means for a clever, rational, and shared enquiry, in line with the zetetic and anti-dogmatic spirit of his reflection.

It is Diogenianus himself who declares the fundamental purpose of the dialogical exchange: to investigate the cause (αἰτία) and the reason (λόγος) for which the oracle has ceased to use the poetic form (ἔπεσι καὶ ἐλεγείοις χρώμενον)[12]. Theon immediately replies that it will be possible to attempt an explanation only at a later time, after the company will have completed its itinerary through the Delphic site. I believe that this suggestion, primarily showing Theon's intention of not offending and neglecting the guides who offered to escort the visitors around, seems also to enclose a deeper meaning: hypothetically, it might signify that only after having considered all the items present in the sacred precinct, and interpreted their symbolic value, it will be possible to attempt an explanation for the central question of the dialogue, i.e., the prosaic nature of the responses.

As the reader does clearly perceive, the intriguing discourses stimulated by the encounter with peculiar sacred objects follow the pace of a relentless philosophical investigation, motivated by the need to decipher sensible realities and discover an ulterior meaning behind the surface of concrete data and facts.

The Delphic reality described in *De Pythiae oraculis* can be effectively defined as 'full of symbols'. The notion of 'symbol' and its power are indeed central in this dialogue, where multiple oblique significations, explicit and implicit references to 'symbolical' objects, and indirect ways of communication are constantly present.

6,475d), which nevertheless in the context of *De Pythiae oraculis* is declined in a positive, appreciative sense.

[10] Cf. *De Pyth. or.* 394F-395A.
[11] Cf. Romilly (1979) 293-307.
[12] Cf. *De Pyth. or.* 397D.

1.2. The role of the symbols

Oblique communication is a common feature in a wide range of contexts in antiquity. In particular, in Greek literature the word 'enigma' (αἴνιγμα) usually refers to a riddling story that conceals a hidden meaning that the attentive reader has to disclose. As the geographer Pausanias points out – while proposing a sort of critical-hermeneutical method for the interpretation of myths and legends –, ancient wisdom typically resorted to riddles: for this reason, myths and stories of earlier times are not to be understood in a literal, straightforward sense, but to be decoded through a process of rational interpretation[13].

The notion of 'symbol' (σύμβολον) can be employed as a useful conceptual tool for the study of ancient texts. This concept is indeed central with regard to the exegetical spirit and method of ancient allegorism, which Peter Struck has defined a "more or less continuous strand of literary thinking", developing from the Classical to the late Roman age[14]. The key term to refer to ancient allegoresis is 'enigma' (αἴνιγμα) and its derivatives; the allegorists employ them to convey their theories on poetry and to refer to, or explain, their hermeneutical methodology[15]. In particular, the use of 'riddle' or 'enigma' (αἴνιγμα) largely exceeds that of 'allegory' (ἀλληγορία), which according to Plutarch was a relatively new term at the time as used to point to a 'veiled kind of language'[16]. Following the 'allegorical' view, poetical exegesis, mystery religions, esoteric philosophy (such as Pythagoreanism) and divination itself seem to share comparable conceptual frameworks, according to which fundamental truths are hidden underneath similarly variable, misleading appearances, and await to be discovered[17].

In antiquity, divinatory items at large are commonly liable to an allegorical and symbolical interpretation. More specifically, during the first centuries AD, the correct exegesis of prophetic utterances (mainly accessible to few inspired, gifted and charismatic individuals) acquires

---

[13] Cf. Pausanias, 8,8,3: Ἑλλήνων τοὺς νομιζομένους σοφοὺς δι᾽ αἰνιγμάτων πάλαι καὶ οὐκ ἐκ τοῦ εὐθέος λέγειν τοὺς λόγους, καὶ τὰ εἰρημένα οὖν ἐς τὸν Κρόνον σοφίαν εἶναί τινα εἴκαζον Ἑλλήνων. For a thorough explanation of this passage, see Hawes (2014) 182.

[14] Struck (2004) 18.

[15] Cf. *ibid.* 151.

[16] Cf. *De aud. poet.* 19E-F.

[17] Jean Pépin's distinction between allegory and sign on the one hand, and myth and symbol on the other, might constitute a valuable critical referent – despite, as we will see, Plutarch's writings do not seem to match this theory. According to Pépin, while allegory (as this very word expresses) and sign point to an external reference, myth and symbol – which do not refer to any external token – have their reference and significance within themselves, for which reason they are called '*tautégories*' (tautegorical expressions) – cf. Pépin (1958) 79-80.

an unprecedented prestige and even becomes crucial for defining the authentic standards of religious belief.

During the Imperial age, implicit and explicit textual interpretations come to constitute the privileged field for philosophical debate: philosophical reflection focuses on the exegetical reading of the works of ancient thinkers, conceived as imperative methodological and theoretical authorities[18]. The systematic reading of authors of the past leads to the composition of collections of *problems* (προβλήματα, ζητήματα, ἀπορίαι): the questions and doubts found in ancient sources are analysed, and a possible solution (λύσις) is formulated, by employing the methods of rational inquiry. Hermeneutic activity is a crucial component of Plutarch's output and reflection; furthermore, in his peculiar case, the exegesis addresses with the same care and intensity philosophical texts as well as religions, cults and myths, included the Delphic reality and tradition, as an accurate reading of the Pythian dialogues strikingly confirms.

As Yvonne Vernière explains, Plutarch never gives a clear, definite assessment of the meaning of myths and symbols, nor he studies these elements in an objective way: instead, he employs them as varying, ambivalent tokens, ready to be used as parts of a wider demonstration. Vernière in particular emphasises that Plutarch intends mythology as a superior kind of language, through which images and rites become a 'reservoir of symbols', out of which a comprehensive general image can be reconstructed[19].

As I believe, it is possible to establish a connection between the hermeneutic activity in which Plutarch engages for deciphering traditional myths on the one hand, and the exegetical methods that he employs for discovering the hidden meaning of ritual elements and customs at the Delphic shrine on the other. At a closer analysis, all these objects of investigation convey, under their variable and misleading appearance, a superior content of knowledge. Human mind can access the precious significance concealed behind phenomena through rational interpretation of symbols and riddles, which resorts to the methods of analogy (παρεικάζειν) and substitution (ἀνίττεσθαι). Any attempt of penetrating into the enigmatic wisdom (αἰνιγματώδης σοφία[20]) 'refracted' on sensible objects must adhere to rigid philosophical principles and high rational standards.

De Iside et Osiride contains important suggestions on Plutarch's opinion on the role of myths in philosophy: he explains that myth (μῦθος) is fundamentally different from historical account (λόγος) and distinct from rigorous scientific methodology. Therefore, in order to disentangle the

---

[18] For an analysis of the methods of philosophical exegesis in this age, cf. Ferrari (2001) 86-94 and Opsomer (2004).

[19] Cf. Vernière (1977) 50-51.

[20] *De Is. et Os.* 354C.

meaning hidden behind myths, one must preserve and analyse only those details and components that comply with a standard of verisimilitude (κατὰ τὴν ὁμοιότητα)[21]. Plutarch conceives myth not as a mere invention: rather, it is an oblique, non-univocal form of communication that orients human mind towards different objects and gives access to a mediate understanding of reality, by pointing to superior meanings in a vague and indeterminate way.

De Pythiae oraculis similarly resorts to, and displays, an oblique and indirect kind of knowledge transmission: the symbolical dimension constantly shapes and substantiates the Delphic reality, despite some formal changes affecting the literary style of the responses there delivered. Evidences of this mode of expression are spread throughout the whole dialogue, from the highest theoretical explanation of the symbolic role of the sun and the moon, to the more 'down to earth' discussion around the custom of substituting people's real names with nicknames and epithets[22].

This work of Plutarch reveals how the Delphic oracle steadily preserves its ancient role as deliverer of divine messages to humankind. At the dramatic time of the dialogue, the responses given by the Pythia have ceased to be poetical and allusive in character and, contrary to the days of old, are formulated in a direct, plain and unequivocal style. Despite this fact, the 'symbolic element' that intrinsically characterises the communication between god and humankind is preserved within the oracular apparatus: the dynamics of divination indeed constitute *themselves* an interrelated complex of symbols that human understanding has to disentangle and decipher, by relying on its own limited capabilities. Plutarch believes that truth is not fully accessible to human soul, due to its incarnation and permanent contact with the mortal element; nevertheless, god, who wants us to partake in superior knowledge, stimulates our never-ending, 'asymptotic', quest for truth through riddles, enigmas, and signs scattered in the cosmos.

The mantic role performed by the Pyhtia, who resorts to a simple prosaic style, enables and facilitates the necessarily *mediated* expression of the thoughts of god within the sensible realm, which is performed without the need of any additional formal artifice or stylistic codification. Accordingly, Plutarch condemns the utterly childish (παιδικόν) and silly (ἀβέλτερον) attitude of those blaming the extreme clearness of the oracles delivered at the Delphic temple at the time[23]. The analogy with childhood is brought even further: children prefer astonishing, unusual phenomena, like the appearances of haloes and comets, to the simple, ordinary vision of the moon and the sun. Nevertheless, these last objects, according to the

---

[21] Cf. *ibid.* 374E.

[22] Cf. *De Pyth. or.* 401A-B.

[23] Cf. *ibid.* 409C.

theoretical framework of *De Pythiae*, are precise and reliable 'symbols' encoding higher divine realities.

Plutarch appears to despise the ancient custom of pronouncing obscure responses, which were in constant need of rational interpretation and allegorical exegesis. He explains that it is exactly a childish nostalgia to make humans regret enigmas, allegories and metaphors previously employed by the Pythia in the mantic session (τὰ αἰνίγματα καὶ τὰς ἀλληγορίας <καὶ> τὰς μεταφορὰς τῆς μαντικῆς): magniloquence and allusions indeed mangle the prophetic message by creating confusing reflections (ἀνακλάσεις) and deceive men by acting exactly on their intrinsically mortal faculty of imagination (τὸν θνητὸν καὶ φανταστικόν), susceptible of sensible perceptions[24].

As I believe, Plutarch's argument seems to imply that the cause of the formal change (τὴν αἰτίαν [...] τῆς μεταβολῆς) of the oracular expression is *itself* one of the main, authentic mysteries and riddles that belong to the religious framework of the Delphic oracle and are in need to be interpreted – on condition of respecting the majesty of the oracular god. Indeed, despite the relative clearness of the present responses, there is enough obscurity as regards the providential plan and hidden intention (διάνοια) of god: his secret purpose follows a totally inscrutable logic, undecipherable by simple human reasoning (λογισμός)[25]. The dynamics of the prophetic act is *itself* an enigma that awaits to be solved: the ancient allegorical phrasing of the Pythia's utterances would only have the negative outcome of adding uncertainty and confusion to the puzzling phenomenon of oracular divination.

1.3. The function of the temple

In *De Pythiae oraculis*, Delphi emerges as the selected place of the encounter between divine wisdom and prescience on the one hand, and human desire for knowledge on the other. The function of the oracle is to control and regulate inspired divination – perceived as a natural, spontaneous, marginal form of prophetic activity, also qualified as potentially dangerous from a socio-religious point of view, given its intrinsically savage and unpredictable character[26].

---

[24] Cf. *ibid.* 409D and also *De Is. et Os.* 358F-359A: "Just as the rainbow, according to the account of the mathematicians, is a reflection of the sun, and owes its many hues to the withdrawal of our gaze from the sun and our fixing it on the cloud, so the somewhat fanciful accounts here set down are but reflections of some true tale which turns back our thoughts to other matters" (Eng. trans. Babbitt).

[25] Cf. *De Pyth. or.* 409D.

[26] With regard to divination, it is fundamental to keep in mind Cicero's account in *De fato* and, especially, in *De divinatione* – bewaring of the chronological distance and conceptual differences between him and Plutarch. Cf. Cicero, *Div.* 1,2,4; 1,50,113. For

Generally speaking, divination is divided into two kinds: technical (τεχνικὴ μαντική) and natural (ἄτεχνος μαντική)[27]. Technical, or artificial, divination works with, and aims to decode, sensible signs, be them provoked or spontaneous (like extispicy, lecanomancy, oracular lot-divination). It is also defined as conjectural, inductive (based on logical inferences which, starting from sensible data, lead to their extended meaning), or deductive (inferred from general axioms), and is mostly performed by a competent professional. It is based on the notion of *sympatheia*, which is the dynamic integration of every single phenomenon within the interconnection of all cosmic events – articulated on the interaction between the *microcosmos* (the circumscribed object examined) and the *macrocosmos* (the general referent). Natural divination, instead, is intuitive and 'internal' in character; it includes dreams, epiphanies, and oracular prophetic enthusiasm – which is held as its most prestigious expression[28] – and sometimes requires a peculiar state of mind of possession, madness, trance[29].

At closer inspection, the distinction between artificial and natural divination proves to be constitutionally blurred and indefinite: for instance, the outcomes of natural divination, corresponding in our case to the Pythia's prophetic utterances, enigmatic and allusive as in ancient times, may be undecipherable in light of common linguistic rules and thus require a complex technique of decipherment[30]. In other words, even in cases of 'intuitive', 'natural' divination[31], one needs to resort to interpretative techniques in order to decipher the content received in inspiration. In *De Pythiae oraculis* these two kinds of divination are both present – explicitly

---

Cicero's account of divination, see the crucial debate between Mary Beard (1986) and Malcolm Schofield (1986).

[27] Cf. Cicero, *Div.* 1,18: Cicero here explains this contrast in terms of that between *ars* and *natura*. Plato in *Ti.* 71e-72b opposes inspired prophets to interpreters (ὑποκρίται) and spokesmen (προφῆται), these last lacking any inspirational power (indeed, οὐδεὶς γὰρ ἔννους ἐφάπτεται μαντικῆς ἐνθέου καὶ ἀληθοῦς). A formal connection between the figure of the prophet and the interpreter is established in Cicero, *Div.* 1,34.

[28] Cf. *ibid.* 1,6,11. In this regard, I would like to remind that Michel Casevitz proposed an etymological connection between μάντις and the root *ma, which is the same root of the verb μηνύω (to reveal). This possible derivation, by stressing the communicative role of the μάντις, shortens the distance between inspired and technical kinds of divination, which – as evidence shows – is *per se* quite blurred. Cf. Casevitz (1992) esp. 11.

[29] For a concise and effective overview, see Burkert (1992) 79-82. Inspired divination – whose complex roots are anyway extremely difficult to reconstruct – was believed to be non-Greek in origin: the activity of frenzied women possessed by the god and speaking according to his will is attested in the regions of Mesopotamia, Mari and Assyria from the II millennium BC – cf. Burkert (1985) 114.

[30] For these two techniques of interpretation see Manetti (1993) 24-25.

[31] Cf. Romeo (1977) 84; Romeo also names this form of divination 'endosemiotic'.

and implicitly, separated and intertwined – and they make up the fabric on which the debate is articulated.

Plutarch's thought and writings are animated by the need to pave a 'wise middle path' between the two extreme philosophical perspectives of the Stoics and the Epicureans[32]. In this dialogue, we can fully observe Plutarch's art of mediation at work. The Epicurean Boethus holds that the gods must have no involvement in the activity of divination, and *a fortiori* in the composition of the responses, whereas the Stoic Sarapion believes in the active engagement of the god, who composes and dictates *himself* the oracular predictions[33]. These two stances are grounded on the more fundamental question of the possibility of divine prescience and human prevision: whilst the Epicurean affirms the arbitrary and unpredictable character of earthly events, the Stoic instead embraces a rigidly deterministic view of the unfolding of destiny, intended as an inescapable causal chain, whose very structure substantiates the predictability of future facts[34].

According to Boethus, reality at large – included the Delphic reality, with its oracles and prodigies – is governed by fortune (τύχη) and chance (αὐτόματον)[35]: the Epicurean modulates his interventions on these two notions, in order to discredit divination and nullify its value, by resorting to some topical arguments of his school. In particular, he explains that sometimes words and sentences uttered by the diviner happen to casually (αὐτομάτως) meet future events and thus to strike the right outcome among infinite possibilities (ἀπειρία). The given precondition is that everything is possible in time (χρόνος) and nature (φύσις). Boethus thus believes that predictions do not foretell (προειπεῖν) but simply *tell* (εἰπεῖν) random facts, and these facts, in some fortuitous cases and by pure chance (ἀπὸ τύχης)[36], happen to come true.

He also very curiously declares that every prediction of future events is false (ψεῦδος), even if it eventually turns out to be true. As Franco Ferrari points out, this stance appears *prima facie* to be based on the Epicurean conception of time: accordingly, predictions refer, in the very moment they are proffered, to things that are neither present nor existent (τὰ μὴ ὑπάρχοντα), and for this reason they are obviously false. Ferrari expresses two criteria generally considered for granting the legitimacy of divination: first, a deterministic view of reality and its related physical-moral overtones; second, the logical aspects implicated in making assertions about future events. With reference to this last criterion,

---

[32] Cf. Opsomer (2006a).

[33] Cf. *De Pyth. or.* 396C-397E.

[34] Cf. *ibid.* 399F.

[35] Cf. *ibid.* 398F.

[36] Cf. *ibid.* 398F-399A.

he demonstrates that Boethus' stance may derive from his application of the binary logic on a late-Epicurean theory – employed by the Epicureans to demonstrate the flaws of divination and attested by Cicero's *De fato*. In brief, this theory proves the falsity of statements regarding the future by means of logical arguments[37], by asserting that both members of a disjunctive sentence concerning a specific event that will happen in the future are always false[38].

According to Boethus, it is rather the heuristic activity of the scientist that embodies a positive model of rational prediction. The only case in which forecasting is acceptable is indeed that of the wise man, who, in a way totally different from the diviner, formulates reliable conjectures in a correct and successful way (εἰκάζων καλῶς), by employing his preparation, profound analysis and sound methodology. This person can be really identified as the best prophet (ἄριστος μάντις), since he founds his investigation of the future on rationality and plausibility, on a dim understanding of the underlying natural laws and on his own trained logical deductive skills[39]. This view obviously counteracts Plutarch's acceptance of the possibility of divination as a non-mediated, irrational form of knowledge acquisition. As *De defectu oraculorum* shows even more clearly, prediction is performed intuitively (ἀσυλλογίστως, ἀλόγως, φαντασιαστικῶς), since the faculty primarily involved in the process – the mantic faculty (μαντικόν) – is a sort of *tabula rasa* (ἄγραφον γραμματεῖον), irrational and undetermined, void of any previous knowledge and competence, and completely receptive of impressions and presentiments[40].

Sarapion explicitly counteracts Boethus' view, which appeals to an extremely simplistic binary logic, and opposes his own explanation that emphasizes the complex and detailed style of the Delphic responses. As I believe, the confrontation between Boethus and Sarapion, sprung from the Epicurean's provoking stance, directly recalls the opposition between two classical modalities of oracular responses: the ones 'binary', and the others 'open'. While the binary mode implies a neat 'yes or no' answer, the open involves a discursive form and a certain amount of accessory information[41]. If we follow Sarapion's account, we come to the conclusion

---

[37] Cf. Cicero, *Fat.* 16,37-38.

[38] See Ferrari (2000) esp. 155-156.

[39] Cf. *De def. or.* 432C; Cicero, *Div.* 2,5,12: *bene qui conciet, vatem hunc perhibeto optimum.*

[40] Cf. *De def. or.* 432C-D.

[41] An example of binary oracle is given in *De frat. am.* 492B. For the 'conversational' character of the Delphic oracle, cf. Johnston (2008) 52. For this topic see also Robbins (1916); Amandry (1950) 29-36, 84-85, 232-233; Parke-Wormell (1956) 18-19; Fontenrose (1978) 219-224. The custom of employing a lot oracle in Delphi would also substantiate

that the answer to the standard formula of the enquires submitted to Apollo – 'Is it better and preferable...?' ('εἴη λώϊον καὶ ἄμεινον;')[42] – was not rigidly binary ('yes or no'), but involved a significant amount of details and specifications.

Recalling Cicero, the Stoic definition on divination corresponds to 'the prediction and presentiment of events that happen by chance'[43]. This idea is found on the assumption of a rigid causal succession underlying all events, and on the conception of 'chance' as a cause fundamentally inexplicable for the human mind. Accordingly, Sarapion stresses that the Delphic responses are not limited to disclose what is going (or not going) to happen (τὸ γενησόμενον); rather, they describe the predicted events in a detailed, complete way – including the modalities, time, and circumstances under which they are expected to come. In this perspective, predictions do not tell what perhaps (τάχα) will happen, but express what is absolutely (πάντως) forced to come. Such is the discrepancy between mere conjecture (εἰκασμός) and authentic prognostication (προδήλωσις): the latter offers a number of specifications and several additional items (καὶ πῶς καὶ πότε καὶ μετὰ τί καὶ μετὰ τίνος), which greatly enrich the prediction, and prove its authenticity and reliability[44].

In order to support his thesis, the Stoic poet reports some past notorious and successful predictions. In this context, the precise chronological order and logical disposition (τάξις) are what sustains and proves the trustworthiness and validity of oracular responses, since the very term 'order' (τάξις) stands in complete opposition to the concepts of 'fortune' (τύχη) and 'chance' (αὐτόματον) – which are exploited, instead, by the Epicurean adversary. In other words, correct predictions represent for Sarapion an empirical proof of the existence and effectiveness of divination, and of its divine origins: they have nothing to share with fortune (τύχη) or indefiniteness (ἀπειρία); rather, they confirm that destiny (τὸ πεπρωμένον) always follows a precise path (ὁδός).

Plutarch, looking at the debate from his 'moderate perspective' – an attitude that testifies to his mild and sincere religious spirit, harmonised with his sceptical rationalism – on the one side rejects the Epicurean position, which denies the value of divination, while on the other counteracts the Stoic admission of a deterministic, precise, consequent and rigorous knowledge of forthcoming events. The Chaeronean through the further development of the dialogue aims to confirm that the continuous

---

the possibility that the oracle was also consulted outside the fixed dedicated days – for this see Parke (1943) 19-22.

[42] Cf. Fontenrose (1978) 222.

[43] Cf. Cicero, *Div.* 2,13: *divinationem esse earum rerum praedictionem et praesensionem, quae essent fortuitae.*

[44] Cf. *De Pyth. or.* 399A-D.

attentive care (ἐπιμέλεια) and providence (πρόνοια) of the supreme god – who resorts to the Delphic oracle as a 'perfect medium' through which he conveys his thoughts and indications to humankind – are completely compatible with the relatively autonomous unfolding of earthly events, in terms of historical contingency, and individual freedom and responsibility.

2. *The concept of* krâsis

The concept of 'mixture' (κρᾶσις) is one of the key-ideas within the theoretical framework of the dialogue, and works as a leading theme bounding together the diverse topics addressed in the discussion. The notion of *krâsis* – that, as we will see, is investigated in greater depth in *De defectu oraculorum*[45] – is directly connected to that of 'medium', which will turn out to be another crucial element of *De Pythiae*. As I aim to demonstrate, the concept of *krâsis* is also emblematic of the interaction among material elements in the physical world, and is especially meaningful in relation to Delphic divination.

The first symbolic element that the characters encounter during their *promenade* is the peculiar flourishing brilliant deep blue patina (τὸ ἀνθηρόν) that covers the surface of the Nauarchs and other bronze works of art in Delphi[46]. The distinctive colour of the bronze statues, which strikes the eyes of the curious Diogenianus, has not ceased to capture the attention of scholars in multiple disciplines until nowadays, and also archaeologists and geologists have attempted to provide accurate analyses of the phenomenon, based on scientific data[47].

In the dialogue, three different explanations of the strange, wonderful tinge are provided. The first two solutions are developed by Diogenianus himself, who explains the phenomenon as an artistic device and gives two reasons for its discovery, respectively connected to the two opposite concepts of 'purpose' and 'chance'. First, he connects the phenomenon to the invention of a dyeing method (τέχνη) employed in bronze tempering, which involves a peculiar 'mixture' (κρᾶσις) and preparation (φάρμαξις). Then, he ascribes the discovery of the blue-tinge technique to a fortuitous circumstance (συντυχία): the burning of a house full of gold, silver, and a large quantity of copper, which accidentally melted together in a special

---

[45] Cf. *De def. or.* 432C; 432E; 437F.

[46] Cf. *De Pyth. or.* 394E-396C. For the blue patina cf. Jouanna (1975): this article proves how the presence of the brilliant blue patina characterizes all the bronze statues in Delphi, and is not limited to the Spartan sculptural group of the Nauarchs.

[47] Franke-Mircea (2005) reports the results of the chemical analysis conducted in order to examine the coloured patina of the Charioteer, which is the only life-size statue of Delphi survived until our time. The authors conclude that the typical bluish appearance was acquired by the statue while underground – so only after it was buried under the soil 2000 years ago – and hypothesise that its blue shades are due to the presence of azurite.

proportion and therefore produced a particular metallic mixture. Theon defines this last account as a 'fictional story' (μῦθος), exactly like the more brilliant and ingenious one that he himself proposes: once, a Corynthian bronzesmith crumbled a large quantity of gold with bronze, and in this way obtained a wonderful 'melange' or 'mixture' (κρᾶσις) that he sold for a high price[48].

Theon himself formulates the final, and apparently definitive, solution, which dismisses all the previous accounts[49]: he explains that the particular colour covering the artefacts requires a twofold explanation, which significantly stresses the importance of the very concepts of 'blending' (μεῖξις) and 'mixture' (κρᾶσις).

Theon explains that the tinge is due to a peculiar mixing (μεῖξις) and preparation (ἄρτυσις), resulting from a combination of specific elements in specific quantities. He defines air, which is constantly in contact with bronze, as the element responsible for enhancing the marvellous brilliance of the bluish tinge of the statues. In fact, the air in Delphi possesses a special, mysterious, property (φῦσις) and power (δύναμις): because of the peculiar repulsing influence exerted by the nearby mountains, the air is compact (πυκνόν), consistent and dense (συνεχῆ καὶ τόνον ἔχοντα). Theon defines the Delphic air in a double, almost paradoxical way: on the one hand, it is delicate, subtle, tenuous (λεπτόν); on the other, it is harsh and pungent (δηκτικόν). Accordingly, its action on the bronze consists of two distinct phases: first, the air, in virtue of its subtlety and pungency, 'cuts' the bronze and scratches out a thick rust; then, in virtue of its heaviness and density, it wraps up the rust, fixes and retains (στέγειν) the powder just created, and so engenders the characteristic luminosity of the bronze[50].

Jean Pouilloux has assimilated this 'cutting' capacity of air to that of fire, similarly intended as a 'cutting' natural element, which cannot be stopped nor retained[51]. He draws this analogy from the analysis of the use of the verb 'to retain' (στέγειν) in Plutarch, as referred to the action of the Delphic air on bronze, compared with the use of the same verb in Plato's *Timaeus*. Pouilloux also stresses the philosophical character of the argument concerning the exceptional nature of the air in Delphi, which is grounded on the following equation: as the bronze produces the astonishing patina under the peculiar influence of the Delphic air, in the same way the Pythia pronounces the oracular responses under the

---

[48] Cf. *De Pyth. or.* 395B-C.

[49] Cf. *ibid.* 395C-D.

[50] Cf. *ibid.* 396A.

[51] Poilloux (1986) explains that the air in Delphi, and its 'cutting' faculty, may be associated to the characterization of fire exposed by Plato in *Ti.* 57a. He also shows interesting connections between *De Pyth. or.* 396A (where the air is also said to influence the digestion of the inhabitants) and Plato's account of digestion in *Ti.* 78a-b.

marvellous influence of the Delphic *pneûma*[52], being both the 'patina' and the 'oracular responses' exceptionally captivating, concrete and directly perceivable elements that catch the attention of the visitors at the shrine.

The explanation here suggested by Poilloux stresses the importance of the concept of 'medium' – which in this framework is represented by the two elements of the Delphic air and the *pneûma*. Admitting the presence of a material medium – which not only connects multiple material elements with each other, but also exerts a transforming action on them – helps Plutarch to find a logically acceptable, rational justification to oracles and prodigies, and to explain these phenomena in line with the most fundamental rules of nature.

In this regard, I would like to stress the importance of two notions that are essential in *De Pythiae* and more generally lie at the core of Plutarch's explanation of natural phenomena: those of 'double action' and 'twofold causation'. I aim to show that Plutarch will give to the key question at the very heart of the dialogue – which concerns the origin and the modalities of oracular inspiration – a scientific explanation that is articulated onto two different levels of causality, exactly like every other earthly phenomenon. We must be aware that also the description of the dynamics of prophetic enthusiasm (ἐνθουσιασμός) is founded on the synergy of two distinct forces, which belong to two antithetic ontological plans.

3. Prodigies

Right in front of the statue of Hiero the tyrant, a discussion on prodigies (ἀναθήματα) arises, as the guides remind the visitors that in the very moment of the despot's death a bronze column that he had erected surprisingly crumpled down. This startling narrative allows the company to engage in the problematic issue of the relationship between god and sensible beings, and more specifically to discuss whether and how divine providence can operate within the natural world and modify its sensible appearance. This passage gives some hints on how Plutarch himself envisions the connection between a transcendent deity and the material world, two entities that – according to his articulated dualistic perspective – represent two opposite ontological poles[53].

The Epicurean Boethus explains prodigies as mere coincidences, created by fortune and chance (τύχη καὶ αὐτόματον). Fortune and chance are exactly the two elements to which he continuously resorts in his explanation of the divinatory phenomena – which confirms his absolute refusal of any intelligent, divinely-constructed plan underlying events. Boethus counteracts altogether the immanentist conception embraced by

---

[52] Cf. Poilloux (1986) 272.
[53] Cf. *De Pyth. or.* 397E-F.

the Stoics and their idea of *sympatheia* (συμπάθεια, according to which the cosmos is a dynamically interacting system). Moreover, the Epicurean strongly and unconditionally refutes the possibility – admitted instead by the Stoics – that god might merge with matter and change it from within. Pierre Boyancé has interestingly shown that the same arguments are found in Heraclides Ponticus, whose account on prodigies and sacred objects is reported by Iamblichus in *De vita Pythagorica*[54].

The solution to this problem is apparently proposed by Philinus, who clarifies a key principle of the mantic dynamics: he proposes an exegesis of the expression 'everything is full of god' (πεπλῆσθαι πάντα θειότητος[55]), which denies that god materially mingles with everything in the cosmos. Rather, he explains the interaction between the transcendent principle and materiality as a sort of 'divine influence' (θειότης) – which is a significant and recurrent concept in *De Pythiae oraculis*.

Considered that the debate is grounded on the fundamental antithesis between providence (πρόνοια) and accident (αὐτόματον)[56] – which characterizes the wider conceptual framework of the Delphic dialogues –, I believe that the theoretical aim of *De Pythiae*, to which the narrator Philinus contributes, is to reach for a balance between the total withdrawal of the god from contingency – which would undermine the usefulness and divine character of oracles – and his presence intended in a 'strong sense' as a 'mixture' with materiality – which instead would degrade his majesty. In line with this purpose, Philinus explains that the votive offerings (ἀναθήματα) in Delphi manifest a kind of 'sympathetic movement' (συγκινεῖσθαι): the objects in the temple seem alive and animated, endowed with sensibility and with 'divine spirit and nature' (θειότης). Inanimate entities are physically affected by god's power, which bestows a superior significance upon them: they express a profound meaning (συνεπισημαίνειν) in accordance with divine providence and foreknowledge (τῇ τοῦ θεοῦ προνοίᾳ)[57].

Votive offerings appear to react to human happenings in an autonomous way, by resorting to their own peculiar language which, following Paul Veyne's original definition, is "made of matter" (metal or marble), and displays a kind of "physics of the supernatural world"[58]. Philinus also compares physical cultic items in Delphi to Homer's words, similarly

---

[54] Cf. Boyancé (1938) 307. In this article Boyancé also offers a valuable account of Boethus' ideas on prodigies.

[55] *De Pyth. or.* 398A.

[56] For a discussion on this opposition cf. Frazier (2010) 76.

[57] Cf. *De Pyth. or.* 398A: καὶ τῶν ἀναθημάτων τὰ ἐνταυθοῖ μάλιστα συγκινεῖσθαι καὶ συνεπισημαίνειν τῇ τοῦ θεοῦ προνοίᾳ, καὶ τούτων μέρος μηδὲν εἶναι κενὸν μηδ᾽ ἀναίσθητον, ἀλλὰ πεπλῆσθαι πάντα θειότητος.

[58] Cf. Veyne (1999); I adapted from French the expressions in quotes.

described as 'living' and 'full of movements' (Ὅμηρον ἔλεγε κινούμενα ποιεῖν ὀνόματα διὰ τὴν ἐνέργειαν); as Boyancé explains, the term '*energeia*' (ἐνέργειαν, 'active power') – employed to refer to the lively character of the words of Homer – will be adopted by the Neoplatonists to express the peculiar virtue that consecrated objects manifest[59].

Now, does this passage of *De Pythiae*[60] – as some interpreters have argued – attest that Plutarch believed in artificial divination? Roger M. Jones holds that Plutarch credited this form of mantic with a high value[61]. Nevertheless, we should remember not only that artificial divination as such was not practised in Delphi, but also that Plutarch's revered master Plato seems not to have embraced this belief: rather, he stressed the superiority of divine, heaven-sent madness and prophetic inspiration over human rational interpretation of *omina*[62]. Frederick Brenk has devoted attention to this subject[63]: Plutarch admits belief in portents just if grounded on a firm religious basis and read through the lens of rational sceptical judgement (ἐποχή). More specifically, miraculous elements can be accepted only in the event that no scientific explanation has succeeded in giving a satisfactory account of the phenomenon taken into analysis.

From a wider perspective, the entire dialogue appears to revolve around the principle that 'god does not mingle with men'[64]. The work therefore seeks to devise strategies to connect the supreme deity with the material cosmos, while attempting to find the correct 'middle way' between the two opposite principles of reciprocal complete mixture (as in Stoicism) and absolute detachment (as in Epicureanism). The clear ontological gap that Plutarch posits between the level of stable being (τὸ ὄντως ὄν) and that of becoming (τὸ γιγνόμενον) makes the interconnection between immanence and transcendence eminently problematic[65]. God is not omnipotent: he can act inside the material realm only while respecting the inferior laws of necessity there at work. Just by acknowledging the intrinsically *limited* character of divine action, human religious faith becomes free from superstition (δεισιδαιμονία).

In order to preserve the transcendence of the supreme god as well as the possibility for him to act within the material world, his influence

---

[59] Cf. Boyancé (1938) 307.

[60] Cf. *De Pyth. or.* 398A-B.

[61] Cf. Jones (1980).

[62] Cf. Plato, *Phdr.* 244c-d. Plato displays a great appreciation for Delphi, a shrine credited with the honourable task of settling religious and political disputes – cf. Plato, *Resp.* 4,427b; 5,461e; *Lg.* 5,738b; 6,759c; 8,828a.

[63] Cf. Brenk (1987b) 316.

[64] Cf. Plato, *Smp.* 203a: θεὸς δὲ ἀνθρώπῳ οὐ μείγνυται. I would like to thank Franco Ferrari for this suggestion.

[65] Cf. *De E* 392E.

in the cosmos must be conceived exclusively as indirect – a position that counters both Epicurean mechanism and Stoic immanentism. The way in which the indirect, necessarily *mediated* character of the divine action in the cosmos has to be conceived is a central concept within the argumentative structure of *De Pythiae oraculis* as well as of Plutarch's philosophy at large, and can be formulated as follows: god only transmits to material entities the initial impulse (ἀρχή) of their movement.

4. *From poetry to prose*

The shared philosophical investigation displayed in Plutarch's dialogue, by building on the problem of the formal decadence of oracular responses, gradually reaches the very essence and foreground of divination. It is the scarce aesthetic relevance of the responses *itself* to suggest that, although oracles are authentically divine in origin, the god is not directly responsible for every single stage of their production. As just outlined, he generates only an 'impulse' (ἀρχή) for human conception of predictions, and by so doing he intervenes in prophecy only in a mediated manner.

This dynamics is explained in Theon's long conclusive monologue, which is aimed at finally overcoming the antagonism between the Stoic and the Epicurean view. He clarifies that the formal decadence of oracles is not a rigid, inescapable rule – given that some oracles in the past were delivered in prose, while some others nowadays are in verse[66]; rather, he underscores that similar impressive changes in communication must be ascribed to some wider modifications in human life. We also know, thanks to a precious evidence found in Strabo, that Delphic prophecy was variously perceived in antiquity as well. Strabo attests that the Pythia, when receiving the inspiring *pneûma* (τὸ πνεῦμα) that was flowing up from a narrow opening of a deep cave (μαντεῖον) upon which the high tripod was placed, pronounced her oracles in prose; afterwards, her sentences were sometimes transformed into verses by the poets (ποιητάς) serving at the shrine[67].

At any rate, Plutarch seems to believe – as his character Theon emphasizes[68] – that benefiting from a convenient rational attitude and from a sound religious spirit is fundamental for trying to solve the central question under examination: no oracular response (be it in prose or in verse) is strange, unacceptable or against reason (παράλογον), provided that our opinions (δόξας) concerning the god are correct and pure (ὀρθὰς καὶ καθαράς). Holding correct ideas on the gods preserves us from unwisely

---

[66] Cf. the examples in *De Pyth. or.* 403B-F; 404A.

[67] Cf. Strabo, 9,3,5,419. Cicero, through the voice of Quintus, confirms the presence of a gas or vapour in Delphi that makes the soul of the Pythia inspired, and is subjected to natural modifications of intensity, cf. Cicero *Div.* 1,38.

[68] Cf. *De Pyth. or.* 397C; cf. also *De def. or.* 414E.

attributing to the supreme deity a direct involvement in the oracular process – which would inevitably lead to diminish god's majesty and undermine his extraordinary status. In this regard we should remind that according to Plutarch's theological reflection, as partly explained in the final section of *De E apud Delphos*, Apollo, as the prophetic deity active in Delphi, seems to also coincide with the supreme god of the Platonic theological scheme.

The theological viewpoint is central within the discussion on poetry and prose reported in *De Pythiae oraculis*, which presents the usual, recurrent pattern of an opposition between the Stoic and the Epicurean stance.

According to the Stoic poet Sarapion – who used to write in verse his philosophical reflections – oracular poetry is perfectly composed, elevated and commendable *a priori* for the simple fact that it is a *divine production*, and in virtue of its beauty (κάλλος) it can compete with the poems of Homer and Hesiod. For this reason, not the oracles but the very judgement and discernment (κρίσις) of humans must be emended[69]: it is the poor taste of the age to be responsible of the scarce appreciation for the oracular responses. Sarapion contrasts Sappho's charming and bewitching poems with the prophetic utterances of the raving Sybil, whose words, despite lacking any aesthetic embellishment (ἀγέλαστα καὶ ἀκαλλώπιστα καὶ ἀμύριστα), have an everlasting life and effect[70]. I want to underline that this formal-linguistic peculiarity of the Sybil's pronouncements closely recalls the power of words as conceived in the context of ancient magic. A good example can be found in the practices of Hellenistic magic attested by the Greek Magical Papyri: there, words do not derive their effectiveness from elegance, sophistication and refinement, but exactly from simplicity, directness and informality.

The positive character of the formal simplification of the responses can be better appreciated, as Theon underlines, if considered from the perspective of god's provident action[71]. Accordingly, two main groups of reasons are provided in the dialogue in order to account for the change from poetry to prose; while the first group is mostly connected to aesthetic-cultural factors, the second is mainly based on religious and diplomatic considerations that specifically refer to the Delphic shrine.

First, the aesthetic-stylistic change is connected to a broader anthropological modification. In the past, differently from the dramatic time of the dialogue, people needed to keep memory of many things, and verses are easier than prose to remember[72]. Everyday communication was in verse, therefore the prophetic activity also followed this trend – as confirmed

---

[69] Cf. *De Pyth. or.* 396D.
[70] Cf. *ibid.* 397A.
[71] Cf. *ibid.* 406B.
[72] Cf. *ibid.* 407F-408A.

by the fact that the god chose exactly Delphi as the home of the Muses[73]. Poetic language, with its metaphors, riddles and ambiguities, worked as a sort of protective shell against failures and mistakes of prophecy[74], but also prevented a full understanding of oracles: it covered truth with obscurity and blended it with vagueness (ἀσάφειάν τε καὶ σκιάν). This image recalls the 'oracular-crater' shared by the Night and the Moon in the eschatological myth of *De sera numinis vindicta*[75]. That mysterious crater, combining truth with falsity and lacking of a single location on earth, sends deceiving dreams and visions to mortals all over the world. It therefore appears as the absolute antithesis of the Delphic oracle of Apollo (god master of 'clarity' and 'solarity'), that is unique on earth and points right to the truth.

The shift from poetry to prose is justified as part of a broader conversion in the lifestyle of people (τοῦ βίου μεταβολή)[76]. Since life engenders changes in human fortunes and natures (ἅμα ταῖς τύχαις καὶ ταῖς φύσεσι), human communication also evolves, according to the inescapable passing of time: common language employed in everyday interactions has itself shifted from ancient sophistication and magniloquence to the current limpidity and exactitude. This stylistic change has also produced, as a positive outcome, a greater accuracy in different sciences – such as philosophy, astronomy and historiography – without damaging their content and significance[77], but rather enhancing their clarity and simplicity.[78]

Second, a historical explanation is proposed, which highlights the prominent social and political function played by the temple in the days of old. During the Classical age, the oracular institution fulfilled a public function: the shrine had to resort to ambiguity (διπλοής), obscurity (ἀσάφεια) and uncertainty, since direct and graceless words – especially if conveying unpleasant predictions – may have risked to provoke the hostility of its distinguished and prestigious consultants. The god, significantly defined as generous and desirous to reveal the truth (ἀληθές), chose poetry as an effective, though obviously transfiguring and ambi-

---

[73] Cf. *ibid.* 406D-E.

[74] Cf. *ibid.* 407A-B.

[75] Cf. *De sera* 564C.

[76] Cf. Toye (2000) 173-181: this article analyses the change from poetry into prose in the light of the results of comparative studies in orality and literacy. It also helps to contextualise this change within the political shift from a tyrannical into a constitutional system.

[77] Cf. *De Pyth. or.* 403A. Philinus underlines the discrepancies between the current widespread use of the prose on the one hand (to which Sarapion constitutes an exception), and the poetical expression previously adopted by philosophers (Orpheus, Hesiod, Parmenides, Xenophanes, Empedocles, Thales) and astronomers (Eudoxus, Hesiod, Thales) on the other.

[78] Cf. *ibid.* 406E-F.

guous, medium for its expression, also useful to protect the oracle and its employees[79]. The absolutely positive formal-stylistic change of the oracular responses has not affected their content: like in the ancient times, Apollo's prerogative is still to offer his valuable help and support (βοηθεῖν) to humankind[80].

Theon therefore points out a crucial historical and political reason for the oracular stylistic 'decline': Greece has reached a state of peace and calmness (εἰρήνη καὶ ἡσυχία), thus ordinary practical problems are expressed through simple, even trivial questions posed by both individuals and cities, which therefore do not require extraordinary, momentous responses[81]. Moreover, Plutarch seems to explain through the words of Theon that the present glory of the Delphic shrine – honoured with votive offerings from barbarians and Greeks, and confirmed by the massive architectonic-artistic restoration promoted by the Amphictyonic Council – may also have a divine, transcendent origin and be part of a providential plan. Theon indeed justifies Delphi's rebirth with the actual 'presence of the god' (τοῦ θεοῦ τὴν ἐπιφάνειαν) in the temple, also attested by the benefits and improvements registered in the surrounding areas.

We can conclude that the form of expression for god's thoughts, which both in antiquity and at the time of the dialogue were transmitted through a human medium, is permanently exposed to modifications – exactly like any other human enterprise and earthly event. The present straightforward, direct style has the particular merit of introducing minimal variations to the 'original content' of the divine message. The present form is thus highly preferable to the ancient, embellished, twisted and allusive, 'less authentic' phrasing. When the god abolished poetry and obscurity (ἀσάφειαν), the Pythia started to express herself in an unequivocal style, similar to the one employed in legislative or educative contexts. Her words, while respecting the criteria of intelligibility and persuasion (τὸ συνετὸν καὶ πιθανόν), are now easier to understand – which has greatly fostered human belief in god. This modification towards clearness (σαφήνεια) had indeed a positive impact on the religious sphere, and oracles in prose – unequivocal, thus not liable to confutation (ἔλεγχος) – enhanced human faith (πίστις) in the gods[82]. From a religious perspective, the confused utterances and sophisticated periphrases (as those introduced into the oracular responses) were perceived as manifestations of the deity, i.e, as expression of *theiotês*

---

[79] Cf. *ibid.* 407D-E.

[80] Cf. *De E* 384E-F.

[81] Cf. *De Pyth. or.* 408B-C. In *De E apud Delphos* (*De E* 386B-C) the priest Nicander reports some trivial interrogations introduced by the particle 'if' (of the kind: if someone will win, get married, go abroad).

[82] Cf. *De Pyth. or.* 408F.

(θειότης)[83]. The word *theiotês* occurs in other two key-passages of the dialogue and refers to the 'divine spirit' that on the one side permeates the objects in Delphi, while on the other underlies the possibility of truthful predictions[84]. Theon, in contrast with the ancient aesthetic-religious taste, praises the positive attitude of the masses and ordinary consultants as the correct reaction to the oracle's stylistic change: people who are eager to learn (μανθάνει ἀγαπῶντες) are inclined to appreciate a direct, unambiguous diction and sentences composed in an easy and clear way (σαφῶς καὶ ῥᾳδίως)[85].

Beside these two main reasons, I believe that it is relevant to point out another minor cause of the oracular decline inferable from Plutarch's text, which is nevertheless crucial for reconstructing the cultural-religious background of the age. I am referring to the so-called 'independent diviners' and 'prophets' (ἀγύρται καὶ μάντεις) of the Great Mother and Sarapis, two successful Oriental deities widely worshipped in Plutarch's time. According to Theon, these deceiving pseudo-prophets (γόησιν ἀνθρώποις καὶ ψευδομάντεσιν) damaged the poetic art and, according to his metaphor, 'made it fall from the truth and the tripod' (ἐξέπεσε τῆς ἀληθείας καὶ τοῦ τρίποδος), thus ruined its reputation as concerns both its content and form.

The activity of these pseudo-prophets, attested even during the Classical age[86], is an important element of continuity within the tradition of Greek religion; the oracular crisis of the I century AD brought the pseudo prophets into greater disrepute. They sometimes tend to overlap with the 'chresmologues' (χρησμολόγοι), but their respective competences and practices are clearly different in kind[87]. Chresmologues sneak into the oracles, steal their prophetic utterances, and turn them into stilted verses and obscure hexameters; they thus violate the physical or virtual sacred space of the shrine in order to spoil, alter and sell the divine oracles there produced. Wandering soothsayers, instead, while working outside the oracular institution and far away from its area of influence, trick their simple and uneducated clients and extort their money in change of invented and badly-composed predictions.

Beside the formal literary contrast between noble oracular poetry on the one hand, and the trivial language of itinerant diviners on the other,

---

[83] Cf. *ibid.* 407A: λοξὸν ἀτεχνῶς καὶ περιπεφρασμένον εἰς ὑπόνοιαν θειότητος ἀνάγοντας ἐκπλήττεσθαι καὶ σέβεσθαι τοὺς πολλούς.

[84] Cf. *supra* 31 and *De Pyth. or.* 398A-F.

[85] Cf. *ibid.* 407A-B.

[86] Cf. Plato, *Lg.* 1,642d; *Resp.* 2,364b-c (ἀγυρτικόν γένος); *Sol.* 12,7; Lucianus, *Alex.* 36,3; *Peregr.* 30,14; *Hermot.* 6,11.

[87] Cf. *De Pyth. or.* 407C; for the figures of independent diviners see Dillery (2005) 170.

we should consider that it was mostly a matter of *power* to oppose the two parts. Oracles and diviners represent two contrasting authorities, whose struggle involves the definition of fundamental concepts, like those of piety towards the gods (εὐσέβεια) and religious faith (πίστις), but also concerns broader issues, such as those of culture and education (παιδεία), and even addresses the very notion of religious or philosophical truth (ἀλήθεια)[88]. Generally speaking, the oracular institution of Delphi performs a paradigmatic civic and religious function within the Greek world, based exactly on the systematic exclusion of foreign wisdom and extraneous influences. Delphic prophecy is *constitutively antithetic* to the action and savage power of independent seers (γόες) – who operate beyond the social, political, and religious boundaries of the civic-political association.

5. Enthusiasm

As Theon explains, two main reasons supported the renaissance of the oracle. These factors belong to two different but concurring causal levels: human attention and dedication (ἐπιμέλεια) *plus* divine inspiration engendered by the god's presence at the shrine (as confirmed by the expression θεοῦ παρόντος and by the recurring term θειότης)[89]. This kind of explanatory pattern, founded on the synergy of multiple causes, often recurs in the dialogue and even serves to explain the mystery central to the debate as well as to the very dynamics of divination: that of prophetic enthusiasm. Theon, conveying Plutarch's own 'moderate' perspective about god's involvement in divination, explains that the deity provides just an impulse (ἀρχή) to which 'each' Pythia reacts in an independent way, according to her own nature and by relying on her own faculties (ὡς ἑκάστη πέφυκε).

At this point, I believe that from the overall discussion of *De Pythiae* we can infer a sort of general rule, whose formulation resembles that of a physical law: the way in which any object, once properly predisposed, reacts to a certain stimulus (ἀρχή) is determined by the nature and qualities of the object itself.

This twofold dynamics involving an 'extrinsic stimulus' and an 'intrinsic reaction' lies at the heart of the notion of 'enthusiastic inspiration' (ἐνθουσιασμός) – which arises at an early stage of the discussion in *De Pythiae*, but is treated at a greater length only in the second part of the dialogue, where enthusiasm is defined as a twofold movement – partly caused by the deity, partly determined by the Pythia's own qualities.

---

[88] For this topic cf. Bendlin (2011).

[89] Cf. *De Pyth. or.* 409A-C. For the historical implications of this passage cf. Swain (1991) and Stadter (2005).

The Pythia is responsible for the voice (γῆρυς), the sound (φθόγγος), the very words (λέξις) and the metre (μέτρον) of the responses, while the god provides only the images (φαντασίας) and the light (φῶς) arising in her soul and favouring the vision of the future[90].

I think that an attentive consideration of Plutarch's psychological conception can pave the way to a better understanding of his account of mantic enthusiasm. In *De Pythiae oraculis*, the qualification of the human soul seems to shift back and forward from a twofold to a threefold structure. These two different psychical configurations rely on distinct (and ultimately irreconcilable) psychological accounts developed by Plutarch in different places of his *oeuvre*[91]. While the chaotic and irrational movements of the Pythia's soul, devoid of a rational guiding principle, directly recall the 'standard' dichotomy found in Plutarch's expositive-exegetical treatises (especially *De virtute morali* and *De animae procreatione in Timaeo*), the intermediary role attributed to the soul in *De Pythiae* seems to be modelled instead on the threefold anthropology of *De facie in orbe Lunae*[92]. *De facie* proposes a tripartition of: body (σῶμα), which originates from the earth, soul (ψυχή), from the moon, and intellect (νοῦς), from the sun. Accordingly, the soul is conceived as an intermediate element between intellect (νοῦς) – active and autonomous, divine in origin – and body (σῶμα) – passive, heteronomous and material. The mediating role of the soul between body and intellect is analogous to that of the moon between the earth and the sun.

Relying on Plutarch's cosmology, the world soul also plays a crucial intermediary role in the cosmos: the *anima mundi* is the medium that allows the god to be present within the sensible realm. Therefore, as expressed by the dichotomic essence of the word soul (which is divided into two principles, one rational and the other irrational) and by its mediatory function, the two aforesaid prerogatives (the bipartition of the individual soul, and its intermediary role between two extremes) become more compatible with each other.

The parallelism between the individual and the cosmic soul, which will prove useful within the present analysis, is deduced from the complex analogy that Plutarch establishes between them – synthesised in the definition of the human soul as a fragment and imitation (μέρος ἤ τι μίμημα[93]) of the cosmic soul.

---

[90] Cf. *De Pyth. or.* 397B-C.

[91] For a clear account of the different divisions of the soul provided by Plutarch, see Opsomer (2012).

[92] Cf. *De facie* 943A. For the role of the moon and psychology, cf. *De facie* 945C-D.

[93] Cf. *De virt. mor.* 441F.

5.1. Body and soul

In order to clarify the notion of enthusiasm, Theon establishes an interesting, special relation centred on the concept of 'instrument' (ὄργανον). He explains that in the same way as the body uses (χρῆται) material instruments (ὄργανα), so the soul uses the body and its parts. This proportion adheres to Plutarch's general psychological perspective – mainly drawn and elaborated from the Platonic and Aristotelian ones – which envisions the body as an instrument of the soul[94]. In particular, this explanation is strongly reminiscent of the notorious passage of Plato's *Alcibiades I*, where Socrates explains that the soul employs (χρῆται) the body as an instrument, by commanding (ἄρχουσα) over it[95].

When applied to the sphere of divination, the aforementioned parallelism shifts from the field of anthropology to the wider, more complex domain of the relationship between material-human and intelligible-divine powers. It therefore comes to refer to a different and extraordinary kind of interaction: in the framework of oracular mantic, the human soul becomes *itself* an instrument (ὄργανον) in the hands of the oracular god, who works as a superior, transcendent agent[96]. The deity, like a musician or an artisan, employs the Pythia's soul, or better the priestess *in her totality*, as a living instrument (ἔμψυχον καὶ αὐτοκίνητον[97]). The prophetess, in her turn, responds to god's directions according to her own particular abilities and constitution: she is thus the body of what we can call the great 'living organism of divination'. Her instrumental role is even confirmed when Theon declares that the god needs, and literally 'makes use of' (χρώμενος, the same verb employed by Plato in the *Alcibiades*, cf. *supra*), humans as attendants and prophets (ὑπηρέταις καὶ προφήταις) at the temple, and therefore he is willing to protect them and to ensure their safety[98].

I believe that the subordinative relationship between the god and the Pythia encloses two fundamental references that must be highlighted.

First, it recalls the hylomorphism that Plutarch establishes at the very fundamental level of the interaction between reason and passions in human soul: reason is a 'form' (εἶδος) exerting its regulative action over passions, which are instead identified with the 'matter' (ὕλη) of moral virtue[99]. In other words, in order to achieve the end of ethical virtue, the irrational part of the soul (παθητικὸν καὶ ἄλογον, which is characterized by inner

---

[94] Cf. especially Aristotle, *de An.* 2,1-2; Plato, *Phd.* 82d-e.

[95] Cf. Plato, *Alc. I.* 130a.

[96] Cf. *De Pyth. or.* 404B. For an analysis of these passages, see Holzhausen (1993).

[97] *De Pyth. or.* 404F.

[98] Cf. *ibid.* 407D.

[99] Cf. *De virt. mor.* 440D. This relationship between matter-irrational principle, and form-rational principle, though apparently Aristotelic, depends instead on a tradition in Platonism, as pointed out in Opsomer (2012).

disordered movements) needs to be disciplined, guided and controlled by practical reason (πρακτικὸς λόγος)[100].

Second, it recalls the creative process of *poiêsis* (ποίησις), i.e., the creative production in which an ideal design (ἔργον) becomes visible through the intermediary of matter, while the raw material employed opposes its resistance and inevitably causes a modification (διαφορά) of the original idea. Accordingly, it can be easily stated that the key concept of paragraph 21 of *De Pythiae oraculis* – a crucial passage for the description of divination – is that of 'contamination': Theon declares that the 'idea' or 'form' conceived by a craftsman, once it is materially implemented, cannot maintain the pure and perfect status (καθαρὸν καὶ ἀπαθὲς καὶ ἀναμάρτητον) that it has when it is in the mind of the creator (ἐν τῷ δημιουργῷ)[101]. Without the active intermediation of an instrument, the design or ideal model would remain hidden and invisible (ἄδηλον); but, in order to become manifest and concrete, the product of the agent's thought (ἔργον τοῦ νοήματος) has to be necessarily commingled with extraneous elements (μεμιγμένον πολλῷ τῷ ἀλλοτρίῳ), by which it is inevitably contaminated[102]. As a consequence, the optimal quality and specific virtue (ἀρετή) of an instrument is to conform (μιμεῖσθαι) to the intention of the agent to the *highest possible degree* – which means that it has to preserve its own intrinsic characteristics.

In this regard, there is a crucial expression employed by Theon that we should take into consideration; this is: 'to be mixed up with' (μείξομαι). In the context of the parallelism with craftsmanship proposed by Theon, this verb refers to the action of impressing and mingling the ideal model onto the raw material – a process that allows the abstract design to become concrete and perceivable. It is worth noting that *meixomai* is also employed in the dialogical context to express the relationship between the god and the Pythia, and specifically how the deity employs the mortal body (διὰ σώματος θνητοῦ) and soul (ψυχῆς <ἀνθρωπίνης>) of the priestess in order to give reality to, and reveal, his own thoughts (τὰς αὐτοῦ νοήσεις). In this process, divine thoughts get literally 'mingled' (μεμιγμένας) with the human living medium – an assertion that is extremely important since it clarifies that just the *thoughts of the god*, and not his essence or spirit, are involved in the process of divination and transferred to the troubled soul of the Delphic priestess. The prophetess is not 'possessed' by the god. Rather, she displays a hybrid nature composed of both transcendent and earthly factors: she shares in god's rationality and prescience, while contributing her own human capabilities. In this complex operation, she also receives

---

[100] Cf. *De virt. mor.* 444B.

[101] Cf. *De Pyth. or.* 404C; also cf. Ildefonse (2006) 296, n. 217. It is well known that a similar scheme characterises the demiurgic creation of the cosmos in Plato's *Timaeus*.

[102] Cf. *De Pyth. or.* 404C-405A.

the necessary material support from the cultic-ritual framework of the Delphic institution.

The altering action performed by the human prophet, who inevitably impresses a modification on the original divine message, is also expressed by a Heraclitean maxim quoted in the dialogue, which stresses the ambiguous and oblique style of god's oracular admonitions: according to this saying, the Delphic Apollo "neither speaks out nor conceals, but signifies"[103]. I think that, in the specific perspective of Plutarch's conception of oracular divination and in the light of the foregoing considerations, this maxim has to be read as follows: divine thoughts reach humankind by passing through the transforming medium of the Pythia, whose individual personality and peculiar faculties cause the original message to be referred in an altered form and in an utterly subjective way.

A further explanation of the enthusiastic attitude of the Pythia clarifies what it means that she is not directly 'possessed' by the god: in compliance with the ritual rules in force at the shrine, the chaste woman becomes the 'perfect medium' for the expression of suggestions, wishes, and decisions that god is eager to share with humankind[104]. His thoughts (νοήματα[105]) need to be expressed by a physical intermediary, with which they mix and by which they are inevitably contaminated. Indeed, as Plutarch explains in a notorious passage of the *Life of Coriolanus*, it is inconceivable that an immaterial entity – be it a soul or a god – may ever talk (διαλέγεσθαι) without making use of a lively physical body (ἄνευ σώματος ὀργανικοῦ)[106].

In Homer Plutarch finds support to the fact that practically nothing happens 'without a god' (ἄνευ θεοῦ)[107]. Nevertheless, god always acts in compliance with the powers (δυνάμεις) and natures (φύσεις) of sensible beings, and respects their peculiar properties and faculties. The prodigies associated to cultic objects and votive offerings in Delphi – as we have seen – require a similar explanation. According to Plutarch, these phenomena

---

[103] *ibid.* 404D (Eng. trans. Goodwin). For the explanation of this maxim within the context of the Heraclitean thought see the very informative Calabi (1977/1978). This article stresses the originality of Heraclitus' stance and attitude towards the temple, which is essentially opposed to Plato's and Plutarch's ones. Plato and Plutarch tend to consider Apollo and the Delphic temple as endowed with a cognitive, religious and political role, while Heraclitus is more concerned with the social aspects of the re-foundation of the shrine and interested in its wider theoretical significance. Interestingly, Calabi puts Heraclitus' ambiguous way of expression in connection with mantic apophantic formulations, which typically resort to enigmas and aphorisms.

[104] Cf. *De Pyth. or.* 404E.

[105] For the sense and meaning of the 'thoughts of god' in this context see Ferrari (1996d) 133.

[106] Cf. *Cor.* 38,2-3.

[107] Cf. *Od.* 2,372; 15,531.

attest to the possibility for god to intervene within the sensible world, by acting always in line with the laws of physics, and by considering the specific qualities of material entities.

The fallible and precarious activity that the Pythia performs appears to be part of the constitutively *imperfect* implementation of the cosmic plan designed by divine rationality (keep in mind in this regard the interrogative formulation of the title of the present research), whose defective character is due to the resistance of matter – primarily corresponding, in the sphere of divination, to the priestess, with her delicate body and mutable soul.

5.2. The soul of the Pythia

The individual soul performs a crucial role within the mantic phenomenon, as a closer look at the arguments developed in *De Pythiae oraculis* will reveal.

First of all, Plutarch defines the soul of the priestess as unable to reach for a peaceful condition *per se* (ἡσυχίαν ἄγειν μὴ δυναμένης). The priestess's soul is unable to be passive, inactive and calm when it offers itself to its divine mover (μηδὲ τῷ κινοῦντι παρέχειν ἑαυτὴν ἀκίνητον ἐξ αὐτῆς καὶ καθεστῶσαν). According to Plutarch's psychology and cosmology (which are strictly interrelated), the psychic principle is intrinsically disordered in nature: the Pythia's soul cannot be serene and tranquil since this disposition is contrary to the intrinsic temperament and complexion of the psychic principle itself. This concept is confirmed by the following general law: it is impossible to use inanimate bodies in a way that goes against their constitution, and *a fortiori* it is impossible to treat an animate (ἔμψυχον) and self moved (αὐτοκίνητον) being against its own character (ἕξις), power (δύναμις), and nature (φύσις)[108]. Although Plutarch's text is not very clear in this respect, we can suppose that the prophetess, beside her irrational soul, also introduces her proper features into the mantic activity, in which she partakes as a living medium (ἔμψυχον), thus contributing her proper *hexis*, *dynamis* and *physis*. The god does not simply make use of the irrational psychic component, but needs the woman in her totality: the Pythia – with both her body and her soul – becomes a living instrument in his hands.

Plutarch's psychological conception is founded indeed on a clear dichotomy internal to the soul, which is divided into a rational and an irrational principle; the imperfect, variable proportion of these two parts constantly strives towards harmony[109].

---

[108] Cf. *De Pyth. or.* 404E.
[109] Cf. *De virt. mor.* 441E-F.

As concerns ethical virtue, Plutarch states that to eradicate (ἐξαιρεῖν) passions is not possible (ἀδύνατον), nor convenient (ἄμεινον); the passionate element is not only indispensable in moral life, but also plays a pivotal role in Plutarch's philosophical reflection at large, and connects his ethical, cosmological and divinatory conceptions with each other.

More specifically, according to Plutarch's ontological and metaphysical perspective as expressed in *De animae procreatione in Timaeo*, the irrational element corresponds to the psychic principle *itself*, which is cause of life and movement. On the basis of the innate disordered character of the soul, we can infer that the violent emotions that capture the Pythia's soul seem to result exactly from a reduced participation of her psychic principle in rationality[110], and from a stronger interaction of her soul with the corporal element[111].

The soul of the Pythia[112], as in a rolling swell, is tossed and agitated like a rough sea, profoundly shaken by passions (πάθεσιν) and movements (κινήμασι). In this framework, it seems to me that the light (φῶς) that illuminates her *psyche*, by donating to her the faculty of gazing into the future, resembles the primordial demiurgic, creative act accomplished by the god, when he transmitted order, harmony and intelligence to the precosmic irrational soul – as Plutarch explains in *De animae procreatione*. In both cases – i.e., in the oracle and in the cosmos – the intelligible divine part, while maintaining its transcendence, also becomes *somehow* present within the material plan.

From Plutarch's cosmological perspective, god belongs to an ontological level which is superior to that of the world soul, without nevertheless being absolutely detached from it. Following the words of the Chaeronean, the cosmic soul is not only a product of the demiurge (ἔργον τοῦ θεοῦ), but also shares in his rationality. It is not merely the production of god as an agent (ὑπ'αὐτοῦ), but it comes from him 'as from a source' (ἀπ'αὐτοῦ), and is generated 'out of his substance' (ἐξ αὐτοῦ)[113]. The preposition *apo* (ἀπό, 'away from') preserves the idea of the transcendence of the deity, whereas *ex* (ἐξ), referring to material causality, indicates the permanence of a fragment of the divine within materiality. The demiurge both gives form to the precosmic soul and bestows a part of his own substance on it – a prerogative that renders his creative activity radically different from simple craftsmanship, in which the final product is instead ontologically distinct from its artisan/maker.

---

110 Cf. *De genio* 591D-F.
111 Cf. *De sera* 566A-D.
112 Cf. *De Pyth. or.* 404D-F.
113 Cf. *Quaest. Plat.* 2,1001C (Eng. trans. Cherniss).

5.3. The dynamics of enthusiasm

The loss of control of the Pythia's soul replicates the same movements characterising the objects that are caught in eddies: eddies do not exert a complete command over the bodies that they capture, which instead sink down while dragged into a deranged spiral (ὡς γὰρ οἱ δῖνοι τῶν ἅμα κύκλῳ καταφερομένων σωμάτων οὐκ ἐπικρατοῦσι βεβαίως)[114]. The key-adverb 'firmly' (βεβαίως) – negated by the particle 'οὐκ' – encloses the profound meaning of the passage: Plutarch here is demonstrating that, as eddies and whirlpools do not have a firm control over the objects that they seize and push downwards, in the same way god does not have a firm control over the Pythia and her soul during the mantic performance, and especially in the course of the enthusiastic inspiration.

In the wider context of Plutarch's scientific conceptions, the eddies-analogy employed by Theon to describe the twofold movement of the Pythia's soul proves to be extremely relevant – as especially the last chapter of the present research will explain. The character indeed declares that bodies caught in eddies *move in a circle* according to necessity (κύκλῳ μὲν ὑπ' ἀνάγκης φερομένων κάτω), while they *sink* according to nature (φύσει ῥεπόντων)[115]. In other words, while according to the laws of nature, any heavy body would simply go downwards, in the peculiar case of eddies the additional, imposed power of the circular whirl contributes to create a composite and ultimately uncontrolled motion. The composition of two different movements (a necessary circular movement *plus* a free/natural vertical one) engenders a motion that is disordered and troubled (ταραχώδης, a term that meaningfully means also 'delirious') and a staggering, frenzied (παράφορος) convulsion.

This captivating image displays what happens inside the Pythia's soul, whose agitation (σάλος[116]) similarly results from the combination (μεῖξις) of two distinct movements (κινήσεων δυοῖν): the first impulse is given by an externally imposed force which affects the Pythia extrinsically (ὡς πέπονθε), while the second impulse pertains to, and is engendered by, the very nature and intrinsic constitution of her soul (ὡς πέφυκε), captured in a confused and relentless agitation. The synergistic combination of these two impulses is what is called 'enthusiasm' (ἐνθουσιασμός)[117].

Frédérique Ildephonse has hypothesised that the passage describing the disordered motion of the Pythia's soul can be compared to the description of the *chôra* (χώρα) in Plato's *Timaeus* – which is equally defined as unbalanced and oscillating (ταλαντουμένην) when agitated

---

[114] Cf. *De Pyth. or.* 404E.

[115] Cf. *ibid.* 404F: ἀλλὰ κύκλῳ μὲν ὑπ' ἀνάγκης φερομένων κάτω δὲ φύσει ῥεπόντων.

[116] Cf. σάλος ψυχῆς in *Amatorius* 758E; 763A.

[117] Cf. *De Pyht. or.* 404F.

(σείεσθαι) by the forms, and as shaking them in turn with her own movement[118].

As I believe, the peculiar dynamism of the priestess's soul mostly reminds the chaotic agitation of the precosmic soul in *De animae procreatione in Timaeo* – a parallelism that I will explore in greater depth in my last chapter. In *De animae procreatione*, Plutarch describes the precosmic matter as animated by a disordered soul (ὑπὸ τῆς ἀνοήτου ταραττομένην αἰτίας); this precosmic nature (φύσις) is characterized by manifold and variable passions (ἐν πάθεσι παντοδαποῖς καὶ μεταβολαῖς)[119]. The precosmic, irrational soul, which is the cause of the disordered movement of the precosmic matter (ψυχὴ γὰρ αἰτία κινήσεως καὶ ἀρχή), is arranged by the demiurge through his cosmopoietic act, and thus brought to order and harmony (τάξεως καὶ συμφωνίας). The demiurge mitigates the destructive power of the precosmic, evil soul by means of persuasion (πείθω), and thus gives origin to the cosmic soul[120]. The cosmic soul nevertheless preserves in its composition the primordial irrational component – defined as divisible (μεριστόν), unstable (πλανητόν), amorphous (ἄμορφον), undetermined (ἀόριστον) and always in contact with matter[121].

Jan Opsomer has thoroughly analysed the complex implications of the analogy that Plutarch establishes between the constitution of the human and the cosmic soul[122]. Relying on this articulated parallelism, it is possible to establish a direct correspondence – displayed in particular in Plutarch's theory of moral virtue – between the disordered part of the cosmic soul (ταχαρῶδες) and the more powerful and prominent irrational element (ἄλογον) present in the human soul.

Starting from these premises, we can infer with some certainty that, according to Plutarch, the psychic status reached by the priestess during the mantic session is neither an uncontrolled, raving frenzy and a chaotic and overwhelming disruption of confused feelings (cf. Erwin Rohde[123]), nor a completely calm, reasonable state of lucidity (cf. Lisa Maurizio[124] and Simon Price[125]). Instead, I believe that the Pythia seems to reach a rather paradoxical, almost oxymoronic condition: a sort of irrational and chaotic inner status that, precisely for its intrinsic lack of order, is

---

[118] Cf. Ildefonse (2006): Introduction, 47-48; 297, n. 220; the passage of the *Timaeus* here recalled is Plato, *Ti.* 52e3-5.

[119] Cf. *De an. procr.* 1015E-F.

[120] Cf. *ibid.* 1015E.

[121] Cf. *ibid.* 1024A-B.

[122] Cf. Opsomer (1994); (2004).

[123] Cf. Rohde (1925) 289-291.

[124] Cf. Maurizio (1995).

[125] Cf. Price (1985).

susceptible to be guided by a rational, superior, divine force – but always in a mediated, indirect, non-deterministic way. The god – far from exerting a complete, encompassing control – engenders a partial and accessory guiding influence, by transmitting to the Pythia's soul some peculiar representations and a spiritual light that clarifies the future.

As stressed by Robert Flacelière[126], Plutarch believes that the status of prophetic enthusiasm is similar to the one caused by the feeling of love, and that both these psychic conditions are radically different from any kind of 'intoxication'. The parallelism between enthusiasm and love is founded on a passage of *De Pythiae oraculis* that presents an important argument concerning poetic inspiration. Theon states that the peculiar nature (φύσις) and temperament (κρᾶσις) of men and women in ancient times made them spontaneously inclined to produce poetry: as a consequence, any element striking their imaginative faculty (φανταστικόν, essential for poetic creation) was sufficient to stimulate it to the highest degree[127]. Love – which naturally inspires poetry, as any other passion – is a stimulus of this kind: it does not instil in one's soul the poetic and musical faculty themselves (ποιητικὴν καὶ μουσικήν), but awakens and solicits one's intrinsic *natural* attitude and poetic *temperament* which otherwise would lie hidden and inactive (λανθάνουσαν καὶ ἀργοῦσαν)[128].

As we can see, in the case of poetic enthusiasm generated by the passion of love, inspiration is also made up of two elements: first, a natural faculty, innate within the soul; second, an external stimulus that solicits the soul from the outside (ἔξωθεν). Prophetic and poetic enthusiasm (ὁ δὲ μαντικὸς ἐνθουσιασμός, ὥσπερ ὁ ἐρωτικός) therefore share the same composite dynamics: they both make use of our innate faculty (χρῆται τῇ ὑποκειμένῃ δυνάμει, here note again our key-verb χράομαι), and move us – their recipients (κινεῖ τῶν δεξαμένων ἕκαστον) – in accordance with our individual nature (καθ'ὃ πέφυκεν)[129].

5.4. The features of the Pythia

I think that the natural condition of the Pythia's soul – who, as we have seen, is unable to be calm and quiet in the first stage of the mantic session – reveals some important features of her ethical and psychological status at large. The soul of the Pythia – who is not supposed to adhere to elevated rational moral standards – appears to be radically different from the soul of the philosopher or the wise man. As a consequence, the inspiration

---

[126] Cf. *De Pyth. or.* §23 (405D-406B) and notes *ad loc.* in Flacelière (1974).

[127] Cf. *ibid.* 405D: σωμάτων ἤνεγκε κράσεις καὶ φύσεις ὁ χρόνος ἐκεῖνος εὔρουν τι καὶ φορὸν ἐχούσας πρὸς ποίησιν.

[128] Cf. *ibid.* 405F.

[129] Cf. *ibid.* 406B.

that she receives is diametrically opposite to the elitist, authentically philosophical enlightenment allowed by an absolute moral purity, as the one received by Socrates. The fundamental reference in Plutarch in this regard is the dialogue *De genio Socratis*. There we read that only some chosen, privileged humans can enjoy the benefits of a direct contact with divine sources of knowledge: exclusively pure souls receive direct extraordinary messages, whereas mediated and riddling signs are destined to common individuals.

What is required from the Pythia is to have a noble character (ἐστι γενναία τὸ ἦθος) and to live in a dignified way (εὐτάκτως). The day in which she first enters the temple and takes on her role, she is a poor and simple peasant, with no knowledge of the outer world (she has no τέχνη, ἐμπειρία, δύναμις). She resembles an inexperienced bride, who must be ignorant and pure (ἄπειρος καὶ ἀδαής) when she settles into the marital home[130]. She has to be similarly unlearned and naive, in order to join her virginal (παρθένος) soul with the god (ὡς ἀληθῶς τὴν ψυχὴν τῷ θεῷ σύνεστιν)[131]. In particular, in light of the anthropology of the mantic session explained in my previous paragraph, according to which the medium actively participates in the process by introducing its specific characteristics and intrinsic limitations, it is impossible that the priestess talks in sophisticated verses, since she has absolutely no knowledge of meter and poetry.

Being so deprived of any sort of preparation, the prophetess lacks high intellectual and moral standards – which, according to Plutarch's pedagogical ideas, mostly depend on having access to refined education (παιδεία). We can therefore say that the rational qualities that she is missing are somehow compensated by what we might call 'templar rationality': the rigorous and austere ritual customs performed at the Delphic temple seem to make up for the extreme simpleness of the prophetess, thus creating a very well-controlled cultic framework and a rationally-organised space in which the connection with divine knowledge and power can take place.

All the people working at the temple engage in a precise ritual orthopraxis. The Pythia, in particular, prior to the consultation, has to follow the purifying procedure established – which is supposedly and ultimately aimed at reducing the amount of external components that might contaminate the original message[132]. She bathes in the Castalia spring and fumigates herself with laurel leaves and barley meal (δάφνην καὶ κρίθινον ἄλευρον)[133]; she wears a white clothing, a laurel crown, and holds a laurel branch. When descending into the cave, she is totally immersed

---

[130] Cf. Xenophon, *Oec.* 7,4,5.
[131] Cf. *De Pyth. or.* 408C.
[132] Cf. *ibid.* 405C-D.
[133] Cf. *ibid.* 397A.

in her duty (πλέον τὸ καθῆκον) – or refilled with truth (πλέον ἀληθείας), if we follow Bernardakis's reconstruction of this *locus desperatus*[134] – thus she completely disregards human taste, praise or blame[135].

6. *The history of the oracle*

As I will demonstrate in the fourth chapter of the present study, Plutarch's writings show that the Delphic ritual apparatus is perfectly integrated within the very structure of the universe and the forces animating it.

I think that one example of this special prerogative of the Delphic shrine is found in the 'threefold dismemberment' of the first Sybil, described in *De Pythiae oraculis*[136]. This digression is occasioned by a peculiar object that the characters encounter in their promenade: the *Bouleterion*, i.e., the legendary rock placed next to the council chamber that was the seat of the first Sybil (Herophiles) at her arrival from the Mount Helicon, where she had been raised up by the Muses[137].

Sarapion recalls the first utterances that she pronounced, which were the first heroic verses ever composed, and explains that when the Sybil died she was divided into three parts, and each one was assigned to a different destiny: it is fundamental to stress that all of them, as I believe, demonstrate her ongoing, after-death involvement in mantic activity (μαντική).

The first part, simply 'she' (αὐτή), without any further qualification, has become the so-called 'face' that appears on the moon: by continuously revolving around the planet, she creates a peculiar visual effect on its surface[138]. In this regard, it is crucial to remind that in Plutarch the moon acquires a fundamental mediatory function with regard to divination and is also in strict connection with the realm of the demons. The second part, her spirit (πνεῦμα), significantly 'mixed' (συγκραθέν) with the air, produces audible prophetic signs, such as voices and kledons. The third part, her body, buried in the earth, enriches the grass destined to feed the sacrificial victims; by passing through the animals' fodder, this particular nourishment produces material modifications in their entrails, which are currently read by humans for prognostication, according to the techniques of artificial divination.

---

[134] Cf. πλέον...ἢ † ἐκείνη μέλει δόξης καὶ ἀνθρώπων ἐπαινούντων ἢ ψεγόντων, in Sieveking (1972) 25-59.

[135] Cf. *De Pyth. or.* 408D. I will examine more deeply the differences between Delphic and Socratic divination in the last chapter of the present study.

[136] For a thorough reading of this passage and an analysis of the after-death dismemberment of the Sybil see Lincoln (1998).

[137] For this place of the temple see Pausanias, 10,12,1-5.

[138] Cf. also *De sera* 556D: here the crater, which symbolizes the lunar mantic activity, is opposed to the Delphic tripod, whose origin is located in the highest region of the sky, flooded with light.

As we can see, the present state of the mantic art constitutes the continuation of the primordial divinatory activity of the Sybil, who still makes her prophetic influence perceived by the senses of: sight (by creating the 'face' on the moon), hearing (by producing prophetic voices) and touch (by modifying animal viscera). This also demonstrates that Plutarch, very peculiarly, aims to describe the sequence of the consecutive 'owners' of the Delphic oracle as smooth and homogeneous, by flattening their rivalries and by appeasing the contrasts among its successive stages. The Earth – former 'owner' of the oracle – passed the baton to the first Sybil, who still continues to exert her power through her peculiar 'threefold activity', allowed by her multiple 'mixture' into different material entities (the moon, the air, the soil).

Since the Epicurean Boethus reacts with a mocking attitude (καταγελῶν) to the aforementioned mythical-cosmological explanation of the Sybil's 'threefold destiny', Diogenianus, desirous to stress the reliability of the Delphic oracle, reminds some successful predictions, like those of the disasters in Cumae and Dicaearcheia caused by the eruption of Vesuvius in 79 AD[139]. It is important to note that, even in this context, the correctness of the responses is linked to the presence of the so-called 'divine spirit' of the god (θειότης) at the shrine. The very concept of '*theiotês*' – meaning 'divine spirit' or 'divine nature' – is assumed as the vital element of every correct prediction, necessary for the accomplishment of any reliable result[140]. This spirit appears to permeate entirely the Delphic set: the word *theiotês* indicates indeed the godly presence necessary for the prophetic activity as well as the peculiar sacred nature and properties that qualify the ritual objects in Delphi and determine their capacity to work as vehicles for divine communication[141].

When Diogenianus decides to interrupt the company's *promenade* through the Delphic precinct, and to sit on the southern steps of the temple, in front of the shrine of the Earth and the sacred spring, the discussion comes to address another main issue related to the glorious past of the oracle. The meaningful spot also inspires Diogenianus to remind the other characters that it is time to discuss the argument at stake: the reason why the Pythia has ceased to deliver oracles in verses and uses instead a negligent prosaic style – a formal change that may dangerously undermine human faith (πίστις) in oracles and even in god.

Diogenianus himself proposes two possible reasons for the formal decline of oracles: either the Pythia no longer approaches the place where god is (τῷ χωρίῳ [...] ἐν ᾧ τὸ θεῖόν ἐστιν), or the prophetic spirit (πνεῦμα)

---

[139] Cf. *ibid.* 566E.
[140] Cf. *De Pyth. or.* 398F: μή τί γε προειπεῖν ἄνευ θειότητος.
[141] See *supra* 31 and 37-38, and *De Pyth. or.* 398A.

and its power (δύναμις) are vanished. I wish to point out that this is the only passage of *De Pythiae* that defines the pneumatic exhalation as an element involved in the mantic sessions and as a factor useful to explain its dynamics. Indeed, in this dialogue, the analysis of the oracular phenomenon is essentially limited to the action of god within the process or divination *plus* the relationship that he establishes with the prophetess. As the next chapter will demonstrate, the *pneûma* is held instead as a key material principle of oracular divination in *De defectu oraculorum*[142]. For this reason, Flacelière has hypothesised a chronological-thematic development from *De Pythiae* – where the god seems to enter into direct contact with the prophetess – to *De defectu* – where the mediated, indirect action of the god upon the soul of the prophetess is explained in more accurate terms, by resorting to the physical agent of the 'pneumatic exhalation'[143].

Boethus stresses that the location, formed by the shrine of the Earth and the spring of water, may *itself* suggest a solution to the problem debated: his approach contributes to emphasize the symbolical meaning of the objects and places in Delphi, as well as the revealing value of their rational decipherment. Significantly, in paragraph 10, the Epicurean adds some detailed, meaningful information, while composing a sort of reverential tribute to the Delphic shrine, as if to prove that even a follower of the Garden can be enchanted by the temple's captivating atmosphere, and by the long and distinguished tradition that it embodies.

Boethus reminds that a shrine of the Muses was placed exactly there in ancient times, next to the well whose water was used for sacred libations and lustrations. By ensuring that this source has nothing to do with the obscure river Styx, he confirms the solar, lively and luminous nature of the Delphic shrine, opposed to the confused, deadly streams of the underworld – an antithesis that, as I think, recalls the already mentioned opposition present in *De sera numinis vindicta*, between the bright, predictive power of Apollo and the obscure, deceiving oracle of the night[144].

At the time when the responses were in musical measures, the Muses played an essential role at the shrine: they were working as assistants and protectors of the mantic art (παρέδρους τῆς μαντικῆς καὶ φύλακας), and for this very reason their place was there, next to the well and the sanctuary of the Earth, the goddess to which the Delphic oracle once belonged (at a later stage, the Earth abdicated in favour of Apollo). Boyancé, who has studied this passage extensively[145], offers an illuminating explanation for

---

[142] Cf. *De Pyth. or.* 402B-C; for the notion of *pneûma* as a varying natural power cf. *De def. or.* 433C-D; 437C.

[143] Cf. Flacelière (1943) 88.

[144] Cf. *supra* 35.

[145] Boyancé (1938) 308.

the role played in Delphi by the Muses: he identifies them with the demons regulating the pneumatic and psychic composition (κρᾶσις) necessary for divination, as explained in *De defectu oraculorum*.

In this regard, I would like to point out that the word *paredros* (πάρεδρος), associated to the Muses in this section where they are described as 'assistants and protectors' of divination, is a significantly recurrent term of magical texts and extremely successful in Plutarch's time[146]. This word indicates indeed the 'assistant' and 'magical helper' of a professional magician; similar familiar, friendly, beneficent spirits are believed to provide magical aid to the practitioner, throughout the course of a long-term association[147].

7. Solar symbolism

One single paragraph (number 12) of *De Pythiae oraculis* contains all the three occurrences of the term 'symbol' (σύμβολον) – a fundamental, although often implicit, element of this dialogue. Paragraph 12 explains the hidden meaning of the bronze palm, the frogs and the water-snakes forged in metal located at the base of the Corinthians' treasure-house. The Stoic poet Sarapion interprets the special decorations as a proof of the origin of the sun from moisture (ἐξ ὑγρῶν)[148], from which it takes its nourishment, inception (γένεσις) and 'breath' or 'exhalation' (ἀναθυμίασις). Here Sarapion, while fully embracing and applying the technique of Stoic materialistic allegorical interpretation, defines Apollo and the sun as one and the same entity.

The first two occurrences of the term *symbolon* serve to explain that the frogs crafted within the aforementioned monumental offering are not a symbol (σύμβολον) of the city of Corinth[149]. These animals, as Philinus will

---

[146] See the satirical report by Ps-Lucianus, *Philops.* 29; for the occurrences of the word in the *Greek Magical Papyri*, see for instance PGM 4,1746-1767; 12,80-85.

[147] I also would like to recall the coincidence established between Moires and Muses by Plutarch. In the *Table talk* (*Quaest. conv.* 743D; 745B) he explains that in ancient times the Delphians believed that the Muses were named according to the division of the universe into three parts: fixed stars, planets, and sublunary realm. Each part, ordered according to harmonic proportions, was presided by a different Muse: Hypate, Mese, and Nete – the same three worshipped in Delphi – also called Remembrances (Μνείας). This is paralleled in Plato, *Resp.* 10,617b-c, where the cosmic functions are associated to the three Moires (Atropos-invisible, Lachesis-Sun, Clotho-Moon) – for this cf. *De facie* 943A-945C. See also *De genio* 590B, where in the final myth, the cosmic structure fully appears (φαίνεσθαι) before the eyes of the protagonist Timarchus, and he accedes to cosmic mysteries: the secrets of rebirth, the order of reality and the principles of being presided by the Moires.

[148] Cf. SVF I 541: *Cleanthes Lycium Apollinem appellatum notat quod, veluti lupi pecora rapiunt, ita ipse quoque humorem eripit radiis.*

[149] Cf. *De Pyth. or.* 399F: ὥστε σύμβολον ἢ παράσημον εἶναι τῆς πόλεως. Frogs cannot even

clarify[150], have instead been crafted and placed there since they symbolise (are a σύμβολον of) the spring, which is the season when the sun dissipates the winter cold. Nevertheless, as Babut has underlined[151], this solution derives from the premise that the sun and the god are identical – an assumption that counteracts the anti-materialistic view that the guide Philinus himself has just expressed and even contrasts with Plutarch's own metaphysical convictions.

The third occurrence of the term 'symbol' appears in connection with the Egyptian mythological symbolism[152], according to which sunrise is represented by the little boy Harpocrates, son of Isis and Osiris, sitting upon a floating lotus flower. Such a symbolic iconography (σύμβολον[153]), founded on the Egyptian belief of the origin of the sun from water, is widespread in Plutarch's era, a time marked by an intense and extensive admiration for Egyptian cultic elements, symbolism, and religion.

Plutarch's dualistic conception – articulated upon the two opposite, incommensurable plans of contingency and transcendence – clearly prevents him from endorsing Stoic immanentistic allegorisation, founded on a direct identification between deities and physical realities, included the cosmic *logos*.

Philinus, while probably conveying Plutarch's own impressions, rejects the identification between Apollo and the sun, and rather suggests that the relationship between the deity and the planet is one of *analogy*, understandable through symbolical meanings and allusive readings. It is very important to point out that, as Philinus declares, the sun differs from Apollo as much as the moon differs from the sun. For this reason, the appearance of the sun – if not wisely and attentively analysed – is dangerous and deceptive for humans: by attracting and deviating their reflection (διάνοια) to sensation (αἴσθησις), the sun leads them to ignore (ἀγνοεῖν) and misunderstand the real essence of Apollo. The shift from real being (ἀπὸ τοῦ ὄντος) to mere appearance (τὸ φαινόμενον) generated by the sun is indeed opposite to the rational process of abstraction. This is the most advantageous gnoseological path for human understanding: ascending from sensible beings to transcendent notions.

---

be assumed as symbols of Apollo. Philinus remarks that on the basis of a widely accepted symbolism the animals that better represent the god's majesty are rather: crows, swans, wolves, sparrow-hawks, and the cock. For the explanation of the symbolic character of these animals cf. Flacelière (1974) 70, n. 4.

[150] Cf. *De Pyth. or.* 400C: οὕτως ἐνταῦθα τοὺς βατράχους ἐαρινῆς ὥρας φαίη τις ἂν γεγονέναι σύμβολον ἐν ᾗ κρατεῖν ἄρχεται τοῦ ἀέρος ὁ ἥλιος.

[151] Cf. Babut (1993) 219.

[152] Cf. *De Pyth. or.* 400A: εἶτ' Αἰγυπτίους ἑωρακὼς ἀρχῆς <σύμβολον καὶ> ἀνατολῆς παιδίον νεογιλὸν γράφοντας ἐπὶ λωτῷ καθεζόμενον.

[153] Cf. Sieveking (1972) *ad loc.*: <σύμβολον καὶ>.

The way in which Plutarch himself envisions the relationship between the material and the intelligible realm is perhaps inferable from a notable passage of *De Iside et Osiride*, a *locus* that clarifies how Plutarch employs symbols and their decoding in order to convey abstract concepts and complex theories. The passage contains the description of the iconographic appearance of the two main deities of the Egyptian pantheon. The variable and variegated colours of Isis' clothes (στολαὶ ποικίλαι) reveal that her power (δύναμις) is in relation with matter and specifically with her capacity to change according to all the different, and even antithetical, forms that it receives (such as: φῶς σκότος, ἡμέραν νύκτα, πῦρ ὕδωρ, ζωὴν θάνατον, ἀρχὴν τελευτήν)[154]. On the contrary, Osiris' robe is simple and monochromatic, and shines of pure luminosity; this special clothing points to the god's supreme simplicity, and suggests that he corresponds with the simple, intelligible (νοητός), highest (πρῶτος) principle (ἀρχή)[155].

The sun, exactly like the clothes of the Egyptian deities, merely *points to* the existence of the god Apollo and *suggests* his character and qualities. The planet, as a variable material element, and the god, completely disentangled from matter, pertain in fact to two different ontological plans[156]: the sun belongs to the sensible world and regulates its ordered life and becoming (γένεσις), while the deity belongs to the intelligible, transcendent, invariable realm of eternity.

The dialectical confrontation presented in *De Pythiae* contrasts Stoic materialism with Plutarch's understanding of the sensible elements as repositories of hidden messages that must be interpreted according to sound hermeneutical principles. The Stoics – by postulating a direct connection between the divine and the physical world – explain the influence deriving from the sun and the moon (whose origin is identified with two material elements, earth and water, respectively) as material kindlings (ἀνάψεις) and exhalations (ἀναθυμιάσεις).

A notorious Platonic reference, quoted as well in paragraph 12 of *De Pythiae oraculis*[157], provides what I believe is an effective example of symbolic relation. I am referring to the analogy between plants turned upside down and humans, which clearly suggests an important interconnection existing between two different levels of reality: the one psychological-individual, the other cosmological-universal. On this basis, the human being is compared to a 'celestial plant' hanging from the sky[158]. Significantly, the original context in Plato's *Timaeus* is that of a

---

[154] Cf. *De Is. et Os.* 382C; cf. also 373A-B: τὸ γὰρ ὂν καὶ νοητὸν καὶ ἀγαθὸν φθορᾶς καὶ μεταβολῆς κρεῖττόν ἐστιν.

[155] Cf. *ibid.* 382C-D.

[156] Cf. Roskam (2007) 144-145.

[157] *De Pyth. or.* 400B-C.

[158] Cf. Plato, *Ti.* 90a: ὡς ὄντας φυτὸν οὐκ ἔγγειον ἀλλὰ οὐράνιον. For an analysis of this

demonological discussion, which also takes into account the ontological status and psychological constitution of human beings. Accordingly, our head hosts the rational (νοῦς) and noblest (κυριώτατον) part of the soul, which is called demon (δαίμων) and is resemblant to the realm of transcendence. The personal demon, by virtue of its privileged position in the top of human body, connects the soul to its transcendent region of provenance, thus proves its divine affiliation and kinship with the sky (τὴν ἐν οὐρανῷ συγγένειαν). Intellect (νοῦς, another name for the individual demon), divine in origin, free from mutation and independent from the physical component, keeps our body straight and oriented upwards[159].

The belief in the identity between Apollo and the sun[160] – which in the following centuries will result in the institutionalised cult of 'solar henotheism' – is already widespread in Plutarch's time[161]. Another votive offering mentioned in the dialogue that refers to the relation between Apollo and the sun is the golden plectrum dedicated by the Athenians to the oracular god. Theon hypothesises that the donors wanted to recall some significant verses by Scythinus – whose poem *On nature* is founded on Heraclitean ideas and principles – based on the analogy between the lyre and the sun. Accordingly, the Athenians' gift perhaps symbolically enclosed a reference to Apollo's virtue of harmonising the universe with his lyre, from its beginning to its end – thus following the same 'ideal path' daily traced by the sun.

It is worthwhile to dwell now on the image of the lyre, extremely meaningful as regards the role of human soul in divination – which, as we have seen, becomes an instrument (ὄργανον) in the hands of god. Ilaria Ramelli explains the connection between Apollo and the golden plectrum, which dates back to Cleanthes, as a transposition of this musical object into the physical world, where it comes to be identified with sunlight[162]. This conception is grounded on the Stoic idea of the absolute perfection and harmony of the cosmos: the sunbeams strike (πλήσσων) the Oriental

---

concept see Timotin (2012) 75-81. This same image is present, and further developed, in Plutarch's *Amatorius* 757E, and also appears in *De ex.* 600F.

[159] As Philinus explains, this Platonic *exemplum* and analogy does not apply to the sun, and therefore counters the Stoic position: it is indeed impossible to conceive the sun as a 'terrestrial plant' that takes its origin from earthly elements.

[160] Cf. *De E* 386B; *De def. or.* 434F-435A.

[161] An important Delphic found works as a concrete iconographic proof of this identification: it is a fragment of a votive relief representing Helios-Apollo. This archaeological evidence confirms the presence of the deity in the area, thus attests its worship since the Hellenistic age – cf. Zagdoun (1995).

[162] Cf. Ramelli-Lucchetta (2004) 90-91; the connection stressed is with SVF I 502: οὐκ ἀνέγνωσαν δ' οὗτοι Κλεάνθην τὸν φιλόσοφον, ὃς ἀντικρὺς πλῆκτρον τὸν ἥλιον καλεῖ· ἐν γὰρ ταῖς ἀνατολαῖς, ἐρείδων τὰς αὐγάς, οἷον πλήσσων τὸν κόσμον εἰς τὴν ἐναρμόνιον πορείαν [τὸ φῶς] ἄγει.

regions and guide the harmonious course of the world[163]. It should also be reminded that the sun is the middle term in the Pythagorean order of the planets – a position that determines its role of a cosmic mediator[164]. Accordingly, a connection can be established between the sun, which is responsible for the cosmic harmony, and the *mesê* as the middle note in the harmonic scale.

The concept of 'mean' (μέσον)[165] – in the sense of 'intermediate term' or 'middle note' typical of the musical theory (περὶ φθόγγους καὶ ἁρμονίας)[166] – and the Platonic image of the chariot[167] – which inspires Plutarch's tripartite vision of the soul, integrated into, and mitigated by, the emphasis that he places on the alliance between reason and the irascible part – are treated jointly in the ninth of Plutarch's *Questiones Platonicae*[168]. Here, by cleverly exploiting the multifaceted meanings of the term *logos*, the Chaeronean identifies this notion not only with the harmonic proportion that reason imposes on passions, but also with reason itself, as principle of regularity and order that controls the whole soul and harmonizes the psychic composition[169]. In light of this digression, if we turn back to the issue of oracular inspiration, it is easier to ascertain the relevance of the concept of 'medium', which comes to coincide with the notion of 'middle term' as well as with that of 'intermediary' between two opposite terms.

According to a clarifying analogy that Plutarch proposes[170], in the same way as the god uses the Pythia to be heard (πρὸς ἀκοήν), so the sun uses the moon to be seen (πρὸς ὄψιν). The moon is the most obedient (εὐπειθέστερον) natural entity[171], and the most perfect instrument present in the physical realm, since it faithfully resembles, and obeys to, its master: the sun. The moon captures the sunbeams and projects them upon the earth with a different intensity – thus inevitably modifying them[172].

---

[163] In this regard, see Borthwick (2003) 279: "In Scythinus, Apollo the sun god with his plectrum has the same function as the sun as *mesê* linking the two tetrachords of the heptachord in a fanciful passage of Nicomachus (p. 242, cf. 272), where he identifies each note of the scale with one of the seven planets, with *mesê*/sun in the middle". Borthwick also draws a parallel with *Quaest. conv.* 745B, where Plutarch attests that in Delphi 'Mese' was the Muse granting the cosmic harmony by supervising the planets.

[164] For the mediating function of the solar deity of Mithras, see Turcan (1975) 11-12.

[165] Cf. Aristoteles, *EN* 2,6,1106a24.

[166] Cf. *De virt. mor.* 444E.

[167] Cf. Plato, *Phdr.* 246a6-7.

[168] For a thorough discussion see Opsomer (2012) esp. 23-28.

[169] Cf. *ibid.* 26.

[170] Cf. *De Pyth. or.* 404D.

[171] Cf. *ibid.* 404D1-3: καὶ γάρ εἰσι <...ἡλίῳ δ'> οὐδὲν οὔτε μᾶλλον <τὴν> ἰδέαν ἔοικεν οὔθ᾽ὡς ὀργάνῳ χρῆσθαι φύσει γέγονεν εὐπειθέστερον σελήνης·

[172] Cf. *ibid.* 404C-D.

If we apply this analogy to oracular divination, we find that the prophetess is utterly similar to the moon when she performs her role of 'perfect medium' between the god and humankind. On the one hand, the Pythia works as an *intermediary* agent: she expresses the thoughts and indications of the god, though slightly corrupted and modified. On the other hand, she occupies an ontologically *intermediate* position between the absolute transcendence of the deity and the ordinary status of common human beings.

When the Pythia submits herself to the action of prophetic inspiration, her intrinsic faculties and intellectual capabilities play a major role, notwithstanding the regulative ritual framework enacted in Delphi, which – as I anticipated – is apparently supposed to compensate the rationality and ordered psychic status that the priestess is missing. Her soul, captured in confused movements and passions, is an indispensable component of the divinatory dynamics: the god illuminates, and partially orders, her *psychê* by bestowing on it a part of his superior rationality – an act that, following the same model of the cosmogenesis as explained in Plutarch's *De animae procreatione in Timaeo*, leads her to an oxymoronic controlled *and* chaotic status.

What has emerged so far is that the explanation of the prophetic activity in *De Pythiae oraculis*, like several other natural phenomena analysed in this dialogue, is founded on two main epistemic assumptions. First, all the elements involved in a natural process, included oracular divination, must be in a perfectly balanced 'mixture' (κρᾶσις) among themselves in order for a given phenomenon to arise. Second, the functioning and explanation of every phenomenon are necessarily articulated upon two different orders of causality. In particular, the twofold division of causes (primary-transcendent *and* secondary-material, which we will find more clearly stated in *De defectu oraculorum*) is grounded on the ontological structure of the world: the sensible cosmos, according to Plutarch, is not pure (καθαρός), but mixed and composed of divine rationality *plus* matter (λόγος and ὕλη)[173]. In fact, as the creation of the world by the demiurge had to pass through disordered matter – given the principle that god cannot create anything from nothing, thus cannot make the incorporeal corporeal –[174], in the same way the communication of his divine thoughts has to pass through the resistance of utterly human, material elements, characterised by peculiar qualities and subject to the unbreakable laws of necessity. In the case of oracular divination, these correspond to the Pythia's mortal body and her simple soul.

---

[173] Cf. *De def. or.* 436B.
[174] Cf. *De an. procr.* 1014C.

Chapter 2
An analysis of *De defectu oraculorum*

1. Introduction

De defectu oraculorum addresses the problem of the quantitative decline of the oracular activity and production in the II century Greece, which dramatically affects also the prophetic role of the Delphic shrine[1].

The Delphic temple[2], at the time when the Pythian games are approaching[3], is the location chosen in *De defectu* in order to debate the historical issue of the decline of oracles, which is undermining both their quantity and prestige. The philosophical and religious aspects of this enquiry are harmonized under the aegis of the Apollinean religion, which contributes to confirm Apollo as the protective deity of rational investigation as well as of mantic activity. In the course of the dialogue, religious beliefs, mythological narratives and geological accounts are all employed to define the Delphic oracle as a unique location on earth, chosen by the deity and recognised by humans, and as the 'perfect place' designed for the encounter between men's desire to know (φιλοσοφία) and god's perfect wisdom (σοφία).

This chapter will show that this dialogue has mainly an apologetic purpose: it intends to prevent that the oracular crisis destroys human belief in the existence of the deity, and in its providential and beneficent character. We will see that the text recursively presents an identical argumentative strategy: the first stage consists in a thorough investigation of concrete data and facts, while their philosophical examination and some tentative

---

[1] A former decline of Delphi dates back to the I century CE: during the Mithridatic wars (88-63 BC), Sulla sacked the city in order to finance his military campaign. The site afterwards benefited from Nero's restoration plan for the Greek cities (continued by Hadrian). Its second major decline corresponds perhaps to the one described by Plutarch in *De defectu oraculorum* (written in *ca.* 85-90 AD), thus dates back to the end of the I century. Nevertheless, the restoration promoted by the Antonines would have soon restored the activity and reputation of the Delphic shrine. Plutarch apparently attests to this rebirth (cf. *De Pyth. or.* 408F-409A), by declaring that numerous Greek and foreign pilgrims were reaching Delphi with rich votive offerings, while new buildings were erected and ancient monuments and statues rebuilt. The impressive spiritual and material flourishing of oracles will last until the middle of the IV century AD; after a short revival under the emperor Julian (361-363 AD), they will be definitively silenced.

[2] Cf. *De def. or.* 412D.

[3] Cf. *ibid.* 410A. The dramatic date of the dialogue is probably 83 AD – for this see Ogilvie (1967).

solutions are provided in a second stage. As the present analysis will show, experiences, narratives and inquiries (ἱστορίαι) are all adopted as solid proofs and starting points for the discussion; only in a second time, their abstract implications are analysed and their theoretical outcomes are developed.

From the dialogue we can infer that all the participants – except the Cynic philosopher Didymus Planetiades – are religious men, initiated into mysteries (οὐδεὶς [...] τῶν βεβήλων καὶ ἀμυήτων): they all share the common belief (and underlying principle of the whole discussion) in the existence of a supreme provident immortal deity[4]. As the present chapter will attempt to demonstrate, this theological conception counteracts the Stoic ideas of divine materiality (πῦρ νοερόν) and periodical destruction of the universe (ἐκπύρωσις, from which just Zeus is preserved as the only eternal and unchangeable god[5]) as well as the Epicurean atomistic theory, which advocates indefiniteness (ἀπειρία) against the rational power of divine providence, discarded as fictitious (μῦθος)[6].

I will point out how this religious belief substantiates and legitimises the hypothesis of demonology, which is crucial in the dialogue, and appears sound and reliable if compared to the absurd pseudo-philosophical and counter-intuitive conceptions of both the Stoics and the Epicureans. As Cleombrotus explains, the demonological theory is firmly anchored in natural science (φυσιολογία); the same assumption is also suggested by Plato in the *Timaeus*[7], in an enigmatic and cautious way (αἰνιγματώδη μετ᾽εὐλαβείας), when he alludes to the possibility of the plurality of worlds. Another world would indeed be the place where the demons could have escaped, thus leaving the oracles mute and uninspired[8].

The present analysis will show that *De defectu oraculorum* brings into focus two main roles that the demigods play within the oracular process: they serve both as 'psychic assistants' that balance the pneumatic combination of the prophetic spirit with the temperament of the Pythia's soul, and as 'metaphorical referents' that constitute an effective point of comparison and a theoretical model for clarifying the psychological dynamics of enthusiasm.

The demonological theory is a constitutive part of the analysis of the divinatory procedure in *De defectu* but, given its speculative and constitutively unverifiable character, it is treated just indirectly and elusively. Plutarch, as Daniel Babut underlines, considers demonology a

---

[4] Cf. *De def. or.* 418D.

[5] Cf. *ibid.* 420B. For the Stoic reference cf. SVF II 1049.

[6] Cf. *De def. or.* 420B.

[7] Cf. Plato, *Ti.* 55c-d; other allusions to this argument are found in *De def. or.* 421F; 422E; 426F.

[8] Cf. *De def. or.* 420F.

mere *hypothesis*, which therefore is impossible to embrace and profess dogmatically[9]. In this sense, the demonological hypothesis plays a role similar to the mythological narratives scattered in the dialogical exchange: as the present analysis also aims to show, demonology and myths similarly display a kind of 'blurred' argumentative strategy – whose 'detached' and 'approximative' character originates from, and reveals, the intrinsic limitedness of human understanding with regard to transcendent truths.

2. *The character of Didymus and the style of philosophy*

The intervention of the Cynic philosopher Didymus Planetiades, although strikingly short and unwelcome, is, as I believe, a key passage of *De defectu oraculorum*[10]. Didymus is the first character who attempts to solve the debated problem, but also the first to abruptly abandon the discussion, as soon as scolded for his hostile and arrogant contempt against the god. At first sight, he embodies the 'living *manifesto*' of all the hideous attitudes and conceptions that must be banished when debating on sacred matters. Plutarch indeed believes that philosophical enquiries concerning the divine must acknowledge the majesty and supreme ontological status of god, while also respecting the intrinsic and impassable limits of human rationality. Didymus, as we will see, offers a perfect antithetical example with regard to these criteria. Plutarch depicts him as the stereotypical Cynic philosopher, who grabs in his hand the walking stick – a symbol of his status of permanent traveller and foreigner – that he hits on the ground a couple of times before starting his diatribe against the wickedness of humankind. The Cynic identifies human naughtiness (κακία) as the main cause of the departure of divine providence (πρόνοια θεῶν) from earth, which has provoked the oracular crisis and the consequent impossibility for humans to predict the future. Incidentally, I wish to point out that Didymus, when ascribing the task and responsibility of the production of oracles precisely to the gods and their '*pronoia*', is the first speaker to introduce the pivotal concept of providence into the discussion.

Didymus also provides a counter-argument for this dreadful decline: he notes that Delphi surprisingly stands out as a unique exception to the general crisis, as confirmed by the fact that it was surprisingly not abandoned by divine providence[11]. He explains that the activity of the Delphic oracle contrasts with the terrible conditions in which it is forced to operate: it is constantly under attack by several irreverent clients

---

[9] Cf. Babut (1994b) 548.

[10] Cf. *De def. or.* 412F-413D.

[11] The episode of Heracles and the tripod is an example of hostile contempt against the shrine; cf. also *De E* 387D; *De sera* 560D. For an interesting philosophical reading of Plutarch's narration, see Lernould (2000).

submitting profane enquiries (ἀθέων ἐρωτημάτων). This happens in two ways: first, people come to test the god in a sophistic manner (ὡς σοφιστοῦ); second, they pose trivial everyday questions on wealth and marriages – a custom also attested in *De Pythiae oraculis*[12] – thus shamelessly showing to the deity their secret wishes and passions[13].

I think it is worth dwelling on the first tendency pointed out by Didymus, that of questioning the god in an inquisitive way, which indeed recalls the attitude of another famous contemporaneous Cynic philosopher: Oenomaus of Gadara (*floruit ca.* 120 AD). Oenomaus in *The Exposure of Frauds* denounces the 'human, all too human' cheating behind oracles and divination, by collecting some mythical and historical *exempla* of incongruous predictions[14]. The philosophical basis of this work lies in Oenomaus' polemical attitude against the Stoics and specifically against their simultaneous and contradictory admission of fate as a deterministic chain encompassing all events (included oracular responses) *and* human freedom (included the freedom of the prophet himself)[15].

Oenomaus reports his own experience at the oracle of Apollo at Claros, close to the Lydian city of Colophon[16], and documents some of its ambivalent, incomprehensible answers, sometimes delivered identical to multiple consultants[17]. Oenomaus' harsh controversy against the authority of official oracles highlights two main historical critical issues concerning divination, which have already been recalled in my previous chapter[18], and can be outlined as follows: first, his testimony indirectly questions the dis-

---

[12] For the low quality of the inquiries made to the oracle cf. *De E* 386C; *De Pyth. or.* 408C.

[13] Cf. *De def. or.* 413B. As Didymus explains, this attitude goes against the Pythagorean principle according to which men show their best in front of the gods. Cf. also *De sup.* 169E: καὶ ὅλως ἀποδείκνυσιτὸν Πυθαγόρου λόγον φλύαρον εἰπόντος ὅτι βέλτιστοι γιγνόμεθα πρὸς τοὺς θεοὺς βαδίζοντες.

[14] Extracts of this work are preserved in Eusebius, *PE* 6,7,1-42.

[15] Cf. *ibid.* 6,7,23.

[16] The oracle of the sanctuary of Apollo at Claros was active since the late IV century BC. Claros' golden age was the II century AD, when Hadrian promoted its reconstruction (an inscription of *ca.* 135-138 AD contains his personal dedication to Apollo), which bolstered the success of the oracle in the Eastern area of the empire. Fox thoroughly analyses the financial-economical conditions behind this revival – see Fox (1995) 171-180. For a general discussion see Johnston (2008) 76-82.

[17] Individual oracular enquiries (opposed to civic enquiries) are widely attested in literature (cf. Xenophon Ephesius, 1,6; Apuleius, *Met* 4,32; Aristides, *Or.* 15,312,5; Merkelbach-Stauber 21). During the Imperial age, questioning the oracle on individual/private issues is a widespread custom – which, nevertheless, is not limited to this period. Indeed, "Ce type de demande adressée à la divinité, à savoir des questions sur des problèmes personnels, a toujours existé" – Busine (2005) 104.

[18] Cf. *supra* 37.

tinction between public religious institutions and fraudulent independent seers (ψευδομάντεις); second, it sheds light on a fundamental aspect of divination, which will acquire an increasing relevance by the end of the Imperial age, and consists in its profound interconnection with the notion of 'authenticity', 'reliability' and 'truth'[19].

Indeed, attracting the 'good faith' of the community is an important prerogative for the success of oracular institutions. Reliability is what the Delphic oracle has attempted to reach throughout the centuries, while constantly fighting against the misconception that a systematic action of propaganda or manipulation was there at work. The *Homeric Hymn to Apollo* emphasizes exactly the role of the Delphic temple as a catalyst for civic interest and a source of long prosperity[20], while ensuring that in that very place the divine power of Apollo, founder of the oracle, will always continue to manifest itself. The god is said to employ this sacral institution in order to communicate his *unfailing advice* (νημερτέα βουλήν) – an expression clearly aimed at encouraging the faith of humans in his voice[21].

The attitude of the Cynic philosopher Didymus testifies to the kind of hyper-rationalistic and irreverent approach usually employed to discredit oracles as expressions of vulgar superstition. His attitude, shared by other contemporaneous intellectuals, first of all Lucian of Samosata[22], strongly contrasts with Plutarch's devout spirit and with his conception of a profound complementarity (συμφωνία) between rationalistic and religious tendencies.

Plutarch generally tends to be critical towards the Cynics' disengagement from the political activity and their detachment from the practical problems of society. The intervention of Didymus Planetiades in this section of the *De defectu oraculorum* helps us, in particular, to understand Plutarch's position with regard to Cynic theological-religious conceptions. While explaining the recent oracular decline as a divine punishment for human wickedness, Didymus implicitly attributes a vindictive spirit and resentful behaviour to the deity: this characterization strongly contrasts with Plutarch's theology and theodicy, according to which the god is an absolutely transcendent and imperturbable being, whose actions can be

---

[19] For an analysis of the relevance of these notions and values in connection to the divinatory practices of this age see Filoramo (2007) 41-56; Couloubaritsis (1990) 113-122.

[20] Cf. *h.Ap.* 531-537.

[21] Cf. *ibid.* 247-485.

[22] Lucian of Samosata notoriously denounces the frauds perpetrated, among the others, by the founder of a personal oracle and mystery cult Alexandros of Abonuteichos. On the role of Alexander as a self-constructed pseudo-prophet see Sfameni Gasparro (1996).

neither reduced to a rigid cause-effect scheme, nor connected to human events in an indisputable, clear-cut way[23].

It is significant that Lamprias' response to Didymus' allegations follows an argumentative line that Plutarch himself may have endorsed: he stresses the ontological distance between god and humans, which prevents any direct causal relations between their respective choices and actions. Moreover, he underlines that divine providence still shows its benevolent character and still provides everything – except divination – that humans need for their survival, as a loving mother who cares for her progeny[24].

To sum up, the intervention of the Cynic philosopher is relevant under three main respects. First, it introduces – despite in highly negative, inappropriate terms – the notion of divine providence, thus anticipating the prominent role that this concept will play in the subsequent development of the dialogue. Second, it sheds light on the importance that diverging theological assumptions might have assumed in Plutarch's relationship with Cynic philosophy, or at least with its followers. Third, it works as an example of how a sound, well-balanced and educated philosophical exchange should *not* be conducted.

Didymus' sudden departure leaves the company in a peaceful condition (ἡσυχίας δὲ γενομένης), ideal for philosophical discussion, as the participants themselves confirm. According to the grammarian Heracleon of Megara just a warm, harmonious expression of feelings allows for the rise of rational and fruitful dialectical exchanges[25]. Lamprias eventually stresses the need to dismiss any provocative attitude and arrogant behaviour when discussing philosophically, and to always show respect towards the god, whose goodness and mildness (εὐόργητος γάρ ἐστι καὶ πρᾶος) are never to be questioned[26]. Later in the dialogue[27], Cleombrotus will provide methodological instructions for dialogical investigation: when debating important matters, relevant principles (μεγάλαι ἀρχαί) should constitute the starting point, while the target should not be truth, but rather opinion and probability (ἐπὶ τὸ εἰκὸς τῇ δόξῃ). Ammonius, in his turn, will appeal to reciprocal understanding and forbearance (συγγνώμη), highlighting the value of authentic freedom of speech (παρρησία) which, opposed to the uncontrolled rage of Didymus, provides the preconditions for real common

---

[23] Dillon (2002) offers a valuable account of Plutarch's theodicy.

[24] Cf. *De def. or.* 413C: οὐδ' ἅμα τὴν πρόνοιαν ὥσπερ εὐγνώμονα μητέρα καὶ χρηστὴν πάντα ποιοῦσαν ἡμῖν καὶ φυλάττουσαν ἐν μόνῃ μνησίκακον εἶναι τῇ μαντικῇ καὶ ταύτην ἀφαιρεῖσθαι δοῦσαν ἐξ ἀρχῆς.

[25] Cf. *ibid.*: τὰ δ' ἄλλ' ἔξεστι τὰς ὀφρῦς κατὰ χώραν ἔχοντας φιλοσοφεῖν καὶ ζητεῖν ἀτρέμα μὴ δεινὸν βλέποντας μηδὲ χαλεπαίνοντας τοῖς παροῦσιν.

[26] Cf. *ibid.* 413C.

[27] Cf. *ibid.* 418F.

research (ζητεῖν) and learning (μανθάνειν), while banishing rivalry (ἔρις) and contentiousness (φιλονεικία)[28].

As Jan Opsomer has pointed out in his seminal contributions on the topic of *Divination and Academic 'Scepticism'*[29], search for the truth in Plutarch is tentative and consciously directed towards provisional achievements; moreover, in line with the dialogical structure frequently employed by the Chaeronean, philosophical investigation is mainly envisioned as a common, dialectical enquiry driven by an aporetic-zetetic spirit and based on the awareness of the provisional character of human knowledge. Caution (ἀσφάλεια[30]) is a key criterion for rational inquiry: only secure intermediate steps count within the path of rational investigation, given that no definitive cognitive goal is attainable by human beings.

Plutarch firmly believes in the need to suspend judgement (ἐποχή) on non-graspable objects of knowledge and to show a deep reverential respect towards the divine (εὐλάβεια[31]) – enriched by a self-aware subjective attitude (σεμνότης) and by the conviction that any groundless certainty in the field of religion would lead to the extremes of superstition or atheism. Rational investigation is limited to probability and verisimilitude: the nature of the sensible world prevents a complete understanding of natural phenomena, while the transcendent realm cannot be grasped by human mind, due to its intrinsic limitations. Plutarch's epistemological stance is greatly influenced by his Academic affiliation[32]: in the fields of ethics and religion human beings cannot reach for a comprehensive knowledge, which – contrary to what the Stoics believe – is reserved only to gods. Opsomer has indeed showed the polemical function of Plutarch's epistemological ideas in his controversy against the Stoics and the Epicureans; in this regard, he has demonstrated the coexistence of scepticism and religious faith in Plutarch, reinforced by the Chaeronean's conviction of the unity of the Academic tradition, throughout which the belief in oracles can be assumed as a constant thread.

As the present research will show, the epistemic framework of Plato's *Timaeus*[33], according to which every discourse on the physical world

---

[28] Cf. *ibid.* 431D.

[29] Opsomer (1996); (1998) 185.

[30] Cf. *De def. or.* 431A.

[31] Cf. *ibid.* 420F.

[32] Opsomer (1996) reminds some Plutarchan lost works, listed in the Lamprias catalogue, related to the thesis of the unity of the Academy and the affiliation between Academic philosophy and the religious-divinatory spirit: *On the Unity of the Academy from Plato* (n. 63); *That the Academic Philosophy allows for the Reality of Prophecy* (n. 71); *On the fact that there is no Conflict between the Principles of the Academy and the Art of Prophecy* (n. 131).

[33] Cf. Plato, *Ti.* 48d.

is inevitably fallible, is a fundamental idea implicit throughout the development of *De defectu oraculorum*[34]. Nevertheless, a striking paradox must be emphasized: while the study of divination must comply with the highest standards of rationality, divination itself is an important element included in god's design to help humans *exceed* their weakness and *do away* with their rational faculty, in order to grasp what is beyond standard comprehension.

3. Narratives and inquiries

Cleombrotus the Lacedaemonian seems to condense in a few words the spirit of the dialogue, when he declares to derive rational arguments from factual-empirical data[35]. He has been travelling extensively, driven by his curiosity and desire to see and learn (ἀνὴρ φιλοθεάμων καὶ φιλομαθής) – and not for business (οὐ κατ᾽ ἐμπορίαν)[36]. In the course of his journeys, he gathered a wide practical knowledge and collected a large amount of historical and geographical information (ἱστορία). These form the basis for his theoretical and philosophical reflection (φιλοσοφία), which, as he believes, is in its turn directed to theology (θεολογία)[37].

Franco Ferrari has pointed out that the hierarchical disposition of these three disciplines is not likely to correspond to Plutarch's own view. The Chaeronean rather considers epoptic science the acme of rational enquiry. Epoptic corresponds to the understanding (νόησις) of the simple and pure, touched and seen just once (ἅπαξ)[38], in a time-limited, extraordinary experience[39]; its object is the supreme end (τέλος) of human quest for knowledge, located beyond the variable and mixed sensible world[40]. While

---

[34] The epistemic status of the sensible and intelligible world in Plutarch are explored in: Ferrari (1996) esp. 368; Bonazzi (2015) 94-104.

[35] The name and features of this character disclose some Platonic allusions, as pointed out in Dušanić (1996) esp. 293.

[36] Such a description reminds the one of the 'stranger' Diogenianus in *De Pyth. or.* 394F, where he is defined as not simply willing to contemplate (φιλοθεάμων), or to listen passively (φιλήκοος) to the guides' explanations, but rather eager to acquire profound knowledge (φιλόλογος) and active comprehension (φιλομαθής).

[37] Cf. *De def. or.* 410B: συνῆγεν ἱστορίαν οἷον ὕλην φιλοσοφίας θεολογίαν ὥσπερ αὐτὸς ἐκάλει τέλος ἐχούσης.

[38] Cf. θιγεῖν in *De Is. et Os.* 382D and ἅψασθαι in Plato, *Tht.* 186d.

[39] Cf. Pseudo-Plato, *Ep.* 7, esp. 344b-c: ἅμα γὰρ αὐτὰ ἀνάγκη μανθάνειν καὶ τὸ ψεῦδος ἅμα καὶ ἀληθὲς τῆς ὅλης οὐσίας, μετὰ τριβῆς πάσης καὶ χρόνου πολλοῦ, ὅπερ ἐν ἀρχαῖς εἶπον· μόγις δὲ τριβόμενα πρὸς ἄλληλα αὐτῶν ἕκαστα, ὀνόματα καὶ λόγοι ὄψεις τε καὶ αἰσθήσεις, ἐν εὐμενέσιν ἐλέγχοις ἐλεγχόμενα καὶ ἄνευ φθόνων ἐρωτήσεσιν καὶ ἀποκρίσεσιν χρωμένων, ἐξέλαμψε φρόνησις περὶ ἕκαστον καὶ νοῦς, συντείνων ὅτι μάλιστ᾽ εἰς δύναμιν ἀνθρωπίνην; on the relevance of this passage for Plutarch, see Zambon (2002) 57.

[40] Cf. *De Is. et Os.* 382D-E: ἐποπτικὸν [...] μέρος [...] τῆς φιλοσοφίας.

'theology' is limited to the knowledge of the supreme divine causes, epoptic is a kind of religious-metaphysical 'illumination' on superior entities (being and god). Claudio Moreschini has similarly stressed that Plutarch conceives philosophy and religion as on the same level, and both of them as equally preliminary for epoptic – for which reason, philosophy cannot be intended as an '*ancilla theologiae*'[41].

In order to have a better insight on the relevance of Cleombrotus' stance in *De defectu*, and in the broader framework of Plutarch's thought, it is worth dwelling briefly on the meaning of the three terms that he employs (ἱστορία, φιλοσοφία, θεολογία) and contextualise them within the argumentative structure of the dialogue. *De defectu* seems to somehow implement Cleombrotus' assertion: as stated in the beginning of the present analysis, a recurrent pattern of the dialogue is indeed to first present and explore practical-concrete data, then to develop their theoretical-abstract consequences.

In particular, some narratives told in the dialogue provide valuable information – concerning the character, nature, and faculties of demons – that will be employed within the subsequent theoretical analysis of oracular mantic. These data were collected by the speakers during extensive, fascinating journeys, which – like votive pilgrimages – also strengthened their piety and worship[42]. Plutarch – in line with the contemporaneous culture and sensibility, encouraged by favourable economical and political conditions – intends travel as a reliable source and fundamental means of knowledge acquisition. Journeys (be they realistic, mysteric, fictitious) are considered a real and effective prerequisite for accessing authentic wisdom, supposedly 'hidden' in far, inaccessible lands. This tendency is attested by numerous works of the time: one need only think of Pausanias' *Periegesis*, where travel emerges as a resource for exploring the world, classifying reality and reconstructing the utopian, idealized Greek past, while the barriers between real facts and imaginary events (θαυμάσια, μυθώδη) become surprisingly permeable.

The image of the 'wanderer' (ἀλήτης) achieves a great success in the first centuries AD: an example is the rhetorician Dio Chrysostomos, who lives as an itinerant Cynic, travels to remote lands, while spreading the knowledge that he has acquired *directly* and witnessed with his own eyes (αὐτὸς ἰδών)[43]. Wandering prophets, charlatans and magicians, as well as the educated (πεπαιδευμένοι) representatives of the Second Sophistic, exert

---

[41] Cf. Moreschini (1996).

[42] Hunt (1984) provides an interesting analysis of travel as a social phenomenon in the Imperial age.

[43] Cf. Dio Chrysostomus, 7,1; for the life of this itinerant philosopher and rhetor, Philostratus, *VS* 1,479.

a kind of spiritual-religious or social-political influence in those areas of the Empire where the official central sovereignty is invisible or ineffective.

Travel is indeed connected to the notion of *historia* (ἱστορία), which corresponds to both the active, dynamic task of investigating (εἶδον), and to the static *corpus* of information gathered in the exploration (οἶδα). This is also evident in Plutarch, who strongly considers our innate desire to know as a constitutive part of our intellectual life. Ernesto Valgiglio has highlighted that – especially in Herodotus, the notorious 'father' of *historia* – the peculiar character of this research activity is to be associated with active quest and solicitation. It is therefore opposite to the 'automatic knowledge' transmitted by tradition, or to the passive gathering of data through accidental sight (ὄψις, θέα) and hearing (ἀκοή)[44].

I would like to focus now on three narratives told in *De defectu oraculorum*. They involve exactly the concept of *historia* and display it according to a gradually higher degree of accuracy: the first is an event not partaken in by the speaker; the second is based on information partly acquired by the narrator and partly told by other witnesses; the third is an encounter with a sort of superhuman individual, experienced by the speaker in first person[45].

The first narrative consists in Philip's description of the death of Pan[46]: as said, this story is twice distant from reality, since Philip reports an event occurred to another man, Epitherses, during a journey – an episode assumed as a reliable proof on demonological subjects. Such a curious experience provides empirical evidence of the mortality of demons, as condensed in the famous adage: 'the Great Pan is dead[47]' ('ὁ μέγας Πὰν τέθνηκεν'), echoed by the wail of many voices. Demons, differently from gods, are not immortal.

The second narrative consists in Demetrius' report on a striking phenomenon witnessed during a journey that he undertook on behalf of the emperor[48]. He was exploring the islands surrounding Britannia and

---

[44] Cf. Valgiglio (1991), esp. 21: "[...] un sapere automatico, il cui ἵστωρ è la fonte della tradizione, di contro al sapere sollecitato, che è la ἱστορίη". Valgiglio's essay offers a thorough examination of the use and development of the term *historia* from Homer to Plutarch.

[45] It is worth noting that all these three episodes display a clear connection with imperial potentates: Epitherses was summoned and interrogated by Tiberius, who was eager to investigate on Pan and his death (419D-E); Demetrius was on an exploration trip (ἱστορίας καὶ θέας ἕνεκα) for account of the emperor (419E); the Barbarian of the Red Sea was regularly consulted by rulers and ministers. This also contributes to prove how imperial power was perceived as a cumbersome presence by intellectuals.

[46] Cf. *De def. or.* 419A-419E.

[47] Eng. trans F. C. Babbitt.

[48] Cf. *De def. or.* 419E-420A. Demetrius will later propose what he will call in another

observing those places with his own eyes, according to the principles of authentic *historia* (ἱστορίας καὶ θέας ἕνεκα). He landed in a territory populated by few holy inhabitants (ἱεροί), where he was welcomed by a number of meteorological signs and omens (διοσημίας πολλάς): as he was told, the impressive portents accompanied the disappearance (ἔκλειψις⁴⁹) of a divine being, presumably a demon. Demetrius also learnt that Chronus was there, confined on a nearby island, where he was watched over by some demigods and Briareus⁵⁰. While the narration as a whole – similarly to the previous one – bears witness to the mortality of demons, this last aspect stresses their caring and supporting capacity, which they also direct towards humans – being this last one among the typical functions of demigods according to Plutarch's demonology.

The third narrative (διήγησις⁵¹) consists in Cleombrotus' direct testimony of a memorable experience that also highlights additional virtues and beneficial services that characterise the demonic nature. The wealthy man, after long wanderings and large amounts paid for reliable information, finally reached the Red Sea shore where he found the long-sought inspired, semi-mythical individual (θεῖος ἀνήρ), depicted as a 'barbarian' but ennobled by evident Pythagorean features, such as the typical Doric accent. It is important to stress that he was committed to any kind of learning and *historia* (μάθησις καὶ ἱστορία), a term that in this context may correspond precisely to 'enquiry' or 'research'.

'real fact' (πρᾶγμα), as opposed to a rational philosophical argumentation (λόγος) and demonstration (ἐπίδειξις), in order to fight scepticism in religious matters. The governor of Cilicia – an insolent, irreligious man (ὑβριστὴς καὶ φαῦλος), sustained in his wrong convictions by the Epicureans and their scientific theories (φυσιολογία) – decided to put the oracle of Mopsus to test (which, according to our sources, was defined a typical barbarian act). The test obviously proved the oracle's effectiveness, baffled the Epicureans and turned the irreverent ruler into a zealous worshipper of Mopsus (cf. *De def. or.* 434C-F). For the analysis of other 'barbaric' consultations, see Price (1985) esp. 152.

The description of the Cilician ruler presents the same topical features typically attributed to barbarians in Plutarch – who is influenced by Classical ideas and standards. As Schmidt (2002) points out, Plutarch tends to disqualify the barbarians by blaming their cruelty (ἀγριότης), arrogance (θρασύτης), recklessness (τόλμα), their excesses in wealth and war, their ignorance and savagery. On the contrary, the Greeks shine for their education (παιδεία), humanity (φιλανθρωπία) and virtue (ἀρετή). Plutarch's idealized depiction of the Greek world is nevertheless rather anachronistic for his times.

⁴⁹ It is worth noting that the same word used here, 'ἔκλειψις' in the sense of 'abandonment', appears in the title of *De defectu oraculorum* (Περὶ τῶν ἐκλελοιπότων χρηστηρίων), where it presumably refers to the oracles' abandonment by the demons.

⁵⁰ Also cf. *De facie* 945D. It is interesting to stress that the Hecatoncheires, the superhuman sons of Uranus and Gaea to which also Briareus belongs, were believed to incarnate the frantic power of earth- and sea-quakes.

⁵¹ *De def. or.* 421F-422E.

Moreover, the 'barbarian' proved to be in strict connection with Delphi: he was aware of its rites, traditional stories and even of its more obscure aspects, also concerning the importance of Dionysus for the temple. According to this stranger (ξένος), demons are responsible for the mantic power, as well as for his own divinatory ability. He assigns a significant hermeneutical role to them: demigods are the real protagonists of those mythical adventures – such as escapades, fights and peregrinations – which would be highly disrespectful to attribute to the gods. These misfortunes are called 'great sufferings' (πάθη μεγάλα – which is the standard mysteric expression traditionally adopted to define divine deeds, performed by 'suffering gods', θεοὶ ἐμπαθεῖς). Accordingly, the 'barbarian' explains that Apollo was not exiled after the slaying of Python, but escaped to another world (εἰς ἕτερον κόσμον); after nine Great Years he returned, completely changed and purified, truly radiant and pure (φοῖβος ἀληθῶς), and took the Delphic oracle from Themis. This explanation constitutes a significant example of the aetiological and exegetical role of demons, whose very existence and functions are employed as 'hermeneutical tools' for the explanation of myths and stories. As the 'barbarian' reveals, this is confirmed by the names that the demons adopt, usually derived from the gods to whom they are connected, and whose power they inherit. Therefore, in the aforementioned story, the name 'Apollo' simply refers to the demon bearing the god's name. This prerogative recalls the custom of attributing 'divine' epithets to humans, as mere nicknames (παρωνυμίαι) that have no relation with the gods[52].

It is important to stress that the idea of gods involved in wanderings, servitude and sufferance (πάθη) is highly incompatible with Plutarch's own theological perspective. Significantly, indeed, Cleombrotus proposes a similar 'demonological hermeneutic' later in the dialogue, thus proving that the hypothesis of demonology helps to appease interpretative problems in popular mythology. A rational *and* religious reading of myths requires to consider demons as the real protagonists of those traditional tales which, if referred to gods, would threaten their majesty and transcendent status. Cleombrotus also labels Apollo and Python as demons, so to define the right account of the foundation of the Delphic shrine – an utterly strange narration (λόγος) of escapades and transformations[53]. The same logic applies to the interpretation of gloomy rites and sacrifices, that would collide with the magnificent status of the immortal gods: the demons are in fact the actual beneficiaries of these rituals, and in particular the evil demons, who constantly require to be propitiated.

The barbarian talks – or better tells his tales (μυθολογοῦντος) – as in a religious initiation or mystery (ἀτεχνῶς καθάπερ ἐν τελετῇ καὶ μυήσει), so

---

[52] Cf. *ibid.* 421C; for 'nicknames' cf. *De Pyth. or.* 401A-B.

[53] Cf. *De def. or.* 417E-418C.

without providing any evident proof or rational demonstration (ἀπόδειξις) for what he is declaring[54]. The cosmological view that he presents (183 worlds arranged in a triangular pattern) suggests his Doric origins, since it was originally developed by Petron of Himera, probably influenced by Pythagorean reflections. As Andrei Timotin points out, this explanation recalls Stoic-Pythagorean interpretations and conceptions regarding the notion of 'Big Year' and the admission of a plurality of worlds[55]. Indeed, when in *De defectu* the discussants analyse his incredible (θαυμαστόν) explanation, they realize that the 'barbarian' might rather be a Greek man, fully competent in Hellenic philosophy and culture.

Starting from the narrative told by Cleombrotus, Daniel Babut stresses the positive role that he plays in the dialogue and acknowledges the reliability of the arguments that he introduces in the discussion[56]. Babut appeals to the serious contempt of the character, who is held in high regard from the other participants, and declares that: Cleombrotus has to be taken seriously ("Cléombrote doit donc être pris au sérieux"[57]). In particular, Babut emphasises the fundamental complementarity between the Barbarian's mythical account (μῦθος) on cosmology and Cleombrotus' rational exposition (λόγος) on the role of demons[58].

A deeper understanding of the concept of '*historia*' in *De defectu oraculorum* can be gained by putting it in connection with the notion of 'myth'. As Cleombrotus affirms, mythical stories as well as rational accounts (μῦθοι καὶ λόγοι), aimed at supporting the demonological hypothesis, are blended together in the dialogue like in a mixing bowl (κρατήρ)[59]. Plutarch's tendency of employing *mythos* alongside *logos* seems to be rooted – exactly like other key-aspects of his philosophical reflection and production – into his personal interpretation of Plato's dialogues, and particularly the *Timaeus*, especially if we assume that the peculiarity of this work is to "overcome[s] the traditional opposition between μῦθος and λόγος"[60].

In Plutarch's philosophical writings – contrastingly from his biographical and scientific texts, where *historia* corresponds respectively to historical and empirical research – practical-sensible data seem to constitute the preliminary level of research, necessary for the subsequent

---

[54] Cf. *ibid.* 422C.

[55] See Timotin (2012) 157 and Dörrie (1983).

[56] Cf. Babut (1994b) esp. 531-536; (1992) 217-218.

[57] Babut (1994b) 535.

[58] Cf. *ibid.* 537. Babut counteracts the scholars (such as Brenk, 1977, 97) who emphasise the negative reception of the barbarian's tale among the other characters, and their accusation of plagiarism.

[59] Cf. *De def. or.* 421A.

[60] Burnyeat (2005) 156.

and resulting theoretical reflection. In *De defectu oraculorum*, the first explicit example of this strategy appears in the beginning of the dialogue, when Cleombrotus proposes a strange case that he came to know precisely during his peregrinations: the perpetual lamp in the sanctuary of Ammon is mysteriously consuming less oil each year[61]. Cleombrotus' explanation is crucial for understanding the spirit of *De defectu*: he suggests that small, apparently irrelevant, facts are signs that lead to major conclusions (τὸ δὲ μικρὰ μὴ διδόναι σημεῖα γίγνεσθαι μεγάλων). He emphasises the great demonstrative (ἀπόδειξις) and predictive (προαγορεύσις) power of this principle, by recalling that it is usually applied in many areas of human knowledge, including science and medicine[62].

After hearing some hypotheses from the other speakers, Ammonius concludes the discussion on the enigma of the ever-burning lamp by declaring that instead of signalling the progressive shortening of the year's length – as supposed by the priests at Ammon's temple –, this phenomenon might rather be determined by peculiar physical conditions. He proposes two options: first, the quality of the air at the shrine might have relented the burning process; second, and more probably, the increased density of the oil employed for the lamp might have slowed down the combustion rate[63]. What we can infer from Ammonius' explanation is that he wishes to correct Cleombrotus' assertion: as I believe, the implicit message behind the words of the Egyptian philosopher is that the heuristic principle according to which 'great conclusions can be drawn from small data' has to be always applied with extreme methodological caution. This means that every physical-scientific investigation must respect some fundamental epistemic criteria, such as: starting from sensible evidence, adhering to rational norms of inquiry and leading towards verisimilitude (instead of certainty).

Hence, the extended burning time of the oil does not allow to conclude anything on the variation of the year's length – a notable phenomenon that would be signalled instead by a complete transformation in the sky (τῷ οὐρανῷ παντί) as well as by other unusual phenomena connected to the hypothetical accelerated movement of the sun. On the contrary, a sound and rational investigation into the striking phenomenon of Ammon's lamp produces some circumscribed results, which specifically concern the physical qualities, and reciprocal interactions, of the materials involved in the combustion process. Ammonius' conclusion thus seems in line with Plutarch's idea of a prudent scientific, and authentically philosophical, explanation of earthly phenomena and their physical causes.

---

[61] Cf. *De def. or.* 410B-411D; for this case, and more generally for Plutarch's treatment of natural phenomena, see the very instructive Meeusen (2017) esp. 133-135.

[62] Cf. *De def. or.* 410D-F.

[63] Cf. *ibid.* 411D.

My analysis has already defined what, according to Plutarch, is the correct modality for philosophical enquiry, which emerges with the utmost vigour in polemical contexts: a 'sceptical' methodological stance is indeed a peculiar feature of Plutarch's argumentative strategy and a constant thread throughout his production. What philosophy *itself* should be for Plutarch, and what its aim and content, is an even more delicate and controversial issue. Roger Miller Jones, who first conducted extensive studies on Plutarch's thought throughout his *oeuvre*, argues that Plato's dialogues, and especially the *Timaeus*, mostly inform Plutarch's philosophical ideas and writings[64].

Plutarch's philosophy is enriched and vivified by a strong religious spirit. Theological concepts are evident throughout the Delphic dialogues, and recur especially in writings devoted to demonology and eschatology (such as *De facie in orbe Lunae*, *De genio Socratis*, *De sera numinis vindicta*), as well as in *De Iside et Osiride*, an exegesis of Egyptian theology and myths (ἡ Αἰγυπτίων θεολογία) in light of Middle-Platonic metaphysics. It is worth reminding that Plutarch in this treatise defines philosophy as an intellectual activity directed towards the acquisition of true knowledge about the gods, achieved by means of learning (μάθησις) and research (ζήτησις)[65].

Plutarch conceives knowledge as a source of happiness, which also sustains the individual moral-intellectual path towards the assimilation to the god – the deity being model of absolute happiness, perfect knowledge (ἐπιστήμη) and wisdom (φρόνησις). The aim of the authentic philosophical life is becoming like god (ὁμοίωσις θεῷ[66]): this presupposes a complete purification, reached by ascending through successive ethical and cognitive stages. Practical concerns surely play a key role in the realization of this 'ascetic' end, as expressed by the emphasis placed on virtuous life and political engagement. Marco Zambon has effectively shown how Plutarch's vision of philosophy is that of a complex and inclusive body of knowledge, where some precisely defined preparatory disciplines are the preliminary step towards intellectual and spiritual fulfilment[67].

Recalling Cleombrotus' words, philosophy finds its completion in theology: but what does the word 'theology' mean in the context of *De defectu oraculorum*? Plutarch employs the expression 'theologians' (θεολόγοι) twice in the dialogue. The first occurrence refers to the theologians in Delphi, some ministers working at the temple and treasuring knowledge of the traditional rites and cults[68]. The second occurrence refers instead to

---

[64] Cf. Jones (1980).
[65] Cf. *De Is. et Os.* 351E.
[66] Cf. *De sera* 550D.
[67] Cf. Zambon (2002) 55-56.
[68] Cf. *De def. or.* 417F.

the earliest generation of thinkers – named 'theologians and poets' (οἱ μὲν σφόδρα παλαιοὶ θεολόγοι καὶ ποιηταί) – who focused their investigation on god as the supreme principle of the cosmos, in contrast with the physical philosophers, who instead explored just the material, inferior causes. In this framework, the word 'theologians' seems to address a wide, undefined category of ancient authors – of whom Orpheus is the only one mentioned explicitly – probably including ancient thinkers such as Homer and the Presocratics, perceived, in Plutarch's time, as authentic and reliable cultural authorities on philosophical and religious subjects[69]. In other places, Plutarch apparently dismisses the theology of the poets – designated as conscious or unconscious liars – and contrasts it with the theology that is developed by the founders of official rites, or that is based on sound philosophical principles[70].

'Theology', in the context of Cleombrotus' assertion, seems to correspond to an investigation and erudite knowledge on the gods, traditional myths, rites and cultic customs. This arguably differs from Plutarch's own conception of theology as complementary to, and interdependent with, philosophy, thus based on rational interpretation of traditional myths, rites and religious contents, and centred on the idea of an incorruptible and eternal deity.

I think that it is possible to spot a hiatus between Cleombrotus' vision of the relationship among *historia*, philosophy and theology on the one hand, and Plutarch's own view on the other. In the framework of *De defectu*, Cleombrotus represents the cultivated traveller of the most flourishing days of the Roman empire, wandering in remote lands in order to acquire detailed and direct knowledge on facts and cultural customs of different peoples. Nevertheless, when it comes to develop, out of his empirical research, correct and well grounded theoretical outcomes, he dramatically fails, due to his lack of rational-philosophical guidelines. Cleombrotus embodies the perfect example of a curious, learned intellectual, who is nevertheless misled by his *naïve* credulity and therefore connects practical data to abstract outcomes simplistically and erroneously. Instead, as Plutarch wants to teach us, inference from concrete to theoretical matters must be supported by solid scientific-philosophical principles (such as the 'double causation theory' that Lamprias will explain later in the dialogue), and placed within a clear and sound epistemic scheme of reference, ultimately illuminated by Platonic ideas and spirit.

---

[69] Cf. *ibid.* 436D; a similar meaning of the term 'theologians' is found in *De E* 388F. Chlup has analysed the occurrences of this word in Plutarch, concluding that "he normally tends to ally theologians with poets rather than philosophers" – Chlup (2000) 145. Chlup includes Hesiod, Empedocles, Heraclitus, and some of the Presocratics in this first group.

[70] Cf. *De aud. poet.* 16A; *Amatorius* 763C.

Cleombrotus seems to conceive philosophy in a radically different way from Plutarch: he intends it as a kind of ingenuous reflection over a chaotically gathered body of information, in the light of some general ideas drawn from popular philosophy and beliefs. I believe that, although the Chaeronean would not disagree completely with Cleombrotus' stance – considered especially the focus that they both place on sensible, physical, ritual realities within the development of theoretical accounts and explanations –, Plutarch's own methodology of processing evidence and data is in fact at odds with the one endorsed by his character.

Although the Chaeronean himself benefits from the knowledge acquired through extensive travels, and accepts the opportunity to learn religious matters through 'unconventional' sources (such as Egyptian or barbarian myths), what guides him is a strong sense of what is rationally admissible according to Platonic Academic standards. Moreover, the relationship that Plutarch envisions between philosophy and theology is more complicated than the simple subordination posited by Cleombrotus: philosophy does not supply material for theology. Rather, it is valuable *inasmuch* as it complies with sound theological standards – and *vice versa* theology must adhere to philosophical-rational criteria. In their highest expression, philosophy and theology are both as separated as possible from the sensible world, and reach their fullest reciprocal enrichment.

De Iside et Osiride, which offers a valuable example of the prominent role played by exegesis in the philosophy of the Imperial age, displays Plutarch's conviction that the correct interpretation and careful reading of myths is the key to authentic religious piety. Real piety (εὐσέβεια) – i.e., the correct belief in the true nature of the gods (ἀληθὴ δόξα) – finds its completion in the pious and philosophical interpretation (ὁσίως καὶ φιλοσόφως) of the stories about the gods, and in the proper observance of the established rites of worship[71].

The overall aim of *De Iside*, as it has been supposed[72], might be to stress that Egyptian elements acquire their proper dignity when read through the lenses of Greek rationalism and philosophical interpretation, which amend false and superstitious elements – a view that emphasises Plutarch's use of the allegorical method as a tool at the service of his own explicative objectives and theoretical ends[73]. In his entire *corpus*, Plutarch appears to promote an ethically acceptable interpretation of traditional myths and poetry, while rejecting the physicalistic-materialist allegorical reading promoted by the Stoics, that distorts the real meaning

---

[71] Cf. *De Is. et Os.* 355C-D: an excessive credulity in sacrifices and other material deeds (θύσειν and ποιήσειν) is closer to superstition.

[72] Cf. Richter (2001).

[73] The concept of *allegoresis* in Plutarch is analysed in Ramelli-Lucchetta (2004) 391-402.

of ancient stories (μῦθοι) and clashes against common sense. As also the analysis of *De Pythiae oraculis* has contributed to demonstrate, Plutarch's exegetical activity is an important hermeneutical means, employed to connect physical data (myths and rites, as well as historical facts and events) to their profound theoretical referent: in other words, it represents a way of dealing with, and somehow reconcile, the dichotomy postulated between the material and the immaterial world.

4. God's responsibility

De defectu oraculorum focuses on the question – also central in the two other Delphic dialogues – as *to what extent* material cultic dynamics, and more broadly the dynamics of the entire sensible world, are to be ascribed to god's responsibility. Cleombrotus points out that it is indeed hard to understand *to what extent* (μέχρι) it is legitimate (τοῦ μετρίου καὶ πρέποντος) to appeal to divine providence and call it into question as an explanatory factor for earthly phenomena[74]. In their respective interventions, Ammonius and Lamprias provide the two main answers to this question. It is important to underline from now that both these characters will acknowledge the providential and beneficial nature of god, while firmly dismissing the assumptions of those detractors, such as Planetiades, who explain the decline of oracles as the repercussion of an irascible, punishing god.

Ammonius ascribes to the god a full responsibility over divination, by asserting that he controls the oracular activity directly through his disposition (θεοῦ γνώμη). God determines its changes in intensity over time, but also decides the appearance and disappearance of oracular shrines in different places. Since no force is more powerful than god, there is no stronger energy (μείζων οὐδὲ κρείττων δύναμις) that may cancel or abolish (ἀναιρεῖν καὶ ἀφανίζειν) divination in his place. Mantic is a product (ἔργον) of god's action and, like any other divine work, is intrinsically characterized by moderation (μετρίου), adequacy (ἱκανοῦ), constraint (μηδαμῇ περιττοῦ πανταχῇ) and self-sufficiency (αὐτάρκους)[75]. In other words, the divine power of god exerts a complete control over the divinatory activity, as an all-inclusive, well-balanced, beneficial and invincible force, never diminished or affected by material, earthly, inferior factors.

I would like to point out that Ammonius' religious explanation resembles the demiurge's speech to the young gods in the *Timaeus*: while he grants their immortality, he significantly declares that nothing that he fabricates can be destroyed without his consent[76]. Therefore, according

---

[74] Cf. *De def. or.* 414F.
[75] Cf. *ibid.* 413E-F.
[76] Cf. Plato, *Ti.* 41a: Θεοὶ θεῶν, ὧν ἐγὼ δημιουργὸς πατήρ τε ἔργων, δι' ἐμοῦγε νόμενα

to the Egyptian teacher, the present oracular decrease is part of a divine plan; it specifically results from god's rational resolution, based on the contingent evidence of the current depopulation of Greece: oracular shrines have disappeared from uninhabited areas, where they have become useless for humankind, while the still active Delphic oracle requires just one priestess in the place of the three needed before[77].

As we can see, Ammonius' account offers a strictly theological perspective on divination, reinforced by an interesting kind of human-oriented teleology, which I will summarize as follows: divination, planned by god according to an intelligent design and for the benefit of humans, is kept alive only if humans are in condition to profit from it. Ammonius indeed stresses how surprising (θαυμάζειν) it would have been if the god had located oracular sources in unreachable places, destined to remain purposeless and unproductive[78].

Ammonius' solution, in his own words, neither blames god nor makes him irresponsible (μὴ τὸν θεὸν ἀναίτιον ποιῶμεν). Rather, god – like an experienced artisan – appears to regulate oracles wisely, by relying on actual practical-contingent factors, while always having human good at stake[79]. The importance that Ammonius attributes to divine action is connected, as I will clarify, to his refusal of a merely physical account of divination – which will emerge in the second part of the dialogue[80]. Moreover, the emphasis that he places on the action of the immortal god, as immune from sufferance and destruction (τὸ ἀπαθὲς καὶ ἄφθαρτον εἶναι)[81], helps to define the supreme deity in contrast to the inferior demonic powers, but also to highlight the gap between the respective roles of divine and human agents in the mantic session.

Differently from Ammonius' account, Lamprias' 'preliminary' explanation of the oracular decline concentrates on material factors: he explicitly points out that the disappearance (ἀναιρεῖσθαι) of prophetic shrines has not to be ascribed to god, but to the power inherent in matter. Specifically, Lamprias' account is based on a dualistic perspective that opposes transcendent and material forces: while the divine power is positive and productive, matter instead is inclined towards corruption and disintegration. Nature (φύσις) and matter (ὕλη) are cause of destruction (φθορά) and

---

ἄλυτα ἐμοῦ γε μὴ ἐθέλοντος. Significantly, Ammonius proves the inconsistency (ἀνωμαλία) of Planetiades' speech: if god was extinguishing only some oracular shrines, he would simultaneously condemn and endorse human wickedness (cf. *De def. or.* 413E).

[77] Cf. *De def. or.* 414A-C.
[78] Cf. *ibid.* 414C.
[79] Cf. *ibid.* 414D-E.
[80] See in this regard Babut (1992) 221.
[81] Cf. *De def. or.* 420E.

deprivation (στέρησις)[82]. It is crucial to point out that the idea that matter has an active detrimental character is attested nowhere else in Plutarch's *corpus*, and may become utterly problematic if considered within the broader context of his metaphysics. Indeed, in *De animae procreatione* he rather underlines that the material substrate is, according to the Platonic theory, 'unqualified matter' (ἄποιος ὕλη), and as such it is neutral in character and devoid of qualities[83].

According to Lamprias, god is the primary cause and origin (ἀρχή) of the material goods that he himself bestows on humankind, whilst the essence (οὐσία) and power (δύναμις) of these goods are located in the natural realm, namely in nature and matter (ἐν τῇ φύσει καὶ τῇ ὕλῃ), and therefore are liable to modification and destruction like every other sensible being.

'Nature and matter', which seems an obscure association at first sight, is later clarified by Cleombrotus: as he states, Plato was the first philosopher who attributed a crucial importance to these concepts, by defining the substrate (ὑποκείμενον) as the underlying element subject to changeable manifest qualities[84]. The pair of terms 'substance and matter', which appears twice in this brief but fundamental passage of *De defectu*, results from Plutarch's interpretation of Platonic metaphysics, and specifically from his re-elaboration of the Platonic concept of receptacle (χώρα) that he assimilates to the notion of 'matter' (ὕλη)[85]. Such a conceptual operation, firstly found in Aristotle's *Physics*[86], was common to other contemporaneous Platonists[87]. According to Cleombrotus, Plato's 'discovery' of the underlying neutral element of 'nature and matter' – useful to solve numerous philosophical problems – can be paralleled to the 'discovery' of the presence of the demigods between the divine and the human world: this very formulation coincides with the Platonic definition of demons in the *Symposium* as intermediaries and messengers between us and the gods, that are located middle way (μεταξύ) between these two opposite poles[88].

The very notions of matter (as substrate) and demigods are meaningful to understand the way in which Plutarch interconnects the transcendent god and the created cosmos. Lamprias' explanation of divination clearly appeals to a rigid barrier between the sensible and the intelligible world – a configuration that prevents any direct contact between these two dimensions. His vision, as he declares, honours the dignity, superior

---

[82] Cf. *ibid.* 414D.
[83] Cf. *De an. procr.* 1015A.
[84] Cf. *De def. or.* 414F-415A.
[85] Cf. also *De Is. et Os.* 372E-F: χώρα καὶ ὕλη.
[86] Cf. Aristoteles, *Ph.* 4,2,209b11-16.
[87] See for instance Alcinous, 162,29-31.
[88] Cf. Plato, *Smp.* 202e.

status and perfect virtue (τὸ ἀξίωμα καὶ τὸ μέγεθος αὐτῷ τῆς ἀρετῆς) of the supreme deity: accordingly, the god does not express his thoughts directly, but through 'material' agents (prophets) employed as living instruments (ὀργάνοις). Lamprias' words seem to me to draw from the famous Platonic *adagio*: 'god does not mingle with men'[89]. This maxim, arguably in line with Plutarch's own convictions, also speaks against those philosophers (the Stoics) who conceive the divine as commingled with human needs and realities (καταμιγνὺς ἀνθρωπίναις χρείαις)[90].

Specifically, Lamprias admits the existence of two natures (δυεῖν ὑποκειμένων φύσεων)[91]. The first nature is mutable and sensible (αἰσθητῆς); it can be moved in different places and changes according to generation and destruction (ἐν γενέσει καὶ φθορᾷ μεταβόλου). The second nature is intelligible (ἐν οὐσίᾳ νοητῆς) and always immutable and identical with itself (ἀεὶ κατὰ ταὐτὰ ὡσαύτως ἐχούσης).

The sensible and the intelligible natures are equally subject to the differentiating power of division (δύναμις ἁπτομένη μείζονας). The proof of the divisibility of the sensible and intelligible reality comes from Plato, and notably from his discussion of the five highest kinds[92]: being, identity, alterity, movement and stability. As inferable from *De E apud Delphos*[93], Plutarch harmonizes the articulation proposed by Plato in the *Philebus* among limit, unlimited, mixed, and the cause of becoming[94], with the just recalled partition into five kinds (γένη). Accordingly, limit, unlimited, and becoming are made correspond to the first three kinds (being, identity, alterity); the combination of limit and unlimited, and the distinction implied in becoming, correspond instead to the last two (movement, stability). Plutarch eventually proposes an ulterior combination of this solution, once again recalling the one proposed in the *Sophist*, in which limit, infinite, becoming, unity and separation come to correspond respectively to stability, movement, being, identity, and alterity[95].

4.1. A plurality of worlds

The hypothesis of a plurality of worlds raised in the centre of the dialogue represents a typical philosophical question (ζήτημα) of the kind of those

---

[89] Cf. *ibid.* 203a: θεὸς δὲ ἀνθρώπῳ οὐ μείγνυται.

[90] Cf. *De def. or.* 414E.

[91] Cf. *ibid.* 428B.

[92] Cf. *De def. or.* 428C-D: τό τ᾽ ὂν εἶναί φησι καὶ τὸ ταὐτὸν καὶ τὸ ἔτερον, ἐπὶ πᾶσι δὲ κίνησιν καὶ στάσιν. Cf. Plato, *Sph.* 256c.

[93] Cf. *De E* 391B.

[94] Plato, *Phlb.* 23c. Opsomer has stressed the importance of the *Philebus* in Plutarch's theory of principles – see Opsomer (2005a) 190; see also Laurenti (1996).

[95] Cf. *De E* 391C.

discussed in Platonist circles of the Imperial age; moreover, it shows how strongly the dynamics of divination are interconnected with broader cosmological and theological issues. Konrat Ziegler has pointed out that this discussion (which occupies six chapters of the dialogue[96]) can be intended just like a section of a commentary to the *Timaeus*[97]. The very *zêtêma* concerning the number of the worlds is drawn from the *Timaeus*, where – according to Lamprias' expression already recalled – it is formulated in a cautious, 'enigmatic way' (αἰνιγματώδη μετ'εὐλαβείας)[98]. The worlds' plurality argument has two main objectives in *De defectu oraculorum*: first, to define the action of providence and its sphere of influence; second, to clarify the role and position of the demigods in the cosmos[99].

Lamprias stresses the plausibility of this hypothesis, since god, divination and providence (θεός, μαντική, πρόνοια) could perfectly extend their powerful action to multiple worlds[100]. He proves this by adducing the following arguments. First, god, who is perfectly good (ἀγαθός [...] τελέως), needs to engage with other worlds and gods in order to practice his social virtues (κοινωνικαῖς ἀρεταῖς) – i.e., justice (δικαιοσύνη) and benevolence (φιλία, χάρις) that by definition arise from interaction with other subjects[101]. Second, our world would be solitary and friendless if alone, lost and lonely in the infinite void (note that the concept of void is vehemently rejected by Lamprias and Plutarch himself). Third, our world, as any other being, cannot be one of a kind, since all beings belong to classes and species (γένεσιν καὶ εἴδεσιν), are defined by a general designation (λόγος κοινός) and composed of homeomeries (ὁμοιομερῶν). Fourth, the concept of providence itself (of which Plutarch often stresses the fundamentally *relational* character) establishes a reciprocal benevolent interaction among different worlds and gods. This last is a key point in Plutarch's philosophy: god's providence and attentive care towards the whole cosmos are fundamental for its life and well-being, but they never undermine human freedom, nor the spontaneous development of contingent events[102].

Lamprias raises some important points of criticism against Stoic theology and cosmology: the hypothesis of a plurality of worlds does not necessarily require the introduction of multiple necessities, providences, and even supreme gods, as claimed by the Stoics[103]. Moreover – as Lam-

---

[96] Cf. *De def. or.* §§22-27 (421F-422C).
[97] Ziegler (1964) 112.
[98] Cf. *De def. or.* 420F; 421F.
[99] Cf. *ibid.* 425F-426A.
[100] Cf. *ibid.* 423C-424F.
[101] Cf. *ibid.* 423C-D.
[102] For Plutarch's conception of providence cf. Opsomer (1997); Ferrari (1999).
[103] Cf. *De def. or.* 425E-F.

prias underlines, while always pursuing an anti-Stoic polemical aim –, gods are completely self-sufficient and independent (ἀδεσπότους καὶ αὐτο-κρατεῖς): they are neither commingled with matter, nor subject to any external control. Therefore, they cannot be identified with the physical power of the elements (air, water, or fire), whose generation and destruction are determined by the cosmic cycles of conflagration[104]. Lamprias also shows that the hypothesis of a plurality of worlds directly counteracts the Aristotelian conception of the world's unity and uniqueness[105].

In this perspective, we realise that the possibility of multiple worlds seems to respond to Plutarch's own need of representing the supreme god as perfectly managing and governing all the possible worlds (provided that they are limited in number), by means of one single destiny and providence (εἱμαρμένη καὶ πρόνοια)[106]. This conception is somehow close to an original, authentic core of philosophical ideas that Plutarch personally embraces and scatters in his works: god, not trapped in self-reflection (the Aristotelian νόησις νοήσεως[107]), engages in a constant contemplation of the created world, while directing his care and attention towards the cosmic body (σῶμα) and reshaping it continuously. Such a beneficial relation between the demiurge and the cosmos, according to Lamprias, can be replicated on the wider scale of multiple worlds, and to a complex network of plural interactions.

The ordering power of providence (πρόνοια) is opposite to the chaotic power of chance (τύχη). Accordingly, Lamprias strongly rejects the hypothesis that the worlds might be infinite in number – being infinite a synonym of chaos in Plutarch's account. Nature does not admit indefiniteness and infinitude (πλῆθος ἀόριστον καὶ ἄπειρον), and not even irrational and disordered motions (κίνησιν ἄλογον καὶ ἄτακτον)[108]. Plutarch – following his master Plato[109] – rejects the possibility of the existence of an infinite number of worlds, either diachronically, as believed by the Stoics, or synchronically, as believed by the Epicureans. Infinity, constitutively connected with disorder, is incompatible with the regular (τάξις) genesis and transformation (γένεσις καὶ μεταβολή) of beings that we can observe in nature[110]. Differently from a well-sorted plurality (which is liable to be governed by divine care and providence, ἐπιμέλεια καὶ πρόνοια), senseless

---

[104] Cf. *ibid.* 426B-C.
[105] Cf. *ibid.* 424B-E.
[106] Cf. *ibid.* 426C.
[107] Cf. Aristoteles, *EE* 7,1245b14; *Metaph.* 12,1074b.
[108] Cf. *De def. or.* 424B.
[109] Cf. *ibid.* 421F-422A.
[110] Cf. *ibid.* 423C.

and irrational infinity escapes any control, and is inevitably interconnected to chance and accident (κατὰ τύχην καὶ αὐτομάτως)[111].

In the broader context of Plutarch's cosmological perspective, disorder is the key-feature of the precosmic state[112]. As he explains in *De animae procreatione in Timaeo*[113], universe is brought into being *by* god (ὑπὸ θεοῦ) and *out of* (ἐξ ἧς) substance and matter (οὐσία καὶ ὕλη) already there available, eventually arranged in an ordered disposition (εἰς διάθεσιν καὶ τάξιν) by the demiurge. Regarding the role of the demiurge as an efficient cause (here expressed by the preposition 'ὑπό'), it is crucial to note that Plutarch takes up from the *Timaeus* the definition of god as the best of the causes (ἄριστος τῶν αἰτίων)[114], which will acquire a crucial relevance in the 'double-causation theory' that Lamprias proposes as an effective solution to the central question of *De defectu oraculorum*.

5. The demons and the moon

Cleombrotus begins his demonological exposition by reporting some demonological ideas, drawn from the ancient tradition, such as those of Zoroaster, Orpheus, the Egyptians and the Phrygians, Homer and (mostly) Hesiod[115]. Based on ancient authorities and sources, Cleombrotus admits the existence of demons (δαίμονας) and defines them as intermediaries placed midway (ὥσπερ ἐν μεθορίῳ) between gods and humans. They are of a mixed nature and possess both human and divine qualities: like humans, they are affected by mortal emotions (πάθη θνητά) and necessary modifications (μεταβολὰς ἀναγκαίας), and are characterized by various degrees of virtue (ἀρετῆς) and irrationality (τοῦ παθητικοῦ καὶ ἀλόγου); like gods, they are revered, named and worshipped following the precepts of traditional religion[116].

According to Cleombrotus – who resorts to what may have been perceived as the standard Platonic definition[117] –, part of the demons' mediating activity lies in their role of interpreters, ministers and helpers of the gods (τὴν ἑρμηνευτικὴν [...] καὶ διακονικὴν [...] φύσιν), of which they act as attendants and secretaries (λειτουργοῖς [...] ὥσπερ ὑπηρέταις

---

[111] Cf. *ibid.* 426D-E.

[112] For a thorough investigation of Plutarch's cosmology and the precosmic soul, cf. Deuse (1983) 12-26.

[113] Cf. *De an. procr.* 1014B.

[114] Cf. Plato, *Ti.* 29a.

[115] Cf. *De def. or.* 415A-B; Hesiod is mostly quoted as a testimony of the demons' mortality.

[116] Cf. *ibid.* 416C-417B.

[117] Cf. Plato, *Smp.* 202e; *Plt.* 260d.

καὶ γραμματεῦσι). Specifically, they act on gods' behalf in oracles, rites, mysteries, and by punishing evil deeds[118].

By drawing on Xenocrates' demonology, Cleombrotus associates gods, demigods, and humans to equilateral, isosceles, and scalene triangles, respectively, thus employing geometrical figures as symbolic references for natural and supernatural entities – an explanatory strategy that implicitly confirms the role of objects of common knowledge as fundamental starting points towards superior theoretical acquisitions. Accordingly, he identifies humans with transient celestial phenomena (beams of light, comets, meteors), and demons with the moon. Interestingly, the moon displays indeed a sort of *demonic* character (μίμημα δαιμόνιον): its mixed body (μικτὸν δὲ σῶμα) shares both in earthly and solar nature, and is constantly subject to modifications[119].

In this respect, I find it crucial to stress this meaningful parallelism between *De defectu oraculorum* – where the moon symbolizes the power of demons, their life cycle and variable status – and *De Pythiae oraculis* – where the moon symbolizes instead the divinatory action of the Pythia. In both cases, the satellite is assumed as a mediating element; its effective, astronomical role of mediation between the earth and the sun – extended to the demons in the one case, and to the Pythia in the other – is employed to exemplify, in two different manners, the connection between the intelligible and the sensible realm[120]. John Dillon has indeed pointed out that the moon is a fundamental element of "mediation and transition in the world scheme", not only with regard to the aforementioned demonological account, but also in the context of the mythological narrative in *De facie in orbe lunae*, where the satellite is defined as the place of the souls, and assumed as a "symbol of the World Soul"[121].

The mediating role performed by the *daimones* is vital for the well-being of the entire cosmos. To brush out the demigods and so to postulate an empty space between the sun and the earth (as well as between gods and humankind) would imply to dismantle the harmonious, coherent structure of the universe[122]. This would lead to a general confusion, while forcing the gods into the limited human world and destroying the essential barrier between the sensible and the intelligible realm. The polemical side of this claim is clear: the feared 'complete chaos' – which evokes the Stoic scenario, since based on the pervasive presence of the divine within materiality – is contrasted with sound Platonic metaphysical principles,

---

[118] Cf. *De def. or.* 417A.
[119] Cf. *ibid.* 416C-D.
[120] See also *De Is. et Os.* 361C.
[121] Dillon (1996) 217.
[122] Cf. *De facie* 935A.

and in particular by appealing to the dichotomy between material-changeable *vs.* divine-unchangeable.

Cleombrotus points out that the demigods are the necessary intermediate element between the immortal god and the changeable reality of the Delphic temple. Demigods mediate the presence and influence of the deity within the sensible world (cf. the notion of 'θειότης' in *De Pythiae oraculis*[123]). The absolutely transcendent ontological status of the god prevents him from being *present* (παρεῖναι) at the temple, from exerting any action straight on the oracle, and from providing any direct inspiration. For this reason – according to this speaker – the demigods are in charge of the oracles, so that when they move away, the shrines lose their inspirational power (δύναμις) and cease their activity. When they return, the temples instead resonate like instruments (καθάπερ ὄργανα), reanimated as by a vivifying psychic principle[124].

The analogy between oracles and instruments is of a great importance. Again, it recalls *De Pythiae oraculis* and the parallelism there established between the Pythia's soul – properly 'tuned' in order to receive the inspiration – and a musical instrument (ὄργανον). Nevertheless, as I think is important to underline from now, Cleombrotus' idea that demons are fully in charge of oracular prophecy is dismissed in the most reliable account of divination developed in *De defectu*: as I will demonstrate, Lamprias – who is the most reliable character in this context – will indeed assign to the demons a mere accessory role.

Cleombrotus' exposition as a whole is valuable especially for two reasons: first, some of his arguments will reemerge in Lamprias' explanation of divination[125], which is apparently the one closest to Plutarch's own convictions; second, his account is nevertheless useful to sketch some aspects of Plutarch's demonology, as attested in other works of his[126], and which we can summarise as follows: first, demons are non-incarnated souls; second, they play a mediating role between the human and the divine; third, their presence and function help us to find a middle-way between the two extremes of gods' complete involvement in[127], or detachment from[128], the sensible reality – endorsed by the Stoics and the Epicureans, respectively.

---

[123] Cf. *supra* 31 *et passim.*

[124] Cf. *De def. or.* 418D.

[125] Cf. *ibid.* 436F. For the importance of Cleombrotus' arguments within Lamprias' exposition cf. Babut (1994b) 540.

[126] Dillon, after quoting Cleombrotus' demonological exposition, declares: "This passage deserved, I think, extended quotation as containing all the basic elements of Plutarch's theory of demons" – Dillon (1996) 217.

[127] Cf. *De def. or.* 416E-F.

[128] Cf. *ibid.* 414F.

5.1. Demonology, the kinds of divination and the structure of the soul

The prominent role provisionally attributed to the demons in the first section of the dialogue serves to account for the non-verbal communication occurring between souls. In this sense – as I anticipated in the beginning of this chapter[129], and I will discuss in what follows – they work as 'metaphorical referents' for exemplifying the psychological dynamics on which divination is founded.

Ammonius explains the special inter-psychic kind of interaction that lies at the core of demonic communication, by reporting it to the field of common-sense experience and everyday practices. In real life, we exchange messages not only orally, but also through writing (γράμμασι), direct contact (touch, θιγόντες) and visual interaction (glance, προσβλέψαντες). Likewise, it is neither irrational (ἄλογον) nor surprising (θαυμαστόν) to suppose that one soul, meeting another soul, is able to transfer impressions of the future to it (φαντασίας ἐμποιοῦσι τοῦ μέλλοντος), without resorting to verbal means[130]. I wish to stress that – in light of Plutarch's broader reflections on this topic, considering first the work *De genio Socratis* – this inter-psychic communication pertains in principle to the individual, demonic way of inspiration. It seems thus extraneous to oracular divination, which resorts to external material agents (the temple, sacrificial animals, the objects required for the preliminary rites, the Pythia herself, and so on). The contrast between the oracular and the Socratic kind of inspiration is ultimately based on the different parts of the soul involved and will be analysed in the last chapter of the present study.

De defectu oraculorum itself offers some reflections on demonology that are precious to understand the role of the soul and of its parts in divination. An analysis of these elements will show the weight that the soul's structure has within the mantic context, in the light of Plutarch's broader psychological-anthropological framework.

The clearest reference to a possible partition of the soul is made by Lamprias when, in order to demonstrate the Platonic thesis of the five worlds, he insists on the presence of the number five in the cosmos[131].

---

[129] Cf. *supra* 60.

[130] Cf. *De def. or.* 431C.

[131] The chapters 31-38 (426E-431A) of *De defectu oraculorum* are devoted to explain the qualities of the number five, connected to: paradigmatic genders of nature (428E), numerological speculations (429B-C), etymological references to the word 'universe' (πάντα-πέντε, 429D), other physical elements that are five in number: senses, parts of the soul, fingers, maximum amount of children in a pregnancy, gods generated by Rhea in the Egyptian mythology, areas of the earth, circles of the sky, and musical intervals (429F-431A). All these arguments prove that nature engenders harmony based on the number five, thus counteracting the spherical model proposed by Aristotle (431A). The insistence

He does so by also reminding the Aristotelian five "senses and parts" of the soul: physical growth, perception, appetite, fortitude and reason (φυτικὸν αἰσθητικὸν ἐπιθυμητικὸν θυμοειδὲς λογιστικόν)[132]. This account, reported only here and in *De E apud Delphos*[133], is nevertheless extraneous to Plutarch's own conception of the structure of the soul – and especially of his 'standard' moral psychology developed in *De virtute morali*[134].

As concerns the aforementioned 'metaphorical role' of demons within the explanation of the psychological dynamics of divination, it is important to remind that in *De defectu oraculorum*, Ammonius and Lamprias, by building on demonological ideas drawn from traditional religion and Platonic philosophy, establish an identification between demigods (δαίμονες) and non-incarnated souls (ψυχαί). Ammonius in particular recalls Hesiod's definition of demons as 'aerial beings'[135]: these souls do not participate in mortal bodies and, as Lamprias specifies again on the basis of a Hesiodic verse ("ἁγνοὶ ἐπιχθόνιοι φύλακες θνητῶν ἀνθρώπων"[136]), live on earth, where they act as holy guardians of mortals[137].

Based on these premises, Lamprias aims to prove that the divinatory power is *intrinsic* and *innate* (σύμφυτον[138]) in human soul. He does so by reporting a conversation on demonology that he had with some strangers, during a consultation day at the oracle of Trophonius at Lebadea[139] – described in the dialogue as one of the few oracular sites still active at the time. Lamprias explains that there are some specific powers (δυνάμεις) that the demigods, as non-incarnated souls, possess in the highest degree; nevertheless, these powers diminish or disappear when the demons/souls are incarnated in mortal bodies. One of them is the mantic faculty (μαντική), which is in charge of the prognostication of the future (προγιγνώσκειν; προδηλοῦν): when demons are mixed (μεμιγμένας) and in permanent contact (ἀνάμειξις [...] καὶ σύγχυσις) with the corporal element (πρὸς τὸ θνητὸν),

---

on the symbolic value of numbers – deriving from Plutarch's absorption of Pythagorean numerological theory – will be also found in *De E apud Delphos*.

[132] Cf. *De def. or.* 429E. For the division of the soul in Plato cf. *Resp.* 3,410b; 4, 440e-441a; *Ti.* 70a.

[133] Cf. *De E* 390F.

[134] Cf. *De virt. mor.* §3 (441C-E).

[135] Cf. *De def. or.* 431B: 'ἢ ψυχὰς ὄντας περιπολεῖν καθ' Ἡσίοδον 'ἠέρα ἐσσαμένους;' Brenk (1998) has contextualised this passage within Plutarch's demonology.

[136] Cf. *De def. or.* 431E; cf. Hesiodus, *Op.* 123.

[137] For this conception also see *De genio* §24 (593A-594A).

[138] *De def. or.* 432C.

[139] The oracle of Trophonius seems to have been really important for Plutarch, who devoted to it one of his lost works (*On the descent into the cave of Trophonios*, Lamprias catalogue n. 181) and set there the notorious myth in the end of *De genio Socratis*.

their mantic capacity is weakened, in the same way as the sun appears less bright when hidden behind the clouds[140]. In other words, the demon-soul, immaterial and immortal, when commingled with the body, material and mortal, changes under two fundamental respects, which can be expressed as follows: its ontological status, and its relation to time.

In order to clarify this point, Lamprias compares the power of prophecy to its complementary (ἀντίστροφον) and specular faculty of memory, thus resorting to a common-sense example resumed from the sphere of ordinary phenomena. While the power of memory preserves (κρατεῖν) the past, the mantic faculty anticipates (προλαμβάνειν) the future. Time, their common dimension, brings everything away in its inexorable flow: everything appears to be created and destroyed simultaneously, while the present is reduced to an imperceptible transition of the future into the past. Nevertheless, the faculties of memory and prediction prevent humans from being lost in the stream of time: memory controls (κρατεῖν) and retains things past, conferring upon them a sort of appearance and essence (φαντασίαν καὶ οὐσίαν), while the predictive capacity anticipates (προλαμβάνειν) future events[141].

What is noteworthy in this regard is that Lamprias defines the nature of the soul as more strongly connected with the future than with the past (προσήκει καὶ τούτοις συμπαθής ἐστι): indeed, the soul has *within itself*, as a peculiar characteristic of its own very nature, a special and constant tendency towards the things that are going to happen (ἐπιβάλλεται καὶ προτίθεται πρὸς τὰ μέλλοντα).

Now, it is important to focus on the relation between the faculty of memory here recalled and Plutarch's theory of recollection, both considered in the light of his psychology. As Jan Opsomer has pointed out[142], the possibility of recollection (ἀνάμνησις) is directly connected to Plutarch's partition of the cosmic soul, which is mirrored in that of the individual soul of humans (an imperfect copy of the *anima mundi*). According to Plutarch's theory, humans can experience *anamnêsis* because their souls enclose a rational part that stems from the divine[143]: exactly this special, immortal psychic part coming from without is responsible for recollection.

---

[140] Cf. *De def. or.* 431E.

[141] Cf. *ibid.* 432B; cf. also *fr.* 23 (*Is Foreknowledge of Future Events Useful?*).

[142] Cf. Opsomer (2005a) 183.

[143] Cf. *De an. procr.* 1016D; *Quaest. Plat.* 2,1001B; 2,1001C; cf. also 1,1000D-E: Plutarch here stresses how, according to Socrates, real wisdom is that concerning the divine and intelligible (περὶ τὸ θεῖον καὶ νοητόν), identified with an erotic tension which derives from recollection (ἀνάμνησις), and not from generation (γένεσις) or discovery (εὕρεσις). The activity of Socrates consists in bringing to light the innate knowledge (τὰς ἐμφύτους νοήσεις) hidden within humans, by means of his maieutic art (μαιωτικὴν τέχνην).

Although the notion of reminiscence is not central in Plutarch's reflection[144], it is nevertheless implied in his innatist theory of knowledge, especially if we take into account the role and function of intellect (νοῦς). The *noûs*, receptive of a sublime form of knowledge, represents a point of tension between different and contrasting anthropological-psychological views emerging from Plutarch's works. A twofold division of human beings and of the soul itself, composed of an irrational and a rational part, is provided in *De virtute morali*; a three-fold partition into body (σῶμα), soul (ψυχή) and the superior element of intellect (νοῦς, immortal and divine) is instead provided in *De genio Socratis* and *De facie in orbe lunae* – two works that nevertheless display two conceptual structures that are significantly different between themselves[145].

This theoretical dissonance becomes even bewildering when we analyse its technical terminology: in Plutarch's *oeuvre*, and especially in the aforesaid texts, the word 'demon' (δαίμων) refers to both the noblest part of the soul (like in the *Timaeus*[146]) and the human disembodied soul as a whole (as, for instance, in Cleombrotus' and Lamprias' accounts in *De defectu oraculorum*)[147].

In the passage of *De defectu* that we are now considering, the faculty of memory is contrasted with, and opposed to, that of prediction. Therefore, as I believe, 'memory' has to be intended here as something radically different from recollection – a distinction that becomes clearer when explored in relation to the structure and division of the soul. While 'recollective memory' is based on the activity of a divine-transcendent element located in the soul, 'common memory', the one recalled by Lamprias, is mostly rooted within the alogical and irrational part of the soul, just like its specular faculty of prediction. Both prediction and common or ordinary memory make use of imagination (φαντασία[148]): memory not only preserves things past, but also suggests their exterior appearance as well as their essence (φαντασίαν καὶ οὐσίαν). Prophecy, on the other hand, is receptive of sensations (δεκτικὸν [...] πάθεσι), images and presentiments (φαντασιῶν [...] προαισθήσεων)[149].

Imagination is inherent in human soul, and – as we read in the exegetical treatise *De animae procreatione in Timaeo* – of the world soul as well, which appears to have a twofold power (δύναμις) divided into a kinetic and

---

[144] For the value of reminiscence in Plutarch's philosophy see Donini (2005).

[145] Cf. Plato, *Ti.* 41c-d; 90a. For this 'inconsistency' and 'tension' between two views of the soul division in Plutarch, see also Dillon (2001a).

[146] Cf. Plato, *Ti.* 90a.

[147] Cf. *De def. or.* 431E.

[148] It must be kept in mind that the most accurate English translation of the notion of φαντασία is 'image-creating faculty'.

[149] Cf. *ibid.* 432D.

an imaginative faculty (κινητική, φανταστική), both permanently in contact with matter[150].

Demetrius meaningfully employs a term related to 'imagination' (φαντασία), in order to explain the psychological process of acquiring prophetic contents: indeed, as he says, human mediums become 'receptive of impressions' or 'representations' (φαντασιαστικούς) when they are under the effect of demonic enthusiasm (κατόχους τοῖς ἐνθουσιασμοῖς)[151]. It is significant that he chooses the expression 'receptive of impressions' (φαντασιαστικούς), which contributes to prove that all the characters of the dialogues attribute a great importance to imagination within the activity of divination. Although Demetrius is seemingly endorsing also the possibility for 'demonic inspiration', the idea that demons are directly responsible for enthusiasm does not belong to the apparently 'correct' account eventually presented by Lamprias – and probably shared by Plutarch.

It is worthwhile to briefly remind the concepts of 'representations' (φαντάσματα, φαντασμοί) and 'imagination' (φαντασία), which appear in Epicurus' corpus and whose meanings closely resembles the one that they have in Plutarch[152]: *phantasia* refers to the *phantasma* of an object that we have perceived and is retained within us. The context of Greek atomism also provides the first occurrence of the notion of 'imaginative *pneûma*' (πνεῦμα φαντασιαστικόν), which is attested in Democritus: the *pneûma phantasiastikon* helps creative delirium to overpower rational reasoning, and thus represents the indispensable precondition for poetic inspiration[153].

Returning to Lamprias' explanation, we learn that dreams attest to the responsiveness of imagination to bodily affections: the oneiric state indeed facilitates the encounter between external factors and the inner disposition of a person. This encounter engenders complex, diverse and variable visions (ὄψεις), according to the temperament and condition of one's body – which is significantly defined κρᾶσις τοῦ σώματος, an expression identical to the one that indicates the physical condition necessary for divination[154].

Lamprias seems to disprove the prophetic virtue of dreams. Indeed, as he says, the melancholic person – whose imaginative faculty (φανταστικόν) plays a major role – is particularly susceptible to receive straight and vivid

---

[150] Cf. *De an. procr.* 1014C.

[151] Cf. *De def. or.* 431B. Demetrius in this regard invites the company to reflect on the cause (αἰτία) and power (δύναμις) exerted by the demigods.

[152] It is striking that the first occurrence of the adjective φαντασιαστικός is in Epicurus, *Nat.* 1398,1 with the meaning of 'receptive of impressions or images' (cf. LSJ, *s.v.* φαντασιαστικός). Occurrences of related terms in *De def. or.* are: 431B (φαντασιαστικούς); 432C (φαντασιαστικῷ); 433C (φαντασιαστικῶς); 438A (φαντασιαστική).

[153] Cf. DK 68 B 17.

[154] Cf. *De def. or.* 437E.

dreams (τὸ εὐθυόνειρον)[155]. Nevertheless, since melancholic people receive numerous dreams and visions, there is a high statistical probability that their arrows sometimes happen (ἐπιτυγχάνουσι) to hit the spot, so they guess the future by pure chance. This argument against the predictive power of dreams, here employed by Lamprias, interestingly recalls the one that the Epicurean Boethus develops in *De Pythiae oraculis*, analysed in the first chapter of this study. There Boethus, while intending to disprove the effectiveness of oracular predictions, asserts that oracles randomly 'guess it right', thus meet future events by sheer coincidence[156]. Furthermore, Lamprias' denial of the mantic potential of dreams implicitly proves how rare it is for humans to receive reliable divine signs, being the non-mediated, authentically illuminating communication with divine entities reserved to a few wise individuals chosen by the god – as explained in *De genio Socratis*[157].

And now a question arises: does Plutarch believe in the prophetic power of dreams? According to Frederick Brenk[158], Plutarch's view of dreams is highly influenced by religious Platonism and Aristotelian materialism. The theory that the soul can acquire a prophetic knowledge in dreams is mostly found in the *Vitae* – although not consistently, which prevents us from ascribing it unquestionably to Plutarch's own convictions. Moreover, the majority of the oneiric episodes in the biographies fulfil a dramatic function – which constitutes a notable example of Plutarch's compositional technique that Christopher Pelling has effectively called "creative reconstruction"[159]. The question thus remains mostly open.

Going back to the concept of 'imagination', considered now in a wider framework, the image making faculty of the soul proves useful to justify the possibility for the transcendent god to exert his influence within the material world. According to Plutarch's epistemological account, god acts in the sensible cosmos just in a mediated way: he cannot directly alter or move human bodies (πλάττοντες, μετατιθέντες), but he can create 'representations' in the imaginative part of human soul – which may lead a person to act according to god's will. Considering the process described in detail in the *Life of Coriolanus*[160], god intervenes within human life while completely respecting human responsibility and independent choice (τὸν ἑκάστου λογισμὸν τῆς προαιρέσεως). He simply makes inceptions, representations and conceptions (ἀρχαί, φαντασίαι, ἐπίνοιαι) arise in human mind: these images generate impulses that have

---

[155] Cf. Aristoteles, *Div. somn.* 463b16.
[156] Cf. *De Pyth. or.* 398F-399A.
[157] Cf. *De genio* 593D.
[158] Cf. Brenk (1987b) 322.
[159] Pelling (1997) 199.
[160] Cf. *Cor.* 32,7-8.

diverse effects on the practical-deliberative part of the soul (τῆς ψυχῆς τὸ πρακτικὸν καὶ προαιρετικόν), which thus becomes encouraged or appeased. The foundations of this account can be also found in the *Adversus Colotem*, where Plutarch distinguishes between three psychic activities: sensation (φανταστικόν), impulse (ὁρμή) – which is sufficient to engender action –, and assent (συγκαταθετικόν)[161].

Plutarch conceives the irrational and the rational parts of the soul as clearly distinct and hierarchically subordinated. Nevertheless, they are in constant interaction and, as explained in *De virtute morali*, it is their reciprocal participation (μετέχειν) to allow for the impulse (ὁρμή) produced by reason to stimulate the bodily parts. The rational impulse shakes the bridle of the soul (χαλινός, ἡνία, ῥυτήρ[162]) and drives the whole body to action: in this way, the end (τέλος) of ethical virtue can be realized[163]. The association that Plutarch posits between the rational impulse on the one hand, and the synergy between the rational and the irrational parts of the soul on the other, counteracts the Stoic account of choice (προαίρεσις) – which results instead from exclusively rational deliberation intended as a deterministically defined act, part of a rigidly predetermined causal chain encompassing all the cosmic events.

6. *The psychology of divination*

Divination is radically different from logical reflection, as well as from scientific evaluation and prediction of outcomes. The antithesis between inspired and standard ways of knowledge acquisition is made explicit by Lamprias' firm rejection of the identification between the prophet and the intelligent man (ἔμφρων [...] ἀνήρ). The latter employs the rational part of his soul (τῷ νοῦν ἔχοντι τῆς ψυχῆς) and relies on probability and verisimilitude – as condensed in the Euripidean maxim: 'the best prophet is the one who guesses well' ('μάντις ἄριστος ὅστις εἰκάζει καλῶς')[164].

---

[161] Cf. *Adv. Col.* 1122B-D. For Plutarch's critical remarks on the connection between the theory of knowledge (based on representation and assent) endorsed by the Stoics and their conception of fate, cf. *De Stoic. rep.* 1055F-1057C.

[162] Plutarch often resorts to terms pertaining to the Platonic image of the chariot, by referring in particular to the notion of 'bridle', which symbolizes the control exerted by the rational principle on the chaotic irrational psychic element (cf. *De virt. mor.* 445C). Opsomer has highlighted the frequent metaphors that express the recalcitrant-disobedient character of the irrational part of the soul (πειθήνιος, ἀπειθής, ἀπειθέω, ὑπείκω), or the power (κράτος) exerted by the rational part, mostly in connection with the concepts of wisdom (σωφροσύνη) and self-control (ἐγκράτεια), and expressed with the images of 'bridle' and 'charioteer' – cf. Opsomer (1994).

[163] Cf. *De virt. mor.* 442D.

[164] Cf. *De def. or.* 432C (Eng. trans. Goodwin). For this maxim cf. also *De Pyth. or.* 399A.

As Lamprias explains[165], human reasoning (θνητὴ φρόνησις) imposes rational caution (εὐλάβειαν) on the soul – being caution, as I have already pointed out in this study, a fundamental epistemological criterion for philosophical investigation according to Plutarch. Instead, in the context of mantic activity, *eulabeia* represents a major hindrance to the effectiveness of inspiration, since it can easily turn off the enthusiastic irrational status necessary for divination[166]. Lamprias defines divination as an irrational way of knowledge acquisition and poses two main reasons for this statement, which correspond to the two different functions performed by the psychic parts involved. First, the rational part of the soul (τὸ λογιστικὸν καὶ φροντιστικόν) gets detached from the present, and the soul turns towards the apprehension of the future pursued in an irrational and fantastic way (ἀλόγῳ καὶ φανταστικῷ), so that alogical-imaginative apprehension substitutes rational reasoning. This happens in some particular circumstances, such as in dreams or in the moment of death, when the body becomes pure (καθαρός) or acquires a favourable temperament (κρᾶσις) for ecstasy[167]. Second, the irrational part arises and prevails over the rational one by means of the *mantikon* (μαντικόν), which is the innate psychic faculty responsible for the apprehension of the future. The *mantikon*, irrational and indeterminate (ἄλογον καὶ ἀόριστον) like a *tabula rasa* (γραμματεῖον ἄγραφον), is receptive (δεκτικόν) of impressions of images and presentiments (φαντασιῶν πάθεσι καὶ προαισθήσεων) and utterly extraneous to logical reasoning (ἀσυλλογίστως). The important role of the irrational component and of the disordered part of the soul within the psychological dynamics of divination must be kept in mind since, as I will show in the last chapter of this study, it constitutes a pivotal element for understanding the central place that oracular mantic occupies within the broader framework of Plutarch's most authentic reflection.

In more detail, the prophetic function of the soul (μαντικόν) drifts apart from the corporal perceptions and the actual bodily status, and opens itself to the impressions suggested by inspiration. Consequently, the whole soul acquires a demonic status and disposition, and gains the special capability of glimpsing into future events[168]. This special temperament – reached when the mantic faculty, normally inactive, is mostly dissociated from the present and the body, and prevails over the rational one – is called enthusiasm (ἐνθουσιασμός). This peculiar condition is sometimes reached

---

[165] Cf. *De def. or.* 432C-F; here Lamprias quotes Euripides, *Ba.* 298 to prove his point.

[166] Cf. Strabo, 9,3,5: Strabo defines the scientific man as totally different from the diviner, given that he relies on his preparation, profound analysis and complicated calculations.

[167] Cf. *De def. or.* 432C.

[168] Cf. *ibid.* 432D.

independently by the body, while other times (such as, in the oracular context) it is favoured by the prophetic *pneûma*, engendered by the earth under the influence of the sun.

7. *The sun and god*

If demons, as previously clarified, symbolically correspond to the moon, then, in a cosmic hierarchy of planetary entities, the sun is identified with Apollo. Nevertheless, while the correspondence between the demonic and the lunar nature does not seem to cause a big controversy – given their similar hybrid character and the overtly metaphorical kind of their relation – the one between the sun, as a material entity, and god, as a superior transcendent principle, appears much more complex and problematic.

Lamprias examines two possible ontological connections between the sun and god: first, god could be the sun itself (εἴθ᾽ἥλιός ἐστιν); second, god could be a superior entity, the master and father of the sun (κύριος ἡλίου καὶ πατήρ), located beyond the visible realm (ἐπέκεινα τοῦ ὁρατοῦ παντός) – an expression clearly reminiscent of the Platonic definition of the good as superior and transcendent to being[169].

Ammonius recalls the common belief according to which the sun and Apollo are one and the same entity[170]. A similar remark occurs in *De E apud Delphos*[171], where a Chaldaean astronomer presents this conception as an idea generally accepted among the Greeks. It is important to point out that, both in *De defectu* and *De E*, Ammonius openly rejects the identification between the sun and the god – a denial that also Plutarch professes. Lamprias recalls and plainly dismisses the traditional religious conception (shared by Philippus as well) according to which Apollo and the sun are identical[172]. As we will see, the analogical relationship between the deity and the planet sheds some light on the correlation established by Plutarch between Apollo on the one hand, and the supreme transcendent principle of Platonic ontology on the other. It is worthwhile to stress here that Lamprias defines the principle of analogy (ἀναλογία) as 'beautiful and wise' (καλὴν καὶ σοφήν), and that Plutarch himself often employs it as a powerful reasoning method and effective clarifying tool[173].

It is important to investigate the role of the sun within Lamprias' explanation of the psychological process that underlies the prophetess's divinatory act. He establishes a parallelism between prophecy and sight,

---

[169] Cf. Plato, *Resp.* 6,509b: οὐκ οὐσίας ὄντος τοῦ ἀγαθοῦ, ἀλλ᾽ἔτι ἐπέκεινα τῆς οὐσίας πρεσβείᾳ καὶ δυνάμει ὑπερέχοντος.

[170] Cf. *De def. or.* 434F-435A: οἴεται γὰρ ὥσπερ οἱ πολλοὶ καὶ αὐτὸς οὐχ ἕτερον εἶναι τὸν Ἀπόλλωνα θεὸν ἀλλὰ τῷ ἡλίῳ τὸν αὐτόν.

[171] Cf. *De E* 386B: ἡλίῳ δ᾽ Ἀπόλλωνα τὸν αὐτὸν ὡς ἔπος εἰπεῖν πάντας Ἕλληνας νομίζειν.

[172] Cf. *De def. or.* 434F.

[173] Cf. *ibid.* 433D-E.

which I will consider in the last chapter of the present study. A joint analysis of the psychology of divination in Plutarch and the physiology of vision in Plato's *Timaeus* will show that sight and prophecy are gifts bestowed on humans by divine wisdom and goodness, so that they can appreciate the order and beauty of the cosmos[174].

According to Lamprias' parallelism, the human soul has a close and intimate connection with the prophetic spirit (πνεῦμα), analogous to the kinship that vision has with light. On this basis, he establishes the following proportion: vision (ὄψις) : light (φῶς) = soul (ψυχή) : prophetic spirit (πνεῦμα). This analogy creates a clear parallelism between the power of vision (ὁρατικὴ δύναμις) and that of prediction (μαντικὴ δύναμις)[175]: as the sunlight activates the eye[176], in the same way the prophetic spirit illuminates the soul and enables it to enjoy the vision of the future. In other words, the latter element of each couple reinforces the former, and facilitates its action[177]. Both the eye and the soul need an element whose substance is similar to their own, which can activate and stimulate them, so that the visual capability and the prophetic power can arise.

This effective analogy stresses that the power of prediction is a completely natural faculty, intrinsic to human soul, which needs a likewise natural power (the *pneûma*) in order to express itself. What is interesting is that the 'material principle' of both phenomena is one: the sun. The sun on the one hand makes human sight effective, whereas on the other prompts the prophetic natural spirit to emerge from the earth, by nurturing the soil with its warm exhalations.

Lamprias' explanatory parallelism is followed by a more complex one, which defines the articulated role played by Apollo and the sun within divination. The connection between the planet and the god appears as mediate and indirect, as shown by the eight-terms analogy (ἀναλογία) proposed:

body (σῶμα) : soul (ψυχή) = vision (ὄψις) : intellect (νοῦς) = light (φῶς) : truth (ἀλήθεια) = power of the sun (ἡλίου δύναμις) : nature of Apollo (Ἀπόλλωνος φύσις)[178].

---

[174] Lamprias' account seems to anticipate the Neoplatonic notion of 'luminosity' of the divine power, employed even within the explanation of divination (cf. Iamblichus, *Myst.* book 3). For the physiology of vision in the *Timaeus*, cf. Plato, *Ti.* 42e-47e.

[175] Cf. *De def. or.* 433E.

[176] Cf. *ibid.* 436D.

[177] For the connection between light and the power of vision, cf. Plato, *Resp.* 6,508a-509b and *De def. or.* 436D.

[178] Cf. *De def. or.* 433D-E.

The hierarchical relation existing between the couples of terms presented in this complex equation reflects the subordinative order between the sun and Apollo, which Lamprias explains in generative terms: the god is the father, and the planet his offspring (ἔκγονος, τόκος) that belongs to the natural world, thus to the inferior level of incessant mutation and becoming (γιγνόμενον ἀεί). The sun and Apollo similarly stimulate specific human capabilities: the former activates the sensible visual capacity (τῆς αἰσθήσεως τὴν ὁρατικὴν δύναμιν), while the latter activates the prophetic faculty of the soul (τῆς ψυχῆς τὴν μαντικήν). According to the analogy proposed, we can conclude that the faculty of divination is nobler than that of vision, since it is more closely connected to the power of god, placed on the same level of soul (ψυχή), intellect (νοῦς) and truth (ἀλήθεια) – against the 'all too physical' terms of body (σῶμα), vision (ὄψις) and light (φῶς).

Lamprias also provides a rational explanation for the fact that in ancient times the Delphic oracle was dedicated jointly to Apollo and the Earth[179]. According to tradition, the oracle was also presided by Poseidon, the Earth-shaker – earthquakes being a recurrent event in Delphic mythology. This may shed some light on the complex issue of Plutarch's beliefs concerning the 'previous owners' of the Delphic oracle. Nicole Loraux has highlighted the following striking, peculiar and contradictory fact pertaining to the story of the foundation of the Delphic oracle: although Apollo overthrew Gaia Protomantis, she preserved her sovereignty over the oracle, while ruling together with the god. Loraux has explained this co-regency as an attempt to harmonize the "Apollonian *logos* with the chthonian depths", two elements embodying the masculine and feminine principle, respectively[180].

The 'harmonization' between these two items is confirmed by Lamprias, who offers a physical interpretation of the interaction of the power of the sun with that of the earth. On the one hand, the sun is responsible to create in the earth the right temperament for the prophetic streams to arise. On the other hand, the earth as a whole is a 'safe seat for all', according to Hesiod's definition (πάντων ἕδος ἀσφαλές[181]); it is thus in a permanent status of balance, ensured by its eternal (ἀΐδιον) and incorruptible (ἄφθαρ-

---

[179] Cf. *ibid.* 421C. This point contrasts with the account of the 'Barbarian of the Red Sea', who asserted that the Delphic oracle originally belonged to the Earth and was conquered by Apollo only in a second stage. In this respect, it is worth reminding that the majority of the Greek oracular shrines were believed to be originally founded or presided over by the Earth (Γῆ) – on this subject, see Sourvinou-Inwood (1987).

[180] Loraux (1995) 184. In this respect, it should be reminded that Xenocrates' metaphysical scheme distinguished the monad from the dyad, identifying the former with the masculine divine principle (Zeus or intellect, νοῦς), and the latter with the feminine divine principle (the cosmic soul).

[181] Hesiodus, *Th.* 117.

τον) nature. Nevertheless, the potencies (δυνάμεις) and material variable entities (lakes, rivers, springs, mines) located above or below its surface are subject to continuous changes in place and intensity[182]. One of these variable potencies is the prophetic *pneûma*, engendered in the womb of the earth and emerging from time to time on its surface, at the Delphic shrine[183].

In *De defectu oraculorum*, the issue of the relation between the sun and Apollo is object of an interesting animated discussion, full of contradictions (πολλὰς ἀντιλήψεις); it does not receive a permanent assessment and is just postponed to another time (ὁ καιρὸς οὐ παρέχει πάσας ἐπεξελθεῖν[184]) – which is probably a reference to *De E apud Delphos*, analysed in the third chapter of the present study. The connection between the planet and the god offers in any respect an excellent, illuminating analogy to explain the *mediated* influence of the divine power within the oracular divinatory process, and the role of divine rationality within the mantic dynamics.

I believe that Lamprias' final explanation as a whole helps to clarify the relation between planetary deities and the functioning of divination, thus shedding light on the planets' more general theological and ontological qualification. He points out that, according to traditional religion (νόμῳ πατέρων), a divine character is ascribed to the sun and the earth, the two main external, sensible entities that provide the material conditions for divination[185]: practically, the power (δύναμις) of the sun alters the intrinsic mixture (κρᾶσις) of the earth, which becomes in its turn stimulated to produce the prophetic streams (ἀναθυμιάσεις). Presumably, the divine character here ascribed by Lamprias to the sun and the earth has no relation with the Stoic materialistic interpretation of natural beings as supernatural entities. Rather, as the text itself clarifies, it is drawn rightly from the classical identification between planets and deities, corresponding to a peculiar conviction of ancient Greek religion, i.e., the 'belief of the fathers' (πάτριος πίστις), whose influence constitutes a fundamental element within Plutarch's theological reflection. Indeed, he feels strongly the great value of national religion for the Greek people, but also participates in first person to festivals and rites, thus exhibiting a sincere and joyful religious spirit[186].

---

[182] Cf. *De def. or.* 433F-434A.

[183] Giulia Sissa, in her thought-provoking study *Greek Virginity* (Sissa, 1990), which provides an original view of the role of the Delphic priestess as a virgin and woman, interestingly connects the pneumatic inspiration to fumigations commonly used for therapeutic purposes in ancient medicine (cf. esp. Ch. 5: *Open to the Spirits*).

[184] *De def. or.* 438D-E.

[185] Cf. *ibid.* 436F.

[186] Cf. *De sup.* 169D; *Non posse* 1102A-D.

8. *The theory of double causation*

It is now time to thoroughly analyse Lamprias' final, well-balanced, rational account[187], which is seemingly the most reliable among those proposed in *De defectu oraculorum* – as is usually the case with the conclusive intervention in Plutarch's dialogues. As a result of Lamprias' explanation, developed on the basis of his 'double causation theory', enthusiasm is neither attributed uniquely to supernatural causes, nor to physical factors. Rather, it results as the product of a complex intersection of favourable conditions, backed by divine endorsement.

It is worth noting that this part of the dialogue resembles the argumentative structure typical of a commentary – a very common philosophical genre during Plutarch's age. This 'commentary section', as Ferrari has pointed out, mainly focuses on passages extracted from the *Phaedo* and the *Timaeus*[188]. After Ammonius has proposed his theological perspective, by stressing the role of divine responsibility within divinatory rites and practices, the focus shifts with Lamprias' explanation to the role of necessary-physical causes and to the analysis of the fundamental function of matter. 'Inferior factors' receive at this point a more extensive consideration than in all the previous accounts. The material principle is described as playing a fundamental role in divination and Plato is accordingly praised as the first philosopher who acknowledged its dignity.

Lamprias calls in Plato himself as a witness and advocate (μάρτυρα καὶ σύνδικον) of the theory that he is going to present, which will clarify the ontological status (οὐσία) and functioning (δύναμις) of oracles as well as god's providential action. He justifies his solution by appealing to the peculiar place gained by Plato within the history of philosophy. Lamprias points out that the first generation of thinkers, that of the ancient theological writers and poets (παλαιοὶ θεολόγοι καὶ ποιηταί), had focused only on the superior divine cause (τῇ κρείττονι μόνῃ), thus leaving aside the necessary and natural causes (ἀναγκαίαις καὶ φυσικαῖς [...] αἰτίαις)[189]. By the contrary, at a later time, the physicists (φυσικοί) disregarded the 'beautiful and divine cause' (τῆς καλῆς καὶ θείας [...] ἀρχῆς), while ascribing instead every phenomenon to the action of bodies (σώμασι), their affections (πάθεσι), reciprocal strokes (πληγαῖς), changes (μεταβολαῖς) and combinations (κράσεσι)[190]. Anaxagoras himself only considered the physical causes (ταῖς φυσικαῖς [...] αἰτίαις) and what happens by necessity (κατ'ἀνάγκην), and so neglected to investigate the superior reasons (βελτίονας αἰτίας οὔσας καὶ ἀρχάς), which correspond to the final and the

---

[187] Cf. *De def. or.* 435F-436A.
[188] Cf. Ferrari (2001) 79.
[189] Cf. *De def. or.* 436D.
[190] Cf. *ibid.* 436D-E.

efficient cause (τὸ δι' ὅ καὶ ὑφ'οὗ, the end and the agent, respectively)[191]. As can be easily seen, both the previous stances were deficient and partial, since the materialistic solution omitted the superior causes, i.e., the final and the efficient cause (τοῖς μὲν τὸ δι'οὗ καὶ ὑφ'οὗ), whereas the theological one disregarded the inferior causes, i.e., the material and instrumental cause (τοῖς δὲ τὸ ἐξ ὧν καὶ δι' ὧν)[192].

Plato stands out in the history of philosophy as the first thinker who combined these two different orders of causation together, and thus developed the most complete epistemic model for the study of the sensible world and of earthly phenomena. As Lamprias shows, Plato harmonized the role of the agent – acting on matter (ποιοῦντι καὶ κινοῦντι) as a craftsman – and that of matter – corresponding to the object *on which* the productive action is performed (ὑποκείμενον καὶ πάσχον)[193].

It is highly probable that the original formulation of the double causation theory pertains to Plutarch's authentic beliefs and conceptions: Pierluigi Donini has demonstrated that this is employed in several other contexts, thus proving that for the Chaeronean a well-founded *scientific* explanation must take into account both material-inferior and divine-superior orders of causation[194]. Plutarch trusts the reliability of human senses, but postulates an additional account superior to the physical one, since he is convinced that only the discovery of divine-superior causes may offer the supreme explanation and the required metaphysical complement for every merely physical account[195]. This attitude confirms the importance that Plutarch attributes to *historia* – in this sense, a *fil rouge* of the dialogue – as a preliminary study and collection of data, which allows for the subsequent development of theoretical arguments.

Epistemological theories involving multiple levels of causation (αἰτίας εἴδη) are shared by other contemporaneous Platonists and taught in the philosophical schools of the time. These doctrines incorporate Aristotelian causes within the Platonic metaphysical scheme, and verbalize them through conventional prepositional syntagms. Plutarch partly resorts to these linguistic standards when expressing the material-secondary level of causality with 'τὸ ἐξ'ὧν καὶ δι'ὧν' and the divine-primary one with 'τὸ δι'ὅ καὶ ὑφ'οὗ'[196].

Donini has identified the two key Platonic passages of provenance for Plutarch's personal development of the double causation theory. These are:

---

[191] Cf. *ibid*. 435F.
[192] Cf. *ibid*. 436E.
[193] Cf. *ibid*.
[194] Cf. Donini (1992) 103.
[195] Cf. Opsomer (1998) 23.
[196] Cf. Donini (1992) 102.

Phaedo 98b-c and *Timaeus* 68e-69a[197]. Another suitable *locus* that scholars often indicate as a possible source for Plutarch's double causation theory is *Phaedo* 97b-c, where Socrates presents Anaxagoras as a promising thinker, who correctly recognised the supreme mind (νοῦς) as the major cause regulating the ordered and coherent emergence of phenomena. Nevertheless, the following passage (98b-c) seems more pertinent and much closer in content to *De defectu* 435F, since here Socrates reveals his dissatisfaction with the way in which Anaxagoras has come to interpret the cosmic reality. Anaxagoras indeed disappointedly took into account only the combination of particular factors and elements (such as water and aether), without exploring the action of the general organizing intelligent principle for the whole (τὸ κοινὸν πᾶσιν).

Above all, I think that – in the context of the present study – it is important to emphasize the value of Plutarch's interpretation of the *Timaeus*, which informs his philosophy and particularly his vision of divination. In doing so, we should always keep in mind that the fundamental source useful to analyse the *Timaeus'* influence on Plutarch's reflection is *De animae procreatione in Timaeo*. It is worthwhile to remind that Gretchen Reydams-Schils has hypothesised a polemical aim behind Plutarch's double causation theory against the Stoic model of explanation (as based on one single material level of causation). Accordingly, two different perspectives would indeed have arisen from two opposite readings of the *Timaeus*: the Stoic one, proposed by Varro and Cicero, and Plutarch's one, more in line with the interpretation of the Platonic dialogue given by Philo and Alcinous[198].

Analysing some particular aspects of Lamprias' theory of the synergy of two different causes will surely help us to understand the importance of the cosmology of the *Timaeus* within Plutarch's reflection as a whole. First, Lamprias proposes an illustrative analogy in order to explain the notion of double causation: in the craft production of a statue, the material cause ('that out of which') corresponds to the bronze used to mould the object, the efficient cause (which, according to Aristotle's definition in *Physics* 2,3,194b29-30, is the ἀρχὴ τῆς μεταβολῆς ἢ στάσεως) to the artisan (ὁ ποιητὴς καὶ δημιουργός) and the superior cause (τὴν δὲ κυριωτέραν ἀρχήν) to art and reason (τέχνη; λόγος)[199]. This analogy also shows the way in which natural phenomena (in this case, the physical characteristics and reactions of iron and pigments) interact with superior causes (in this case, the rational author).

Ferrari, while stressing the importance of the *Timaeus* within the so-called 'rebirth of transcendence' that characterises Middle-Platonism, has

[197] Cf. Donini (2002).
[198] Cf. Reydams-Schils (1999) 169.
[199] Cf. *De def. or.* 436B-C.

focused on the Middle-Platonic re-reading of some of the key notions of the *Timaeus*: the *chôra* (χώρα) has been assimilated to the concepts of 'matter' (ὕλη) and 'material cause' (τὸ ἐξ' οὗ); the demiurge, instead, to the efficient cause (τὸ ὑφ' οὗ); the ideas to the paradigmatic cause (πρὸς ὅ) subordinated to the demiurge[200].

A similar scheme is found in Lamprias' explanation. Accordingly, Plato attributed to the deity everything that happens according to reason (κατὰ λόγον), whereas he ascribed to matter (ὕλη) the role of necessary cause of what comes into being and is subject to becoming. Lamprias, who grounds his theory on Plato's ontology, declares that the sensible universe (τὸ πᾶν αἰσθητόν), despite its ordered appearance (διακεκοσμημένον), is not pure in its essence, but always presents a combination of matter (ὕλη) and reason (λόγος) – which is necessary for the material coming into being (γένεσις) of the whole universe[201].

This cosmological account probably coincides with what Plutarch may have conceived as an authentically Platonic vision of the universe. Assuming that the world is an admixture of *hylê* and *logos* plainly counteracts the Epicurean idea of the world as infinitely distant from, and neglected by, the gods, as well as the Stoic viewpoint, in which the concepts of divinity and materiality and those of providence and natural necessity all merge together.

9. *The theory of double causation applied on oracular divination*

In the following paragraphs I will explain how Lamprias applies the double causation theory to the dynamics of divination. Fundamentally, he identifies the matter (ὕλη) of the divinatory process with the human soul (ψυχή), and the enthusiastic spirit and exhalation (ἐνθουσιαστικὸν πνεῦμα καὶ τὴν ἀναθυμίασιν) with the efficient cause acting on the soul as an instrument (ὄργανον) or plectrum (πλῆκτρον)[202]. What he underlines, and we have to keep in mind, is that this rigorous scientific explanation does not make divination neither irrational (ἄλογος) nor godless (ἄθεος), for the fact that demigods and gods (included the planetary deities of the Earth and the Sun) are involved into the mantic process.

9.1. The *pneûma*

In summary, in the first half of the dialogue two different explanations for the decline of oracles are provided. The first attributes the prophetic power to the demons, as the principal agents of the divinatory inspiration. The second – sketched in the first part, and eventually re-integrated in

---

[200] Cf. Ferrari (1996c) 366.

[201] Cf. *De def. or.* 436A.

[202] Cf. *ibid.* 436E-F.

Lamprias' final explanation – is seemingly opposed to, and incompatible with, the former and associates the mantic power to physical entities: the prophetic stream and its material manifestations such as winds (πνεύματα), vapours (ἀτμοί) and exhalations (ἀναθυμιάσεις)[203].

Ancient testimonies prove a general agreement on the existence of the Delphic *pneûma*[204]. It might be interesting to recall that, for instance, in Pseudo-Longinus' *De sublimitate*, some emanations (ἀπόρροιαί τινες) flowing from the 'elevated spirit' (μεγαλοφυσία) of ancient authors into the souls of the readers are compared to the inspiration that the Pythia receives from the earth. In Delphi, as the author of *De sublimitate* declares, an intoxicating vapour (πνεῦμα) comes up from a rift in the earth (γῆς ἀναπνέον) and fills the priestess with divine power (δαιμονίος), which enables her to pronounce the oracular responses[205]. Implicitly, the analogy equates literary and mantic production – as both associated to a semi-conscious state and, once recorded, in need of rational decipherment and interpretation, necessary to decode the original message that they enclose.

That of *pneûma* proves to be an extremely useful conceptual tool in Lamprias' treatment of divination, since the prophetic stream engendered by the earth is regarded as the main factor responsible for the prophetess's enthusiasm and divinatory inspiration. *Enthusiasmos*, as Lamprias explains, results from a peculiar composition (κρᾶσις) and disposition (διάθεσις) or modification (μεταβολή) of the Pythia's soul. The human soul is capable *per se*, under special conditions, to reach the peculiar status (διάθεσις) of enthusiasm, which allows for an insight into the future. In oracular divination, this same transformation becomes submitted to a superior control, and somehow tempered and directed by divine rationality itself, although through intermediate material instruments. In the case of the Delphic temple, indeed, the Pythia attains the ecstatic state since her soul is solicited by the material streams engendered there by the

---

[203] Cf. *ibid.* 435A.

[204] Cf. *ibid.* 432D. It seems interesting to me that Cicero defines the pneumatic exhalation in rather similar terms, as a natural force springing from the earth (cf.: Cicero, *Div.* 1,8: *Potest autem vis illa terrae, quae mentem Pythiae divino adflatu concitabat, evanuisse vetustate, ut quosdam evanuisse et exaruisse amnes aut in alium cursum contortos et deflexos videmus*; 1,79: *Nam terrae vis Pythiam Delphis incitabat, naturae Sibyllam*; 1,115: *Credo etiam anhelitus quosdam fuisse terrarum, quibus inflatae mentes oracula funderent*). He also underscores, through Quintus, the need of detaching the soul from the body – described in more extreme terms than in Plutarch: *Ergo et ei, quorum animi spretis corporibus evolant atque excurrunt foras, ardore aliquo inflammati atque incitati, cernunt illa profecto quae vaticinantes pronuntiant* (Cicero, *Div.* 1,114). Although pertaining to the very different context of the I century BC Rome, Cicero's arguments help to confirm the Stoic influence on Plutarch's development of a philosophical explanation of mantic inspiration.

[205] Cf. [Longinus], *Subl.* 13,2.

earth (πηγαὶ δυνάμεων). The prophetic breath (μαντικὸν ῥεῦμα καὶ πνεῦμα) that comes through air and flowing water – therefore by employing two natural elements as vehicles and material supports – stands out for its divine origin and sacred character (θειότατόν ἐστι καὶ ὁσιώτατον), distinguished among numerous streams, benign or malicious, produced in the world[206].

The prophetic spirit – as a concrete, material, natural force – first commingles with corporeal matter and becomes mixed with the body (καταμιγνύμενον γὰρ εἰς τὸ σῶμα); once there, it influences the immaterial psychic element, driving it to an absolutely peculiar (ἀήθη καὶ ἄτοπον) disposition (κρᾶσις). An analogy illustrates the way in which the stream operates: the heat opens some pores, through which the impressions of the future (φανταστικοὺς τοῦ μέλλοντος) come inside, in the same way as the heat engendered by wine opens the bodily pores, thus stimulating unusual inner movements and bringing back to memory things previously forgotten.

The mantic faculty has to become pure in order to function properly and to receive and reflect faithfully the images cast upon it. This status of purity is reached in two possible ways. The first is based on the Heraclitean notion of the 'dry soul'[207]: accordingly, the sensory powers get sharpened by dryness and weakened by moisture[208], so that high temperature renders the prophetic spirit (πνεῦμα) dry and sharpened, ethereal and pure (αἰθερῶδες καὶ καθαρόν). The second option is that low temperature might cool down the prophetic stream (πνεῦμα), thus stretching and hardening the soul's 'predictive part' (προγνωστικὸν μόριον) as toughened iron: the exhalation (ἀναθυμίασις) then, given its peculiar physical-structural affinity with the soul, would penetrate into its openings. The same phenomenon, as Lamprias explains, happens when tin is mixed with bronze: tin penetrates into the porous structure of bronze, thus rendering it stiff and bright – due to their mutual compatibility[209]. This is a fundamental principle: in nature – and in divination, as an ordinary earthly phenomenon – specific preliminary conditions need to be satisfied, so that the qualities of the substances involved in a given process react in the proper, auspicable way. Accordingly, as Lamprias underlines, exclusively the material streams (ῥεύματα) that arise exactly in Delphi are capable to prepare and dispose (διατίθησι) the soul towards the enthusiastic and fantastic (ἐνθουσιαστικῶς [...] καὶ φαντασιαστικῶς) apprehension of the future[210].

---

[206] Cf. *De def. or.* 432D-E. It should be kept in mind that while air is often mentioned as a medium for the movement and action of the *pneûma* (ἀέρος καὶ πνεύματος), water is just neglected in the explanation of the prophetic act. Maybe Plutarch has in mind Delphi's sacred well, employed in preliminary rites?

[207] Cf. DK 22 B 118; *De esu* 995E.

[208] Cf. *De def. or.* 432F-433B. For the notion of moisture also see *Quaest. conv.* 736A-B.

[209] Cf. *De def. or.* 433A.

[210] Cf. *ibid.* 433C.

The scientific validity of this explanation is reinforced by means of some explicit references to the Aristotelian theory of exhalation (ἀναθυμί-ασις)[211]: Lamprias resumes the Peripatetic thesis of earthly modifications and applies it to the prophetic streams and their functioning – thus proving in this way that the pneumatic streams are subject to the ordinary laws of physics. Indeed, when violent forces torn the earth (such as rains, thunderbolts, and especially earthquakes), the prophetic streams are also affected – as proven by the extinction of the oracle of Teiresias and the simultaneous outburst of the plague (λοιμός) in the nearby Orchomenos[212].

The pneumatic exhalation (ἀναθυμίασις) is subject to variations in intensity, exactly like every other natural stream. For sustaining this assumption, Lamprias offers a proof (τεκμήριον), which will be soon discarded for its weakness (μὴ [...] πιθανόν), but is nevertheless interesting for the present research, while constituting a notable intertextual reference to another passage of *De defectu oraculorum*. He recalls a phenomenon often witnessed by the consultants and the priests at the Delphic shrine: at times, randomly (ὡς ἔτυχη διὰ χρόνων), the room where the enquirers seat (οἶκος) is filled with a sweet fragrance arising from the secret prophetic cave or room (ἄδυτον) – a fragrance probably produced by warmth (θερμότης) or by another force (δύναμις)[213]. It is important to stress that, in this context, just like in the aforementioned characterization of the 'Barbarian of the Red Sea'[214], the concept of 'fragrance' (εὐωδία) works as a powerful 'symbol' of a divine force and essence – in line with a widespread ancient belief associating a delicious scent to everything divine, pure, beautiful, good and incorruptible[215].

If we focus on the physical description of the nature and function of the Delphic *pneûma*, we find that Lamprias employs the Stoic technical-conceptual vocabulary, as shown by the following and most recurrent terms: effluence (ἀπόρροια), exhalation (ἀναθυμίασις), mixture or temperament (κρᾶσις)[216]. The Stoics (who notoriously developed a very coherent and influential theory of divination) and Plutarch thus appear to share a

---

[211] Cf. Cicero, *Div.* I,19,38; 2,57,117.

[212] Cf. *De def. or.* 434B-C.

[213] Cf. *ibid.* 437C.

[214] Cf. *ibid.* 421B.

[215] Regarding geological surveys, it is worth nothing that Boer has hypothesised that the reason for supposing a 'fragrant source' in Delphi may have been founded on the presence of some leakage of ethylene – cf. Boer (2007). For a general study on the ancient notion of 'fragrance' and its divine connections, see Deonna (1939). For a thorough analysis of this concept in Plutarch, see the very instructive Tusa Massaro (2005).

[216] Other terms employed in *De defectu oraculorum* in relation to the *pneûma* are: περίψυξις, πύκνωσις, στόμωσις (433A), διάθεσις, διάχυσις (432D-E), ἀνάμιξις, σύγχυσις, σύγκρασις, σύμπεξις (433D).

common conception of the *pneûma* and consequently to assign a fundamental role to this natural agent. According to both views, earthly material exhalations are of great importance in the oracular process: they become commingled with the human soul and thus engender the proper combination (κρᾶσις) necessary for prophetic enthusiasm to arise.

Ernest Will, in his fundamental contribution on the Delphic *pneûma*[217], stresses that the actual existence and material nature of the prophetic exhalations, as well as the connection between the *pneûma* and the legend of Earth as the founder of the oracle, were taken for granted in antiquity and generally accepted by writers and philosophers. Nevertheless, as Will points out, a paradox lies behind the literary-scientific treatment of this phenomenon in ancient times: although the pneumatic exhalation was accepted as a hard fact, we (as well as the ancients) do not have at our disposal any material proof for its functioning and even for its very existence.

Modern researchers have developed some possible accounts of the nature of the Delphic *pneûma* – ranging across different disciplines, from humanities to natural sciences – but an agreement is far from being reached. For instance, the historian Adolph Oppé has denied the existence of a 'mephitic vapour' – postulated by modern scholars – thus providing evidence that no sacred chasm was located just under the shrine, and that the Pythia did not descend into an underground room[218]. The geologist Luigi Piccardi, instead, after analysing the tectonic framework and the geological features of the area, has confirmed the presence of the chasm, and has proved that the temple was constructed on a seismic fault trace[219].

Peter Green, for his part, in a famous article[220], has proposed a very balanced interpretation of the mantic practice in Delphi. He has also significantly remarked the essential diversity between modern and ancient sensibility, rationalistic norms and scientific conceptions. Green first intends to discard the idea that the oracular predictive activity was heavily vitiated by international political instances, and to get rid of the suspect that it only served diplomatic purposes and thus that it was perpetuating a fraud in which the Pythia was consciously participating. Rather, he stresses the universal paradigmatic role played by the temple, which was

---

[217] Will, who devotes a large section of his article to the Chaeronean and to the theory of *pneûma* in *De defectu oraculorum*, points out that in *De Pythiae oraculis* (which is assumed as the last of the Delphic dialogues in chronological order) Plutarch dismisses the concept of material exhalation (ἀναθυμίασις) and adheres to a more definite dualistic scheme, thus attributing an essentially spiritual character to the prophetic stream – cf. Will (1942) esp. 174.

[218] Cf. Oppé (1904) 216.

[219] Cf. Piccardi (2000).

[220] Cf. Green (2009).

to offer valuable responses to human practical doubts. Furthermore, by relying on sound psychological and historiographical data, he proposes a convincing explanation of the effects that the slight toxicity of the telluric exhalation might have exerted on the body of the Pythia, already weakened by ritual privations. As for the geological explanation of the phenomenon, Green suggests that Jelle de Boer and John Hale have produced the most relevant surveys available[221], which he also incorporates into his own account.

Despite the fascinating interest of geological research, the philosophical basis of Plutarch's view of the pneumatic force as presented in *De defectu oraculorum* shows its relevance when analysed in light of his psychological and cosmological theory, which are strictly interconnected. The prophetic *pneûma*, although divine in origin, is not eternal and invariable, but instead is subject to perennial transformations and rebirths (μεταβολαῖς καὶ παλιγγενεσίαις) – just like any sublunary being or, as some believe, like any material being also above the moon[222]. This statement of Lamprias appears to match Plutarch's cosmological account, which is based on two assumptions: first, the sensible world as a continuously variable domain, where every being is overwhelmed by the stream of time; second, the transcendent world as stable and immutable.

9.2. The role of the demons in the temple

Demons take an active part in the divinatory process, as overseers and guardians (ἐπιστάτας καὶ περιπόλους καὶ φύλακας) of divination – a function that Lamprias judges neither irrational (ἄλογον) nor impossible (ἀδύνατον). He deprives them of the leading role of inspiring directly the prophetic message through possession or illumination; instead, they are in charge of balancing the 'harmonic combination' (οἷον ἁρμονίας τῆς κράσεως) between the prophetic stream and the human soul[223]. Demons realize the harmonic mixture by taking away (ἀφαιροῦντας) the superfluous and irrational elements (τὸ ἄγαν ἐκστατικόν [...] ταρακτικόν [...] κινητικόν) on the one hand, and by introducing (καταμιγνύντας) the useful and beneficial ones on the other. Their task thus recalls the function of the 'intermediate' and altogether 'active' character that Alberto Bellanti has ascribed to the notion of virtue as a 'middle term' (μεσότης) – intended as a mathematical and musical proportion ('middle note'), in line with the Pythagorean theory. Bellanti proposes this interpretation in his important contribution on *De virtute morali*, where he convincingly demonstrates that Plutarch re-reads Aristotle under Pythagorean categories. According to Bellanti's original

---

[221] Cf. Boer-Hale, (2000); (2001); Boer (2007).
[222] Cf. *De def. or.* 438C-D.
[223] Cf. *ibid.* 436F-437A.

and captivating reconstruction, virtue is not just an intermediary element between two opposite practical choices, but has also the *power* to actively harmonize the two extremes[224].

We can see that the very notion of 'middle term' (μέση), once transferred into the framework of oracular divination, perfectly applies to demons for two main reasons: first, they are defined – in a cosmological sense – as necessary intermediaries between the sensible and the intelligible realm, and occupy a midway position between humankind and the gods; second, they have also an *active* function, since they *create* the balanced combination between the soul and the *pneûma*, by bringing the various components into the right proportion.

With regard to Plutarch's moral theory, it is worth dwelling on the peculiar kind of hylomorphic relation established in *De virture morali*: here, reason corresponds to the 'form' that imposes limit and order on passions; passions, instead, correspond to the 'matter' or 'substrate' of moral virtue[225]. In line with such an 'informing', 'shaping' function performed by reason, Plutarch defines virtues – following the Aristotelian definition[226] – as intermediate between the excessive and the deficient. The Chaeronean contrasts the Stoic concept of '*apatheia*' (ἀπάθεια) with the Aristotelic notion of '*methriopatheia*' (μεθριοπάθεια), according to which passions are essential for moral virtue. (Virtues are therefore μεσότητες; they are not ἀπάθειαι, as in Stoic rationalist monism according to which passions are merely perversions of reason and have no real existence)[227]. The importance of the passionate element of the soul extends beyond ethics, and involves the very cosmic structure – as it is clear from *De animae procreatione*. The irrational component can never be abolished, since it is an essential, vital element within the composition of the world soul as well as of the human soul; it corresponds to the irrational *psychê* or 'soul in itself' (ψυχή), principle of movement and life[228]. Divination is just one of the numerous areas of Plutarch's reflection where the irrational element proves its crucial importance.

It is worth noting that Plutarch presents the notion of *methriopatheia* as pertaining to an unbroken tradition starting with Pythagoras and including Plato. Christian Froidefond has underlined that both Plato and Plutarch re-employ the Pythagorean notion of 'middle term' (μέσα) as an element that connects an inferior principle to a superior one, according to determined proportional rules[229]. He adds that in Pythagoras this

---

[224] Cf. Bellanti (2003).
[225] Cf. *De virt. mor.* 440D.
[226] Cf. Aristoteles, *EN* 1104b24.
[227] Cf. *De virt. mor.* 441D.
[228] Cf. Plato, *Lg.* 10,896a; *Sph.* 249a.
[229] Cf. Froidefond (1987) 206.

notion is applied precisely to the role performed by the demons, while it is conceived as a bond of union (δεσμός) in arithmetical series, and geometrical (a/b = b/c) and enharmonic (a-b/b-c = a/c) analogies (ἀναλο-γίαι).

Plutarch, probably relying on these notions drawn from Pythagorean numerology and musical theory, intends *methriopatheia* as a 'dynamical musical harmony' that creates balance within the soul[230] – a concept that can be also found in neo-Pythagorean treatises. In this regard it is also striking to note the identification proposed by Pierre Boyancé between the demons regulating the pneumatic and psychic composition (κρᾶσις) for divination and the role played by the Muses at the temple, as masters of the poetical activity – a form of literary and prophetic creation which is similarly regulated by mathematical rules[231].

The idea of a balanced psychological combination as a prerogative for divination seems to draw from the Pythagorean view of the soul as a musical instrument, and specifically from Simmias' explanation of the soul-*harmonia* in the *Phaedo*[232], all the more so considering that Lamprias' entire explanation of the dynamics of inspiration revolves around the very concept of harmony. He declares that the preliminary cause and condition for enthusiasm is that the imaginative-prophetic power (ἡ φαντασιαστικὴ καὶ μαντικὴ δύναμις) is in a state of balance, and is perfectly harmonized with the *pneûma*, like a drug (ὅταν οὖν εὐαρμόστως ἔχῃ πρὸς τὴν τοῦ πνεύματος ὥσπερ φαρμάκου κρᾶσιν). If this condition is satisfied, inspiration necessarily arises (ἀνάγκη γίγνεσθαι τὸν ἐνθουσιασμόν) in those who are prepared to prophesy (ἐν τοῖς προφητεύουσιν)[233].

Finally, it is important to stress that the demons intervene at the 'crucial moment' (ἐν καιρῷ) – a key-concept in the phenomenon of oracular divination, and in Plutarch's philosophy at large[234]: this precise sign indicates the proper moment in which the Pythia can give herself to the pneumatic influence. In this way, the role of the demons as divine immaterial agents can be easily conciliated with the material, physical causality of the prophetic streams of *pneûma* that emerge from the earth[235].

---

[230] Cf. *De an. procr.* §§21-33 (1022E-1030B).

[231] Cf. Boyancé (1938) 308; also cf. *supra* 51-52.

[232] Cf. Plato, *Phd.* 86b-c.

[233] Cf. *De def. or.* 438A.

[234] For a thorough analysis of the importance of the notion of καιρός in Neoplatonic divination see Addey (2014).

[235] The harmonization between the material and the demonic, super-human factor in the process of divination is a complicated issue frequently addressed by scholars; cf. for instance Moreschini (1989).

9.3. Preliminary sacrifices and the concept of '*kairos*'

Lamprias ensures that the sacrifices performed prior to consultations in Delphi have a precise function, and that they perfectly fit within the rational and philosophical explanation (τῷ λόγῳ τούτῳ) of the mantic phenomenon that he is developing.

As largely attested by historical sources, the preliminary rites are a central component of the mantic process. Lamprias highlights their theological relevance, as understood by the Delphic priests (ἱερεῖς καὶ ὅσιοι), who claim that the animal's trembling is a sign (σημεῖον) indicating that the god is disposed to prophesy (θεμιστεύειν, which is the technical verb expressing the action of 'delivering oracles')[236].

This coincides with Ammonius' explanation: as the Egyptian philosopher has stated earlier in the dialogue, the priests believe that the exceptional, total trembling of the victims in Delphi is a sign that a divine entity (be it a god or a demigod) is the cause (αἰτία), so the real agent, responsible for divination[237]. Ammonius highlights that the violent shaking (διασεῖσαι) of the animal's head, which is also required in other sacrifices, is not sufficient for the consultation in Delphi. Here the victim, instead, once sprinkled with the water of libation, must respond with a vivid trembling and quivering, a 'tossing motion[238]' (σάλος), a vibrating movement (παλμός), a complete agitation of the entire body[239]. As can be inferred from the description above, the positive outcome of these special preliminary sacrifices confirms the oracle's extraordinary ontological status of intermediary between humanity and the god. On the contrary, if this divine sign is missing, it means that the shrine (τὸ μαντεῖον) is deprived of that peculiar status, it is ontologically deficient and therefore incapable to produce oracles (χρηματίζειν) – for which reason the Pythia must not be brought inside the temple[240].

Lamprias adds some important technical details: in Delphi the victims have to satisfy the ritual requisite of being completely pure, uncorrupted and sound (καθαρὸν εἶναι καὶ ἀσινὲς καὶ ἀδιάφθορον), both in their body (σώματι) and soul (ψυχῇ). While the physical purity is relatively easy to assess, precise practical procedures are prescribed in order to verify if the animal's soul is in its natural state (κατὰ φύσιν)[241].

---

[236] Cf. *De def. or.* 437A-B. The important notion of physical 'trembling' is expressed by means of diverse technical terms in the course of the exposition, such as: κίνησις, τρόμος, σείσασθαι.

[237] Cf. *ibid.* 435C.

[238] LSJ, *s.v.* 'σάλος'.

[239] The same word 'παλμός' is employed by Epicurus to express the internal vibration of bodies; cf. Epicurus, *Ep.* 43,7.

[240] Cf. *De def. or.* 435C-D.

[241] Cf. *ibid.* 437A-B; according to Plutarch, these techniques include offering grain to bulls, and peas to billy-goats.

From the standpoint of animal psychology, in the wider perspective of Plutarch's reflection, the issue of psychic and bodily purity acquires a deeper philosophical connotation, which exceeds the limits of mere ritual requirements. Against the Stoics and their self-contradictory arguments, Plutarch strongly believes that animals partake of reason[242]. As he argues in *De Iside et Osiride*, every single sensible being is a divine instrument (ὄργανον) and a reflection of the god's intellect and majesty. Every sentient creature is provided with a soul (ψυχή), emotion (πάθος) and character (ἦθος): animals, who live, see, move and have a sense of possession, prove to contain an emanation (ἀπορροή) or portion (μοῖρα) of the divine intellect (φρονοῦν) that guides the entire universe, since every single cosmic element contains a reflection of the creator[243].

Contrary to the Stoic assumption[244], animals are endowed with a peculiar form of rationality, language and emotions. As Plutarch writes in *De sollertia animalium*, beasts are prevented from developing rationality to the highest degree – which would require study and education – but they nevertheless display all the key features commonly employed by philosophers as proofs of rationality: they have purpose, memory, emotions, they care for their offspring and show gratitude as well as hostility; they also know how to obtain what they need and how to manifest their virtues[245].

The principle of 'vitality' (ψυχή) was held by the Greeks as the main condition for assessing an animal's suitability for sacrifice but, as just emphasised, the 'total trembling' experienced by the victims in Delphi appears as an absolutely peculiar kind of reaction, nowhere else attested in the Greek religious world[246]. A possible explanation of this absolutely peculiar event will be provided in the last chapter of the present study.

If the moment chosen by the ritual practitioners does not match divine temporality (τοῦ δὲ καιροῦ διαφεύγοντος), then the god sends special signs (σημεῖα) in order to discourage the consultation: the animal does not

---

[242] Cf. *De soll. an.* esp. 960B; cf. also *De def. or.* 420D-E.

[243] Cf. *De Is. et Os.* 382A-B.

[244] Cf. *De soll. an.* 962C.

[245] Cf. *ibid.* 966B.

[246] Fred Naiden has delved into "The Fallacy of the Willing Victim". In his article, he questions Walter Burkert's commonly accepted view on the 'nod' that a supposedly 'willing' animal victim was expected to express when tested prior to sacrifice (a custom justified with the need of appeasing the human sense of guilt). Resorting to both literary and visual evidence, Naiden provides an alternative view: he proves that what was really expected from the animal was a reaction showing its vitality (ψυχή) and physical well-being. No nod then, but a manifestation of its integrity and dynamism. Moreover, gods, and not the worshippers, were believed to be the owners of animals' vitality – cf. Naiden (2007).

move and remains unaffected (ἀπαθής) and unaltered (ἀκίνητος)[247]. As the analysis of *De Pythiae oraculis* has contributed to demonstrate, it belongs to Plutarch's deepest convictions that the god sends his messages to humankind through special signs, thus resorting to an oblique, cryptic and fundamentally *mediated* style of communication.

I wish now to underline that the concept of 'appropriate time' (καιρός), which I mentioned above, acquires a great importance in *De defectu oraculorum*. According to Lamprias, the animal's trembling in the ritual context – an unmistakable sign of the god's availability to prophesy (θεμιστεύειν) – indicates precisely the propitious moment and favourable occasion (καιρός) for the consultation. I think it is worth noting that the balanced combination realized by the demons must also happen in the opportune moment (ἐν καιρῷ). This moment also marks the positive disposition of the Pythia's soul, which is significantly not characterized in every single moment (ἐν παντὶ καιρῷ) by the same temperament or harmony (μίαν ἀεὶ κρᾶσιν ὥσπερ ἁρμονίαν)[248].

According to a wider principle, there is a propitious time in which (σὺν καιρῷ) every faculty or energy (δύναμις) fulfils its proper function at best[249]. This stance is also inferable from the case study of the lamp at Ammon's temple, in the beginning of *De defectu oraculorum*, and subsequently from Lamprias' detailed description of the action and mixing of the *pneûma* within the human soul, which can happen only in the 'right moment'.

It may be interesting to integrate this principle within the 'general law' emerged from the analysis of *De Pythiae oraculis*, developed in the first chapter of the present study, and which I phrased as follows: the way in which any object, once properly predisposed, reacts to a certain stimulus (ἀρχή) is determined by the nature and qualities of the object itself[250]. By merging together these two maxims we find that: there is a *precise moment* in which a natural entity, once prepared, reacts with its proper nature and powers to a given stimulus in the best possible way. This general physical law, as I think, regulates divination and all the other earthly phenomena, according to Plutarch.

9.4. Delphi as a unique place

Similarly to other oracular shrines in antiquity, Delphi was located in a breathtaking natural landscape and at a remote distance from the influence and control of powerful cities; its place was on the slopes of Mount Parnassus, the home of the Muses, right in the centre of the Greek world.

---

[247] Cf. *De def. or.* 437B.
[248] Cf. *ibid.* 437A-B.
[249] Cf. *ibid.* 437D.
[250] Cf. *supra* 38.

In the preamble of *De defectu oraculorum* we soon encounter two extraordinary (ἱεροί) men and travellers: Demetrius of Tarsus and Cleombrotus of Sparta. In order to introduce them, Plutarch recalls the traditional mythological *topos* of the oracle's foundation, according to which Zeus made two eagles or swans fly from the opposite sides of the Earth and meet in its centre; they met precisely in Delphi, where the place of their encounter was marked by the sacred navel, still enshrined there[251]. This narrative, together with the symbolic element of the sacred *omphalos*, has contributed to define the peculiarity of the oracular location.

In the course of the dialogue, the unique, outstanding character of the Delphic location is further substantiated by the legend of the shepherd Coretas, reported by Lamprias[252], who nevertheless gently dismisses this mythical account and replaces it with his rigorous scientific explanation.

Ammonius, in his turn, aims to prove the eminently divine nature of the mantic phenomenon by focusing exactly on the Delphic temple as a unique place of worship and cultic institution, whose extraordinary character is nevertheless not established once and for all, but has to be repeatedly reconfirmed. He offers a profoundly religious account of the rites performed at the shrine, thus rejecting any simplistic material or psychological explanation. As he points out, to attribute all the prophetic power to material agents would undermine the divine character of divination; it would also damage our idea of the sublime status of the gods and our opinion (δόξα) about them[253]. Ammonius denounces that a merely physical account of oracular mantic degrades divination to a mechanical encounter of the prophetic faculty (μαντικὴ δύναμις) intrinsic to the soul with the pneumatic stimulation exerted by some combination (τίς [...] κρᾶσις) of the air and the winds (ἀέρος [...] πνεύματος). A similar hypothesis would even lead to the abolition of the ritual role of the Delphic oracle, its cultic norms and its practical rules[254].

---

[251] Cf. Plato, *Resp.* 6,427c: οὗτος γὰρ δήπου ὁ θεὸς περὶ τὰ τοιαῦτα πᾶσιν ἀνθρώποις πάτριος ἐξηγητὴς [ἐν μέσῳ] τῆς γῆς ἐπὶ τοῦ ὀμφαλοῦ καθήμενος ἐξηγεῖται.

[252] Cf. *De def. or.* 433C-D. Diodorus Siculus provides the traditional version of the foundation of the Delphic oracle, which stresses its geological peculiarity. Some goats, while grazing in the area where the Delphic temple would have been built, came close to the chasm (where the *adyton* was to be placed), and started to leap and bleat strangely, and to behave like possessed (ὅμοια ποιεῖν τοῖς ἐνθουσιάζουσι). The goatherd also approached the chasm, became inspired and started to predict the future. The site then attracted a number of people wishing to experience its miraculous earthly stream, and made everyone become inspired (ἐνθουσιάζειν). For its seismic-chthonian character, the Delphic oracle – erected right upon the chasm – was dedicated to the Earth (τῆς Γῆς εἶναι τὸ χρηστήριον; Diodorus Siculus, 16,26).

[253] Cf. *De def. or.* 435B.

[254] Cf. *ibid.* 435B-C.

The absolutely special status of Delphi, as Ammonius explains, prevents that its origin (ἀρχή) and human discovering (εὕρεσις) might ever be ascribed to chance and accident (κατὰ τύχην καὶ αὐτομάτως). Rather, it is clear that it was the god to create the oracle – whose location was only found out by humans! – according to a precise teleological plan, guided by the divine power of providence (θεῷ καὶ προνοίᾳ)[255]. These two opposite explanations – respectively ascribing the responsibility of earthly events to chance and providence – comply with two different causal systems and even correspond to two antithetical world-views: while chance and accident are connected to the Epicurean account (they are often employed as explanatory factors by Boethus in *De Pythiae oraculis*), god and providence are instead connected to the (Platonic) belief in an ordered reality presided over by divine rationality. According to this last explanatory model, the birth, discovering and functioning of the Delphic oracle are almost 'sacred events', part of a providential plan, and it would be terrible (δεινόν) to ascribe them to the mechanistic action of irrational principles, especially considering – as an empirical proof – the numerous benefits that the oracle has constantly provided to the Greeks in history. Nevertheless, this view – surely embraced by Ammonius – is not completely ascribable with absolute certainty to Plutarch's own convictions.

It is well known that the Delphic shrine has represented for centuries a milestone for religious, civic and military decisions. While offering valuable cultic and political support to Greek cities throughout the Classical age, it prescribed how to preserve or restore the harmony with the gods. The oracle continues to fulfil its function also under the Roman domination, serving as a diplomatic location, a bulwark of (a sometimes idealized) tradition and an emblem of the construction of Greeks' own identity[256].

Among the arguments raised by the Egyptian philosopher that seem to be mostly in line with Lamprias' final explanation, there are some special prerogatives that contribute to shape oracular divination as a religious

---

[255] Cf. *ibid.* 435D-E.

[256] Cf. Price (1985). The long history of the Delphic oracle dates back to the VIII century BC, when its boundary wall was built (cf. *Il.* 9,404-405; *Od.* 8,79-82); nevertheless, the first attested response dates back to the IV century (cf. Pausanias, 7,5,3). One century later, the temple was apparently rebuilt. The VI century recorded its 'golden age', when the city of Delphi (one of the most important centres of Greece) was home to the Pythian games. The Greek Amphictyony – still existing under the late Roman empire – was gathering there every Autumn. It was in the V century that twenty-seven special buildings were added to the initial core; nevertheless, at the same time the oracle's success was weakened for its ambiguous role in the Persian wars and the dialectical attacks against it unleashed by the sophists.

activity, necessarily connected to a precise ritual time and place, subject to specific rules, and implemented by qualified practitioners. All these conditions are provided by the official institution of the Delphic temple.

Plutarch's description of the mantic session has contributed to fashion a commonly accepted account according to which the priestess, sitting on the tripod placed upon the deep chasm within the innermost area of the Delphic temple (ἄδυτον), is driven into an altered state of mind by the vapour exhaling from the earth. In the dramatic time of *De defectu oraculorum*, one Pythia suffices, but, in the golden age of Delphi, up to three priestesses were required[257]. Plutarch's testimony is exceptionally precious since it indicates the other main participants involved in the consultation: the delegation of the consultants (θεόπροποι), i.e., the public messengers which present civic inquiries to the oracle; one or more interpreters (προφῆται), who are probably responsible for turning the prophetic utterances into understandable sentences; the 'holy men' (ὅσιοι[258]), in number of five and charged for life, who offer a secret sacrifice (ἀπόρρητον θυσίαν) to Apollo, while the inspired maidens Thiades (Θυιάδες), devoted to Dionysus, 'wake up' their god[259]; two other priests (ἱερεῖς) named for life are also in charge at the temple[260].

In Ammonius' speech, we can point out two main notable factual evidences proving the extraordinary character of the Delphic shrine: first, the peculiar nature of the preliminary sacrifices performed at the temple – which I have considered above; second, the special figure of the Pythia, and the complex conditions that she must satisfy in order to act as an effective prophetic medium. I believe it is pivotal to stress that the divinatory process can be performed just and only by the priestess(es) in charge of the shrine, given that the exhalation (ἀναθυμίασις) alone is not sufficient to produce the prophetic inspiration (ἐνθουσιασμός) in every soul and to infect it with its power. Only one special woman (μιᾷ γυναικί) is designed to prophesy: she is the Pythia, who has to comply with rigorous standards of ritual purity, and to be constantly chaste and flawless (ἁγνὴν διὰ βίου καὶ καθαρεύουσαν)[261].

10. *The Pythia*

Lamprias defines the temperament of the Pythia's soul as perpetually mutable, exactly like the *pneûma*: over time, they both display continuous variations, being both subject to the universal laws of nature – in the same

---

[257] Cf. *De def. or.* 414B.
[258] *Ibid.* 437A.
[259] Cf. *De Is. et Os.* 365A.
[260] Cf. *Quaest. Graec.* 292D-F.
[261] Cf. *De def. or.* 435D.

way as every other earthly entity. As a consequence, the variable outcomes of the divinatory phenomenon are caused by the constantly mutable action of both the *pneûma* and the psycho-physical status of the Pythia: as it is natural, they never remain unchanged. This peculiarity directly recalls the effects of music and wine, which affect even the very same person with a stronger or weaker intensity[262], thus producing different degrees of ecstasy depending on one's own temporary inner state and temperament (κρᾶσις)[263].

The diverse passions (πάθεσι καὶ διαφοραῖς) arousing in the Pythia's soul are more inclined to affect exactly that psychic part (μέρος) devoted to divination, i.e., her irrational soul. It is useful to consider in this regard that the nature of the irrational soul is defined as utterly similar (συγγενές) to that of the prophetic spirit (πνεῦμα), and thus predisposed to merge with it[264] – based on a 'like attracts like' dynamics.

A question arises here, pointing to a significant contradiction: in what sense the pneumatic stream and the psychic element might be 'similar'? The prophetic spirit, as we have seen, is a material entity and telluric force, while – both for Plutarch and Lamprias, the latter always appearing to reject hyper-materialistic stances – the soul is immaterial. The *pneûma* and the soul do not seem to belong to the same ontological domain, therefore how can they blend together so easily and naturally?

This contradiction is partly due to Plutarch's employment of Stoic technical terminology – which conveys clearly materialistic notions – in the framework of his Platonic psychology and eschatology. At any rate, in order to better understand this paradox, we must acknowledge that Plutarch develops an ambivalent, hybrid and fluid conception of 'matter' – as proven in particular by his notion of *pneûma*[265]. Plutarch's typically 'elastic' conceptions of the physical structure of the *pneûma* serves to justify the possibility of a *mediated* influence of god within the sensible world, as well as to found upon a solid theoretical basis the principle of the continuity of matter, as explained by Paul Veyne. Veyne interestingly emphasises the problem of the contact (ἐπαφή) between the spiritual and the material as a crucial philosophical-religious question in Plutarch's time[266].

Gerard Verbeke, as concerns Plutarch's use of the concept of *pneûma* outside the divinatory context, notes that the Chaeronean does not employ often this term with reference to human soul – since it would recall the Stoic materialistic doctrine, substantially opposed to his own spiritualistic

---

262 Cf. *ibid.* 436B.
263 Cf. *ibid.* 437E.
264 Cf. *ibid.* 437D.
265 Cf. Will (1942) 172.
266 Cf. Veyne (1999).

anthropology. Verbeke thus demonstrates that Plutarch rather employs the image of *pneûma* in an a-technical sense, mostly in connection with psychological, low-order vital functions. On the other hand, he stresses the original and meaningful character and development of this notion within Plutarch's divinatory account[267].

The prophetic *pneûma*, by virtue of its material consistence, seems to first affect the body, and just from there to reach the Pythia's soul – in which it creates a special disposition (κρᾶσιν ἐμποιεῖ)[268]. The mantic power of the soul, as every earthly element, is not always (ἐν παντὶ καιρῷ) in the same immutable temperament and invariably perfect harmony (μίαν ἀεὶ κρᾶσιν ὥσπερ ἁρμονίαν). Disordered disturbances (δυσχέρειαι καὶ κινήσεις) agitate the Pythia's body and consequently her soul, affecting especially her imaginative faculty (φανταστικὸν [...] τῆς ψυχῆς) – the one most receptive of corporal alterations engendered by sense perceptions of external objects. Imagination must be completely pure and uncontaminated in order to perform its fundamental prophetic role, which is to efficiently capture and reflect the divine messages[269].

For ensuring the purity of the imaginative faculty of the Pythia – a necessary condition for the successful outcome of the prophetic session –, she has to be devoid and clean (καθαρά) from irrational forces and interferences. This prerogative partially fulfils the requirements of the double causation theory, as regards the inferior level of causation (the material-necessary one), which also includes human actions, preparations and efforts necessary to solicit and meet divine benevolence and wisdom. Accordingly, the Pythia has to be tuned as an instrument (ὄργανον), in order to acquire the apt disposition (κρᾶσιν καὶ διάθεσιν), so that she can be stimulated by the *pneûma* as by a plectrum (πλῆκτρον)[270].

The mantic mechanism described here, especially in light of the peculiarities of the soul's parts and of the assimilation of the Pythia to an 'instrument' (ὄργανον), may be fruitfully put in relation to some aspects of Plutarch's psychology and anthropology – with particular reference to the conception of the body as the 'instrument' of the soul, as already highlighted in my analysis of *De Pythiae*. The psychic principle, assumed as an intermediary between the corporeal (σῶμα) and the intelligible (νοῦς) element – if we rely on the account of the topic that Plutarch develops in *De facie in orbe Lunae* – displays a complex relationship with these two opposite terms. I would like to remind the way in which John Dillon deals with Plutarch's treatment of the problem of the body-soul contact and relation. Dillon takes into account a passage of *De genio Socratis*

---

[267] Cf. Verbeke (1945) 267, and the chapter *Plutarque*, 260-287.
[268] Cf. *De def. or.* 433E.
[269] Cf. *ibid.* 437D.
[270] Cf. *ibid.* 438C.

where the Chaeronean, seemingly resorting to "his Pythagorean imagery", simplistically explains the action of the soul on the body merely in terms of an "impulse"[271]. It is important to stress that the same theory is present in *De virtute morali*, where an 'impulse' (ὁρμή) is said to be responsible for the action of reason (λογισμός) on the bodily parts, which are *per se* irrational [272].

In *De defectu oraculorum* Plutarch faces the opposite problem: that of the action of the material on the immaterial – namely, of the body on the soul, and of the *pneûma* on the priestess's irrational *psychê*. While in the demonic and 'Socratic' kind of divination (cf. *De genio Socratis*) both the participants taking part in the process (a demon and a human soul) are immaterial in nature, in oracular divination the Delphic temple provides the *material* external framework, and the *pneûma* works as the *material* external agent. Plutarch thus needs to explain the influence exerted by the material telluric *pneûma* emerging in Delphi on the Pythia's psychic constitution. This influence seems to be performed through her body, which acts as the first recipient of the prophetic spirit and as the intermediary element responsible for its transmission to her inner psychic components.

To sum up, the encounter between the Pythia's inner disposition and the external power of the *pneûma* has an utterly unpredictable outcome: the changeable strength of the exhalations affects her in always different ways, depending on her temporary status. Nevertheless, as previously clarified, the preliminary rites performed at the Delphic temple provide the material signs (σημεῖα) useful to assess whether the Pythia is in the right temperament and disposition (κρᾶσιν καὶ διάθεσιν) to receive the inspiration without any danger (ἀβλαβῶς ὑπομενεῖ τὸν ἐνθουσιασμόν)[273]. Lamprias adds that the Pythia has to be pure in two respects: first, her body (σῶμα) must be chaste (ἁγνόν); second, her life (βίος) must be free from any contact with strangers (ἀνεπίμικτος, ἄθικτος).

The Delphic oracular institution – also thanks to its complex ritual apparatus – works as a perfect receiver of the signs sent by the god and therefore effectively helps to assess the right time (καιρός) for a propitious consultation; furthermore, it provides the ideal conditions for the Pythia's propitious disposition to arise, on which basis she can act as a 'perfect' divinatory minister and medium.

If the necessary conditions are not satisfied, the consultation is disastrous in two possible ways: either the enthusiastic inspiration (ἐνθουσιασμός) does not arrive, or it is not harmonious and balanced, but reeling and frenzied, agitated and disturbed (παράφορον καὶ οὐκ ἀκέραιον καὶ ταρα-

---

[271] Dillon (1996) 221; cf. *De genio* 588F-589B.
[272] Cf. *De virt. mor.* 442D.
[273] Cf. *De def. or.* 438C.

κτικόν)²⁷⁴. This description, characterizing any uncontrolled and irrational form of inspiration as an utterly wrong and destructive eventuality, definitely proves how firmly Plutarch rejects the widespread idea that the Pythia falls into madness and is captured by an out-of-control, raving chaotic frenzy²⁷⁵.

Other ancient authors were concerned with the issue of the rational and controlled *versus* the irrational and frenzied prophetic attitude of the Pythia. Herodotus depicts her as usually lucid and calm, in full possession of her faculties, while she delivers understandable oracles and spontaneously talks in verse²⁷⁶. Plato instead affirms that the priestesses, both in Delphi and Dodona, when inspired and frantic (ἱέρειαι μανεῖσαι, i.e., in their state of ecstasy and madness), procured numerous and great benefits to Greece – in contrast to when they preserved their lucidity and rationality²⁷⁷.

In *De defectu*, a concrete piece of evidence from the recent past of the Delphic shrine offers a counter-check to this theory, proving how an evil form of *enthusiasmos* might be even lethal for the Pythia. In that specific occasion, although numerous inauspicious signs warned about the inadvisability of the prophetic act, the sacerdotal body proceeded defiantly. The alarming signals regarded the animal victim, which did not react to the aspersion, remaining still and calm (ἀκίνητον ὑπομεῖναι καὶ ἀπαθές), but also the Pythia who, full of a strong, negative spirit (κακοῦ πνεύματος), descended into the prophetic cave (τὸ μαντεῖον) reluctantly (ἄκουσα) and unprepared (ἀπρόθυμος). Once there, she started to speak with a strange rough voice. Her sufferance – that Lamprias compares to that of a labouring ship, pressed and urged by a hostile wind – recalls the description of the Pythia's inner status in *De Pythiae oraculis*, where the movements of her soul are compared to a rolling swell²⁷⁸, but here, where the priestess is completely out of control, it causes an extremely dramatic outcome. The conclusion of this event is striking: the Pythia, in a frightening hysterical state, ran with a scream to the door and threw

---

²⁷⁴ Cf. *ibid.* 438A. It is interesting that the same word 'disturbing' (ταρακτικόν) is used to express those elements that the demons remove from the psychic-pneumautic complexion (cf. *ibid.* 437A).

²⁷⁵ Christian authors tended to emphasize the irrational character of the Pythia's activity, and particularly described the *pneûma* as coming in through her sexual organs; cf. Origenes, *Cels.* 3,25; 7,3; Ioannes Chrysostomus, *In Ep. I Cor. Hom.* 29,1, p. 61.

²⁷⁶ Cf. Herodotus, 1,65; 67; 6,34; 36; 66; 7,169; 220; 8,51.

²⁷⁷ Cf. Plato, *Phdr.* 244a-b; 265b. Plato distinguishes four types of μανία: the divinatory one (μαντική) inspired by Apollo, the mystical one by Dionysus, the poetical (ποιητική) madness enhanced by the Muses, and the best kind of madness – that of love (ἐρωτική) – generated by Aphrodite and Eros.

²⁷⁸ Cf. *De Pyth. or.* 404D-F.

herself on the floor. After that, she survived only few days[279].

All the material elements analysed so far – especially those in connection with the inferior level of the double causation theory, such as the function of demons and animal sacrifices, the notion of 'propitious moment', the ritual orthopraxis put in place at the Delphic temple as a unique location on earth, and the role of the Pythia as a privileged human medium – will be combined together in the last chapter of the present study and considered in light of a doctrine that, as mentioned before, has been highly influential in Plutarch's philosophical thought: the cosmology exposed by Plato in the *Timaeus*.

---

[279] Cf. *De def. or.* 438A-C.

Chapter 3
An analysis of *De E apud Delphos*

1. Introduction

De E apud Delphos represents a challenging attempt to solve the fundamentally *unsolvable* enigma (ἀπορία) of the meaning of the mysterious 'E' placed on the Delphic temple. As Ammonius soon explains, this inscription has engendered numerous philosophical reflections, similarly to other two famous advices (προγράμματα) impressed on the shrine: 'know yourself' (γνῶθι σαυτόν) and 'never too much' (μηδὲν ἄγαν)[1].

The dialogical form of *De E* offers the perfect structure for a shared, multifaceted and potentially never-ending investigation, made up of consecutive attempts to solve the enigma. Lamprias, Plutarch's brother, Eustrophus, one of his old fellow students, Ammonius, his teacher, together with the philosopher Theon and the Delphic priest Nicander, partake in the animate, challenging discussion. They offer a chain of tentative solutions, which resort to an always superior level of expertise and are gradually more elevated in content – a compositional structure that recalls the one displayed by some Platonic dialogues, such as the *Symposium* and the *Phaedrus*. Through this hierarchical chain of arguments, Plutarch somehow exhibits his own formation process and personal intellectual development – which aligns with Mauro Bonazzi's proposal that such a dynamical series reproduces the way of a *cursus studiorum*[2], leading from practical to theoretical knowledge, through the successive major steps of logic, physics and theology.

The subsequent elements that the reader encounters in the dialogue – and that display an always increasing degree of sophistication, adequacy, and importance – are the following: personal belief (Lamprias, 385E-386A), astronomy (the 'Chaldaean', 386A-B), religious thought (Nicander, 386B-D), logical reasoning (Theon, 386D-387D), numerological theory (Eustrophus, 387D-F and Plutarch, 387F-391E), and finally an intensely religious and reverential ontological and theological reflection (Ammonius, 391E-394C).

The dialogue is set in Plutarch's youth, at the time when Nero paid a visit to Delphi in 66/67 AD. Some decades later Plutarch[3], as a mature

---

[1] Cf. *De E* 385D. For these two maxims in Plutarch, cf. *Cons. ad Apoll.* 116C and *Sept. sap. conv.* 163D; Plato, *Prt.* 343a-b; *Chrm.* 165a; Pausanias, 10,24,1.

[2] Cf. Bonazzi (2008).

[3] *De E apud Delphos* was probably written in 90 AD; cf. Ziegler (1974) 75.

family man, reports the informed discussion held at the temple long time before, thus acting as an extradiegetic narrator of a diegematic dialogue – a literary form that he often employs. As stated in the introduction (381D-385B), he is solicited to narrate the exchange by his sons and some visitors eager to learn more about the notorious enigma of the 'E' before leaving the sacred place. Plutarch, as a virtuous, cultivated and sociable man and philosopher, dedicates himself to the gentle and decent (εὐπρεπές) act of sharing what he knows, and willingly satisfies their initial curiosity, while the very suggestive location of the Delphic oracle – where the original discussion also took place – offers the perfect setting for the emergence of his memories[4].

In the beginning of the dialogue, the reader soon encounters the renown expression 'some Pythian discourses' (τῶν Πυθικῶν λόγων ἐνίους[5]), usually associated by scholars to the triad of writings analysed in the present study: *De E apud Delphos, De Pythiae oraculis* and *De defectu oraculorum*[6]. Daniel Babut has convincingly demonstrated how these three works share a communal inspiration and are grounded on a unitary theoretical structure. *De Pythiae* and *De defectu* similarly aim to prove "l'origine divine et providentielle de la divination" as well as "la piété et [...] la foi" to which divination is necessarily and strictly linked, while providing at the same time "une explication philosophique et rationelle des choses". According to Babut, *De E apud Delphos*, despite its first appearances, is fully in line with such prerogatives, since it includes a rational-philosophical investigation, developed in the first chapters, as well as a religious and reverent declaration of god's transcendence, expressed in Ammonius' final speech. *De E* also fundamentally revolves around the main question

---

[4] Cf. *De E* 385A-B. For a philological analysis of this passage and a general assessment of Plutarch's sacerdotal service in Delphi, sustained by textual and epigraphical references, see Casanova (2012) esp. 155-157.

I would like to point out that the characterisation of the visitors as 'eager to listen' (ἀκοῦσαί τι προθυμουμένους) – whose inquisitiveness ideally fosters the composition of the dialogue – recalls the role of the 'stranger' Diogenianus, praised for his intelligent questions in *De Pythiae oraculis*, or the adventurous voyager Cleombrotus and his challenging arguments in *De defectu oraculorum*. The importance of these figures implicitly defines intelligent questioning as a welcome and healthy sign of philosophical curiosity.

[5] *De E* 384E. For this expression see Flacelière (1943).

[6] Françoise Frazier has proposed to include *De sera numinis vindicta* within this dialogical group, for its content, setting and composition – cf. Frazier (2010). Konrat Ziegler has suggested to also add in the Delphic dialogues the lost treatise *On self knowledge: whether the soul is immortal* (Lamprias 77); this work would have formed a couple with *De E*, since respectively devoted to the topics of human limitedness and divine transcendence – cf. Ziegler (1964) 192.

characterising all the Delphic dialogues: what the relation is between faith and reason[7].

As we read in the introduction of *De E apud Delphos*, these 'writings' will be sent as gifts to the Stoic poet Sarapion[8], the dedicatee of the dialogue. These literary works are quite strikingly presented as 'spiritual offerings' and 'first fruits' – in Greek 'ἀπαρχαί', a term clearly stressing the religious framework in which the dialogue is envisioned. The primary meaning of this word is indeed connected to cultic practices, since it refers to the 'primal offerings' donated to the god before the real sacrificial act; this signification also points to the fact that more numerous and better discourses are expected in return from the recipient.

The precious spiritual-literary-philosophical gift represented by *De E apud Delphos*, sent from the Platonic priest Plutarch and set in the small peripheral municipality of Delphi, will reach the Stoic poet Sarapion in Athens, a major cultural centre depicted – by implicit contrast – as a big university city that offers rich librarian collections and numerous possibilities for cultivated discussions[9]. There Plutarch received his own Academic formation, studying with the philosopher Ammonius, star of *De E* and its '*princeps dialogi*'[10].

These *logoi* – exchanged between two dear friends who nevertheless embrace two different philosophical views – are intended as authentically honourable gifts, significantly defined as superior to any material good in terms of reason and wisdom (λόγου καὶ σοφίας). Contrary to concrete donations, it is indeed virtuous (καλόν) and ennobling to exchange and reciprocate them. Considering Plutarch's approval and preference for *immaterial* goods[11], and transposing this attitude to the field of hermeneutics, the general compositional and argumentative strategy of the dialogue clearly emerges: the 'body' has to be overcome in favour of

---

[7] Cf. Babut (1992) 233-234. Hendrik Obsieger stresses instead the diversity among these dialogues, and refuses the idea that the expression 'Pythian dialogues' may point to them as a unitary collection – cf. Obsieger (2013) 97-98.

[8] For the image of the poet Sarapion cf. *De Pyth. or.* 396D; *Quaest. conv.* 628A; and *supra* 18, n. 4.

[9] Cf. *De E* 384D-E.

[10] The presence of a '*princeps dialogi*' is a typical feature of Plutarch's compositional technique. Moreover, in Plutarch's works, Ammonius often plays the role of the mature, wise and prepared intellectual, who incites the dialogical exchange with his intelligent questions and informed arguments. For an in-depth analysis of Ammonius see Opsomer (2009).

[11] Cf. *De Is. et Os.* 351C: "All good things, my dear Clea, sensible men must ask from the gods; and especially do we pray that from those mighty gods we may, in our quest, gain a knowledge of themselves, so far as such a thing is attainable by men. For we believe that there is nothing more important for man to receive, or more ennobling for God of His grace to grant, than the truth". (Eng. trans. F. C. Babbitt)

the 'spirit', since the true meaning of material-sensible beings is located beyond their simple semblance – so beyond the literal meaning of a text and, more generally, beyond the physical appearance of things.

2. Importance of symbols and riddles for philosophy and rational reflection

In the beginning of the dialogue, Plutarch stresses the 'oracular side' of the god Apollo, as well as the continual support and benevolent advice that the god offers to individuals by means of the shrine. In such a context, the Delphic temple is intended and implicitly characterised as an effective, chosen and apparently infallible communication channel between god and humankind. The god's suggestions regard the troubles of human life (τὰς μὲν περὶ τὸν βίον ἀπορίας): they address and solve practical concerns. Nevertheless, it is possible to notice from the beginning that a further operational level is at work, implicitly defined as somehow nobler and superior: an additional endeavour of Apollo is indeed to create intellectual (περὶ τὸν λόγον) doubts and enigmas in the mind of those who are philosophers by nature (τῷ φύσει φιλοσόφῳ): the desire (ὄρεξις) that he instils in this way in their soul invites them to reach for the truth (ἐπὶ τὴν ἀλήθειαν). Plutarch seems here to articulate and specify a double level of understanding of divine matters, coupled with two 'intellectual classes' of receptors: those who are philosophers by nature (φύσει φιλοσόφῳ) – intellectually stimulated by god-sent riddles –, and the mass of common believers – comforted, instead, by god-sent solutions[12].

This twofold preliminary description of the activity of Apollo at the temple defines the first two prerogatives attributed to the god in the dialogue. He is a prophet (μάντις) – since he discloses his prophetic knowledge to humankind – as well as a philosopher (φιλόσοφος) – since he stimulates human desire to know by creating a craving within the souls of some selected individuals[13]. Apollo's double-face of 'prophet' and 'philosopher' recurs in Plutarch's whole production and, as we will see, will reappear in the course of *De E apud Delphos*, enriched by several other qualifications.

Some additional features of the god are immediately suggested by Ammonius' 'preliminary depiction' of Apollo. This consists of a series of names (the first over four lists of epithets present in the *De E*), explainable by specific pseudo-etymological connections: Apollo is 'Inquirer', encouraging those who are beginning to learn; 'Clear' and 'Disclosing', sustaining those who have already started to see the light of the truth; 'Knowing', guiding those who possess science (ἐπιστήμη); 'Conversation-

---

[12] Cf. *De E* 384E-F; cf. also *Quaest. conv.* 673B.
[13] Cf. *De E* 385B.

alist', watching over those who enjoy philosophical conversations[14]. As I believe, this succession, by tracing a sort of 'escalation', and shifting its focus from more simple to more complex divine qualifications and human activities, virtually guides us towards the most sublime form of cognitive endeavour: the philosophical exchange, which – rather than focussing on a once-for-all conquered truth – draws its lifeblood from constant debate.

Interestingly, the series of epithets presented by Ammonius complies with the definition of philosophy that he offers next, which is also extremely helpful in order to understand Plutarch's own conception of the nature and aim of philosophical research. Ammonius defines wonder (θαυμάζειν) and uncertainty (ἀπορεῖν) as the sources of inquiry (ζητεῖν), which in its turn represents the beginning of philosophy (φιλοσοφεῖν)[15].

The hierarchical path leading towards philosophical reflection is therefore the following:

$$[θαυμάζειν + ἀπορεῖν] \rightarrow ζητεῖν \rightarrow φιλοσοφεῖν$$

This sequence – which, as we will see, forms part of the theoretical background of Ammonius' final speech – recalls the very structure of *De E apud Delphos*: a zetetic investigation over a primary, surprising, puzzling symbol, whose tentative decipherment potentially leads towards a superior kind of philosophical exchange. From a gnoseological perspective, this assumption invites us to discover, through rational investigation (λόγος), the underlying cause of natural phenomena (διὰ τί καὶ διδασκαλίαν τῆς αἰτίας), while from a theological standpoint, it is connected to a view of the divine as concealed in riddles[16].

In a famous passage of the *Quaestiones convivales*, a similar definition of philosophy is proposed by Lucius Mestrius Florus, in a discussion concerning the 'wicked eye'. He claims that the existence of a relation between two events, if proven by facts, cannot be doubted simply because its cause is obscure and apparently unexplainable. Indeed, when looking for a *probable* explanation of a given phenomenon, we should never

---

[14] Cf. *ibid.* 385B-C. Πύθιος – explained by Plutarch as from πυθέσθαι, 'to inform / look for' – is connected to Πυθώ, the alternative toponym for Delphi; Δήλιος – associated to 'clear', δῆλος – refers to Δῆλος, the island where Apollo was born; Φαναῖος – linked to 'show', 'φαίνω' – comes from Φάναι, a hill of the island of Chios where the god was worshipped. Finally, Ἰσμήνιος is related to ἰδ-, the root of the verb 'to know', and Λεσχηνόριος to λέσχη, place of gathering and discussion. For these etymologies cf. Lozza (1983) 224, n. 6 and Strobach (1997) 59-60. Valgiglio has collected the epithets that Plutarch associates to Apollo here and in other of his works, and studied their parallels in other authors – cf. Valgiglio (1988a) 209-222.

[15] Cf. Plato, *Tht.* 155d; Aristoteles, *Metaph.* 1,982b12-20.

[16] Cf. *De E* 385C.

deny the existence of things that our reason can not explain – given the constitution of the material and the immaterial world, which are much wider than ourselves and our cognitive faculties. The 'unpredictable' and 'fantastic' are essential to our knowledge, so much so that real philosophy starts where the cause eludes our intelligent thinking. In such a conceptual framework, open and intelligent 'doubting' (τὸ ἀπορεῖν) becomes equal to 'philosophising' (τὸ φιλοσοφεῖν)[17].

In *De E apud Delphos*, the chosen symbol and principal expression of the enigmatic and challenging nature characterising both the earthly phenomena and the divine world is precisely the inscription of the 'E'. The '*epsilon*' indeed, enclosing a hidden meaning, is *per se* conceived as a philosophical *aporia*: this is the real protagonist of the dialogue, of which it constitutes the first and most important riddle. I would like to point out from the beginning that Plutarch values the letter as a precious object of inquiry exactly because its mystery, fundamentally unsolvable, stimulates a prolific quest for truth and restless philosophical discussions.

Plutarch believes to be *likely* (τοῦτο γὰρ εἰκός, note the Academic resonance of this adjective) that the 'E' was placed there neither by chance (κατὰ τύχην) nor through a random selection (ἀπὸ κλήρου). The argumentative strategy opposing chance and purpose is consistently employed in the Delphic dialogues and refers to two opposing systems of thought that respectively attribute supremacy to each of these cosmological forces. As Plutarch emphasises, the choice of the 'E' was made according to a precise purpose: that was evidently held as the one and only letter that constituted a worthy and meaningful offer (ἀνάθημα) for the god, so was placed there *intentionally* in order to be clearly noted and contemplated by the visitors. The first of those who were investigating on the god (περὶ τὸν θεὸν φιλοσοφήσαντας) consciously chose it as a suitable symbol (σύμβολον), given its powerful significance (δύναμις) and its status of an object worthy of study (σπουδή)[18].

A second and likewise important element of the dialogue is the power of divine names: exactly like the symbol of the 'E', if correctly interpreted, they disclose precious information concerning the transcendent world. The belief in the power of names has its most remarkable 'theoretical' precedent in Plato's *Cratylus*[19], and its 'religious-mysteric' one in the *Derveni papyrus*, specifically attesting to the Greek common conception that words are efficacious operative tools and 'seals' that capture the

---

[17] Cf. *Quaest. conv.* 680D: ὁ ζητῶν ἐν ἑκάστῳ τὸ εὔλογον ἐκ πάντων ἀναιρεῖ τὸ θαυμάσιον· ὅπου γὰρ ὁ τῆς αἰτίας ἐπιλείπει λόγος, ἐκεῖθεν ἄρχεται τὸ ἀπορεῖν, τουτέστι τὸ φιλοσοφεῖν. Also cf. Opsomer (1998) 78-82; Meeusen (2017) 242-244.

[18] Cf. *De E* 384F-385A.

[19] For a discussion on the role of words and names in this dialogue, cf. Natoli-Sini-Vegetti (1995) 201-249.

essence (οὐσία) of things. In magic, the strength of *verba* and *voces* is paramount, since they are believed to point – although in an obscure and enigmatic manner – to hidden powerful contents[20].

In this regard, it is worth reminding that Marina Cavalli has interestingly proved the influence of the oracular style on Plutarch's linguistic choices and literary expression, which clearly reproduce oracular verbal customs – precisely in force of the fundamental *coincidence* between words and the reality that they represent, typical of the Greek culture and mindset[21]. Ancient theories (like the one concerning the power of divine names) are re-interpreted by Plutarch according to his own religious spirit, cultural sensibility and philosophical background, but also in light of the great influence exerted by 'Oriental religions' in his time – as we will see in the present chapter.

The idea that unsolvable intellectual doubts and enigmas (ἀπορίαι) foster philosophical investigation – which has to be always guided by a deep, reverential respect towards the divine (εὐλάβεια πρὸς τὸ θεῖον) – is arguably part of Plutarch's most sincere and profound convictions. Philosophy in *De Iside et Osiride* is equated to the 'αἰνιγματώδης σοφία[22]' of the Egyptian priests – a definition somehow applicable to Ammonius' conception as well, that also resonates with his Egyptian origins. Plutarch often employs the very word 'enigma' (αἴνιγμα) – a Pythagorean key-word – to refer to allegorism[23].

---

[20] In the composite texts of the *Papyri Graecae Magicae* – cf. Betz (1986) – traditional deities (like Hermes, invoked as πολυώνυμος, εὐεργέτης and φαρμάκων εὑρετής, bestowing χάρις and μορφή) are transformed and invoked by unusual epithets including *nomina barbara* (like the famous Ἀβρασάξ).

Amulets and magical gems display a similar syncretic power, showing divine or demonic creatures extraneous to the classical *pantheon*, while the traditional ones are inserted in an original iconographic frame. Signs (χαρακτῆρες), invocations, spells or oracular pronouncements, associated to symbols and signs, create obscure combinations, comprehensible just to knowledgeable practitioners. Words often employed include: non-Greek names, mostly Semitic (such as Ἰάω, Σαβαώθ, Ἀδωναι), and long strange chains of terms that constitute the *voces magicae*, βάρβαρα and ἀσήμια ὀνόματα, as well as Ἐφέσια γράμματα – mysterious sayings supposedly inscribed in the temple of Artemis at Ephesus, also cited by Plutarch in *Quaest. conv.* 706E.

[21] Cf. Cavalli (1991).

[22] *De Is. et Os.* 354C. Similarly, the issue of the plurality of worlds, presented by Plato in an 'enigmatic way' (αἰνιγματώδη μετ'εὐλαβείας, *De def. or.* 420F; 421F), is introduced in *De defectu oraculorum* also as a possible proof of the existence of demons as non-incarnated souls, as well as to acknowledge the providential and beneficial nature of god.

[23] In *Quaest. conv.* 727B-C Plutarch writes that Pythagoreans observe ethical principles enclosed in σύμβολα. For the importance of the notion of symbol and allegory in antiquity cf. Struck (2004) esp. 103.

In the same work Plutarch reports that Pythagoras[24], together with other wise Greek men (such as Solon, Thales, Plato, Eudoxus, and perhaps Lycurgus), personally consulted the Egyptian priests in their homeland – guided by the conviction that Egyptian wisdom was the one closest to the divine[25]. Pythagoras, entertaining a reciprocal admiration for the priests encountered in that mythical land, absorbed their symbolism and their esoteric wisdom (τὸ συμβολικὸν αὐτῶν καὶ μυστηριῶδες) and reshaped his own doctrines according to the enigmatic character and allusive form of the Egyptian sayings (ἀναμίξας αἰνίγμασι τὰ δόγματα)[26]. Plutarch stresses that it was especially from hieroglyphics that Pythagoras took inspiration for composing his prescriptions (σύμβολα)[27] – a mythical-historical remark that contributes to clarify the ancient consideration of Pythagoreanism as an elitist, sectarian, almost mystery philosophy, reserved to initiates.

The belief in the existence of a superior kind of wisdom inaccessible to the mass and the idea that the divine is fundamentally unknown (but just partly knowable by chosen men through a complex ethical-intellectual process of self-cultivation) both characterise the philosophical production of this age, and are shared and re-elaborated by popular thought, magic and religion. Secret knowledge, in this epoch, comes to be perceived as a key-feature of a peculiar 'kind of rationality', according to which true meanings are hidden behind complex associations of seemingly arbitrary symbols, unknown names, sublime words; from a general perspective, every material entity has an enigmatic character and hidden meaning that awaits decipherment.

Following Ammonius' definition of philosophy, wonder and uncertainty are generated by enigmas (ἔοικεν αἰνίγμασι κατακεκρύφθαι), by mysterious elements in need of a rational-logical explanation, enclosing some hidden references to superior realities[28]. This principle can be extended from the cultic-monumental setting of the Delphic temple to the whole sensible world, intended as a repository of enigmas pointing to the divine and to the providential harmony pervading the universe. As *De E apud Delphos* illustrates, humans must resort to a wide range of concepts, definitions and qualifications in order to reach for the essence of god – although only in an approximate, insufficient way. In this process, intermediate, varying elements (for instance, the symbol of the sun) are extremely important,

---

[24] A reference to the Pseudo-Plutarchan work *De liberis educandis* can be instructive in this regard: the author, while explaining how to keep young people away from dishonourable acquaintances, reminds the educative value of Pythagoraean allegories (αἰνίγμασιν; cf. *De lib. educ.* 12D-E).

[25] Cf. *De Is. et Os.* 354D-E.

[26] Cf. *ibid.* 354F.

[27] Cf. *ibid.* 354E.

[28] Also cf. *Quaest. conv.* 745B.

since they work as indispensable cognitive bridges that help humans in the advancement of their knowledge. A symbol is an element midway between contingency and transcendence, characterised by a peculiar status and position; this is in line with Plutarch's firm division among different ontological realms (divine-demonic-material), and with the centrality of the notion of 'intermediary' (μέσα, μεταξύ) in his philosophical reflection – as well as in that of his master Plato[29].

De E apud Delphos appears to be built on the fundamental division between the human and the divine dimension, and displays our tension towards transcendence, our strenuous attempt to bridge this gap by means of our limited cognitive faculties. The god – incorporeal and eternal – and humans – belonging to the world of appearance, materiality and mutability – cannot enter into direct communication with each other. For this reason, their reciprocal contact and exchange is necessarily indirect and must resort to enigmas (αἰνίγματα) – which humans have to interpret through rational investigation.

In such a conceptual framework, the extraordinary ontological and gnoseological status of Delphi arises: the oracle is a chosen, potentially 'perfect' channel to the 'wholly other', whose functioning shows its almost complete 'estrangement' from ordinary life. I believe that, in the context of Plutarch's Delphic dialogues, Delphi's most relevant 'mysterious' and 'symbolic' elements, objects of rational examination and philosophical discussion, are the following: first, its ritual customs, in the guise of cultic traditions and, especially, prophetic dynamics; second, its concrete, architectural, material construction – as attested by the discussion on the symbol of the 'E', as well as by the promenade in *De Pythiae oraculis*, analysed in the first chapter of the present study[30].

In Plutarch's view, signs are scattered everywhere – in cultic objects, revealed data, ritual practices and formulas, myths and even in the words of literates and philosophers. Their meaning is brought to light through exegesis. Similarly to what happens in artificial divination, the interpreter should possess either the charismatic gift of inspiration, or the knowledge of specific hermeneutic rules. In particular, authentic belief in the gods (εὐσέβεια) and a correct opinion (ἀληθὴ δόξα) are required for interpreting

---

[29] For the importance of the concept of 'intermediary' in Plutarch and Plato, see Froidefond (1987) esp. 205-206.

[30] According to Ammonius, other ritual peculiarities of the oracle that under their uncommon appearances hide special significance are: the fact that at Delphi pine wood is burned in the undying fire, while laurel is used for offering incense; two Moires (instead of three) have their statues there (cf. Pausanias, 10,24,4); no woman is allowed to approach the prophetic shrine (cf. Euripides, *Ion* 222); the use of the tripod as a seat for the prophetess. This list confirms how the external appearance of the Delphic oracle is *itself* a repository of meaningful symbols.

myths in a pious and philosophical manner (ὁσίως καὶ φιλοσόφως), and for establishing correct religious practices[31].

Plutarch employs allegorical exegesis for explaining, and giving ground to, his own theoretical ambitions and needs. He notoriously tends to promote an ethical-religious interpretation of traditional stories and poems – while rejecting the atheistic undertones implicit in the Stoic physicalistic-materialistic allegorical reading, which he considers irreverent and erroneous[32]. Basically, while the Stoics constantly confuse the intelligible with the sensible, Plutarch establishes a clear dualistic scheme on the basis of a radical distinction between the material and the immaterial world – whose reciprocal contact, as we will see, has nevertheless to be somehow guaranteed.

The notions of intermediation, hierarchy and graduation are pivotal in *De E apud Delphos*, under three main respects, which we can call: compositional, theoretical-intellectual, and ontological. First, the dialogue is composed in such a way that increasingly 'better' arguments follow one another, so that an always more accurate and reliable answer dialectically counteracts the preceding one. Second, from a theoretical perspective, the text sketches an itinerary of individual intellectual improvement and cultural development through an ascending path of knowledge, that leads to higher philosophical and religious acquisitions. Third, the gap between the human and the divine level is repeatedly and clearly emphasised; these two ontological domains are nevertheless 'bridged together' by some elements that, if correctly analysed and interpreted, can shed light on the superior world and extend our knowledge of the cosmos.

It is important to underscore that Plutarch does not articulate a hierarchical divine system, as those later developed by the Neoplatonists, but postulates one single god, characterised by both a demiurgic and a paradigmatic power. As this analysis intends to show, the image of the supreme god emerging from *De E apud Delphos* is that of a henotheistic deity that collects together all the qualities not only described in Ammonius' final speech, but also resulting from all the preceding contributions and definitions offered in turn by the different speakers.

---

[31] Cf. *De Is. et Os.* 355C-D.

[32] Daniel Babut has underlined that Plutarch does not reject the Stoic allegoresis as such, but the dangerous irreligious consequences that could be drawn from it – cf. Babut (2003) 424. This attitude is confirmed by Plutarch's treatment of the identification between Apollo and the sun. Plutarch's refusal of the consequences deriving from the excessive use of allegories in the Stoic materialistic reading of myths is also expressed in *De facie* 922A-E, where Lamprias counters the Stoic theory (stigmatised as an ἀτοπία) of the face and nature of the moon.

3. Tentative solutions

The main idea sustaining my analysis is the leading conviction that it is possible to attempt an 'inclusive' reading of all the different solutions to the enigma of the 'E' progressively advanced by the participants – a feature typical of the zetematic structure of this dialogue. What I especially intend to point out, as eminently relevant for the purpose of my study, is that all the visions proposed by the characters of *De E apud Delphos* must be considered *together*, since they *all* concur to create a complex, multifaceted and dynamic image of the god Apollo. It is therefore the 'theological meaning' implied in every single explanation that I aim to bring to light, because I believe that the composite, many-sided portrait of the god emerging from this dialogue is strictly connected to Plutarch's own idea of oracular mantic and may help us assess the place that divination occupies in his broader philosophical reflection.

The most interesting aspect of the overall picture finally outlined in *De E apud Delphos* is that no single characterisation presented in the dialogical exchange has to be totally rejected, but each of them can be at least partly saved. What I want to stress is that these diverse depictions, if taken all together, constitute a 'collective effort' to define the sublime god Apollo, with the highest possible level of accuracy.

Moreover, acknowledging the meaning of the god's multiple aspects and the intrinsic value of his articulated characterisation is of a paramount importance for our comprehension not only of Plutarch's thought, but also of the wider religious background of his time, across various social strata and intellectual classes. Fritz Graf – in his monograph devoted to Apollo that significantly encompasses all the different facets of the god – defines this deity exactly as "complex and contradictory, in the myths and cults of the Greek and Roman world as much as in his later reception"[33].

The attitude of assembling together multiple divine features and persons into one single divine entity currently goes under the name of 'syncretism'. This is a typical trait of imperial religiosity, generally coupled with a deep tendency towards 'henotheism', namely, the belief that one god is superior for his power and prestige to the whole pantheon. The idea, widespread in the religious panorama of the time, of a universalistic entity ontologically located beyond particular powers (δυνάμεις) is shared by contemporaneous Middle-Platonic theoretical constructions. The remaining gods of the

---

[33] Graf (2009) 146. And even: "Music and dance, divination, healing, the young, and the polis denote areas where Apollo played a major and sometimes a unique role, different in importance from city to city. The historian feels an intellectual pull to construct these fields into an underlying unity. Such a construction might satisfy a thinker's need of neatness; but it sacrifices so much historical diversity that it loses all value for the historian of religion" (*ibid.*).

pantheon and the demons, as individual religious powers invested with specific prerogatives, form a hierarchical scheme subordinated to the supreme henotheistic deity. The highest god therefore has one single divine substance (οὐσία) *plus* a multiple, variegate appearance (ὑπαρξία). This twofold, oxymoronic qualification becomes even more problematic when conjuncted with the paradoxical depiction of god as simultaneously unnameable and polyonymous (thus worshipped under different names), present in various sources of the Imperial epoch, such as inscriptions, treatises, hymns and aretalogies.

The following part of this analysis will take into account the various solutions presented in *De E apud Delphos*, in order to highlight their usefulness for defining the image of the supreme god and his multiple characters[34].

3.1. Apollo. The god of popular devotion

The first two explanations, respectively offered by Lamprias and by an unnamed Chaldaean astronomer, shed light on Apollo as the god of religious devotion, involved in traditional myths and stories, and object of popular belief.

3.1.1. Wisdom, legend and history

Lamprias, Plutarch's brother, presents the first solution to the enigma of the 'E'. He reports an explanation apparently received from some guides in Delphi: the *epsilon*, as the fifth letter of the alphabet, points to the original number of the mythical 'Wise Men'. Five out of the 'Seven Sages' (traditionally designed as 'οἱ ἑπτὰ σοφοί') decided to peacefully

---

[34] Recently, two notable studies on *De E apud Delphos* have been published by two German scholars, helping to advance our knowledge of this dialogue. Obsieger (2013) proposes an in-depth philological and linguistic study of the text. He aims to prove that the various explanations offered in *De E* have a fundamentally non-serious and even humoristic tone. Accordingly, Plutarch purposely deforms traditional philosophical concepts and views (based on the freedom of speech allowed by the dialogical circumstance) in order to first entertain the readers, and then to surprise them with Ammonius' final speech, devoid of any conclusive or authoritative tone. Thum (2013), instead, convinced of the seriousness of Plutarch's approach, intends to offer a new, comprehensive reading of the work, more accurate and substantiated with respect to all the previous ones, by stressing the compositional dynamism and argumentative polyphony of the dialogue. Thum explores its literary-philosophical background and possible intertextual connections, contextualising *De E apud Delphos* within Plutarch's production and wider cultural milieu. Both Tobias Thum and Hendrik Obsieger maintain that no interpretation offered in the dialogue can be held as definitive nor revelatory of Plutarch's own thought, and assume the 'E' as a protreptic element, at the core of a fundamentally aporetic dialogical-philosophical investigation.

exclude two of them – Cleobulus of Lindos and Periander of Corinth; they then gathered together and dedicated the letter 'E' to the god as an offer representing their number[35]. Cleobulus and Periander were removed for their tyrannical and unjust behaviour: they had indeed resorted to unfair means (δυνάμει καὶ φίλοις καὶ χάρισι) in order to achieve power.

I would like to point out that it is really meaningful that the first explanation presented in the dialogue refers to the mythical group of the Seven Sages: they embody a pre-philosophical tradition of sublime wisdom and are associated to the figure of the Delphic Apollo, who indeed rewarded with the tripod the winner of their competitions. They supposedly also authored a number of 'judgements' or '*apophthegmata*', which enclosed a hidden, cyphred significance – including those impressed on the Delphic temple. It is worthwhile noting that, in a work dedicated to the decipherment of symbols, and employing sensible objects as repositories of hidden meanings and of a superior knowledge, the first external reference is to the ancient legendary Sages, who used to express themselves in cryptic lapidary words. According to Lamprias' version, the very first *epsilon* – made of wood – was donated by 'the five' as a votive gift (ἀνάθημα) to the god. This original 'E' was then followed by the bronze and the golden ones offered by the Atenians and Augustus' wife Livia, respectively.

It is fundamental to point out that, while Lamprias' account is soon dismissed by Ammonius as an unacceptable, and probably invented story based on his personal opinion (ἰδία δόξα)[36], it does nevertheless contain some important veridical and interesting elements. First of all, the very specific conviction that the 'E' is a sacred offering (ἀνάθημα) is explicitly shared by Plutarch himself[37]. Moreover, Apollo, as presented by Lamprias, coincides with the god of popular devotion, honoured with material gifts – in this case the 'E', whose different materials attest to the different social status of the givers. Finally, this explanation reveals Apollo's political face, by means of implicit references to public interest and diplomatic relations. Cleobolus and Periander, the two 'wise men' excluded from

---

[35] Cf. *De E* 385E-386A; cf. *Sept. sav. conv.* See Plato, *Prt.* 343a-b: "Such men were Thales of Miletus, Pittacus of Mytilene, Bias of Priene, Solon of our city, Cleobulus of Lindus, Myson of Chen, and, last of the traditional seven, Chilon of Sparta. All these were enthusiasts, lovers and disciples of the Spartan culture; and you can recognize that character in their wisdom by the short, memorable sayings that fell from each of them they assembled together and dedicated these as the first-fruits of their lore to Apollo in his Delphic temple, inscribing there those maxims which are on every tongue – 'Know thyself' and 'Nothing overmuch'." (Eng. trans. W.R.M. Lamb).

[36] Cf. *De E* 386A.

[37] Cf. *ibid.* 384F-385A.

the legendary group, are clearly stigmatised as tyrants: since they share nothing in virtue (ἀρετή) and wisdom (σοφία), they are unworthy of the ideal fellowship and approval of the wise and peaceful god Apollo. Shifting to the historical present, Livia's offering attests to the tight diplomatic relations existing between the temple and the Roman power, and also recalls her husband Augustus' resolution of supporting the Delphic shrine. The diplomatic ties between Greece and Rome, on the background of the Delphic temple, are even stressed in the introduction of *De E*, where Plutarch dates the dialogue to the time of Nero's visit to Greece – an event that the philosopher associates with the emperor's concession of freedom to the province, declared in Corynth in 67 AD[38].

The *Lives* clearly display Plutarch's conception of the 'historical' Apollo and of his 'oracular influence' within historical events – a theme that acquires a special importance at the time of the Roman domination. The god's interventions do not directly shape and modify human deeds; rather, the interpretation (and even manipulation) of the oracular utterances delivered at the Delphic shrine works as a significant and efficient means of power and control[39]. So much so that, according to Plutarch, some rulers are fully legitimised to make use of superstition as an instrument for influencing and controlling the mass[40].

As for Plutarch's political activity in connection with the Delphic oracle – despite the scarce references that we find in his works – we know that he was serving not only as a priest and administrator (ἐπιμελήτης) at the shrine, but also as a diplomat, sustaining concretely its activity and flourishing by creating fruitful connections with the central rule (especially with the *gens Flavia*)[41]. Probably, he personally met Vespasian in Greece and Alexandria, while benefits and concessions for Delphi seem to have derived from his relationship with Lucius Mestrius Florius[42]. It is indeed a fact that during Plutarch's life the Delphic oracle was registering an impressive increase in prestige and prosperity.

Generally speaking, in this age it is a common custom for intellectuals to benefit from the double-status of philosopher *and* priest in order to obtain greater prestige and social recognition. It is almost surprising how representatives of the upper class of the Eastern Roman Empire

---

[38] Cf. *De sera num.* 568A.

[39] Cf. Stadter (2015) 94: "There is a tension between Plutarch's glorification of Apollo and Delphi in the 'Pythian dialogues' and his treatment in the *Lives*".

[40] This procedure is found, among the others, in Plutarch's *Themistocles, Numa, Lysander, Alexander*.

[41] For the diplomatic activity performed by Plutarch cf. Stadter (2004).

[42] Stadter indicates some of these benefits: "the archonship of Titus, the rebuilding of the temple of Apollo, the construction of new buildings in the sacred precinct, and Nigrinus' decision on the boundaries of the civic land" – Stadter (2004) 31.

are eager to acquire "*multiple identities*" in order to increase their power and popularity[43].

It seems to me that this process reminds the one that involves the deities worshipped at the time, who gain increasing success and greater recognition as many are the names and the facets under which they are venerated.

3.1.2. Apollo and the sun

The second solution proposed in *De E apud Delphos* consists in the largely accepted astrological belief declaring that the sun and Apollo are the same entity[44], proposed by a Chaldaean astronomer who came to Delphi one day before the dialogue took place. Based on the correspondence between the seven planets and the seven vowels, the 'E', which is second to the 'A' in the alphabet, refers to the sun, second to the moon in the astronomical order[45]. While this argument is soon discarded as an example of quackery and charlatanism (παντάπασιν ἐκ πίνακος καὶ πυλαίας), the controversial relationship between Apollo and the sun (which, as we have seen, is one of the leading themes of the Delphic dialogues) will be recalled in Ammonius' final speech[46].

Oracular centres in the first centuries AD encourage and promote a henotheistic theological view, according to which the god presiding over the shrine usually occupies the top of the divine pyramid. *De E apud Delphos* – where the idea of a 'multifaceted Apollo' is combined with a henotheistic theological conception – may contribute to endorse the hypothesis that Apollo is conceived as the highest deity of the pantheon in Delphi.

The success of the identification between the god and the sun in the following three centuries will be fostered by the religious propaganda carried on by the priests in Delphi and other oracular shrines (especially Claros)[47]. The 'Solar henotheism' will soon come to sustain, and give credit to, the

---

[43] For the notion of 'multiple identities' acquired by intellectuals, often characterised by the double status of philosophers *and* priests see Haake (2008) esp. 164-165. For Plutarch, see Jones (2004).

[44] This identification will be also discussed in *De E* §21 (393C-394C). For the Chaldaean astronomers, also see Cicero, *Div.* 1,41,91.

[45] Cf. *De E* 385B-386B. The Delphic priests counter the opinions of Lamprias and the Chaldaean, by stressing that the letter's symbolic value (σύμβολον) is enclosed in its name (ὄνομα), so neither in its aspect (ὄψις) nor in its sound (φθόγγον).

[46] Cf. for instance *Apollon et le soileil*, a chapter of a recent book dedicated to the philosophy of the Delphic dialogues: Brouillette (2014) 113-125.

[47] Robin Lane Fox describes the activity of the Delphic priests as follows: "They raised these questions for visitors but did not answer them exactly. Visitors then put the problems to the god" – Fox (1986) 185.

imperial political-religious ideology where the Sun (under the names of Attis, Adonis, Bacchus or Pan) is celebrated as a polymorphous, pantheistic deity. A votive relief found in Delphi, representing Helios-Apollo, offers the iconographic, tangible confirmation that this identification was already part of the accepted beliefs, currently promulgated at the temple[48].

3.2. Religion and logic

The third and fourth explanations in *De E apud Delphos* are based on the sound of the letter 'E', which is pronounced in Greek in the same way as the diphthong 'ει', which corresponds to the hypothetical conjunction 'if'. Nicander and Theon respectively focus on the interrogative-optative and hypothetical value of this particle.

3.2.1. Prophecy and prayers

Nicander, priest of the Delphic temple, provides a religious account for the 'E': the vowel represents the form and the 'sensible aspect and shape' (σχῆμα καὶ μορφή) of the questions posed to the god, which are normally introduced by the conjunction 'if'. The inquiries mostly concern simple everyday problems (such as marriage, navigation, agriculture, travels). The custom to consult the god on personal issues – recalled in the other two Delphic dialogues – receives strong historical confirmations from the activity of other oracular centres of the ancient Greek world: gods are interrogated and 'put to the test' precisely because one of their fundamental 'duties', and even the condition of their very existence – as cleverly pointed out by Aude Busine – is to listen to human words and possibly offer practical positive feedbacks[49].

Nicander explains that the habit of starting questions with the hypothetical particle 'if' shows how the templar-religious logic, effective in the oracular context, harshly collides against the strictly rational logic, according to which every proposition starting with 'if' is deprived of truth-value. Such a contrast implicitly reveals the oracle as an enclosed, extraordinary space, regulated by rules that are extraneous to human common sense, knowledge and cognition. In this specific ritual frame, the god holds the questions made by the consultants as real facts (πράγματα) despite, or better *precisely because*, they are introduced by the word 'if'.

On the other hand, Nicander stresses the desiderative-optative value of this conjunction, as shown by the prayers frequently submitted to the deity[50]. We know that the god, from the beginning of the oracular activity,

---

[48] This confirms that such a deity was worshipped in the area, even since the Hellenistic age; cf. Zagdoun (1995); *supra* 55.

[49] Cf. Busine (2005) esp. the section 2,1,B: *Contextes privés*, 100-125.

[50] Cf. *De E* 386C-D.

has been receiving interrogations concerning spiritual-ritual renewal and purification from murders. Apollo was considered a protector of the entire civic community, and invoked also for his apotropaic functions – as signalled by the topical elements of the sacred source and the laurel tree present in Delphi. Nicander's position, in particular, recalls the Platonists' conception of prayers as endowed with an 'exchange value' and devoid of the ethical meaning that the Stoics associated to them. It should be reminded that the god, despite his benevolence and power, is never defined in Plutarch as a thaumaturge and, as a general rule, his action always needs to comply with the laws of necessity that regulate the world of phenomena.

I want to stress that Nicander's depiction of Apollo, by lowering the god at the level of humankind and of human troubles and desires, is the one among those presented in *De E* that mostly stresses the interconnection between the transcendent and the immanent plan: Apollo, from a ritual-religious standpoint, is a generous god who delivers practical suggestions to humans and satisfies their demands. More in detail, Nicander provides a twofold qualification. In his speech, the double meaning of the particle 'if' – interrogative and optative, thus respectively employed in questions and prayers – appears to be connected to the very double nature of the god: first, Apollo is a seer (μάντις) who helps us to cope with the uncertainties of life, by answering our questions; second, he is a god (θεός), a beneficent deity who listens to our words and fulfils our hopes, by listening to our prayers.

3.2.2. Logic and truth

Theon, determined to defend logical reasoning, also against Nicander's religious perspective, discards the dubitative-optative meaning of the particle 'if' and stresses instead its logical-hypothetical value. His solution is grounded on Stoic logic, thus based on the conception of a deterministic structure of reality.

Theon connects the obscure and enigmatic character of some oracles with the image of god as a logician, 'dialectical to the highest degree' (διαλεκτικώτατος ὁ θεός ἐστιν), creator and solver of enigmas (ἀμφιβολίας)[51]. In other words, the deliverer of ambiguous oracles and the founder of dialectics are one and the same god. The dialectic art is therefore a tool that allows not only to decrypt prophetic messages, but also to achieve an

---

[51] An example recalled by Theon (*De E* 386E) is the oracle delivered to the Delians that ordered to double the volume of their altar, which – according to Plato's dialectical interpretation – conveyed the injunctions of dismissing their belligerent attitude and dedicating themselves to the study of geometry. For this story cf. also *De def. or.* 413A.

accurate knowledge of the god[52]. Generally speaking, logical reasoning is an essential prerogative of human beings and marks the distinction between the animal and the human world: while the animal mind is limited to the simple knowledge of the existence of things, the human mind instead, possessing the theoretical faculty (θεωρία) and judgement (κρίσις), understands logical successions and conceptual connections between facts[53].

Apollo's knowledge, in Theon's perspective, encompasses the entire succession of earthly events. In his vision, the god's absolute wisdom (often emphasised by Plutarch) is reduced and flattened on the causal mechanism underlying contingent facts. Theon is convinced indeed that reality is made up of a series of causally interconnected events. Accordingly, divine knowledge (and foreknowledge, πρόγνωσις) is grounded on the ordered sequence of facts, and based on the criteria of causality (αἰτία) and rationality (λόγος); the wisdom of god encompasses the whole flow of time, linking together the present with the past and the future[54]. Logical reasoning hence offers the basis for all foresight: since everything has a cause, reliable knowledge of the ordered sequence (ἀκολουθία) is attainable[55].

It is particularly striking that Lamprias' explanation of divination in *De defectu oraculorum*, which seemingly overlaps with the one embraced by Plutarch himself, assumes its primary faculty, the *mantikon* (μαντικόν), to be irrational and indeterminate (ἄλογον καὶ ἀόριστον), a *tabula rasa* (γραμματεῖον ἄγραφον), whose nature and activity are utterly extraneous to logical reasoning (ἀσυλλογίστως). Lamprias – in contradiction with what Theon asserts on corporal perceptions – requires that the prophetic faculty eludes the sensible realm and that it escapes from the present, thus becoming completely susceptible to the power of inspiration[56]. We should remind that in *De Pythiae oraculis* Theon himself – arguably the character

---

[52] Cf. *De E* 386E-F.

[53] Cf. *ibid.* 386F-387A.

[54] Cf. *ibid.* 387B.

[55] Cf. *ibid.* 387A-C. As Theon declares, syllogism is the key for every prediction: it starts from the present and addresses either the future or the past. While sensation (αἴσθησις) provides the mental picture or preconception (πρόληψις), the technical rational element (τὸ γὰρ τεχνικὸν καὶ λογικόν) corresponds to the knowledge of the consequence (γνῶσις ἀκολουθίας). The hypothetical proposition, which constitutes the premiss in a syllogism (συνημμένον) and its primary token, and logical reasoning constitute the basis for every demonstration (ἀπόδειξις). The process of demonstration is described in detail: the *logos* fixes the connection of the consequent with the antecedent (τὴν τοῦ λήγοντος πρὸς τὸ ἡγούμενον ἀκολουθίαν θέμενος), adds to the abstract reasoning the actual existence (εἶτα προσλαβὼν τὴν ὕπαρξιν), and thus obtains the conclusion of the demonstration (ἐπάγει τὸ συμπέρασμα τῆς ἀποδείξεως).

[56] Cf. *De def. or.* 432C-D.

whose perspective is closest to the one of Plutarch – believes that the god throws a light in the Pythia's soul that allows her to see the future (φῶς ἐν τῇ ψυχῇ ποιεῖ πρὸς τὸ μέλλον). In Theon's speech in *De E*, instead, the immaterial, a-rational light of inspiration is replaced by the cognitive light associated to logical demonstration. Theon moreover defines logical demonstration as that which guides philosophy towards its aim, which is *truth* (φιλοσοφία μέν ἐστι περὶ ἀλήθεια) – an idea that probably would be disregarded by Plutarch, whose research is animated by a relentless zetetic spirit.

The knowledge succession inferable from Theon's speech – indirectly appealing to the Stoic logical model of reasoning – therefore is the following:

$$\sigma υ ν η μ μ έ ν ο ν \rightarrow \dot{\alpha} π ό δ ε ι ξ ι ς \rightarrow [\dot{\alpha} λ ή θ ε ι α + φ ι λ ο σ ο φ ε ῖ ν]$$

The idea of divination that Theon embraces is founded on the following paradigm: logical reasoning is necessary for rational demonstration, which in its turn has its aim in philosophy intended as the knowledge of truth. This explains Theon's double qualification of Apollo as simultaneously a 'logical philosopher' and a 'seer' (μάντις)[57]: these two faces are bounded together exactly by logical reasoning conceived as the 'tripod of truth' (εἶναι τὸν τῆς ἀληθείας τρίποδα τὸν λόγον), a symbolical expression in which philosophy and divination are harmonised[58]. According to Theon, hence, the essential logical connection 'if' was consecrated to Apollo in order to celebrate and honour his love for truth.

It is worthwhile to notice how Theon's definition of philosophy clashes against Ammonius' one, which I will briefly remind:

$$[\dot{\alpha} π ο ρ ε ῖ ν + θ α υ μ ά ζ ε ι ν] \rightarrow ζ η τ ε ῖ ν \rightarrow φ ι λ ο σ ο φ ε ῖ ν$$

I want to underline that these two schemes of thought belong to two radically different worldviews: while Theon evidently relies on logical connections as the key for understanding the material world, Ammonius instead emphasizes the amazement generated by our encounter with the unpredictable, surprising nature of contingency. Nevertheless, both Theon and Ammonius fundamentally agree when it comes to the non-incompatibility and (even) the convergence between religious faith and rational-philosophical investigation. For this very reason, and for their step- or hierarchical-structure, both the ideal philosophical paths proposed

---

[57] Cf. *De E* 387A.

[58] Cf. *ibid.* 387C-D. It should be reminded that Theon makes a brief reference to one further and well-known aspect of Apollo: his affiliation with music (he is said to enjoy the sound of swans and the lyre). This fundamental feature will be later recalled by Plutarch.

by these two characters recall the itinerary of progressive knowledge described by Cleombrotus in *De defectu oraculorum*. Cleombrotus' approach – analysed in the second chapter of this book – has identified theology as the end (τέλος) of philosophy[59], which in its turn takes its material (ὕλη) from historical-scientific investigation:

ἱστορία → φιλοσοφία → θεολογία

Despite their apparent diversity, all these definitions comply with an idea of philosophical reflection as a gradual, progressive and patient path towards the divine. For this reason – especially keeping Theon's definition in mind – I think that the episode of Heracles and the tripod inserted in *De E apud Delphos* can be intended as the authentic expression of a deeply anti-philosophical behaviour, since it displays a rebellious spirit that refuses to comply with any diligent and slow improvement or gradual disclosure of knowledge.

This anecdote shows the insolent, 'underdeveloped' reaction of the young hero, which vehemently contrasts with the 'mature' and 'superior' character of rational reasoning and rigorous thinking, promoted and protected by the oracular god Apollo. As an impatient and unadvised young man, Heracles rejects cautious thinking and analytical reflection, thus displaying "la négation de la philosophie par son contraire, la brutalité"[60].

Nevertheless, while in his youth Heracles ridiculed logical reasoning ('εἰ' τὸ πρῶτον, τὸ δεύτερον), by overturning the tripod and insolently confronting the god, later, as a grown up man, he has become experienced and talented in both prophecy and logic. As I believe, Heracles' intellectual development strikes the readers of *De E apud Delphos* as a 'double' of Plutarch's own: the 'writer' Plutarch, i.e., the 'grown up' Platonist philosopher who narrates the dialogical exchange, displays his 'young self' as an inexperienced yet passionate man, at the beginning of his way of training, seen through indulgent and almost affectionate eyes.

3.3. Numerology and Pythagoreanism

The fifth and sixth accounts – offered by the two fellow students Eustrophus and Plutarch, respectively – both resort to the numerological theory in order to decipher the enigma of the 'E'.

---

[59] For the notion of 'theology' in Plutarch see Valgiglio (1988) esp. 260-263.

[60] For the interpretation of the episode of the tripod in Plutarch as *"une erreur de jeunesse"* (against Flacelière): Lernould (2000) here 148. For a general reading of the mythical cycle of Heracles at Delfi, see Defradas (1954) 123-159.

The Athenian Eustrophus explains that neither the letter's meaning (δύναμις), nor its form (μορφή), nor its sound (ῥῆμα) have to be taken into account in order to find out its authentic meaning; rather, the secret significance of the 'E' lies in its symbolic numerological value[61]. Eustrophus, talking in plural, is speaking in behalf of the 'young' Plutarch, as a fellow-follower of Pythagoreanism (who, in his turn, will define Eustrophus' solution a splendid attempt to solve the enigma)[62]. At the dramatic time of *De E apud Delphos*, Plutarch was indeed devoting himself to mathematics with passion (ἐμπαθῶς) and had not turned yet to the Academic philosophy and its hallmark principle 'avoid extremes' / 'never too much' (μηδὲν ἄγαν), prescribing caution and moderation in research[63].

Eustrophus explains in a serious way (οὐ παίζων) – as the 'old' Plutarch-narrator underlines – that, from their Pythagorean perspective, all existing things, natural phenomena and divine principles (πράγματα καὶ φύσεις καὶ ἀρχὰς θείων) are to be understood according to number (ἐν ἀριθμῷ) and the numerological theory (φίλη μαθηματική), whose fruits he intends to offer to the god as votive gifts (ἀπάρξασθαι; note in this regard that *aparchai* is how the dialogues are called at the beginning of *De E*, as I stressed at page 121)[64].

The 'E' is venerated as the symbol of the number five, a supreme and magnificent number (μεγάλου πρὸς τὰ ὅλα καὶ κυρίου σημεῖον ἀριθμοῦ), endowed with a crucial value, and performing a fundamental function as concerns the universal order. From this number, called *'pempad'* (πεμπάς), comes the expression *pempazein* (πεμπάζειν), literally meaning 'counting on the fingers'[65].

The 'mature' Plutarch takes this opportunity to put his 'young-self' on display: the young Plutarch is depicted as experienced in the arithmological theory, of which he explores the multiple applications by composing a sort of encomiastic speech to the number five and thus delivering the longest answer to the debated question. I will briefly recall the main numerological arguments that Plutarch advances to praise the virtues of number five. Afterwards, I will focus on those arithmological

---

[61] Cf. *De E* 386B-387E. Eustrophus' solution is in line with the preliminary warning made by the Delphic priests, according to which the letter's name (ὄνομα), rather than its aspect (ὄψις) or sound (φθόγγον), should be taken into account in order to discover its significance.

[62] Cf. *ibid.* 387F.

[63] Cf. *ibid.* 385D; 392A; 394C; *De def. or.* 431A.

[64] Cf. *De E* 387E.

[65] Cf. *De Is. et Os.* 374A: "And *panta* (all) is a derivative of *pente* (five), and they speak of counting as 'numbering by fives'" (Eng. trans. F. C. Babbitt); cf. also *De def. or.* 429D.

aspects especially connected with the cosmic order and the Delphic temple – which will demonstrate that Plutarch intends to establish a parallelism between the dynamics of the cosmos and the ritual functioning of the shrine.

Plutarch recalls the 'musical' nature and character of the god Apollo, to which Theon has already cursorily alluded[66]: music, dearest to the god (τῆς δὲ δὴ μάλιστα κεχαρισμένης τῷ θεῷ μουσικῆς), participates in the number five. By recalling the different kinds of chords on which the harmonic science is based, Plutarch illustrates that all musical ratios are steadily founded on mathematics, and specifically on the number five. Five are the intervals employed in music (μελῳδούμενα) that are truly harmonic and euphonic.

Plutarch then resorts to psychology. As concerns the individual soul, he connects the numbers four and five to the inanimate body and the soul entering into it, respectively. The human soul itself has five faculties: nutritive (τὸ θρεπτικόν), perceptive (τὸ αἰσθητικόν), appetitive (τὸ ἐπιθυμητικόν), spirited (τὸ θυμοειδές) and rational (εἰς δὲ τὴν τοῦ λογιστικοῦ), the last being the *fifth* and the noblest. Considering all the souls in the cosmos, five is the number of the hierarchical classes into which they are divided: gods, demons, heroes, men, beasts[67].

What Plutarch presents as the most sublime (μέγιστον) 'proof' for the perfection of the number five is the 'ontological argument'. He reminds us that Plato in the *Sophist* indicates five supreme principles – being, identity, divergence, motion and rest – which Plutarch harmonizes with the *Philebus* doctrine[68]. Moreover, Plato believes that the Good reveals itself under five forms: moderation (μέτριον), proportion (σύμμετρον), intellect (ὁ νοῦς), true knowledge of the soul (αἱ περὶ ψυχὴν ἐπιστῆμαι καὶ τέχναι καὶ δόξαι ἀληθεῖς) and pure pleasure (τις ἡδονὴ καθαρὰ καὶ πρὸς τὸ λυποῦν ἄκρατος). The 'E' was accordingly placed on the temple by someone who anticipated Plato's theories and believed that the number five was the sign and symbol of the universe (δήλωμα καὶ σύμβολον τοῦ ἀριθμοῦ τῶν πάντων)[69].

As anticipated, it might be fruitful to treat separately some extraordinary qualities of the number five defended by Plutarch, whose relevant consequences specifically fall within two fields that – as I believe – are strongly interconnected between themselves: the cosmic order and the Delphic ritual.

In the first place, we find references to the cosmic order in the beginning of Plutarch's discussion, where he focuses on the concepts of odd and even, explaining that unity takes part in both, and that it transforms the

---

[66] Cf. *De E* 389C-F.
[67] Cf. *ibid.* 390C-F.
[68] Cf. also *De def. or.* 428C and *supra* 79.
[69] Cf. *De E* 391C.

one into the other. Five, an indeed 'exceptional' number, is the sum of the first odd (number 2) and the first even number (number 3), associated in the Pythagorean theory with the feminine and the masculine, respectively. The number five, which results from their union, is consequently called 'nuptial number' (γάμος)[70]. The special virtue of five is to always reproduce itself, for which reason it is called 'nature' (φύσις). This happens when squared (since whenever multiplied it gives itself again) as well as when added to itself (resulting either in a number ending with five, so of its own nature, or with ten, so a perfect number, thus never engendering anything imperfect or extraneous)[71]. Plutarch also defines five as the sum of the unit (1) plus the first odd number squared (2^2), or of the first two numbers squared (1^2+2^2) – if the unit is considered itself as squared[72].

For these reasons, as he explains, the number five imitates the ordering cause of the universe (ἀπομιμουμένου τοῦ ἀριθμοῦ τὴν τὰ ὅλα διακοσμοῦσαν ἀρχήν), which gives origin to the entire world, out from itself, through variations (μεταβολάς). The parallelism between the number five and the cause of the world is clarified by referring to Heraclitus' idea of fire: fire transforms itself into all material things, which in their turn become fire again ("καὶ πῦρ ἁπάντων, ὅκωσπερ χρυσοῦ χρήματα καὶ χρημάτων χρυσός")[73]. Similarly, five corresponds to fire and reproduces itself into ten, a number that symbolises the cosmic order[74].

Plutarch, in order to stress the cosmological value of this number, also recalls the hypothesis of the five worlds of Plato's *Timaeus*[75]; alternatively, if we admit with Aristotle that there is only one world, the number five can be associated to the earth, water, air, fire and sky making up this world. As Plutarch then explains, Plato linked these five elements to the geometrical solids (pyramid, cube, octahedron, icosahedron, dodecahedron), but some thinkers instead link them to human senses (touch, taste, hearing, smell, sight)[76].

In the second place, it is particularly important to focus on the elaborate relation that Plutarch posits between the numerological theory on the one hand, and the Delphic religious complex on the other – in the guise of cultic procedures, ritual practices and the character of the deities presiding over the shrine. The cosmological overtones of the numerological theory

---

[70] Cf. *ibid.* 387F-388C.

[71] Cf. *ibid.* 388E.

[72] Cf. *ibid.* 391A.

[73] Cf. *ibid.* 388D-E and DK 22 B 90.

[74] Cf. *De E* 389C-D.

[75] Cf. Plato, *Ti.* 55c-d.

[76] Plutarch in *De E* 390C briefly reminds that Homer also divided the world into five parts (cf. *Il.* 15,187-193).

are associated to the traditional alternation between Apollo and Dionysus at the shrine, and help us to grasp some other significant elements defining the overall image of Apollo in Plutarch's thought.

Plutarch clarifies that Dionysus partakes in Delphic activities as much as Apollo does[77]. We know indeed that, on the Parnassus, a festival dedicated to Dionysus was celebrated during the winter – which was the period of the god's tenure. This rite, called 'Herois', was executed by some Thiades sent from Athens, and included a mystical performance evoking the reawakening of Semele[78]. The cyclical trieteric nature of the cult, regulating the Greek calendar, can be probably connected to fertility cults, while the seasonal one-year cycle may result from a contamination with the Oriental octennial calendar[79]. The overall ritual period was named *enneateris*, a word that, as attested by Plato's *Meno*, also has a ritual meaning associating it with blood guilt[80].

Plutarch interestingly reports a doctrine whose original formulation is attributed to some theologians that expressed it in prose and in verse. According to this theory, god is incorruptible and eternal according to nature (πεφυκώς), but subject to transformation according to necessity (εἱμαρμένης γνώμης καὶ λόγου). Sometimes he is exempt from corruption and immortal (ἄφθαρτος ὁ θεός καὶ ἀΐδιος); other times he enters the sensible realm, where he assumes different shapes and acquires varying properties and states (παντοδαπὸς ἔν τε μορφαῖς καὶ ἐν πάθεσι καὶ δυνάμεσι διαφόροις γιγνόμενος) – in this last sense he becomes 'world' (κόσμος), which is the most sublime of the epithets referred to his material appearance[81]. Wise men (οἱ σοφώτεροι) assign special secret names to the god according to his sensible facets – which as a consequence remain hidden (κρυπτόμενοι), and the mass cannot understand them. I would like to note in this regard that the custom of employing secret 'cryptic' names in order to refer to the plural material manifestations of the deity appears to be fully in line with the general spirit and meaning of *De E apud Delphos* that the present analysis intends to bring to light.

---

[77] Cf. *De E* 388E. For the foundation of Dionysian cults in Delphi, see Delcourt (1955) 116-117 and Price (1985) 135.

It is worth noting that Plutarch was initiated into the mysteries of Dionysus (cf. *Cons. ad ux.* 611D) and perhaps in those of Isis (cf. *De Is. et Os.* 364E). For an account of Plutarch's philosophical, and namely Platonic, reading of the traditional image of Dionysus, see the excellent article by Roskam (1999).

[78] Cf. *Quaest. Graec.* 293C-D: τῆς δ' Ἡρωίδος τὰ πλεῖστα μυστικὸν ἔχει λόγον, ὃν ἴσασιν αἱ Θυιάδες, ἐκ δὲ τῶν δρωμένων φανερῶς Σεμέλης ἄν τις ἀναγωγὴν εἰκάσειε.

[79] As explained in Lévêque (1973).

[80] Cf. the expression 'ἐνάτῳ ἔτεϊ' in Plato, *Men.* 81b and especially its ritual-purificatory meaning as clearly explained in R. S. Bluck's edition of Plato's *Meno*: Bluck (2011) 280-281.

[81] Cf. *De E* 388F.

The character 'Plutarch' expounds this technique when composing the second list of divine names that we find in the dialogue. When the god turns into fire, he is called Apollo and Phoebus – two epithets that stress respectively his uniqueness (from privative 'α' plus πολλά, 'many') and purity (from φοῖβος, 'clear')[82]. When instead he becomes every other element or even the cosmos itself, theologians resort to enigmatic expressions (αἰνίττονται) and describe this transmutation as a tearing into pieces (διασπασμόν τινα καὶ διαμελισμόν). As the young Plutarch declares, the names employed in this second case include: Dionysus, Zagreus, Nyctelius and Isodete, and generally refer to the chthonic character and physical dismemberment of the god[83]. He also underlines that the god's transformations are hidden under enigmas and tales (αἰνίγματα καὶ μυθεύματα) of deaths and regenerations (which recalls the πάθη μεγάλα of the mysteries)[84], that need to be read in an allegorical manner.

Plutarch takes the time to examine in depth the opposition between Apollo and Dionysus. To Apollo they sing the paean, to Dionysus the dithyramb; Apollo is depicted as eternally young, while Dionysus under multiple shapes; Apollo is associated to order and purity (ὁμοιότητα καὶ τάξιν καὶ σπουδὴν ἄκρατον), while Dionysus to a complex mixture of playfulness, seriousness, and frenzy (μεμιγμένην τινὰ παιδιᾷ καὶ ὕβρει [καὶ σπουδῇ] καὶ μανίᾳ)[85]. Emerges in this discussion another pivotal connection between the Delphic cult and the universal order that I would like to signal: it concerns the natural cycles of 'abundance' (κόρος) and 'sterility' (χρησμοσύνη) – the former of which is three times longer than the latter. This alternation corresponds to the nine months dedicated to Apollo against the three winter months dedicated to Dionysus – a meaningful proportion, which is reproduced on the cosmic scale, being nine to three the ratio between the ordered cosmos and conflagration.

In Plutarch's perspective, Apollo and Dionysus themselves are two modifications of one and the same god (οὐ φαύλως ἑκατέρας μεταβολῆς τὸ οἰκεῖον λαμβάνοντες)[86]. The god therefore has two faces, the one transcendent and immutable, the other immanent, mutable and contaminated with the laws governing the material world, thus always subject to disorder and destruction.

At this point, it is interesting to consider Dionysus' possible relation with Apollo in the context of divination, as concerns his inspirational virtues and prophetic character. Plutarch, in *De defectu oraculorum*,

---

[82] Cf. *ibid.* 389A.
[83] For an explanation of these epithets see Lozza (1983) 231-232.
[84] Cf. *De E* 389A.
[85] Cf. *ibid.* 389B.
[86] Cf. *ibid.* 389B-C.

through his brother Lamprias, presents a parallelism between the effects engendered in human soul by the mantic *pneûma* on the one hand, and by inebriation from wine on the other: in order to explain this parallelism, he significantly recalls Euripides' *Bacchants* and the Dionysian madness[87]. Indeed, based on Plutarch's works and historical testimonies, Dionysian inspiration seems to be considerably different from the Apollonian one[88]. Plato, for instance, in the *Phaedrus*[89] distinguishes between a 'prophetic madness' associated to Apollo, and a 'telestic madness' associated to Dionysus (μαντικὴν μὲν ἐπίπνοιαν Ἀπόλλωνος θέντες, Διονύσου δὲ τελεστικήν)[90]. All this proves how the yet complicated debate concerning the mental state of the Delphic priestess and the literary value of her responses is even compounded by the simultaneous presence of Apollo and Dionysus at the shrine, and by the different kinds of inspiration that they were believed to cause[91].

It must be reminded that the radical distinction drawn between the rational, harmonious and crystalline expression associated to Apollo, and the frenzy, irrational one generated by Dionysus is mainly rooted within the XIX century literary-stylistic dispute between Classicists and Romantics. This antithesis has been notoriously "popularized" by Friedrich Nietzsche who – as harshly affirmed by Kurt Latte – "overstated it in his usual way" in *The Birth of Tragedy*[92]. The rigid opposition between the two deities,

---

[87] Cf. *De def. or.* 432E-F: ὡς οἶνος ἀναθυμιαθεὶς ἕτερα πολλὰ κινήματα καὶ λόγους ἀποκειμέ-νους καὶ λανθάνοντας ἀποκαλύπτει (Euripides, *Ba.* 298)· 'τὸ γὰρ βακχεύσιμον καὶ τὸ μανιῶδες μαντικὴν πολλὴν ἔχει' κατ' Εὐριπίδην, ὅταν ἔνθερμος ἡ ψυχὴ γενομένη καὶ πυρώδης ἀπώσηται τὴν εὐλάβειαν, ἣν ἡ θνητὴ φρόνησις ἐπάγουσα πολλάκις ἀποστρέφει καὶ κατασβέννυσι τὸν ἐνθουσιασμόν.'

[88] For the 'institutionalised' image or Dionysus see Chirassi Colombo (1991).

[89] Cf. Plato, *Phdr.* 265b. The Muses deliver the poetic madness, while the supreme erotic one is bestowed by Eros and Aphrodite.

[90] It may be interesting to remind that Walter Burkert explains the opposition between Apollo and Dionysus by associating a peculiar "peripheral phenomen(on) of consciousness" to each of them: to the former 'divination', to the latter 'initiation'. Zeus – their father – stands over them with thinking (φρονεῖν) – cf. Burkert (1985) 110. Further in the same book (222-225) Burkert offers an interesting account of the figure of Dionysus and of his relationship with Apollo.

[91] Fontenrose (1978), who generally proposes a sceptical view on ancient divination, holds that the priestess was calm and that she preserved her rationality, while delivering clear, plain binary (yes/no) responses. Amandry (1950) similarly believes that the Pythia, when inspired, is calm and preserves her rationality – as attested by ancient Greek vases depicting her – and that her ecstatic madness is a later invention.

[92] Latte (1940) 9. Latte also offers a critical account against Rohde's interpretation, which is based on the traditionally assumed (and artificial) opposition between Apollo (as balanced-classical) and Dionysus (as chaotic-barbarian) – then emphasised by Nietzsche. Nevertheless, we should remind that Rohde fully acknowledges the exceptional union of Dionysus and Apollo taking place in Delphi, and conceives it as an extremely relevant

and their schematic division into two definite roles, therefore results from a modern artificial and extreme polarization, based on the symbolism associating Apollo and Dionysus with two antithetical poetic styles: the one controlled and harmonious (expressed by the 'Olympian' poetry of the old Goethe), and the other impulsive and irrational (characterizing the production of German romantics like Schlegel).

Pierre Amandry, aware of the prejudices that distort our vision of the ancient relationship between the two gods, reports the two main sides of the controversy over the leading deity in Delphi: some (such as Bouché-Leclercq and Rohde) believe in the pre-eminent role of Dionysus over Apollo; others (such as Latte and Nilsson) downgrade Dionysus' importance and deprive him of the prophetic function[93]. If we follow Dietrich's study, instead, Apollo himself, at the dawn of Delphic oracular activity, appears to display relevant common traits with Dionysus' own character and nature[94].

Apollo and Dionysus seem to have cooperated at the Delphic shrine[95], although it is apparently impossible to assess with accuracy the precise nature of their synergy and their respective roles. Plutarch warns us that Dionysus, as Ammonius' concluding speech similarly seems to imply, is ontologically inferior in nature to Apollo and occupies a subordinated position[96]. Nevertheless, the Chaeronean, without clarifying the ritual function of Dionysus, indicates that his statue is in the very sanctuary of Apollo, by stressing that the Delphians believe the tomb of Dionysus to be located right in the Delphic temple[97].

In this regard, I will remind a quite surprising fact: the religious panorama of the age attests even to a possible *identification* between these two deities. The general syncretistic trend in religious practices and beliefs, leading to an always greater overlapping of Apollo and Dionysus in the following centuries, stands clearly at odds with the post-Nietzschean antithesis. I wish to call into account a precious testimony of Dio Chrysostomos who, in the course of an oration delivered in Rhodes, explains that the gods, differently from men, can be joined and merged into

---

factor in Greek religion as a whole. He also properly stresses the ecstatic element in Delphic divination as caused by the Dionysian spirit and presence at the shrine – cf. Rohde (1928) esp. 282-303.

[93] Cf. Amandry (1950) 196-200: *Dionysus et l'oracle*; Bouché-Leclercq (1963) I,352-363.

[94] Cf. Dietrich (1992) 45.

[95] For a recent important study that contextualises this antithesis within the theory of music see Reibnitz (1992).

[96] Cf. *De E* 394A-C.

[97] Cf. *De Is. et Os.* 365A. For a recent study of the union of the two gods in Delphi – neglected by many modern scholars after Nietzsche's interpretation – cf. Detienne (2001).

one single entity and power, thus do not need to be honoured singularly with individual statues. He also interestingly reports a syncretistic vision of the deities that has led to combine the Sun, Apollo, and Dionysus into one single entity[98]. This testimony can be put in relation with a meaningful 'theological' response delivered at the Apollonian shrine of Claros, to a man who questioned the oracle about the nature of god. The oracular response defined Zeus, Hades, Helios and Dionysus as one and the same deity[99]. Similar syncretistic combinations of multiple divine entities will become always more widespread in the following centuries – as Macrobius' *Saturnalia* notoriously attest[100].

The 'Delphic frame' defined by Plutarch's speech is finally completed by some puzzling details: another reason of the dignity of the number five is found in the mysterious ritual custom of the drawing of the lots on the sixth day of the month, when the Pythia is brought to the Prytanaeum and five names are randomly selected, two by the priest and three by the prophetess. As added by Nicander (who, as a priest, performs the draw), it is forbidden to reveal to strangers the reason of this rule (ἡ δ' αἰτία πρὸς ἑτέρους ἄρρητός ἐστιν), which may not even be comprehensible to profanes but only to initiates (ἱεροῖς, literary 'divine men'). At this point, as Plutarch states, the praise of the arithmetical and mathematical qualities of the number five comes to an end[101].

As I believe, it is remarkable that – in a dialogue built on the very concepts of symbol, allegory, secrecy and complex decipherments – the last example that Plutarch presents to conclude his lengthy numerological account hints exactly at an elitist and initiatory kind of wisdom, connected to incomprehensible and ultimately unspeakable ritual customs.

4. Ammonius' explanation

Although Ammonius appreciates the value of mathematics for philosophy[102], he nevertheless discards arithmology[103], and thus renounces to

---

[98] Cf. Dio Chrysostomus, 31,11: Καίτοι τὸν μὲν Ἀπόλλω καὶ τὸν Ἥλιον καὶ τὸν Διόνυσον ἔνιοί φασιν εἶναι τὸν αὐτόν, καὶ ὑμεῖς οὕτω νομίζετε, πολλοὶ δὲ καὶ ἁπλῶς τοὺς θεοὺς πάντας εἰς μίαν τινὰ ἰσχὺν καὶ δύναμιν συνάγουσιν.

[99] Cf. Merkelbach-Stauber 28.

[100] Cf. Macrobius, *Sat.* 1,18,1-8.

[101] Cf. *De E* 391E.

[102] For Ammonius, cf. Whittaker (1969). Scholars have generally noticed some points of contact between Ammonius' exposition and the philosophy of thinkers such as Philo or Eudorus – cf. Dillon (2002); Ferrari (1995) 51-61. For a reconstruction of the image of Ammonius cf. also Dillon (1977) 189-192; Jones (1967); Donini (1986a), and especially the fundamental Opsomer (2009).

[103] It is interesting to remind that also in the *Quaestiones convivales* Ammonius invites Lamprias to discard the numerological theory, and instead to discuss *in a serious way* and

counteract precisely (ἀκριβῶς ἀντιλέγειν) the arguments presented by the young men (τοῖς νέοις) Eustrophus and Plutarch. He rejects numerological explanations, while stressing that every number could be similarly praised for its virtues – first of all the much celebrated number seven, which symbolizes the majesty of Apollo[104].

Ammonius' speech is an articulated exposition of theological and metaphysical arguments (combining Platonic, Stoic and Pythagorean elements), which attempts to counteract and dialectically surpass all the previous solutions. He pronounces his long explanation *ex cathedra*, without any interruption – a compositional-stylistic choice that constitutes an exception in Plutarch's entire corpus. Ammonius' 'lecture' resembles a sort of private lesson (διάλεξις) delivered by a master who wishes to provide his pupils with philosophical instruction but also spiritual enlightenment. Ammonius' attitude testifies to a typical custom of the teachers of philosophy of this time, who also intended to convert their students to a nobler, more virtuous way of life.

The Egyptian philosopher Ammonius worked as a private teacher in Athens[105]. His philosophical thinking and his teaching activity may have been influenced by Alexandrian Platonism (he lived in the same age of Philo of Alexandria). Ammonius is named 'the Academician' for his knowledge of the Platonic philosophy, often enriched with a religious-mystical character. Apparently, he initiated Plutarch into Platonism, at the time of his Athenian formation. Based on *De E* and other dialogues of Plutarch, Ammonius can be defined a man interested in religious issues, and a believer in oracles and divination[106]. Ammonius is also named 'the Peripatetic', for his grounding in Aristotelian philosophy, especially regarding natural problems: in Plutarch's writings, he is indeed mostly concerned with scientific questions and research. As anticipated, he also admits Neo-Pythagorean mathematics, but believes that it should not be taken too seriously.

In order to better understand the weight that Ammonius had in Plutarch's upbringing, we should consider the wide educative role that teachers of philosophy play during this era. The authority and confidence that they gain is an important element of their broad intellectual work, also in light of the permanent contrast opposing different schools, which

---

according to reason: ἡμῖν δὲ μὴ παίζων ἀλλ'ἀπὸ σπουδῆς, ἐπεὶ τὸν λόγον ἑκὼν ἐξεδέξω, δίελθε περὶ τῆς αἰτίας (*Quaest. conv.* 740A); cf. also 744B.

[104] Cf. *De E* 391F.

[105] Cf. Eunapius, *VS* p. 346 (Wright); Ammonius is the only one of his teachers that Plutarch names explicitly. For further details, and for Plutarch's appreciation towards him, cf. *Quaest. conv.* 646A; 747A-748D. The relationship between Plutarch and his master, and their respective philosophical views, are analysed in Thum (2013).

[106] Cf. Opsomer (2009) 175: cf. *De E* 385B; *De def. or.* 413E; 431B-432B.

involves notions such as 'true' and 'false beliefs'[107]. In such a context, the tasks of the masters include the ability to concretely change the life of their pupils: with specific regard to Platonism, Harold Tarrant has underlined that the ultimate goal for the student is to reach for an "insight" founded on a combination of faith (πίστις) and demonstrative reason. The students are required to develop a firm belief "in certain core ideas of Platonism, many of a religious nature, which were strongly felt within the individual.[108]" This kind of educational program is in line with the strong interdependence between reason and authority – also manifest in the custom of frequently invoking the mythical founders of various disciplines – which acquires an always greater importance from the Hellenistic period to the late Imperial age.

If we come to Ammonius' explanation, the 'E' corresponds to the perfect (αὐτοτελής) way to address and greet the god. Therefore, it does not represent a number, nor an element in a succession, nor a conjunction, nor any other deficient particle (οὔτ' οὖν ἀριθμὸν οὔτε τάξιν οὔτε σύνδεσμον οὔτ' ἄλλο τῶν ἐλλιπῶν μορίων οὐδὲν οἶμαι τὸ γράμμα σημαίνειν). When looking closely at Ammonius' interpretation, one may say that the 'E' works as a kind of 'magical word' – which, only by being pronounced, immediately instils within us the notion of divine majesty: as he himself declares, its simple utterance suffices to give to the speaker the idea of god's power (εἰς ἔννοιαν καθιστᾶσα τῆς τοῦ θεοῦ δυνάμεως). In line with the general theoretical framework of the dialogue, according to which multiple meanings are hidden behind the symbol of the 'E', Ammonius offers his own interpretation: the 'E' encloses the ineffable, transcendent character of the divine, and our ontological-gnoseological relation with the intelligible realm[109].

As Ammonius explains, the god virtually gives the warning 'know thyself' ('γνῶθι σαυτόν', also impressed on the temple) to the man who is approaching the shrine; the visitor replies 'thou art' (being the *epsilon* read as the second person of the verb 'to be': 'εἶ'). 'You are' is the real and truthful (ἀληθῆ καὶ ἀψευδῆ) appellation appropriate to god who really *is*, and exists eternally (ὄν διὰ παντός), as well as a way in which the visitor is greeting the god (τὴν τοῦ εἶναι προσαγόρευσιν), while acknowledging his supreme ontological status[110]. This sort of dialectical exchange poses the Delphic temple at the very heart of the relationship between humankind and the god, and defines the shrine as the ideally 'perfect' physical place for the interconnection between the material and the transcendent realm.

---

[107] Cf. Tarrant (2000).

[108] *Ibid.* 48.

[109] Cf. *De E* 391F-392A.

[110] Cf. *ibid.* 392A. Bonazzi describes this as a kind of 'devotional truth' that acknowledges both human weakness and divine power – cf. Bonazzi (2008).

Ammonius' interpretation of 'Know thyself', the admonition spoken by the god by means of the inscription placed on the temple, radically emphasises the weakness of humans; this reading nevertheless contrasts with some 'Egyptian' elements present in his intervention. Indeed, as stressed by Hans Dieter Betz[111], the possible interpretations of this saying fall under two main meanings: the first can be phrased 'Know you are mortals', which stresses our humanity and limitedness; the second 'Remember you are a god', which acknowledges the divinity of the supreme part of our soul (the intellect, νοῦς). The former is thus the one embraced by Ammonius and leans on Greek traditional wisdom, whereas the latter is widespread in Oriental (and particularly, Egyptian) religion and thought.

Ammonius' reading of 'You are' complies with the famous theory of the flux that he presents in his speech, which, as Pierluigi Donini underlines[112], was familiar to the Middle-Platonists. Ammonius explains that humans have no share in being (εἶναι). All nature is mortal (πᾶσα θνητὴ φύσις) and, placed between generation and corruption (ἐν μέσῳ γενέσεως καὶ φθορᾶς γενομένη), is just a phantasm and a mere semblance (φάσμα παρέχει καὶ δόκησιν ἀμυδρὰν καὶ ἀβέβαιον αὐτῆς).

Everything mortal comes into existence and passes away, and only displays an uncertain appearance: perceiving any sensible being is like grasping water. Earthly things are affected by tumultuous variations; they have a fleeting existence, as attested by the instability of human senses. Nothing ever remains, nothing really exists (οὐδενὸς [...] μένοντος οὐδ' ὄντως ὄντος)[113]. Accordingly, reason (διάνοια) takes hold of nothing, since everything is subject to differing influences and perpetual change. Ammonius' approach recalls Heraclitus' one, condensed in the notorious sentence "It is impossible to step twice in the same river"[114]; this maxim – quoted by Ammonius – defines mortal substance as constantly characterized by continuous dispersion and reunification[115].

---

[111] Betz (1970) stresses the importance of Philo's interpretation (who lived in Alexandria, and Egypt seems the place where the *Hermetica* have been most likely composed) in order to understand the second reading of the admonition. Philo's and the Hermetic view seem nevertheless to stem from a common Greek root (probably identifiable with Posidonius and Plato) according to which self-knowledge consists in discovering our indwelling divine intellect, an awareness that leads to a complete asceticism and to the ascent to the father-god.

[112] Cf. Donini (1986a) 169-170.

[113] Cf. *De E* 392B.

[114] Cf. DK 22 A 6; cf. *De sera num.* 559C.

[115] Cf. *De E* 392B-C. It must be observed that Plutarch employs the Heraclitean maxims "παλίντροπον ἁρμονίην κόσμου ὅκωσπερ λύρης καὶ τόξου" (DK 22 B 51) in three other places (*De an. procr.* 1026B; *De tranq. an.* 473F; *De Is. et Os.* 369B), always with the anti-Stoic aim of stressing the impurity and variability of the human world as opposed to the transcendent

The image of human existence emerging from Ammonius' reflection is peculiar: life consists of incessant transformations that cause one form to disappear into another. Our life is discontinuous and turns us into many persons, with differing ideas, experiences, emotions. Deceived by our sense perception (ψεύδεται δ'ἡ αἴσθησις ἀγνοίᾳ τοῦ ὄντος εἶναι τὸ φαινόμενον)[116], we dramatically fail to realize that we mistake appearance for real being (which remains fundamentally unknown). We are never the same, but undergo several transformations and perennial deaths. Strictly speaking, we *are* not; rather, we always *become*, while constantly changing from one into another (εἰ δ'ὁ αὐτὸς οὐκ ἔστιν, οὐδ'ἔστιν, ἀλλὰ τοῦτ'αὐτὸ μεταβάλλει γιγνόμενος ἕτερος ἐξ ἑτέρου). In other words, Ammonius' refusal of the continuity of our biographical narration endorses a view of the human self as diachronically fragmented, which radically denies its unity and singularity.

Such a striking, radicalised image of the miserable condition of humans, and of the huge gap that separates us from the absolutely transcendent supreme god, is common among other authors of the age; it may suffice to remind Apuleius, who incisively contrasts the majesty of god (defined *summus atque exsuperantissimus*) against the misery of man (considered *ignavus et pessimus*)[117].

Nevertheless, what is of a fundamental importance for the purposes of the present study is to constantly bear in mind that – notwithstanding the arguably pessimistic ontological view emerging from Ammonius' intervention in *De E apud Delphos* – divination can always be considered an extraordinarily useful tool for overcoming the constitutive limitedness of human ontological structure and cognitive capabilities, and thus for reducing the incommensurable distance dividing us from divine perfection and somehow for bridging the gap between the distant plans of contingency and transcendence.

In Ammonius' speech, the ontological partition between the divine and the human corresponds to the temporal division between eternity and time. Real being is eternal: it has neither beginning nor end, and it never changes[118]; time instead is always moving, and its movement is simultaneous with that of matter (κινητὸν γάρ τι καὶ κινουμένη συμφανταζόμενον ὕλη). It continuously flows and goes (καὶ ῥέον ἀεὶ καὶ μὴ στέγον) – a concept that Ammonius clearly explains through the image of a 'vase', which assimilates time to a 'receptacle', a 'vessel' of birth and decay.

---

realm – cf. the analysis of *De tranquillitate animi* in Babut (2003). A clear antecedent is: Plato, *Tht.* 152a-160e.

[116] Cf. *De E* 392E.

[117] Cf. Apuleius, *De mundo* 27. Apuleius' *De deo Socratis* is also extremely significant with regard to the immeasurable distance between humankind and the god.

[118] Cf. *De E* 392E: Τί οὖν ὄντως ὄν ἐστι; τὸ ἀίδιον καὶ ἀγένητον καὶ ἄφθαρτον, ᾧ χρόνος μεταβολὴν οὐδὲ εἰς ἐπάγει.

In Plato's *Timaeus*, Plutarch finds the essential ontological and temporal distinction between authentic being (τὸ ὄντως ὄν) and becoming (τὸ γιγνόμενον) – a hierarchical division that creates an unbridgeable gap between us and the god, and constitutes a hindrance for our apprehension of the divine. This ontological dualism gives rise to an epistemological dualism, which causes direct consequences on our knowledge capabilities. The opposition between authentic being on the one hand, and becoming on the other[119] – as well as of χρόνος as a copy of αἰών, its eternal model[120] – displays time as permanently unstable, without substance and impossible to comprehend. The epistemic consequences of this conception are clear: in the world – always hovering between becoming and decay – no stable knowledge is attainable[121].

The very existence of time is possible just in relation to eternity (ἔστι κατ'οὐδένα χρόνον ἀλλὰ κατὰ τὸν αἰῶνα)[122], although time and eternity are incompatible with one another. The fundamental hiatus existing between the human and the divine realm – with all its theological-ethical overtones – is also present in other works by Plutarch. We read in *De sera numinis vindicta* that only human time can be perceived as long or short in duration. Human 'quantitative time' and its chronological divisions are negligible if compared to the endless existence of gods, in whose eyes human life is almost nothing[123].

With reference to time, words themselves are affirmations of not being. Every expression involving the consideration of time, such as adverbs ('after', 'before') and verbs ('it has been', 'it shall be'), confirms that past and future things lack actual existence[124]. Ammonius points out that, since nature is in strict relation with time (by which it is measured), nothing is stable and really existent in the cosmos, but everything is subject to being generated and destroyed. It is impossible, as well as irreverent (οὐδ' ὅσιον), to define 'real being' as something that 'was' or 'will be' – two expressions that rather convey the changes (ἐγκλίσεις τινές εἰσι καὶ παραλλάξεις) affecting sensible realities and occurring in the material world[125].

This conception collides against Lamprias' idea of time in *De defectu oraculorum*, which – as we have seen in the second chapter of this research – is extremely relevant for assessing Plutarch's account of divination. In

---

[119] Cf. Plato, *Ti.* 27d-28a.

[120] Cf. *ibid.* 37c-38c.

[121] Cf. *De E* 392A. Ferrari believes that Ammonius in *De E* also seems to refer to the central section of the *Timaeus*, and in particular to be relying on a Neo-Pythagoreanizing commentary – cf. Ferrari (2001) 79.

[122] Cf. *De E* 393A.

[123] Cf. *De sera num.* 554D.

[124] Cf. *De E* 392F: 'πρότερον' καὶ τό 'ἔσται' λεγόμενον καὶ τό 'γέγονεν'.

[125] Cf. *ibid.* 393A.

order to understand the dynamics of oracular mantic, Lamprias stresses the ontological and structural connection between the substance of the soul and the essence of the future, as the temporal dimension which is the closest and most available to our apprehension. Then comes the knowledge of the past, similarly inherent to our soul, but to a lesser degree. The present, instead, like in Ammonius' account, permanently eludes our understanding[126]: fast as a flash of light and completely lost between the future and the past, it cannot be grasped.

Time and theology are deeply interrelated: god, who is one (εἷς ὤν) and really *is*, according to Ammonius' effective description, has filled the 'always' with a continuous present (ἐνὶ τῷ νῦν τὸ ἀεὶ πεπλήροκε). Simplicity (ἁπλότης) is a feature that explicitly applies to the divine: the supreme god and the supreme being are identified, while otherness corresponds to becoming (absence of being). The stress placed on the uniqueness of god refers to the fact that he is one in essence, in the metaphysical sense of not blended, incorruptible and pure. Similar assumptions underlie the ritual custom of employing phrases such as 'you are' ('εἶ') or 'you are the one' ('εἶ ἕν') to honour the god[127].

Ammonius' view, rather than monotheistic, can be more correctly defined henotheistic. Henotheistic tendencies characterise indeed the informed theoretical reflections of the intellectuals as well as the popular religious sensibility of the age, as attested by numerous epigraphs found both in Asia Minor and in the Latin area of the Empire. The god worshipped as the supreme one and indicated as superior to the whole pantheon has often the names of Zeus, Sarapis or Helios. Defined 'πάνθεος' or 'εἷς καὶ μόνος θεός', he shines against the indelible background of other still venerated polytheistic deities[128].

Ammonius completes his theological explanation by presenting a new series of divine epithets; this is the third one appearing in the dialogue, after the first that he himself has proposed in the beginning, and the second presented by Plutarch in the midst. The names that Ammonius

---

[126] Cf. *De def. or.* 431F-432B.

[127] Cf. *De E* 393B. Whittaker takes into account the formulas 'εἷς καὶ μόνος' (referring to a personal deity), and 'ἐς καὶ μόνον' (referring to an impersonal principle); he defines them as typically non-Greek, and a mark of Alexandrian Neo-Pythagoreanism – cf. Whittaker (1969) 188. For other interesting remarks concerning Plutarch's Pythagorean connections, see Hershbell (1984).

[128] Cf. Moreschini (2013) 13-29: *Monoteismo ed enoteismo*. This chapter also focuses on the differences and similarities between pagan Henotheism and Christian Monotheism. See for instance p. 16: "la possibilità di signoreggiare su una moltitudine di figure di rango inferiore sembrava suggello e garanzia della potenza di simili divinità, ed è forte la polemica contro il monoteismo 'esclusivista' giudaico-cristiano considerato alla stregua di una diminuzione, o privazione divina".

employs to qualify the highest god, and by means of which he aims to capture his essence, are the following: Apollo, an epithet that he explains as 'simple and not multiple'; Ieius, as 'one and alone'; Phoebus, as 'pure, shining and undefined'[129]. If one compares these last denominations to the first that Ammonius mentioned in the beginning of the dialogue, the striking contrast between the two series emerges clearly: while Ammonius' first series makes explicit reference to the path of human knowledge, guided by divine wisdom, this last focuses exclusively on the definition of the characters and essence of the supreme god – and thus contributes to compose the multifaceted depiction of Apollo emerging from *De E*.

That of 'mixture' or 'composition' (κρᾶσις) – as we have already had the chance to show – is a pivotal concept in Plutarch. It proves its extreme significance from both a practical and theoretical standpoint within the framework of Plutarch's treatment of divination – as I will highlight in the final chapter of this study. Ammonius mainly dwells on its *theological* significance (the opposition between purity and contamination is fundamentally ritual in character[130]), and employs some terms such as mixture (μῖξις), contamination (μιασμός), corruption (φθορά), in order to define the realm of matter and change[131]. Ammonius condemns those thinkers (such as, the Stoics) who believe in the mutability of the divine and in the periodical and cyclical conflagration (ἐκπύρωσις) and reformation (διακόσμησις) of the cosmos[132]. God is never commingled with matter (ἀναμεμιγμένον, ἐγκπεκρασμένον), being the concept of mixture (κρᾶσις) primarily and uniquely characteristic of the sensible cosmos. It is a given and precise 'combination' among diverse material elements that determines their effectiveness and enhances their properties.

Differently from the material world, made up of multiple components, the divine is one, pure, simple and uncontaminated[133]. The same qualification of the supreme intelligible principle is found in *De Iside et Osiride*, where the supreme god is defined as far removed from the sensible cos-

---

[129] Like in *De Is. et Os.* 354B, 381F, and *De E* 388F, the name of Apollo is connected to the following etymology: Ἀπόλλων as denying many/multiplicity (ἀ-πολύς, ἀ-πολλά). 'Ieios' comes from 'ἰή', a sound used for invoking Apollo. Plutarch instead associates it with 'ἴα', 'ἴης' – words drawn from the epic language, whose meaning is 'one'. 'Phoibos' comes from 'φοῖβος', which means 'pure' and 'bright' (cf. *De def. or.* 421C).

[130] For the relation between Apollo and purity, cf. Parker (1983), esp. Appendix 8: *Gods Particularly Concerned with Purity*.

[131] Cf. *De E* 393C. Plutarch employs these words in examples concerning combinations of materials and colours.

[132] Cf. *De Stoic. rep.* 1075B-C.

[133] Cf. *De E* 393C: τὸ δ᾽ ἓν εἰλικρινὲς καὶ καθαρόν [...] οὐκοῦν ἕν τ᾽ εἶναι καὶ ἄκρατον ἀεὶ τῷ ἀφθάρτῳ καὶ καθαρῷ προσήκει.

mos, absolutely distant from everything subject to death and destruction, and therefore from the sensible world[134].

4.1. Ammonius: Apollo and the sun

Ammonius' dense speech also discusses the relation between the god and the sun. On the one hand, the philosopher expresses his respect towards those who identify the planet with the god, while on the other he denounces the incoherence of this presumed identification and stresses the need of reading it only in a metaphorical way. The sun is rather a suitable 'symbol' to point to the god, which represents effectively his benevolent and altruistic character[135]. Nevertheless, the sun is simply an image that reflects the supreme majesty of the deity (ἐμφάσεις τινὰς καὶ εἴδωλα)[136], which, immaterial and immortal, is far beyond the physical realm. It is just a physical figure perceived by our senses, which mirrors the blessedness of the real essence (οὐσία) of the god.

It is worth reminding that – as Plutarch himself explains in the *Amatorius*[137] – the Egyptians believed in the existence of three 'Eros': one terrestrial, one celestial (τόν τε πάνδημον καὶ τὸν οὐράνιον), and a third one, identified with the sun. Soclarus, the character in question, clarifies that the assimilation between the sun and Eros is based on the fact that they both bestow nourishment, light and energy (τροφὴν καὶ φῶς καὶ αὔξησιν), on the body and on the soul, respectively[138]. While the sun shows to humans all earthly beings without distinction, Eros sheds light just on beautiful individuals[139]. As Soclarus himself explains, the distinction between Eros and the sun (being the former intelligible, νοητός, and the latter visible, ὁρατός) is rooted within the more fundamental one opposing the soul and the body. The planet and the god exert opposite effects: while the sun

---

[134] Cf. *De Is. et Os.* 382D: ἡ δὲ τοῦ νοητοῦ καὶ εἰλικρινοῦς καὶ ἁπλοῦ νόησις; 382F: ὁ δ᾽ ἔστι μὲν αὐτὸς ἀπωτάτω τῆς γῆς ἄχραντος καὶ ἀμίαντος καὶ καθαρὸς οὐσίας ἁπάσης φθορὰν δεχομένης καὶ θάνατον.

[135] Geert Roskam proposes a very interesting account of the concept of 'symbol' and of its use in Plutarch, by choosing the identification between the sun and the highest god (Apollo, Eros, Zeus, etc.) as a relevant case study. Roskam points out that every effective symbol respects three conditions: first, it is nothing more than an εἰκών or εἴδωλον, and belongs to the 'phenomenal' world as opposed to the 'noumenal'; second, it has *fundamentum in re* and its link with the deity – based on its 'bipolar' nature – is 'well-balanced' (μεσότης), so neither too close as in Stoicism, nor too far as in Epicureanism; third, the connection between the symbol and the god determines the official integration of the symbol within cultic customs – cf. Roskam (2006) 184-185.

[136] Cf. *De E* 393D.

[137] Cf. *Amatorius* 764B.

[138] These two kinds of Eros are also commonly accepted in the Greek culture; cf. Plato, *Smp.* 180d-182a.

[139] Cf. *Amatorius* 764C-D.

diverts our attention from the spiritual realm and directs it towards the sensible beings (ἀπὸ τῶν νοητῶν ἐπὶ τὰ αἰσθητὰ τὴν διάνοιαν), Eros on the contrary helps us to reach for the supreme intelligible realities, and solicits us to find only in himself the truth as well as any other good (αἰτεῖσθαι τά τ' ἄλλα καὶ τὴν ἀλήθειαν, ἑτέρωθι δὲ μηθέν)[140].

The passages here recalled show the importance of the image of Eros, as presented in the dialogical context of the *Amatorius*, in order to better understand the role of the sun as an effective symbol of the god. Interestingly, in the *Amatorius* divine goodness is also said (by Daphnaeus) to manifest itself through an intermediary power, corresponding to a particular beneficent deity (τοῦ θείου τοῦ φιλανθρώπου), which assists us in the practical problems of life and works for us as a good guardian (ἀγαθοῦ καὶ φύλακος[141]) – an idea that is absolutely central in divination, and characterizes Apollo's immanent face of a 'prophet' (μάντις). As we can see, even in the *Amatorius*, the gap between the sensible and the intelligible is emphasised; nevertheless the material entity, if correctly read, clarifies – instead of confusing – the qualities and essence of the superior referent, and thus works as a precious and powerful *symbol*. In addition, the characteristics attributed to both the sun and the god in the *Amatorius* closely resemble the ones proposed in *De E apud Delphos*, and brought to light in the present chapter.

Interestingly, John Dillon has defined Eros the "Middle-Platonic Logos in its anagogic aspect, presiding over the noetic cosmos, the realm of Ideas, but also exerting its influence upon our souls to lead us up to that realm"[142]. In particular, Dillon stresses how Plutarch's purpose seems to "identify Eros with the intelligible archetype of the Sun, and thus in fact the Good of *Republic* vi"; the identification with the Platonic Good is also implicit in Ammonius' concluding speech in *De E apud Delphos*[143].

In *De defectu oraculorum*, Plutarch, through the voice of Lamprias, defines god as 'beyond everything that is visible' (ἐπέκεινα τοῦ ὁρατοῦ παντός)[144]. Xavier Brouillette has effectively explained Plutarch's debt to Plato's reflections in this regard: the Chaeronean attributes to the supreme principle all the qualities belonging to the Sun and the Good in the *Republic*[145]. Brouillette also pinpoints as a peculiarity of Plutarch's approach the fact that he merges together three fundamental Platonic ideas: the distinction between the visible and the intelligible world; the

---

[140] Cf. *ibid.* 764E; cf. also *De Pyth. or.* 400D.

[141] *Amatorius* 758A.

[142] Dillon (1977) 201.

[143] Cf. *ibid.* 200.

[144] Cf. *De def. or.* 413C. For an analysis of the Platonic derivation of this image see Brouillette (2010).

[145] Cf. Brouillette (2010) 41-42.

coincidence between god (Apollo) and the idea of Good; god as a primary cause, which also exerts a providential action. The theoretical-polemical aim of the Chaeronean is thus to counteract Stoic immanentism and popular theology on the one hand, and Epicurean materialism and atheism on the other, while outlining and embracing an original Platonic stance (balanced between materiality and transcendence), based on a faithful reading of Plato's writings[146].

Franco Ferrari significantly points out that Plutarch identifies god with the totality of the eidetic-divine world[147]; he is located at the highest level of the noetic reality and is endowed with a paradigmatic function. God is not structurally ineffable; rather, human nature and intelligence are incapable of accessing to a radically other ontological level, which is that of the divine.

Nevertheless, god for Plutarch is not 'beyond being' (ἐπέκεινα νοῦ καὶ οὐσίας) – as instead it is for Eudorus and Philo of Alexandria, and later for Plotinus. Plutarch never conceives the supreme principle to be beyond the ontological dimension. Rather, as explicitly stated in *De E apud Delphos*[148], the supreme principle corresponds to the *authentic being*, as well as to a demiurgic providential intellect, responsible for the creation and for the present existence of the world.

Another field of reflection where Plutarch exploits the symbolic value of the sun in a challenging way is that of political philosophy, and especially in those wise suggestions to the statesman collected in the pamphlet *Ad principem ineruditum*. There Plutarch counteracts the Stoic idea of god as commingled with matter and necessity[149], hence introduces a definition of the deity as completely transcendent, separated from the corruptible world, located 'up there' (ἄνω που), and whose essence is exempt from any variation – all qualities recalling the Platonic theoretical framework and mostly expressed through the Platonic terminological apparatus.

Ad principem ineruditum presents a doctrine, extraneous to the tradition of Hellenistic political thought, based on an original relationship between the sovereign and the sun: the unwritten law (which is not the positive law of the state, but an interior, spiritual law) exerts its hegemony within the very soul of the wise governor, who has achieved a sufficient level of philosophical education. The ruler, by proposing himself as a positive example, guides all the citizens towards moral virtue. The sun is placed in the sky as an imitation and an image of god (μίμημα, εἴδωλον, εἰκών). It is

---

[146] Cf. *ibid.* 44-46.

[147] As Ferrari explains, Ammonius collates in one same entity: τὸ ἀγαθόν, ὁ θεός, ὁ δημιουργός, ἰδεα, παράδειγμα, ὁ νοητόν, τὸ ὄντως ὄν, νοῦς, τὸ ἔν – cf. Ferrari (2002) 50; (2005) 13-26.

[148] Cf. *De E* 393E.

[149] Cf. *Ad princ. iner.* 781E.

available to sight for a mainly ethical-practical aim: inviting humans – and especially those who are the best (οἱ μακάριοι καὶ σώφρονες) – to modify and shape themselves by means of philosophy (ἐκ φιλοσοφίας), in accord with the most beautiful sensible being (πρὸς τὸ κάλλιστον τῶν πραγμάτων), which is the sun itself[150]. The theological and paradigmatic value of the symbol of the sun is therefore confirmed in the political writing *Ad principem ineruditum*: the sun shines for us, and invites us – through the image of the good statesman – to follow the path of virtue.

4.2. Ammonius' explanation of the 'E'

Based on Ammonius' ontological qualification of the supreme principle, it is now clear why 'thou art' is the proper salutation for the deity: this expression represents the most accurate way to address the god, since it directly points to his essence, while expressing the fact that he belongs to the realm of authentic being. The 'E' is defined a 'προσαγόρευσις' – from 'προσαγορεύω', which means 'address' or 'greet as', and more importantly 'call by name': I believe that it is crucial to underline that this last meaning – by defining the 'E' as a way of calling, or naming, the god – creates an implicit contrast with all the other epithets previously presented in the dialogue, and thus contributes to emphasise that the syntagm 'you are', enclosed in the mysterious *epsilon*, is superior to them all.

Ammonius specifies that, below the supreme god, simple and unique (as expressed by the appellation 'E'), there is a second principle, which belongs to a different ontological level: this corresponds to an inferior deity, or better a *daimôn*, who is associated to perpetual change and disintegration (ἔκστασις, μεταβολή, φθορά, γένεσις), and operates within the natural-material world (φύσις)[151]. Ammonius denounces the chaos caused by humans who, by mixing these two distinct ontological realms, create a dangerous confusion between the divine and the demonic world. The opposition between the principle of identity-being and that of mutation-becoming is incisively exemplified by a double series of names (the fourth and last of the dialogue) that Ammonius employs to pinpoint and describe these two different entities: the one superior, immortal and unchangeable, the other inferior, perishable and subject to change.

Following Ammonius' epithets, the first god is: simple (Ἀπόλλων), clear (Δήλιος), radiant (Φοῖβος), associated to the Muses and the goddess of Memory, 'observing' (Θεώριος) and 'disclosing' (Φαναῖος). The second, Hades, is characterised by multiplicity (Πλούτων); he is hidden (Ἀϊδωνεύς), obscure (Σκότιος), and associated to Oblivion and Silence[152]. While the

---

[150] Cf. *ibid.* 781F-782A.
[151] Cf. *De E* 394A.
[152] Cf. *ibid.* 385B.

former is luminous and revealing, the latter is obscure and concealed. While the former is celebrated with joy and songs, the latter is accompanied by sorrow and lamentations (some poetical *loci topici* are quoted to stress the opposition[153]). This two-sided theological view immediately recalls the corresponding passage in Plutarch's exposition, concerning the alternate exchange between Dionysus and Apollo in Delphi[154].

At this point it clearly appears how the research path traced by the subsequent interventions composing the dialogue finds its completion in Ammonius' speech[155], where religion and rationality are finally harmonised, and so is the contrast between philosophy and theology. 'Thou art', as a sign of respectful awe towards the god that acknowledges his eternal existence (ὄν διὰ παντός), is mirrored in the admonition 'Know thyself', which reminds to humans their transience and fragility (ἀσθένεια)[156]. The sense of this interpretation has been effectively connected by Heinz Gerd Ingenkamp to the notion of 'σεμνότης': our reverential respect towards the deity is based on the awareness that our knowledge concerning god is strictly subjective, not founded on a match between copy and facts. By referring just to a copy, it does not represent an objective state of affairs[157].

It is important to notice that the maxims present at the temple (ἐπι-γράμματα)[158], such as 'Know yourself', 'Never too much', as well as the praise 'You are' are believed by Plutarch to convey Academic-Platonic moral-epistemological principles of moderation and caution (εὐλάβεια, ἀσφάλεια, τὸ μηδὲν ἄγαν)[159]. Respecting our limited human comprehension is one with acknowledging the unreliability of sensible impressions[160], so with observing the principle of suspension of judgement (ἐποχή) as the most preferable and authentically philosophical stance when discussing about (especially, obscure) religious or scientific subjects[161]. Fully in line with these assumptions, Ammoinius' final discourse does not disclose a definite, certain knowledge (ἐπιστήμη), but rather – by confirming his definition of philosophy formulated in the

---

[153] Cf. *Il.* 9,159; Pindarus, *Pae.* 16,6; Euripides, *Supp.* 975-977; Stesichorus, fr. 50,3,24 Bergk; Sophocles, fr. 765 Nauck.

[154] Cf. *De E* 388E-389C. For the opposition between two principles in Plutarch, cf. Dillon (2002).

[155] Cf. Opsomer (2009) 135: "[Ammonius] usually raises the discussion to a higher level by pointing towards a form of causality that surpasses the level of material causes".

[156] Cf. *De E* 394C. Cf. also Plato, *Chrm.* 164d.

[157] Cf. Ingenkamp (1985).

[158] Cf. *De Pyth. or.* 395A: Ἐπέραινον οἱ περιηγηταὶ τὰ συντεταγμένα μηδὲν ἡμῶν φροντίσαντες δεηθέντων ἐπιτεμεῖν τὰς ῥήσεις καὶ τὰ πολλὰ τῶν ἐπιγραμμάτων.

[159] Cf. Plato, *Chrm.* 164d-165a; *Phd.* 95e; *Phdr.* 229e; *Lg.* 10,885b-888d.

[160] Cf. Donini (1994).

[161] For suspension of judgement on issues of natural philosophy cf. *De prim. frig.* 955C.

beginning of the dialogue ([θαυμάζειν + ἀπορεῖν] → ζητεῖν → φιλοσοφεῖν) – it defines philosophy as a shared and potentially endless research (διαλέγεσθαι καὶ φιλοσοφεῖν πρὸς ἀλλήλους), solicited by god's invitation, and conducted under his aegis (πρὸς τὸ σκοπεῖν τι καὶ ἀκούειν καὶ διαλέγεσθαι)[162].

Despite the pessimistic tone of the first part of Ammonius' speech, the last part, as pointed out by Jan Opsomer[163], proposes a kind of *moderate* scepticism: notwithstanding the cognitive unreliability of sensation and our constitutive limitedness, the world *can be known* inasmuch as it participates in divine harmony. Ammonius' final discourse, while embracing the Heraclitean theory and representing the sensible realm as overwhelmed by a continuous stream of destruction, on the other hand underlines god's stability, eternity and transcendence, and the foundational function of the intelligible dimension with regard to the advancement of our knowledge.

This optimistic spirit resembles very closely the one that emerges from Plutarch's *De audiendo*, especially considering a key-passage where he states that philosophical *logos* effectively leads to the knowledge of the cause of every object examined (περὶ ἕκαστον αἰτίας). In this perspective, philosophical research silences the wonder that comes from inexperience and ignorance (ἐξ ἀπειρίας καὶ ἀγνοίας) and preserves our peace and moderation, thus helping us to ascend the path of virtue[164].

Ammonius' rational *and* religious-reverential definition of the supreme god reflects Plutarch's own attitude of blending together into one divine entity his 'personal' oracular god Apollo and the first deity of the Platonic pyramidal ontology. Frederick Brenk has explained how Ammonius enriches the philosophical image of the Middle-Platonic god with the fundamentally religious-ritual concepts of 'oneness' and 'purity'. His speech in *De E* accordingly stresses, in its first part, the god's identification with the supreme being and the One, while highlights, in its second part, the god's demiurgic role. The convergence of such distinct characteristics into one same divine entity stresses the importance of the relation between the god and the material cosmos, and more generally sheds light on the relevant conceptual role that the material cosmos (κόσμος αἰσθητός) plays within Plutarch's reflection[165].

Indeed – notwithstanding Ammonius' devaluation of the human condition (unparalleled in the entire Plutarchan output) and his radicalisation of god's transcendence – the god-supreme being always maintains a benevolent relation with the cosmos, which in its turn manifests a 'revelatory'

---

[162] Cf. *De E* 385C-D.

[163] Cf. Opsomer (2009).

[164] Cf. *De aud.* 44B-C. I am very grateful to Geert Roskam who invited me to consider this extremely meaningful reference. See his analysis in Roskam (2005) 351-352.

[165] Cf. Brenk (2005).

function with regard to the divine, provided that its phenomena are studied in depth and correctly interpreted.

5. *The final image of Apollo and Plutarch's god*

Greek deities are generally characterised by a multifaceted aspect; this is especially true for Apollo, as confirmed by one of the first and most important literary testimonies of his manifold nature: the *Homeric Hymn to Apollo*[166]. An additional, 'ominous' character – rooted into popular religion – makes the image of Apollo even more controversial than is commonly believed. As pointed out by Christopher Faraone[167], deities like Apollo, but even Artemis and Heracles, are perceived as both beneficial and dangerous, in antiquity; their powerful 'dark' side is expressed in mythical stories and reflected in iconography. They are invoked in order to both cause and reject plagues, according to the principle: 'like banning like'. Statues of Apollo the Archer – considered as the most potent and effective deity against the plague, which he scares away with his portentous arrows – are placed at the civic threshold, probably as a protection (φυλακτήριον) for the entire community: as the epidemics are attributed to Apollo's anger, people require his very help for the purpose of either purifying or preserving the city from further risks. Indeed, the consecration of healing statues usually serves two main aims: the one expiatory, the other apotropaic. In this respect, it must be reminded that oracles are similarly endowed with a healing-resolutory power: they often suggest how to defeat a plague (λοιμός), by also introducing ritual and cultic improvements.

Jacques Boulogne has clarified how Plutarch's original and multifaceted theological approach is substantiated by a so-called "unité multiple de dieu", developed according to what he effectively defines "un traditionalisme non conservateur, un éclectisme non syncrétique et un hénothéisme inclusif"[168]. Bernard Boulet, similarly intending to explain why Plutarch's Apollo has "many faces", defines the god's polymorphic and even conflicting appearances scattered in Plutarch's *oeuvre* as the result of some purposely constructed "intelligent contradictions", an oxymoronic expression that does justice to Plutarch's brilliant intellectual creativity and re-evaluates his (only apparent) inconsistencies[169]. Boulet demonstrates the sound theoretical reasons for the "fluctuations" that constantly affect the image of the god, throughout diverse works and periods of Plutarch's production, according to which the Chaeronean defines Apollo from

---

[166] For an in-depth analysis of the hymn see Miller (1986).

[167] Cf. Faraone (1992) 61-66. In *Iliad* I, Apollo (patron deity of archery) sends the plague and then heals it himself. Cf. also Belaiche (2007) 171-191.

[168] Boulogne (2004) 96.

[169] Cf. Boulet (2008) 169.

time to time: an Olympian deity, an oracular god, a rational transcendent principle beyond the sensible world, or an astute politician supporting (fraudulent) statesmen.

As we have seen, the several characters and powers of the oracular Apollo are well depicted in *De E apud Delphos*: each explanation proposed in the dialogue appears as inadequate *per se*, but all of them taken together contribute to offer an overall valuable series of qualities effectively defining the god and his features.

In the beginning, Ammonius significantly describes Apollo as a philosopher *and* a prophet. Lamprias' explanation, although imprecise, stresses the god's traditional-mythical aspect and his political character, as strictly interconnected with popular belief and devotion. The Chaldaean astronomer reports the widely accepted – but not acceptable *tout court* from a Platonic perspective! – identification between the sun and the god, which nevertheless, if read metaphorically, suggests some key-features of Apollo, such as his beneficial power and altruistic attitude in favour of humans. The Delphic priest Nicander emphasises the extraordinary character of the temple – as a precinct where an utterly peculiar kind of 'ritual logic' is at work – as well as god's philanthropic attitude: Apollo is a generous deity that gives us practical instructions, and listens to our prayers and requests. The Stoic philosopher Theon, in his turn, presents a strongly deterministic view of reality in which the god emerges as a protector of logic and dialectic, and ultimately as a supreme 'prophet' and 'lover of truth'. Eudorus and Plutarch provide a wider and more complex survey. While the former indirectly acknowledges the 'universal' importance of the deity, honoured with the number five, which indeed determines the numerical ratios governing the natural world, the latter praises the number's virtues, implicitly recognising the Delphic temple as a symbolic place where all the cosmic dynamics fruitfully merge, and all the fields of human knowledge (psychology, music, theology, cosmology, ontology, *etc.*) come into completion and are unified under the aegis of Apollo as a supreme powerful deity. Ammonius' deep and reverential ontological-theological definition of Apollo finally qualifies the Delphic temple as a sensible repository bearing impressed on its surface the absolute proof (i.e., the 'E') of the unbalanced relationship between the god and humankind. The temple also embodies the most effective means for their reciprocal interaction and communication[170].

---

[170] Franco Ferrari, instead, believes that Plutarch mostly shares the precepts and theories that Ammonius expresses in the conclusion of the dialogue. Ferrari particularly emphasizes the work's 'programmatic nature' and defines it a *manifesto* of Plutarch's thought and intellectual evolution, which even accounts for all the main cornerstones of his philosophy, such as the relationship between positive-dogmatic and sceptical-aporetic elements, or that between philosophical reasoning and religious faith – cf. Ferrari (2010).

As I intended to show, the different interventions composing the dialogue, and recalling some phases of Plutarch's own formation path, can be seen as a succession of always more sophisticated ideas concerning Apollo. Dialectically overcome and therefore saved in part, these diverse definitions still survive somehow in the final idea of god, as strongly influenced by the theological and epistemological approach derived from Plutarch's 'conversion' to Academic Platonism, and illuminated by a sincere devotion towards the oracular deity.

The multifaceted image of Apollo, as presented in *De E*, is built on a primary fundamental duality: that between his immanent aspect and his transcendent nature. In order to understand this basic double-qualification, it is essential to consider the second of Plutarch's *Quaestiones Platonicae*. This *zêtêma* analyses *Timaeus* 28c3-5, a passage that attracted the theoretical interest of other contemporaneous Platonists: "Now to discover the Maker and Father of this Universe were a task indeed; and having discovered Him, to declare Him unto all men were a thing impossible"[171]. Plutarch focuses on the main qualities of the supreme god, of which he stresses some typically non-Platonic characters: his transcendence, unknowability and ineffability. As Franco Ferrari has pointed out, Plutarch's original interpretation of the Platonic passage, if compared to the scholastic reading that was common in his age, combines into one single entity the images of 'maker' (ποιητής) and 'father' (πατήρ) of the cosmos – ultimately equated to the supreme god, according to a theological approach that excludes any ontological gradation among different divine entities. As a consequence, Plutarch merges into one single divine being the supreme causative power of god and his demiurgic action – two prerogatives that are radically different in nature and effects[172]. Indeed, Plutarch never makes a distinction between the supreme god and the 'demiurge' that operates within the cosmos and in contact with matter – a peculiar interpretative choice that sets him apart from Eudorus, Numenius and other Middle-Platonists. Although the Chaeronean, as Marco Zambon has pointed out, is aware of the classical three-principle scheme (demiurge – paradigm – matter), he chooses the dualistic configuration, thus opposing the demiurge *plus* the paradigm to the material-psychic principle[173].

As we have seen, in *De E apud Delphos* the 'double face' of Apollo, as simultaneously transcendent and immanent, clearly emerges. On the one

---

[171] Eng. trans. W.R.M. Lamb.

[172] Cf. *Quaest. Plat.* 2. Ferrari reminds that Numenius, for instance, refers the notions of 'maker' and 'father' to two different metaphysical subjects, placed on two distinct levels, thus anticipating post-Plotinian metaphysical schemes – cf. Ferrari (1996e).

[173] Cf. Zambon (2002).

hand, he is identified with the One and the Good[174], the supreme intelligible principle, whose existence is in accordance with timeless, durationless, instantaneous eternity (αἰών), and opposed to human time (χρόνος). On the other hand, he is a popular deity, object of personal devotion, that concedes prophetic notions to humans and supports them with his provident attention (ἐπιμέλεια καὶ πρόνοια). This last and fundamental aspect, also endorsed by Plutarch throughout his whole production, necessarily leads him to dismiss the idea of god as isolated in self-reflection, and thus to refute the doctrine – generally embraced by other Platonists of the age – that identifies the 'thoughts of god' with the Platonic ideas[175].

Plutarch's notion of a double *facies* (on the one side purely ontological, on the other personal-ritual) of the highest god also shapes Apollo's oracular role: to admit – beside his transcendent aspect – his devoted, practical care towards the cosmos allows for the acceptance and plausibility of miracles, prodigies, portents and divination. Indeed, to consider the cosmic structure and the harmonizing function performed by the divine *logos* in the world is crucial for understanding some key aspects of divination, and more specifically for founding or assessing the possibility of predicting future events. All this can be clarified by examining Plutarch's conception of the relation between god and the material cosmos, both in terms of knowledge (i.e., if he is aware of future contingent events), and influence (i.e., if he can effectively modify the sensible world) – on the background of the relationship between the material and the immaterial cosmos that emerges from Plutarch's philosophical thinking.

As Plutarch states in the *incipit* of the *De Iside et Osiride*[176], god's existence is *real* life. The god is in a state of bliss (μακάριον τὸ θεῖον) precisely because he possesses true knowledge and intelligence (ἐπιστήμη καὶ φρονήσει). Differently, his life would not be real life, but simple eternity. He has a perfect knowledge of the truth, which is intelligible and immutable, but "the things that come to be do not, through knowledge, fail in advance[177]" (μὴ προαπολιπεῖν τὰ γινόμενα) – being god's knowledge of contingent events one of the reasons for his absolute happiness (he is defined perfectly εὐδαίμων)[178]. Osiris, who possesses both a transcendent and a historical aspect (his soul is pure and unchanging, while his body is subject to dismembering and reconstruction), can be assumed as the emblem of the relation between sensible reality and intelligible essence. Significantly,

---

[174] Cf. *De E* 393B-C and *De def. or.* 432D.

[175] Cf. Opsomer (1997); Ferrari (1999); (2004).

[176] Cf. *De Is. et Os.* §§1-2 (351C-352A).

[177] I have reported here a possibly faithful translation of this passage that Geert Roskam has generously suggested to me.

[178] Cf. *De Is. et Os.* 351E.

he is represented with the key-attributes of an eye and a mirror: the former symbolizes his providence (πρόνοια), while the latter his immanent power (δύναμις)[179].

God's interventions into the physical world are always mediated and indirect, and are aimed at producing only slight corrections. All his 'interferences' comply with the norms of physical necessity as well as the intrinsic peculiarities (τέχνη καὶ δύναμις) of each object[180]. With regard to divination, this principle has been scrutinised in the analysis of *De Pythiae oraculis* proposed in the present study[181]. In that dialogue, indeed, prophetic inspiration is clearly defined as radically distinct from possession – which would instead imply a *direct intervention* of the god, who would be required in this case to enter into the body of the Pythia. Apollo, instead, simply inspires the images (φαντασίαι) and a prophetic light in the soul (φῶς ἐν τῇ ψυχῇ) of the different prophetesses, who react according to their innate character, cultural preparation, and psycho-physical disposition[182].

From a cosmological perspective, god's creative activity is an ongoing process: his constant providential care and *indirect* intervention – through which he is *somehow* present in the world – refrain matter's inclination towards disorder[183]. Since god can not act on matter directly, he exerts his providential action by recurring to intermediaries: the inferior gods, the demons, or the world soul – whose mediatory-demiurgic role reflects Plutarch's idea of the soul as possessing a mediating function between intellect and matter[184].

Plutarch accurately delineates the interrelation between god and the world – directly connected to the notion of 'providence' (πρόνοια) – along a wisely and cautiously built 'middle path' between Epicurean chaos and Stoic determinism. The cosmological-theological accounts of Epicureanism and Stoicism would respectively lead to the dangerous extremes of atheism and superstition.

The Chaeronean constantly shows his aversion against Epicurean atomism, materialism, hedonism and atheism. Contrary to what the Epicureans declare, the correct attitude towards the gods is an emotional blend of reverential respect and fear (αἰδοῦς καὶ φόβου), the first nourishing

---

[179] Cf. *ibid.* 371E-F.

[180] Nevertheless, it must be kept in mind that according to Plutarch the primary cause of every event is a divine efficient cause, and that nothing happens without god (ἄνευ θεοῦ, *De Pyth. or.* 405A).

[181] Cf. *De Pyth. or.* 405A-B.

[182] Cf. *ibid.* 397C.

[183] Cf. *Quaest. conv.* 720B-C. For Plutarch's idea of god, see Ferrari (2005) and Hirsch-Luipold (2005c).

[184] Cf. Opsomer (2005b) 94-95 and Karamanolis (2014).

our hope for divine help and support, while the second keeping alive our fear for divine punishment[185].

As for the Stoics, Plutarch has a largely comprehensive and strikingly detailed, technical and specialistic knowledge of their philosophy. He largely employs Stoic arguments and terminology in a variety of contexts and for diverse aims (be they polemical, rhetorical, or neutral), without the presence of Stoicism ever becoming predominant in his writings. Daniel Babut has distinguished three main phases of Plutarch's production: during the last one, corresponding to his maturity – that of the Delphic dialogues and *De Iside et Osiride* – his polemical attitude against the Stoics seems to have become milder[186].

As Jan Opsomer has demonstrated[187], *De E apud Delphos* contains a firm, although not openly declared, criticism against the Stoics, which – especially when applied to divination – appears to be strictly connected to Plutarch's defence of the unity of the Academy[188]. The Chaeronean is convinced that the Academic tradition, throughout its long history, has supported faith in oracles and prediction, and has displayed a strong commitment to its own original rational *and* religious spirit. Moreover, Plutarch places confidence on the fact that divination and dialectic stand in a harmonic relation to one another. Against the Stoics, who claim that Academic suspension of judgement undermines divination, Plutarch asserts that it is rather their deterministic conception of a fixed and inescapable chain of events that leads to deny the action of divine providence, and thus to undermine the predictive function of oracles[189].

Opsomer argues that Plutarch, who also presents some key Stoic views and ideas through the speaker bearing his name in *De E apud Delphos*, probably aims to get the Stoics on his side, by demonstrating that the contrast between Stoicism and Platonism is not completely irreconcilable[190]. Nevertheless, on the other hand, he may use his opponents' arguments in order to "destroy Stoicism from inside and with its own weapons"[191].

---

[185] Cf. *Non posse* 1101B-C.

[186] Cf. Babut (2003). To the 'second phase' dates back Plutarch's violent confrontation against Stoicism expressed in the anti-Stoic treatises, while in the 'first' (his youth) he appears as partly against, and partly influenced by, the Stoics. Babut nevertheless warns us against the vagueness of this scheme (based on the uncertain chronology of the *Moralia*) and defines the aforesaid transition as mainly "expressive".

[187] Cf. Opsomer (2006a).

[188] Opsomer (*ibid.*) recalls the unfortunately lost treatise: Περὶ τοῦ μὴ μάχησθαι τῇ μαντικῇ τὸν Ακαδημαικὸν λόγον (Lamprias 131).

[189] Cf. Opsomer (1996).

[190] Cf. Opsomer (2006a).

[191] Donini (1988) 129.

The idea of the divine presented by Ammonius' intervention in the end of the dialogue displays some points of contact with the Stoic theological conception, according to which the god is identified with a principle, but also with a power that sustains the world actively and constantly. Focussing instead on the anti-Stoic aim of Ammonius' interpretation of the relation between Apollo and the sun (which recalls in particular Cleanthes' cosmology), it is easy to notice Plutarch's refusal of any materialistic, immanentistic and pantheistic conception, as especially those expressed by the Stoic theories of divine *logos* and universal conflagration.

Daniel Babut has stressed also the Stoic overtones of Plutarch's syncretistic attitude: Stoic syncretism within the field of religion – a counterpart of cosmopolitanism within that of politics – gives voice to the desire to conciliate the philosophical and the popular belief, and to harmonize them under a monotheistic view[192].

In this respect, it can be instructive to remind that Plutarch sharply distinguishes between one single 'god' (θεός) and multiple 'gods' (οἱ θεοί), a plural substantive that usually refers to the traditional gods worshipped in diverse religions, downgraded to servant powers (δυνάμεις, ὑπουργαί) and subordinated to the highest deity, thus to one single ordering supreme principle (λόγος) and providence (πρόνοια). Plutarch believes that the 'gods' of different religions, although adored under different names, are always the same in essence – a theological view that safeguards the validity of a plurality of cultic phenomena, as well as the effectiveness and reliability of a broad range of rites[193].

5.1. Fate-providence-freedom

Plutarch makes an original contribution to the contemporaneous animated, wide debate on the interrelation of fate-providence-freedom. He aims to safeguard the power of divine providence, its relational character with respect to humans and the material cosmos, and the existence of human freedom as well as of historical contingency. This approach directly counteracts the Stoic (originally Chrysippean) identification of god (Zeus) with fate and providence as the one and only principle governing the whole cosmos[194].

Since the knowledge of the future is based on the admission of its, at least partial, pre-determination, it is fundamental to consider Plutarch's conception of the cosmic order – and of the nature of the control that the deity exerts over the material world – in order to assess human capability of

---

[192] Cf. Babut (1969) esp. ch. IV.
[193] Cf. *De Is. et Os.* 377F-378A.
[194] Cf. *De stoic. rep.* 1035B.

precognition. The relationship between the god and the world is articulated on the basis of the complex dualism developed by the Chaeronean[195].

In Plutarch's perspective, the order of the events seems to result from the threefold intertwining of: necessity, which is the general causal, inescapable rule governing all mundane events; fortune, a fleeting, random, irrational force; 'what depends on us', namely, what is caused by us as free human agents[196]. As explained in a notorious passage of *Quaestiones convivales*[197], the choice of a life is in our power (τὸ ἐφ'ἡμῖν), while the consequences of this choice are determined by necessity (καθ'εἱμαρμένην). Necessity, defining the cause-effect relationships in natural-biological processes, is a physical law subordinated to providence, which is instead a comprehensive force governing the cosmos at distance, gently leading it towards its good[198].

Human actions, shaped by rational choices and guided by wisdom (φρόνησις) – not immune, nevertheless, from the misleading influence of passions – fall into the domain of 'what is in our power'[199]. The power of human intelligence is superior to that of fortune (τύχη), which escapes any rational comprehension (under its varying faces of τύχη θεία, τύχη δαιμόνιος) and presides over events that are 'without a cause'. Fortune is never the direct cause of our actions; rather, our virtue has to measure its strength against it[200].

De fortuna Romanorum offers an effective example of this approach. There, the beneficent political order founded by the Roman power is described as directly organised by the will of the god[201], and as originated

---

[195] Cf. *De Is. et Os.* 369B-D.

[196] It must be noted that the use of the term 'providence' (πρόνοια) is sometimes quite indiscernible in Plutarch from concepts such as fortune (τύχη) or demon (δαίμων) – cf. Frazier (2010) *Introduction*: III-XXIII. Also see Aristoteles, *EN* 3,3,1112a32: nature, necessity and chance are followed by mind and free will (τὸ ἐφ'ἡμῖν).

[197] Cf. *Quaest. conv.* 740C-D: Lamprias here resumes (from the Myth of Er in Plato, *Resp.* 10,614b-621d) what Plutarch may have conceived as representative of Plato's doctrine on fate and free will (cf. especially the expression 'choice of life').

[198] Cf. *De facie* 927A, where Plutarch through Lamprias, and probably with an anti-Stoic aim, clearly distinguishes between fate (as natural order) and providence (πρόνοια).

[199] Cf. *De Stoic. rep.* 1056A. For an analysis of τὸ ἐφ'ἡμῖν, cf. Eliasson (2008) esp. 130-168: "*The Notion of ἐφ'ἡμῖν in Plutarch*".

[200] This division recalls the introduction of the 'third kind' in the *Timaeus* (cf. Plato, *Ti.* 48e-52d). For an analysis of the notion of fortune in Plutarch and its relationship with virtue, cf. Becchi (2008). Becchi effectively highlights how intelligent thinking and moral responsibility (φρόνησις, εὐβολία) determine the value of our life; our inner part – strengthened by philosophical παιδεία – is the most resistant against the attacks of fortune. Our moral character (ἦθος) is thus completely in our hands. For this topic, see Scannapieco (2010).

[201] Cf. *Rom.* 8,9: [...] καὶ τὰ Ῥωμαίων πράγματα λογιζομένους, ὡς οὐκ ἂν ἐνταῦθα προὔβη δυνάμεως, μὴ θείαν τιν'ἀρχὴν λαβόντα καὶ μηδὲν μέγα μηδὲ παράδοξον ἔχουσαν.

from the harmonic encounter between fortune (τύχη) and virtue (ἀρετή). In this context, virtue corresponds to 'wisdom' (σοφία) and 'foresight' (πρόνοια), this last declined in two different meanings: the one divine (as providence), the other human (as intelligent prevision). Nevertheless, the precise relation between providence (πρόνοια) and other earthly powers (such as fortune, or human deliberation) remains fundamentally obscure.

De sera numinis vindicta is another relevant work for the purpose of exploring the relation between the transcendent god and the sensible world in Plutarch[202]. It concerns the methods followed to achieve a 'providential educational plan', based on the axiom of the immortality of the soul: human life is too short to allow for proper praise and punishment[203]. This work seeks to find a reason for god's delay in punishing evil deeds; it does so by examining the action of providence in the world, as specifically framed around the life of single individuals. *De sera* is fundamentally built upon the concepts of model (παράδειγμα) and imitation (μίμησις), which respectively belong to two opposite ontological dimensions (immaterial and material) and temporal levels (eternity and time). The notion of '*kairos*' is also crucial in this context (as it is in oracular divination): divine punishment happens in the perfect time and, similarly to a drug, it is dispensed in the right moment and dosage. The *kairos* is thus an effective and dynamic mediating element, which intervenes to connect the divine and the human world in some points. It is interesting to note that, within the conceptual framework of this work, Apollo is defined as a luminous deity, as the paradigm of all goods. This theological view complies with a peculiar concept of assimilation to god, which mirrors his double-qualification of a transcendent principle and a beneficent deity active within the cosmos. Accordingly, on the one hand god represents the perfect model of virtue, on the other he bestows virtue to those who have been able to follow him[204].

---

[202] This work was written at the end of the I century AD – so it predates the pamphlets against the Stoics. For a general reading see Torraca (1991) esp. 91: "L'opera, più che un trattato sistematico sulla provvidenza, può essere considerata come un'altissima ed illuminta teodicea, culminante nel rapimento estatico di una visione che schiude i misteri dell'invisibile". Frazier, stressing the similarity between *De sera* and the 'canonical' Delphic dialogues, interestingly states: "la réflexion du *De sera* se meut dans le même orbe que les *Dialogues Pythiques*, où s'articulent étroitement aussi «divination, providence et causalité»" – Frazier (2010) 72.

[203] Cf. *De sera num.* 560F.

[204] Cf. *ibid.* 549F and 550D-E. Ethics plays a key role in Plutarch's philosophy, for the aim of virtue (ἀρετή) and happiness (εὐδαιμονία). Its final τέλος is to realize the ideal of *imitatio dei* (ὁμοίωσις θεῷ). For an original perspective on Plutarch's ethics, see Opsomer (2011).

6. Plutarch's dualism

De Iside et Osiride, offering an original and sophisticated reading of the Isiac myth (ἡ Αἰγυπτίων θεολογία) through Middle-Platonic theological and metaphysical categories, is the key work for the purpose of understanding Plutarch's dualistic conception. In one of its classical and most famous *loci*[205], Plutarch combines the Iranic dichotomy between Ormuzd and Ahriman with some dualistic formulations drawn from the history of Greek reflection – such as those developed by Heraclitus (harmony of opposites), Empedocles (love and strife), Pythagoras (monad and dyad), Anaxagoras (νοῦς and ἄπειρον), Aristotle (form and privation), Plato (identical and different) – intending to demonstrate the continuity of the dualistic doctrine in the Greek (and barbarian) tradition.

Radek Chlup has devoted a valuable contribution to Plutarch's dualistic conception in relation to the Delphic cult[206]. What is especially relevant is the emphasis that Chlup places on the parallelism between Apollo and Dionysus on the one hand, and the concepts of intellect (νοῦς) and soul (ψυχή) on the other. On this theoretical basis, he establishes a correspondence between *De Iside et Osiride* and *De animae procreatione in Timaeo* – where *noûs* (the monadic principle of order) and *psychê* (the dyadic principle of irrational movement) correspond to the two parts composing the world soul according to Plutarch's simplified reading of the structure of the world soul in Plato's *Timaeus*[207]. His dualism therefore is founded on a perennial and cyclical fluctuation between two extremes, on which the cosmic harmony is grounded. Indeed, an opposition exists just in the inferior ontological level of reality (evil is only extant in the sensible world), while the highest spheres are governed by unity and peace. Chlup interestingly stresses how Plutarch has never composed all these aspects into a coherent metaphysical scheme; the reason he gives for this is that the main aim of the Chaeronean is to make reference to metaphysics only while he is treating topics that really matter to him – such as ethics and religion.

As we have seen, in *De Iside et Osiride* (which was written after *De E apud Delphos*), Plutarch presents a dualistic theory – rooted within a respectable tradition and always embraced and supported by wise men – as generally based on the opposition between good and evil. Some believe that the good and the evil are both divine in character, and thus belong to the same onto-theological level (νομίζουσι γὰρ οἱ μὲν θεοὺς εἶναι δύο καθάπερ ἀντιτέχνους, τὸν μὲν ἀγαθῶν, τὸν δὲ φαύλων δημιουργόν), while others defend the superiority of the good over the evil, and therefore identify the

---

[205] Cf. *De Is. et Os.* 369D-371A.
[206] Cf. Chlup (2000).
[207] See esp. *De an. procr.* 1026E-F.

former with a god and the latter with a demon (οἱ δὲ τὸν μὲν ἀμείνονα θεόν, τὸν δὲ ἕτερον δαίμονα καλοῦσιν). Zoroaster belongs to this second group: he distinguishes Horomazes, who is associated to light and knowledge, and is venerated with votive offerings, from the inferior Areimanus, who is instead linked to darkness and ignorance, and honoured with gloomy offerings[208].

An element of extreme relevance, which attests to Plutarch's profound knowledge of the Zoroastrian doctrine and to the reliability of the sources that he employs, is his detailed explanations of the practical overtones that the Zoroastrian dualistic theoretical approach produces within the study of the natural realm, in which the different species of plants and animals are all divided into two classes, each one placed under the aegis of either Horomazes or Areimanus[209].

The intermediary role that Plutarch attributes to Mithra, instead, is not attested in the official sources; it rather seems to be connected to the association between the god and the sun – which occupies the fourth place in a kind of astronomical model widely employed in post-Hellenistic times[210].

Ugo Bianchi has masterfully explained how the complex dualistic construction developed by the Chaeronean in *De Iside et Osiride* is articulated along a cross-scheme of two orthogonal axes: the vertical axis opposes the terms Osiris-absolute-divine-ideal to Isis-relative-demonic-*chôra*, while the horizontal axis opposes Horos (the ordered, 'ideal', visible world) to Seth-Typhon (the principle of chaos, deficiency and destruction). Within this diagram, Isis calibrates the balance of opposite powers, and is divided between the love for perfection on the one hand, and the force of evil on the other. While the vertical axis refers to a 'nuptial' relationship, the horizontal points to an 'antagonistic' one. Bianchi defines Plutarch's 'mythical-theological' dualism as radical (non-mitigated) and dialectical (non-eschatological). At any rate, the notion of 'imperfection' (firstly conveyed by the image of Seth) is absolutely central, as an element necessary for the harmony and completeness of the entire cosmos[211]. Bianchi, in a previous study[212], has also analysed in greater detail the figure of Seth as a 'trickster', an archetypical divine image common to diverse

---

[208] Cf. *De Is. et Os.* 369D-E.

[209] Cf. the very detailed Boyce-Grenet (1991) 458.

[210] Cf. *ibid.* 478-479; see also the two references there given: Cumont (1899) 303 and Beck (1988) 6.

[211] Cf. Bianchi (1986) 113-116. Interestingly, Bianchi – dismissing the idea that Plutarch proposes a 'gnosis', and rather stressing the deeply Platonic character of his mythological reading – rejects any attempt to compare Isis to the Gnostic notions of *psychê* and Sofia, or Osiris to the Hermetic-Gnostic *Anthropos* (cf. esp. 118-119).

[212] Cf. Bianchi (1971) 114. In particular, Bianchi deals here with – and compares Seth to

ethnic groups, thus interestingly displaying the fruitful interconnections between 'cultivated' and 'folkloric' forms of religions.

Nicolette Brout, in an interesting contribution that offers a comprehensive summary of the different readings of the role played by Typhon in *De Iside et Osiride*, stresses how, according to Plutarch's original account in this text, the evil in the universe results from an *active* power. This view radically differs from Plato's cosmology, according to which wickedness is associated to the inertia inherent in matter[213]. Brout also focuses on the way in which Plutarch employs both Persian religion and Middle-Platonic conceptual apparatus in order to give an account of the Egyptian myth. In particular, he inherits from the Persian cults the conception of an ontological and qualitative subordination of the principle of evil under the principle of good (the asymmetry between Horomazes and Arimanius is paralleled with that between Osiris and Seth), while he draws from Platonism the dualistic theoretical framework. Plutarch's 'Platonic dualism' mainly originates from his original re-elaboration of the notorious passage of Plato's *Laws* (X 996d-998c), which describes the world as ruled by a beneficent and a maleficent soul, and from the *Timaeus*' cosmogony and its tripartite 'familiar' model of creation of mother-father-son, transferred into the triad: Isis-receptacle, Osiris-ordering ideal principle, Horus-sensible image of the intelligible world[214].

As Plutarch states in *De Iside et Osiride*, nothing in the sensible cosmos is free from admixture. The force of evil (intrinsic to the maleficent part of the soul, which coincides with Seth in the Egyptian myth[215]) persists in the present status of the world and fights against the better part, thus subverting the cosmic order. Plutarch accounts for the presence of this chaotic, irrational part within the world soul: it is innate – defined as the 'soul as such' – and still present in the cosmic blend. By doing so, he makes god not responsible (ἀναίτιος) for the evil[216].

It is of utmost importance to stress the different ranks on which these two opposing principles and antagonistic forces are located: the better is indeed always predominant and placed on a superior level, while the evil is always inferior, deficient and subordinated.

– the Renard Pale, i.e., the demiurge-trickster of the Dogon of Mali, based on interesting intercontinental ethnographical studies.

[213] Cf. Brout (2004) 71-106.

[214] Cf. *De an. procr.* 1026D: Αἰγύπτιοι μὲν οὖν μυθολογοῦντες αἰνίττονται, τοῦ Ὥρου δίκην ὀφλόντος τῷ μὲν πατρὶ τὸ πνεῦμα καὶ τὸ αἷμα τῇ δὲ μητρὶ τὴν σάρκα καὶ τὴν πιμελὴν προσνεμηθῆναι. τῆς δὲ ψυχῆς οὐδὲν μὲν εἰλικρινὲς οὐδ᾽ ἄκρατον οὐδὲ χωρὶς ἀπολείπεται τῶν ἄλλων. The construction of Isis and Osiris, their role, cosmic relation, and nature, also appears to be influenced by a cross-reading of the *Timaeus* and the *Symposium*. For this topic, see Chiodi (1986) esp. 121.

[215] For the relation between dualism and the traditional Egyptian cult see Velde (1967) esp. 75-77.

[216] Cf. Opsomer-Steel (1999).

6.1. Egypt and Oriental religions

As the analysis of Plutarch's dualism has helped me to show, foreign wisdom plays a key role in his philosophical thinking. If we focus on 'Oriental religions' as an effective cultural means of communication and knowledge transmission, we realize that the Chaeronean is fully aware of the success gained by Oriental, foreign cults in his days[217]. He appreciates in particular (in fact, almost exclusively) Mazdeism and Isism, of which he acknowledges the exigent moral standards. The cult of Isis, introduced in Greece before 330 BC, is indeed present and flourishing in Chaeronea as well as in Delphi in Plutarch's time – as also attested by the biography of Clea, dedicatee of *De Iside et Osiride*, who is a Delphic priestess also consecrated to the Egyptian goddess Isis[218].

Plutarch has an accurate knowledge of Egypt: he has visited that land, where he directly consulted priests and books[219]. He is probably influenced by Hermetic writings as well, with their seemingly-Egyptian content, character, and spirit[220]: in *De Iside et Osiride* he cites some so-called 'Hermes Books', a cursory reference that constitutes one of the first testimonies of Hermetism[221]. The seminal work by Jean Hani, devoted to the role of Egyptian religion and culture within Plutarch's thought, has the fundamental merit of highlighting how Plutarch has both witnessed the desperate attempt made by the Greeks to save their own religious universe, widely perceived as dramatically decaying, and contributed to prepare the birth of a 'syncretistic mysticism', which will acquire an immense success during the following three centuries[222].

---

[217] For a thorough analysis of Plutarch's connection with 'Oriental' cults, and their influence on future Gnostic doctrines, cf. Ries (1982). An extremely informed and interesting discussion on the relation between Plutarch's thought and Oriental wisdom is found in Hani (1964). For Oriental religions in the Imperial age see the dated but still useful Turcan (1989).

[218] *De Is. et Os.* 364E. Clea is also dedicatee of *Mulierum virtutes*. For a study on the priestess Clea as a historical figure see Bowersock (1965).

[219] Cf. *Quaest. conv.* 678C.

[220] According to Cumont, Plutarch's invention of eschatological myths (like in *De facie in orbe Lunae*, *De genio Socratis*, *De sera numinis vindicta*) could display a possible Hermetic imagery – cf. Cumont (1966) 199-200. Vernière observes that Plutarch is partly influenced by Hermetism – cf. Vernière (1977) 336-340. Dillon stresses his possible connection with esoteric Egyptian doctrines, in particular for the theory of the 'separable intellect' – cf. Dillon (2001a). Boulogne has then pointed out meaningful contacts between Plutarch's writings and Hermetic doctrines, remarking that this topic has not received the scholarly attention it deserves; his analysis mainly focuses on three significant passages of *De Iside et Osiride*: §§ 2-3; 77-78; 80 – cf. Boulogne (2008).

[221] Cf. Festugière (1950) I: 67-88, esp. 78; (1954) II: 28-50 (*Le "Logos" Hermetique d'Enseignement*).

[222] Hani (1976) esp. 476. It is worth reminding two interesting points made by Hani: first,

In the composite historical-political context of the first centuries AD, the official religion intersects a far-reaching soteriological anxiety and the urge of establishing a direct, personal relationship with the divine. This finds an expression in new religious phenomena – mostly spreading over the peripheral areas of the empire – that attest to a structural refusal against the imperial cult imposed on the *oikoumenê* as well as to a shared quest for a superior and valuable support in the troubles of everyday life. In 'Oriental religions', the god is generally characterised as endowed with practical powers (δύναμις and ἐνέργεια), which he beneficially employs in favour of human beings. He is object of personal piety and of a sincere, hopeful devotion, but also represents the ideal goal of a complex process of individual soteriology, which is aimed at achieving a spiritual-mystical ascent[223]. The distinctive feature of Oriental religions in the Roman empire lies precisely in their initiatory-soteriological character, to which they owe their definition of 'mystery cults'[224].

In these cults, the supreme deity, located beyond history and opposed to chaos and materiality, represents an ethical model of perfection to be reached through a constant rigorous practical-spiritual exercise (ἄσκησις). A god so conceived supports those who make themselves worthy of his help through a constant ritual-religious or (at a higher degree) ethical-intellectual improvement. Isis is a successful Oriental deity in this age, especially adored as Isis-Tyche, a divine image that also impersonates *iustitia* and *fortuna*; she supports humans on a daily basis but has also a portentous power of salvation, held even superior to the force of destiny.

The space between the sensible and the intelligible realm is bridged by a hierarchical chain of mediating elements, so to allow for the absolutely transcendent god to act in favour of humanity and to interact indirectly with the cosmos. The highest god – often qualified at the same time as 'unknown' (ἄγνωστος) and eager to be known – throws a beam of light on the world, indicating the path to follow.

In this context, barbarian knowledge provides a cultural standard for the Greeks and helps them to define their new condition under the Roman control. It also works as a powerful tool for re-discovering their own identity and for restoring that primeval, remote closeness with Oriental wisdom that dates back to the dawn of Greek thought. Non-

---

the Egyptian religion reinforced the Hellenic one, by means of concepts like personal piety, adoration, contemplation; second, Alexander's political universalism turned into a religious universalism during the Roman period, thus fostering the creation of a transcendental unity of all religions.

[223] "Isisme, dionysisme, orphisme semblent constituer, chez Plutarque, trois maillons d'une même chaîne, aimantée par le pythagorisme. Dans les trois cas, il s'agit de soteriologie", Boulogne (2004) 100.

[224] For Plutarch's relation with mysteries, see Roskam (2001).

Hellenic cultures (such as Jewish, Egyptian, Babylonian, Chaldaean traditions) are greatly estimated, to the extent that the term 'barbarian' tends to loose its classical negative connotation, and begins to indicate a kind of authoritative, exotic, primeval wisdom. This determines a fruitful contamination of classical *topoi* with original and extraneous elements. Regional and barbarian features coexist even within the mainly Hellenocentric perspective of Greek historians, geographers, sophists, philosophers, who appreciate the barbarian thought and wisdom, also read and explained through the Hellenic theoretical apparatus. Accordingly, the probable aim of *De Iside ed Osiride* is to merge Egyptian cultural categories and Greek rationalistic standards and concepts, in order to disclose new meaningful theoretical perspectives, suitable for the religious and cultural sensibility of the readers of the time.

7. *'Conclusion' and value of the dialogue*

Thus men make use of consecrated symbols, some employing symbols that are obscure, but others those that are clearer, in guiding the intelligence toward things divine, though not without a certain hazard[225].

Exegesis is a way of doing philosophy and of reaching for a superior kind of knowledge concerning the gods: every *correct* and *correctly analysed* symbol is endowed with the power of leading human intelligence (νόησις) towards the divine[226]. Taken as a whole, the discussion narrated by Plutarch and transcribed in *De E apud Delphos* – as I believe – works *itself* as a symbol. Its special function of a sort of collection of reminders (ὑπομνήματα, a genre frequently employed for philosophical writing during the Imperial age) is also confirmed by the two meaningful *hypomnêmata* 'Know thyself' and 'Thou art' sealing its conclusion, and symbolically enclosing its overall and ultimately elusive meaning[227].

One may notice a Pythagorean influence within the use of maxims as 'symbols', thus as ethical reminders enclosing complex prescriptions in few words, understandable just to 'initiates'. Luc Brisson has investigated the influence of Pythagoreanism in imperial Platonism; despite the objective difficulty of reconstructing the practical-historical modalities of this contamination, it is possible to pinpoint its principal Platonic representatives: first of all Eudorus and Philo, then the astronomer Trasyllus, and especially Plutarch, but also Moderatus of Gades and Nichomacus of Gerasa. As Brisson explains, the primary original element

---

[225] *De Is. et Os.* 378A-B (Eng. trans. F. C. Babbitt).
[226] Cf. *ibid.* 378A.
[227] Cf. *De E* 394C: τὸ δ' ὑπόμνησίς ἐστι τῷ θνητῷ τῆς περὶ αὐτὸ φύσεως καὶ ἀσθενείας.

introduced by Pythagoreanism is secrecy, employed as an 'instrument' as well as a 'means of formulation'. Doctrines are hidden in symbols, and composed in an enigmatic way (σύμβολα, αἰνίγματα), incomprehensible to the majority of the readers. Platonists similarly come to resort to a kind of knowledge transmission mainly based on oral direct teachings (ἀκούσματα) and brief written reminders (ὑπομνήματα)[228].

In line with this orientation, we can observe two different levels of Apollo's action disclosing themselves throughout the whole dialogue: on the one hand, he helps ordinary humans to cope with their everyday troubles; on the other, he engenders, by means of enigmas, a sublime intellectual urge in the souls of some chosen individuals, who possess mind and reason (λόγος καὶ ψυχή[229]) and are philosopher by nature.

The aporetic exchange staged in *De E apud Delphos* practically demonstrates the value of Ammonius' definition of philosophy, as a communal, potentially infinite quest for truth, always limited, provisional, subjective, liable of endless progressive adjustments, constantly fostered by wonder and doubt. According to this view, in *De Iside et Osiride* Plutarch claims that the gods have generously given to us all blessings and even bestowed on us a share of their perfect intelligence and wisdom, in which we are admitted to participate (νοῦ δὲ καὶ φρονήσεως μεταδίδωσιν). Our strife towards truth, especially that concerning the gods, expresses our desire for divinity[230]: rational research, always tensional and imperfect, represents nevertheless the fundamental instrument at our disposal to approach and honour the deity. The idea of a direct connection with the divine by means of a *unio mystica* – expressed by later Neoplatonists – is nevertheless still excluded in Plutarch[231]. Indeed, due to our limitedness, we can never reach the god: discursive language (λόγος) does not get to the truth; rather, real knowledge is super-intellectual, thus necessarily located beyond rational discussion. The apperception of truth, which is expressed in cognitive terms (ἡ τοῦ πρώτου καὶ κυπίου καὶ νοητοῦ γνῶσις[232]), is like a flash of lightening, shining into the soul just once, through a kind of spiritual touch and sight (ὥσπερ ἀστραπὴ διαλάμψασα τῆς ψυχῆς ἅπαξ ποτὲ θιγεῖν καὶ προσιδεῖν παρέσχε) – an 'intellectual contact' significantly reached by means of philosophical investigation (πλὴν ὅσον ὀνείρατος ἀμαυροῦ θιγεῖν νοήσει διὰ φιλοσοφίας)[233]. Plutarch's epistemological and theological approach thus

---

[228] Cf. Brisson (1999) 157.

[229] Cf. *De E* 385D: τοῖς μὴ παντάπασιν ἀλόγοις καὶ ἀψύχοις ὑφειμένα δελεάζει καὶ παρακαλεῖ πρὸς τὸ σκοπεῖν τι καὶ ἀκούειν καὶ διαλέγεσθαι περὶ αὐτῶν.

[230] Cf. *De Is. et Os.* 351C-E.

[231] For Plutarch's personal religious ideas and their connection with his philosophical thought see Burkert (1996).

[232] *De Is. et Os.* 351F-352A.

[233] *Ibid.* 382D-F.

proves that truth exists, and is located in the metaphysical realm, beyond the sensible world and its variable appearance.

The reverential respect due to the gods (εὐλάβεια) – hallmark of Plutarch's Academic spirit – can be extended to, and conciliated with, the faith in oracles and portents but also with the endorsement of extraneous mythical-religious traditions (combined with Greek philosophical doctrines and religious ideas). Plutarch's main 'personal' interest, as a minister in Delphi, is to both prove the existence of, and promote the faith in, a supreme deity – namely, Apollo – that remotely and actively sustains the oracular activity.

The belief in the presence and action of the divine within human existence is widespread and convincingly embraced by individuals in Plutarch's age: gods are expected to accomplish specific tasks – such as to manifest themselves, heal illnesses, foretell the future through official and unofficial forms of divination – in order to preserve their dignity and their very existence. Oracular interrogations range from personal doubts to religious controversies and often arise from the contemporaneous philosophical reflection or theological debates. Humans are constantly exposed to what Paul Veyne calls the "informelle et multiforme" presence of the divine, expressed and conveyed by numerous signs coming from above. Veyne effectively explains this constant communication as an 'international relationship', an articulated interconnection in which the human and the divine world correspond to two different nations that permanently confront, exchange and negotiate their respective interests[234].

Oracles determine the future rather than merely predicting it – which is confirmed by frequently raised demands asking for practical suggestions rather than for previsions[235]. The predictive-prescriptive function of the oracular Apollo seems to me to represent the *ritual* counterpart of Plutarch's qualification of god as possessing a perfect knowledge of the whole stream of time: as a benevolent deity, he wishes to partly extend his absolute wisdom to humans (through predictions), and to help them to face their actual difficulties (through prescriptions).

Plutarch conceives the highest god as *both* a supreme ontological principle and a personal deity at the top of a henotheistic pyramid, who makes his presence felt and his influence visible within the cosmos. What I think is most important for the purposes of the present study is that Plutarch's idea of god results from his complex, learned and detailed reading of *actual ritual customs* through philosophical concepts, and it is rooted exactly within the diverse historical-sociological aspects and functions associated to the *oracular activity*.

---

[234] Cf. Veyne (1986) 261.
[235] Cf. Bloch (1984).

Moreover, as I believe, Plutarch's view of Apollo, as having a transcendent essence and an immanent power, reflects the simultaneously 'localised' and 'universal' nature of the cult devoted to the oracular god: one of the god's traditional and distinctive features is his simultaneous connection to the city of Delphi as well as to the entire Greek land, where he is celebrated in numerous local festivals[236].

De E apud Delphos can be then assumed as the expression *par excellence* of Plutarch's attempt of collating into one single picture the multiple faces and features of Apollo – resumed from philosophical reflection as well as from traditional belief; he assembles and harmonizes them together in order to approach as much as possible the most complete and exhaustive idea of the supreme deity.

---

[236] Cf. Dietrich (1978). Dietrich in this study interestingly considers the Delphic as well as the Delian Apollo.

Chapter 4
Divination and the soul

My objective in the present chapter is to prove that Plutarch's theory of the soul (both the world soul and the individual soul) is central to his idea of divination; the soul, indeed, by virtue of its mediating function (recalled multiple times in the present research), is primarily responsible for the connection between the transcendent realm and the material world. This last section will show how divination *itself* is an effective, almost 'perfect', medium between humankind and the god, as well as between becoming and being, temporality and eternity, and between the multiple other elements involved in Plutarch's original dualistic theory. Relying on this basis, I will stress the pivotal role that divination plays in his thought.

As I will try to demonstrate, analysing Plutarch's idea of divination in the light of his psychological theory – which I will briefly present in the first part of this chapter – has two advantages. First, it helps us to distinguish among different prophetic modes according to the different psychic parts involved, and thus to account for the peculiar character and mechanism of oracular divination in contrast to those of individual divination (developed in *De genio Socratis*). Second, as I will show in a second stage (by referring to Plato's *Timaeus* and its influence on Plutarch's thought), it provides insight into Plutarch's conception of an authentically rational, scientific and religious, foundation of divination and into the wider, cosmic framework in which prophetic oracular mantic operates.

I. Plutarch's psychology: the individual soul and the world soul

Plutarch's works that have survived to the present day and are specifically devoted to divination are the Delphic dialogues and *De genio Socratis*. They respectively address institutional and individual divination. Given their dialogical form, they do not allow for a full understanding of Plutarch's own perspective, especially with regard to his complex psychological and demonological theory: in these texts, indeed, the philosophical arguments are assigned to the polyphonic, when not contradictory, interventions of different *personae dialogi*, or expressed through cryptic mythological narratives.

Therefore, in order to attempt a reconstruction of Plutarch's doctrine of the soul and to assess its influence within the divinatory theory, it is necessary for me to start with a careful examination of some of his treatises, where he presents his own reflections with his own voice. The ones that I have selected for the specific purposes of the present investigation are the following: *De virtute morali, Quaestiones Platonicae, De animae procreatione in Timaeo*.

1.1. The individual soul

In *De virtute morali* Plutarch gives a full account of his ethical-psychological theory, to which he will remain substantially faithful throughout his entire literary-philosophical production. While countering the psychological monism and ethical rigorism of the Stoics, he combines Peripatetic and mostly Pythagorean elements, and develops a doctrine that is ultimately consonant with his spirit of committed Platonist.

This treatise aims to demonstrate that human nature, beside the clearest dichotomy (ἐμφανεστέραν) between body and soul (which, as Plutarch explains, was identified as such even by the Stoics), is really dual and composite (διττός, σύνθετος) at a deeper level: that of the soul itself. The soul is divided into two parts: one rational, intelligent and logical (λόγος, τὸ νοερὸν καὶ λογιστικόν), the other irrational, disordered and variable (ἄλογον μέρος, τὸ παθητικὸν καὶ ἄλογον καὶ πολυπλανὲς καὶ ἄτακτον)[1]. Introspection confirms the fundamental distinction between these two parts and attests to their perpetual mutual contrast[2].

The ordering, controlling principle of reason (ἡ λογιστικὴ ἀρχή), external and divine in origin, is unitary and simple; it is independent (αὐτοκρατές) from the irrational soul but not immune to the consequences that the irrational soul causes. The irrational soul, in line with Plato's *Republic*[3], is divided into an irascible (θυμοειδές) and a desiderative (ἐπιθυμητικόν) part[4]. The irascible part associates either with reason or with the desiderative part. The desiderative part performs instead the fundamental function of connecting the irrational psychic principle to the body.

Drawing from the Aristotelian distinction between dianoetic and ethical virtues[5], Plutarch ascribes to the soul two cognitive faculties: the one theoretical (θεωρητική), oriented towards the intelligible realm, and the other practical (πρακτική), oriented towards the material realm.

Theoretical wisdom (σοφία) is the virtue of the contemplative faculty of the soul (ἐπιστημονικὸν καὶ θεωρητικόν); it is oriented towards the first principles, which exist absolutely (ἁπλῶς) and are the most sublime and divine objects of human knowledge. *Sophia* is rooted within the pure intellectual activity; it is immune to the influences of irrational elements,

---

[1] The second part, which lacks order and measure, somehow tends towards the directive principle; cf. *De virt. mor.* 441D-442C.

[2] Cf. *ibid.* 441F-442A.

[3] Cf. Plato, *Resp.* 6,434d.

[4] This partition is typical of the human soul, and is not found in the cosmic soul.

[5] Cf. Aristoteles, *EN* 6,1,1139a7.

such as passions and corporeal stimuli (it is εἰλικρινές, ἀπαθές), and is constitutively extraneous to deliberation and fortune – two prerogatives that instead characterise human practical life. Theoretical wisdom relies on the perfect autonomy and self-efficiency of reason, of which it expresses the intrinsic, superior power (αὐτοτελής τίς ἐστιν ἀκρότης τοῦ λόγου καὶ δύναμις)[6].

Practical wisdom (φρόνησις), on the other hand, requires that the contemplative faculty (θεωρητικόν) stands in an active relation with the practical, passionate element (πρακτικὸν καὶ παθητικόν)[7]. It operates within the material, contingent world – governed by instability and error – and within the field of fortune (τύχη) and rational deliberation (βουλή). Its decisions (κρίσεις) are inevitably influenced by the irrational component of the soul (ἄλογον)[8].

In this framework, moral virtue is defined as founded on an active and balanced cooperation between the rational and irrational parts of the soul. Namely, the irrational element corresponds to the very psychic principle, responsible for the life and movement of the soul. As a consequence, it is neither possible (δυνατόν) nor advantageous (ἄμεινον) to silence it, which means to eradicate (ἐξαιρεῖν) passions[9]. This precept clearly counteracts the Stoic doctrine of *apatheia*, which – according to Plutarch – rather than promoting moral virtue, engenders inactivity and insensibility (ἀπραξία, ἀναισθησία)[10]. The ethical ideal proposed by the Chaeronean is one of moderation and inclusion of passions, performed in a wise, controlled way (μετριοπάθεια). According to his view, the spirited, desiderative component (θυμός) is an indispensable ally of reason. Passions cannot be excluded from moral life (their φθορά or ἀναίρεσις must thus be avoided), since they are *indispensable* for realizing the end of ethical virtue (ἦθος)[11]. Ethical virtue is a permanent state that corresponds to a quality of the irrational part of the soul (ποιότης τοῦ ἀλόγου τὸ ἦθος) imposed by reason, which informs and harmonizes it (τὸ ἄλογον ὑπὸ τοῦ λόγου πλαττόμενον)[12].

In the ninth of his *Quaestiones Platonicae* Plutarch employs the Platonic image of the chariot in order to present a tripartite view of the soul[13], which he nevertheless mitigates by placing emphasis on the alliance of reason with the irascible part. In the same *quaestio* Plutarch presents

---

6 Cf. *De virt. mor.* 444A-D.
7 Cf. *ibid.* 443D.
8 Cf. *ibid.* 444A.
9 Cf. *ibid.* 443D.
10 Cf. *De tranq. an.* 465C.
11 Cf. *De virt. mor.* 444D.
12 Cf. *ibid.* 443C.
13 Cf. Plato, *Phdr.* 246a6-7. Cf. *supra* 56 and 91.

the concept of 'mean' (μέσον)[14] – in its acceptation of 'middle term' or 'intermediate note', as a technical word of musical theory (περὶ φθόγγους καὶ ἁρμονίας)[15]. Plutarch here calls '*logos*' both the harmonic proportion of passions imposed by reason, and reason itself, as the regulative principle that adjusts the whole soul by mitigating the irrational components and preserving them from excess and defect[16]. The Chaeronean therefore reads the notion of 'correct mean' (μεσότης) between the extremes of two passions – derived from Aristotelian and Peripatetic ethics – in a Platonic perspective. Accordingly, reason (λόγος) is the superior principle of order, harmony and limitation (τάξις, ὅρος)[17], which submits the irrational part to its leadership, and guides it with its reins (thus rendering it εὐήνιον) in a way more effective than any constriction.

As explained in Chapter I of this book[18], the just recalled theoretical structure at the basis of Plutarch's moral psychology complies with the idea of a 'hylomorphism' between reason-form (εἶδος) and passions-matter (ὕλη). This form-matter model, beside its Aristotelic resonance, rather recalls the Platonic cosmology: practical reason indeed has a regulative function with respect to the chaotic movements of the irrational part[19]. This hierarchical relationship between the rational and the irrational component, also called intellect and necessity (νοῦς – ἀνάγνη) respectively, constitutes an important and recurrent explanatory pattern in Plutarch's reflection[20], and also lies at the core of his account of divination – as I will soon highlight.

1.2. The cosmic soul

Our reconstruction of Plutarch's cosmology should naturally start with an attentive consideration of *De animae procreatione in Timaeo*, a crucial exegetical treatise, where he expresses his own perspective and ideas without dispersing them in the multiple voices of a dialogue. The treatise contains Plutarch's personal and literal reading of the *Timaeus* psychogony (31a1-36b5). Jan Opsomer has significantly defined the theory of the world soul as extremely meaningful and well-integrated within Plutarch's philosophical thought: this doctrine appears indeed to sustain

---

[14] Cf. Aristoteles, *EN* 2,6,1106a24.

[15] Cf. *De virt. mor.* 444E; Opsomer (2012).

[16] Cf. Opsomer (2012) 326.

[17] Cf. *De virt. mor.* 442C-443D; cf. 444B: τὴν δ᾽ ὁρμὴν τῷ πάθει ποιεῖ τὸ ἦθος, λόγου δεομένην ὁρίζοντος, ὅπως μετρία παρῇ καὶ μήθ᾽ ὑπερβάλλῃ μήτ᾽ ἐγκαταλείπῃ τὸν καιρόν.

[18] Cf. *supra* 40.

[19] Cf. *De virt. mor.* 444B-D.

[20] Sven-Tage Teodorsson has provided a thorough study on the influence of Plutarch's interpretation of Plato's cosmology within his personal development of ethical and eschatological theories – cf. Teodorsson (2010).

his metaphysical and religious reflection, to interconnect his psychological and ethical conceptions, and even to have a place within the theoretical structure of the *Lives*[21].

The world soul, according to Plutarch's exposition of its genesis and constitution, is divided into two parts: an intelligent, rational component (ἀκίνητος, ἀπαθής, ἁπλοῦς, εἰλικρινής), which is the cause and principle of order and harmony, closer to the immutable essence; a non-intelligent, irrational component (μεριστόν, πλανητόν, ἄμορφον, ἀόριστον), which instead is the cause and principle of movement, in contact with matter[22]. The first part, the monadic ordering principle (τὸ μέσον, μέτριον, καλόν), is indeed opposed to the second, the indeterminate dyad, characterized by excess (ὑπερβολή) and defect (ἔλλειψις)[23].

According to Plutarch's literal interpretation of the *Timaeus*, the demiurge created the cosmos in a one-time definite act. From this point of departure, the Chaeronean develops an utterly original and personal view of the process of the *psychogonia*. Accordingly, god imparted to a pre-cosmic soul his own intelligence and rationality (νοῦς καὶ νοητόν), which he took out from himself. He employed 'sameness' and 'otherness' (ταὐτὸν καὶ θάτερον) as ordering instruments; by applying number and reason, he introduced limit and form (πέρας καὶ εἶδος) into the chaotic precosmic soul[24]. The action of the rational principle on the irrational psychic component (this last is also called necessity, ἀνάγκη[25]) is described as 'persuasion' (πείθω)[26].

In the framework of Plutarch's thought, the hierarchical relation between reason and necessity might be connected to the one between providence (πρόνοια) and destiny (ἀνάγκη or εἱμαρμένη). Nevertheless, in his works, the interaction between *pronoia* and other cosmic forces in general, including that of 'fortune' (τύχη, αὐτόματον), remains fundamentally obscure – especially since his main writings on this topic have not survived. At any rate Plutarch, like other contemporaneous Platonists[27], conceives providence as a supreme power and a beneficent force that governs the entire universe, and destiny as a subordinated law that regulates the physical realm through its cause-effect logic[28].

---

[21] Cf. Opsomer (2005a) esp. 177 and also Opsomer (2004). For this treatise see Deuse (1983) 12-47; Hershbell (1987); Ferrari (1996a); (2004); Demulder (2015).

[22] Cf. *De an. procr.* 1024A.

[23] Cf. *De virt. mor.* 441E-442A; *De an. procr.* 1012B; Plato, *Ti.* 35a.

[24] Cf. *De an. procr.* 1015D-F: ἁρμονίᾳ καὶ ἀναλογίᾳ καὶ ἀριθμῷ χρώμενος.

[25] Cf. *De facie* 928D: ἐν παντὶ δὲ κρατεῖ τὸ βέλτιον τοῦ κατηναγκασμένου.

[26] Cf. Plato, *Ti.* 48a; cf. also *supra* 46.

[27] For an exhaustive and thorough account of the doctrine of fate in Middle-Platonism, with special reference to the Pseudo-Plutarchan *De fato*, see Opsomer (2014c).

[28] Some other Platonists developed a partition of the cosmic forces at work in the

In particular, I think that it is crucial to point out that the word '*anagkê*' in *De animae procreatione* seems to adhere to two meanings. First, '*anagkê*' corresponds to the disordered force of the irrational soul, which displays similar characteristics to those of the *causa errans* (πλανωμένη αἰτία) in the *Timaeus*. Second, in a notorious passage[29], it is strikingly identified with 'destiny' (εἱμαρμένη), probably for an anti-Stoic purpose: this identification stresses indeed that *anagkê* is not the only force that deterministically guides the cosmos – as the Stoics believe. Rather, it is simply a force inferior to that of divine rationality, by which it gets 'persuaded' in the moment of the cosmogenesis.

The cosmic soul (μέρος θεοῦ, ἔμφρων καὶ τεταγμένη) is composed of a monadic (ταὐτό, τὸ ἀμερές) and a dyadic element (τὸ ἕτερον, τὸ μεριστόν): intellect (νοῦς), principle of order and rationality, is opposed to soul (ψυχή), principle of disordered movement. The evil and disordered soul (ἄτακτον καὶ κακοποιόν[30]) – devoid of form, intelligence and rationality (μορφή, νοῦς and λόγος[31]) – is the psychic principle *itself*, which incessantly moves the precosmic matter[32]. The struggle between the ordering action of divine reason (λόγος) and the chaotic necessity intrinsic in matter (ἀνάγκη) still characterizes the present life of the cosmos. God constantly introduces adjustments and corrections – while always respecting human

---

universe, thus settling a threefold scheme composed of hierarchically ordered powers. For a detailed account of this doctrine in Apuleius, Ps.-Plutarch and Numenius, see the very clear Sharples (2003). For an analysis of Plutarch's reading of the Stoic theory of providence, see Algra (2014), who identifies Stoicism and Platonism as ultimately "two philosophical relatives who both have Plato as an ancestor" (p. 35) and shows their points of contact in Plutarch.

[29] Cf. *De an. procr.* 1026B: [...] λόγος ἄγων πειθοῖ μεμιγμένην ἀνάγκην, ἣν εἱμαρμένην οἱ πολλοὶ καλοῦσιν.

[30] *Ibid.* 1014E.

[31] Cf. *Ibid.* 1015B: ἀκοσμία δ'οὐκ ἀσώματος οὐδ'ἀκίνητος οὐδ'ἄψυχος ἀλλ'ἄμορφον μὲν καὶ ἀσύστατον τὸ σωματικὸν ἔμπληκτον δὲ καὶ ἄλογον τὸ κινητικὸν ἔχουσα.

[32] Plutarch draws from Plato's *Laws* the notion of two souls, one good and the other evil (κακοποιὸς ψυχή, Plato, *Lg.* 10,896d: δυοῖν μέν γέ που ἔλαττον μηδὲν τιθῶμεν, τῆς τε εὐεργέτιδος καὶ τῆς τἀναντία δυναμένης ἐξεργάζεσθαι. Cf. also Plato, *Ti.* 35a). The image found in *De animae procreatione* of an 'innate soul' and 'soul in itself' (ψυχὴ ἀγένητος, ψυχὴ καθ'ἑαυτήν, also called: ἀπειρία, ἀκοσμία, ἀνάγκη) derives from Plutarch's interpretation of the 'innate desire' of the *Politicus* (σύμφυτος ἐπιθυμία, Plato, *Plt.* 272e), the 'infinity' of the *Philebus* (ἀπειρία in Plato, *Phlb.* 16c), and the indefinite dyad of the Platonic ἄγραφα. The coincidence among all these different notions, evidenced by recent scholarship, is founded on the hermeneutic principle – based on Plutarch's conviction of the systematic and coherent character of Plato's thought and production – of 'explaining Plato from Plato' (*Platonem ex Platone*). Following the same hermeneutic stance, Plutarch harmonizes the definition of the soul as eternal and non-generated (ἀγένετος), as found in the *Phaedrus*, and generated (γενομήνη), as found in the *Timaeus*, by making these two qualifications correspond to the precosmic and the cosmic soul, respectively (cf. *De an. procr.* 1015F-1016A).

self-determination and the limits imposed by physical necessity – since the irrational component, trying to prevail, makes the world periodically deviate from its harmonic status[33]. The evil soul (whose existence justifies the presence of evil in the world) nevertheless confers to the cosmic soul three fundamental functions, which account for its kinetic, imaginative and judgemental capacities (κινητικόν – φανταστικόν – κριτικόν)[34]. By virtue of these faculties, the world soul performs a mediating function between the ideal and the material world.

Plutarch draws from Plato the notion of the soul as intermediary between matter and god, and therefore characterises it as in permanent contact with both the sensible and the intelligible substance[35]. The irrational soul, also called 'becoming' (γένεσις), is subject to perpetual change and motion (ἐν μεταβολαῖς καὶ κινήσεσιν). It is located in between 'what impresses' and 'what is impressed' (τυποῦντος καὶ τοῦ τυπουμένου μεταξὺ τεταγμένην) and transmits into this world the images coming from above (διαδιδοῦσαν ἐνταῦθα τὰς ἐκεῖθεν εἰκόνας). Placed between the transcendent forming cause and the sensible thing formed, it transfers immaterial shapes and figures on matter[36].

1.3. The analogy between the individual and the cosmic soul

The parallelism established by Plutarch between the individual soul and the cosmic soul is fundamental with regard to his entire cosmological and psychological reflection[37]. The Chaeronean conceives the human soul not only as a part (μέρος), but also as an imperfect imitation (τι μίμημα), of the world soul[38]: they are both divided into a rational and an irrational component, with the difference that the irrational component is stronger in the human soul[39].

The active providential care of the deity is constantly present within the universe, from the act of the cosmopoiesis performed by the demiurge onwards, and provides a valuable paradigm for human moral life: as the god constantly regulates the combination of the world soul and disciplines its irrational component (ψυχή), in the same way we must harmonize

---

[33] Cf. De an. procr. 1023D. In this approach, the 'two faces' of god (the one immanent, the other transcendent – analysed especially in Chapter 3 of the present study, with reference to the image of Apollo in De E apud Delphos) are conciliated: by inserting a part of himself into the world soul, god becomes somehow immanent in the cosmos.

[34] On these three functions, see Ferrari (2011/2012) 20.

[35] Cf. De an. procr. 1015B.

[36] Cf. ibid. 1024C.

[37] For the analogy between the individual and the cosmic soul in Plutarch, see Baltes (2000); Ferrari (1996a); (1996b); Opsomer (1994); (2004); Phillips (2002); Thévenaz (1938).

[38] Cf. De virt. mor. 441F-442A; Plato, Ti. 69c.

[39] Cf. De virt. mor. 441F; De an. procr. 1025D.

our own soul in order to achieve our ethical end (τέλος). This permanent balancing intervention is indispensable, since the cosmic (as well as the human) irrational part recursively destroys the psychic harmony with disorder (τὸ ταραχῶδες) and necessity (τὸ κατηναγκασμένον). Both the irrational component (ἄλογον μέρος) of the human soul and the dyadic disordered part of the cosmic soul lack limit, reason, order, and are subject to passions and affections. For these reasons, they are in need of a guiding rational principle[40].

As we will see in the second part of this chapter, the cosmic harmony and, particularly, the ordering function exerted by the divine *logos* on the world are two crucial concepts useful for our tentative understanding of Plutarch's view of the mantic activity performed at the Delphic temple.

2. The psychology of individual divination

As I explained above[41], human cognitive capacities are normally oriented towards either the sensible or the intelligible world, in which way they realize the aim of practical or theoretical wisdom, respectively. Now, I will take into account individual divination, a special mantic activity that displays one further capacity of the soul: that of accessing to a superior, extraordinary domain of knowledge[42]. Through this kind of mantic activity, one person can reach a superior kind of wisdom by only relying on her own faculties, thus without the need of the institutional framework of the temple, and without resorting to any material, external means. As I believe, *De genio Socratis* is centred exactly on the conceptual relation between contemplation and practice (θεωρία-πρᾶξις), and – as a closer investigation reveals – it accounts for the important philosophical question as to if, and to what extent, theoretical principles can be applied within human life.

De genio is the reference work for analysing Plutarch's conception of individual inspired divination, as an independent, autonomous prophetic practice, performed by extraordinary individuals and detached from official cultic institutions. Socrates embodies the perfect example of this kind of inspired mantic[43]. His philosophical mission is also deeply connected to the Delphic context: it has its first impulse or *hormê* (ὁρμή) in the famous Delphic response that declared him the wisest man of all, and its guiding principle in the oracular maxim 'know yourself' (γνῶθι

---

[40] Cf. *De an. procr.* 1026A-E.

[41] Cf. *supra* 180-181.

[42] It is worth noting that the 'effective content' of the messages received through demonic divination remains fundamentally obscure in the dialogue.

[43] For a discussion on the success of the image of Socrates in Late-Ancient philosophical reflection, see Döring (1979).

σεαυτόν) – which, as emphasised in the analysis of *De E apud Delphos*, is of a crucial importance for Plutarch's own reflection, also considering its function of a concise and effective reminder of our human, limited condition[44].

This dialogue endorses the idea that the most sublime part of the human soul is 'demonic' in nature – as confirmed by the eschatological myth narrated in its conclusive section[45]. Human intellect (νοῦς) – divine and immortal – becomes completely purified through a real philosophical life: he who takes care of his inner demon achieves happiness (so becomes authentically εὐδαίμων)[46]. Despite the manifold aspects and sometimes contradictory implications of Plutarch's complex demonological theory, the identification between the supreme part of the soul and a demon appears in other places of Plutarch's *oeuvre* and is almost certainly ascribable to his own convictions and original reflection[47]. This doctrine (νοῦς = δαίμων) draws from the notorious passage of Plato's *Timaeus*[48], where the demon (δαίμων) is identified with the most sublime part of the soul (περὶ τοῦ κυριωτάτου [...] ψυχῆς), divine in origin and located in the top of the body. The god sustains human beings and raises them upwards by means of their interior demon, according to their nature of celestial plants whose roots are oriented towards the sky.

Based on a comprehensive reading of *De genio Socratis*, divination emerges as a privileged cognitive vehicle that allows only a few, chosen individuals to obtain an extraordinary kind of knowledge. This divinatory practice complies with a peculiar conception of the soul, which is structurally different from the one developed in *De virtute morali*[49].

While in *De virtute morali* intellect (νοῦς) is an 'active' element and power, which achieves the theoretical and contemplative wisdom (σοφία), in *De genio Socratis* it is instead a 'receptive', passive element, which receives a superior and inspired kind of knowledge, if kept pure and uncontaminated (ὁ νοῦς καθαρὸς ὢν καὶ ἀπαθής)[50]. In *De genio*, indeed, intellect (κρείττων νοῦς) appears to exert its power much more easily when it

---

[44] Cf. *Adv. Col.* §12 (1113B-D).

[45] Cf. *De genio Socr.* 589F-592E.

[46] For an accurate account of the term εὐδαίμων see Centrone (2011).

[47] Cf. Brenk (1973) 11.

[48] Cf. Plato, *Ti.* 90a. This same passage is recalled in *De Pyth. or.* 400B-C; cf. *supra* 54.

[49] With 'comprehensive reading' I intend the interpretation that emerges from collating together all the different arguments proposed in *De genio Socratis* – which, exactly like *De E apud Delphos*, belongs to the literary genre of the *zêtêma*. An attentive analysis of all the arguments developed in *De genio* – although not completely coherent among themselves – displays that they all contain a part of the truth. Therefore, when all these 'veridical kernels' are collated, they offer a reliable solution for the topic debated.

[50] Cf. *De genio Socr.* 588D.

is kept flawless and sound: when this condition is realised, the soul looses its typical indomitable and recalcitrant character, and stops opposing resistance to the rational part of the soul[51].

The notion of 'bridle' is absolutely crucial in *De genio*, where it accounts for a peculiar theoretical and psychological framework: while in *De virtute morali* the bridle symbolises the guide and control exerted by reason over the irrational soul for the sake of virtue, in *De genio Socratis* – based instead on a 'demonic' conception of the soul – the bridle comes to be identified with a controlling element that is external, divine and transcendent[52]. This element works as a guide for some chosen individuals, by leading them towards the understanding of superior truths – otherwise hidden and inaccessible – but even sustains them in their everyday, practical life, by working as a precious source of worldly wisdom and by orienting their existence according to a sort of 'divine educational plan'.

The peculiar psychological structure underlying individual divination is partly clarified through the myth of Timarchus that Simmias narrates in the dialogue[53]. In this narrative, a 'demonic voice' reveals to the protagonist – during a portentous consultation of the oracle of Trophonius – that every soul (a term that in this context indicates the entire individual soul, and not only the irrational psychic principle) partakes of intellect (ψυχὴ πᾶσα νοῦ μετέσχεν). Nevertheless, every soul is also irrational, to the extent to which it is immersed into, and confounded with, the corporal element (σάρξ-σῶμα)[54].

The *noûs* in the myth is associated to the image of a 'buoy' – which effectively captures its extraordinary character and emphasises the difference with the treatment of the same concept in *De virtute morali*. According to the demonic disembodied voice appearing in the myth, souls that are partially immersed into the body leave outside their purest element (τὸ καθαρώτατον, i.e., intellect), as a buoy. This (the νοῦς), once purified, is correctly called demon (δαίμων), since it remains separate from corporeality; when it descends into the body, it is instead named reason (λόγος)[55].

Daniel Babut, in a very useful article for our understanding of *De genio Socratis*[56], has convincingly demonstrated that the psychical structure inferable from the mythical narrative is, at least in its main aspects, compatible with the philosophical arguments presented by the characters

---

[51] Cf. *ibid.* 588E.

[52] Cf. *De virt. mor.* 443D; 445B-D; *De genio Socr.* 592A.

[53] Cf. *De genio Socr.* 590B-592E.

[54] Cf. *ibid.* 591D.

[55] Cf. *ibid.* 591E.

[56] Cf. Babut (1984).

in the dialogue, especially Simmias himself and Theanor. Accordingly, the main aim of *De genio* is arguably to explain that few selected individuals – by virtue of the purity of their intellect (νοῦς) – are worthy of receiving a special kind of education: the divine messages that they capture guide their reason, easily conducting them towards a happy, virtuous life.

According to Plutarch's metaphysics, god – as already explained in the present study – does not directly intervene in contingency and can not violate the laws of necessity. Therefore, even in the case of independent divination, he needs to resort to an intermediary: this role is performed by demons, who (as Theanor explains) communicate to virtuous human souls by means of a special language composed of symbols (λόγῳ διὰ συμβόλων εὐθύνοντες)[57]. On the contrary, ordinary men, unable to receive and make shine in their impure intellects the luminous messages sent by the demons, have to make use of a kind of technical, indirect and inductive divination, which is based on rational decoding and understanding of oblique messages and riddles – as confirmed by the practice of artificial divination (including the interpretation of prodigies and portents)[58].

In this framework, Socrates is the eternal *exemplum* of an exceptionally wise man, who always kept his *noûs* absolutely pure and uncontaminated, and has been led from his childhood by that divine guide – which is something that, as explained by the 'voice' in the myth of Timarchus, also happens with soothsayers and inspired men (τὸ μαντικόν ἐστι καὶ θεοκλυτούμενον γένος)[59]. Socrates' *noûs* is extremely sensitive, receptive, free of passions and loosely connected to his body – as very well explained by Simmias[60]. We can see that one essential condition that must be respected in order for demonic illumination to arise is hence the following: intellect must be pure and disengaged from the body – which is the result of an authentically virtuous-philosophical life.

Moreover, from Simmias' rational-philosophical explanation of the concept of δαιμόνιον, we learn that those who, thanks to both their virtue and education, have reached for a status of inner perfection, are capable of capturing direct prophetic messages coming from above. The individuals belonging to this class are called 'sacred' or 'demonic men' (ἱεροὺς καὶ δαιμονίους ἀνθρώπους[61], while Theanor defines them θεῖοι and θεοφιλεῖς[62]). Simmias explains, indeed, that having a virtuous and peaceful soul is the

---

[57] Cf. *De genio Socr.* 593B.

[58] Cf. Plato, *Ti.* 71d-72b. I think that a good reference to this kind of divinatory practice is given in *De genio Socr.* 577D, a passage in which the characters discuss "σημεῖα καὶ μαντεύματα δυσχερῆ καὶ χαλεπὰ προτεθεσπίσθαι τῇ Σπάρτῃ".

[59] *De genio Socr.* 592C.

[60] Cf. *ibid.*, 588D-E.

[61] Cf. *ibid.*, 589D.

[62] Cf. *ibid.*, 593D.

necessary moral-psychological precondition for having access to demonic communication[63]. The echo and peculiar sound of demonic messages, which manifest themselves through a special demonic light (δαιμόνιον [...] φέγγος), can resonate only in those men whose soul is quiet and pure, like if they were played on a well-tuned lyre – an image that recalls the musical metaphor of moral virtue also employed in *De virtute morali*[64].

I think that this psycho-anthropological division between ordinary humans and divinely chosen individuals perfectly complies with what the Pythagorean Theanor says later in the dialogue, concerning the distinction between natural-inspired and artificial-interpretative divination. According to Theanor, god loves the best of us (who are defined authentically blessed, μακάριοι, and divine, θεῖοι) and bestows on them a special kind of education (παιδαγωγία), transmitted through a special language made of symbols (σύμβολα). This corresponds to 'natural' or 'artless' divination. The rest of us have instead to practice artificial divination (μαντικὴ τέχνη) in order to interpret the oblique signs and omens (σημεῖα) sent from above[65].

Relying on Simmias' account, we can try to reconstruct – at least partially and hypothetically – the modalities of inspiration through 'demonic contact': a noble, demonic power takes control of the rational part of the individual, while the soul – become mild and malleable – can be guided with no constraint. Based on the general principle of the action of the like on the like, one mind (νοῦς) can be moved by a superior and more divine mind; accordingly, Socrates' intellect, completely pure and only loosely connected to the body, can be moved by a demon. When this occurs, the superior, external demonic power, by acting on intellect (νοῦς), moves the entire person to action. Simmias, in order to explain this complex dynamics, compares it to the ordinary one (defined no less surprising) according to which the body is moved by a thought (λόγος) coming from the rational soul[66].

Simmias explains that the demonic prophetic language (λόγος) has no sound and is composed of light (φέγγος); it does not need ordinary physical means to express itself – such as an acoustic impact (φθόγγον) or voice (it is transmitted ἄνευ φωνῆς). Rather, it resorts to air, a malleable element

---

[63] Cf. *ibid.*, 588D.

[64] Cf. *ibid.* 589D; see also *De virt. mor.* 444F: γίγνεται δὲ μεσότης καὶ λέγεται μάλιστα τῇ περὶ φθόγγους καὶ ἁρμονίας ὁμοίως, and 451F-452A: οἷον γὰρ ἐν φθόγγοις μουσικὴ τὸ ἐμμελὲς οὐκ ἀναιρέσει βαρύτητος καὶ ὀξύτητος, ἐν δὲ σώμασιν ἰατρικὴ τὸ ὑγιεινὸν οὐ φθορᾷ θερμότητος καὶ ψυχρότητος, ἀλλὰ συμμετρίαις καὶ ποσότησι κραθεισῶν ἀπεργάζεται, τοιοῦτον ἐν ψυχῇ τὸ νικῶν, ἐγγενομένης ὑπὸ λόγου ταῖς παθητικαῖς δυνάμεσι καὶ κινήσεσιν ἐπιεικείας καὶ μετριότητος.

[65] Cf. *De genio Socr.* 593A-D; for the distinction of two kinds of divination in antiquity, cf. *supra* 24-25.

[66] Cf. *ibid.* 589A-C.

that gets transformed by the thoughts of the demons[67]. The 'demon of Socrates' is therefore not a visual impulse; rather, it is a strange perception of a thought that does not pass through sensory faculties. The demonic contact happens in a dreamlike status: while dreaming, our body is calm and serene, physical impressions are silent, and the voices that we hear are only illusion or fancy (δόξα)[68].

It is important to stress that in *De genio Socratis*, Simmias presents individual inspiration as a communication mode antithetic to human language: while the former is clear and consistent, the latter is pessimistically defined dark (οἷον ὑπὸ σκότῳ), ambiguous, tentative and imperfect[69]. Human ordinary language resorts to verbs and names as symbols (συμβόλοις), and engenders fundamentally approximate and illusory verbal exchanges. The majority of us is therefore relegated to the obscure world of deception; nevertheless, we can resort to the precious gift of inductive-artificial divination, which is founded on the interpretation of omens and signs (σημεῖα, μαντεύματα[70]).

It is possible to notice that the Socratic mantic activity, as described by Plutarch, shows remarkable points of contact with divination as conceived by the Neoplatonists, especially considering the relation between wisdom and theurgy[71]. Moreover, by placing the focus on intellect and on its qualities of passivity and receptivity, we can find relevant points of contact with the Aristotelian notion of 'passive intellect' as elaborated by the Neoplatonists[72].

The passages of *De genio Socratis* here recalled help us to define Socratic divination as an individual form of mantic activity, clearly different from the institutional-oracular Delphic kind of prophecy. Nevertheless, down to the level of their respective (although ultimately nebulous) psychological functioning, they both share an inspirational dynamics. This dynamics appears to follow in both cases a musical model based on the couple plectrum-instrument: while in individual divination an immaterial demonic light hits like a plectrum the well-tuned intellect of some

---

[67] *Ibid.* 589C.

[68] Cf. *ibid.* 588C; cf. also Cicero, *Div.* I,129.

[69] Cf. *De genio Socr.* 589B.

[70] Cf. *ibid.* 577D.

[71] For Neoplatonists and divination see the outstanding examination proposed in Addey (2014). Remind, nevertheless, that Neoplatonists tended to show a critical attitude against Plutarch, especially as regards his cosmology, based on his personal interpretation of Plato's *Timaeus*, as clearly explained in Opsomer (2001).

[72] The Aristotelic notion of 'passive intellect' (cf. Aristoteles, *de An.* 3,4-5) acquires for the Neoplatonists the connotation of '*phantasia*', as demonstrated in Sorabji (2004) 121-123, and esp. 121: "The passive intellect is identified with *phantasia* by some, even though Aristotle distinguishes *phantasia* as a perceptual faculty."

wise individuals, in oracular divination – relying on our analysis of *De defectu oraculorum*[73] – it is an active material stream engendered by the earth in Delphi (μαντικὸν ῥεῦμα καὶ πνεῦμα, ἀναθυμίασις, ἀπόρροια) to hit the simple soul of the priestess like a plectrum[74], and to create a harmonic composition favourable for inspiration.

Finally, I think that it is worth noting that, with regard to the division of human souls into three classes presented in the mythical narrative of *De genio Socratis*, the virtuous souls, calm and manageable, are identified with stars that have a disciplined, ordered motion (εὐθεῖαν καὶ τεταγμένην κίνησιν)[75]; on the other hand, the demons that are inclined mostly towards the irrational element (τὸ ἄλογον) are described as captured in a chaotic, uncontrolled motion (ἀνωμάλως καὶ τεταραγμένως ἐγκλίνοντας)[76]. As the analysis that I will propose intends to show, the presence of an uneven motion (although devoid of the ethical overtones of *De genio Socratis*) is one of the essential components of oracular divination: a chaotic movement characterises exactly the status of the Pythia's soul, as a simple and 'non-philosophical' divinatory agent.

3. Plutarch and the Timaeus

The view of divination as an element of interconnection between the human and the cosmic plan is particularly evident in the works of the Chaeronean – but this is far from being an isolated case. Dario Sabbatucci has analysed and explained the links between divinatory practices and systematic representations of the world, on which basis he proposed to define divination as a way of both 'writing' and 'reading' the world[77]. In particular, with regard to ancient Greek divination, he has identified oracular consultations and mystery initiations with the only two exceptional cases in which it is rite, instead of myth, to perform a fundamental 'cosmicizing' function. Sabbatucci has also stressed the extraordinary character of the Delphic priests and their special dignity and importance, if compared to all the other sacerdotal bodies in Greek antiquity. He has effectively defined the practice of consulting the oracle as a 'cultural act', which bestows cultural value on human actions; accordingly, the oracle is responsible for religion and religious normativity – indeed, its responses are often turned into laws (θεσμοί)[78].

---

[73] Cf. *supra* 101-102.
[74] Cf. *De def. or.* 436E-F.
[75] *De genio Socr.* 592A.
[76] Cf. *ibid.* 592B.
[77] Cf. Sabbatucci (1989).
[78] Cf. Sabbatucci (1992).

In order to assess the 'cosmological value' of oracular prophecy for Plutarch, I think that it is essential to focus on his reading of Plato's *Timaeus*. Plutarch's philosophical reflection is fundamentally guided by the leading idea that a coherent philosophical system is hidden in Plato's dialogues and can be reconstructed out of them: the *Timaeus* appears to constitute Plutarch's reference-work in this hermeneutical operation, and thus to exert a strong influence on his entire output. This dialogue – as I strongly believe – also plays a crucial role in Plutarch's explanation of divination, with regard to both its practical procedures, and its cosmological framework of reference – two aspects of the mantic activity that are strictly interconnected with each other. Plutarch appears to use some key elements of the *Timaeus* in order to investigate the mechanics and foundation of Delphic divination: he incorporates them into his philosophical reflection and adapts them to his own theoretical needs, while re-elaborating Plato's concepts and metaphysics in an utterly creative and original way.

The Chaeronean draws primarily from the *Timaeus* the ontological distinction between becoming (τὸ γιγνόμενον) and being (τὸ ὄν) – reflected in those between the human and the divine realm, and between the sensible and the intelligible world – and reformulates it according to his own dualistic perspective. Plutarch's dualism, a constant thematic thread of all the Delphic dialogues, notoriously emerges from Ammonius' final speech in *De E apud Delphos* – although, we must remind, this monologue is not conclusive nor completely faithful with regard to Plutarch's own views. Also one famous passage of *De defectu oraculorum* provides a clear reference to the 'mixed' nature of the material world: there, Lamprias defines the sensible cosmos as the product of the 'conjunction and fellowship' of reason (λόγος) and matter (ὕλη): god is the supreme cause of order and reason, while matter is the necessary, inferior cause[79].

I believe that the apologetic strength of *De Pythiae oraculis* and *De defectu oraculorum* is grounded exactly on the fundamental ontological distinction between being and becoming. Accordingly, Plutarch's essential objective in these two dialogues is twofold: on the one hand, to affirm the divine origin of divination; on the other, to ascribe its material modifications to its ineluctable phenomenal character. The divine and the material plan are clearly distinct, especially in one respect: no material (qualitative or quantitative) crisis of divination might ever undermine the

---

[79] Cf. *De def. or.* 435F-436B. Lamprias explains that the world is provided with a limited amount (μέτρον) of substance and matter (οὐσία καὶ ὕλη, *ibid.* 424A) and is ordered by a single controlling principle (λόγος ἐγκρατής). Indeed, only one god suffices for impressing a perfect organization (διάταξις) on the cosmos; he acts through his intellectual power (νοῦν καὶ λόγον), as a master, a father (κύριος ἀπάντων καὶ πατήρ), or a commander (ἄρχοντα πρῶτον καὶ ἡγεμόνα, *ibid.* 426A-B).

belief in the providential and beneficial character of god, and in his very existence. Mantic operational dynamics belong to the world of becoming, which is regulated by the natural laws, and are thus subject to perpetual variations, due to the material components involved. In this context, god, the superior agent, eternal and uncontaminated, exerts slight variations on the sensible cosmos from afar, by making use of intermediaries and while always maintaining his transcendent status.

Since divination is grounded on a (strictly mediated) interaction between the divine and the material world, its contingent aspects need to be analysed within a wider metaphysical framework.

3.1. A 'likely account'

In the *Timaeus*, the ontological distinction between becoming and being accords with the epistemological distinction between the plausible knowledge of the earthly reality and the perfect knowledge of being[80]. The correspondences between an ontological and an epistemological kind of dualism are expressed in the twofold kind of explanation proposed in this Platonic dialogue (of which *Ti.* 29b-d is the classical *locus*), and crystallized in the long-debated expressions of 'εἰκὼς μῦθος' and 'εἰκὼς λόγος'.

Some relevant studies on the topic can help us to visualize the possible relation between the two fundamental concepts of 'μῦθος' and 'λόγος', and to better understand the notion of 'εἰκὼς' itself – a word that (with all its derivatives) is largely employed by Plutarch in his writings.

According to the recent research of Myles Burnyeat[81], the *Timaeus* can be seen as a combination and harmonization of a rational account (λόγος) and a mythical narrative (μῦθος). Burnyeat stresses that in this Platonic dialogue the traditional distinction between *mythos* and *logos* appears to be overcome. Indeed, the cosmological explanation that it contains is simultaneously a "likely / probable myth" (εἰκὼς μῦθος) *and* a rational account (λόγος), for which reason it can be defined with the expression of "rational / reasonable myth".

Gabor Betegh[82], starting from Burnyeat's results, notes that in the phrases 'εἰκὼς λόγος' and 'εἰκὼς μῦθος' the adjective 'εἰκὼς' not only points to a positive explanatory model with which every account of the natural world should comply, but also fixes its highest possible standard of certainty and accuracy. 'Εἰκὼς' has both a positive *and* a limitative value: it conveys the idea that the world is a divine product, which god wants to be as good as possible, and is produced to be *likely* with respect to its ideal model.

---

[80] Cf. *Quaest. Plat.* 3,1002B-C; Plato, *Ti.* 27d-28b.
[81] Burnyeat (2005).
[82] Betegh (2010).

Accordingly, the word helps to testify to a teleological scheme that holds on reality and orients the cosmos towards perfection.

Jenny Bryan, in her book on *Likeness and Likelihood in the Presocratics and Plato*[83], clarifies that the cosmology of the *Timaeus* has to be intended as 'εἰκώς', but neither because it is a deficient account of the sensible world, nor because it reveals the unstable nature of the cosmos. Rather, the word 'likely' expresses that the world was created as a likeness (εἰκών) of a transcendent paradigm: the 'representative' λόγος of the *Timaeus* is 'likely' since it depicts the material cosmos as an image of the perfect, divine model. Therefore, the word firstly refers to this intrinsically *positive* kind of relation[84].

When applying these results to Plutarch's works, the notion of 'εἰκώς' similarly appears to identify a positive paradigm and norm for natural enquiry, while suggesting, on the other hand, the hypothetical character to which any account of the physical world is nevertheless confined. Plutarch's anti-dogmatic spirit also draws its nourishment from Plato's *Timaeus*: any scientific discourse on the physical realm is constitutively inferior to those concerning the ideal world. He derives from the *Timaeus*[85], indeed, the ontological-epistemological partition between the realm of becoming (τὸ γιγνόμενον) and opinion (δόξα), and the realm of being (τὸ ὄν) and science (ἐπιστήμη). When transcending the domain of opinion, likelihood and probability, and moving up to the domain of science, human understanding shows its constitutive flaws. There, suspension of judgement intervenes, as an act of piety and respect towards the divine (εὐσέβεια, σεμνότης, εὐλάβεια, ἀσφάλεια)[86].

As Jan Opsomer has masterfully explained, Plutarch often displays a 'sceptical' spirit and an aporetic-zetetic approach, in accordance with Academic epistemological standards. It is also from the *Timaeus* that he draws his 'sceptical' epistemological framework for the study of nature, according to which it is impossible to investigate back into the very primary and fundamental elements of knowledge – a field where suspension of judgement (ἐποχή) needs to be applied. What is important is that truth *exists* for Plutarch, and it is rational and intelligible in principle, but human reason, constitutively weak and limited, is mostly prevented from accessing it[87].

It is significant to remind that in *De defectu oraculorum* Lamprias, applying the standard of plausibility to the explanation of earthly phenomena, suggests that the inquiries regarding the physical world should be

---

[83] Bryan (2012) ch. 3.
[84] Cf. Plato, *Ti.* 29b-d.
[85] Cf. *ibid.* 27d-29d.
[86] Cf. *De sera num.* 549E; in this regard cf. Opsomer (1998) 178-184.
[87] Cf. Opsomer (1998) 178-184. See also *supra* 158.

guided by 'reasonable probability'[88]. Furthermore, he explicitly admits his Academic affiliation[89], while stressing the importance of caution (ἀσφά-λεια) in complex questions on the physical world. His approach may be revealing of Plutarch's own 'Academic spirit': the Chaeronean indeed conceives the Socratic-aporetic attitude as central to philosophical reflection, and suspension of judgement (ἐποχή) as a precious tool to identify a wise 'middle path' between the extremes of Epicureanism and Stoicism.

Plutarch's sceptical attitude is reflected in the compositional techniques that he adopts in his works, and emerges with greatest evidence in his dialogues. In particular, as confirmed by the analysis of the Delphic dialogues made in the previous chapters of this study, the dialogue form is the perfect means of expression for Plutarch's sceptical attitude: it is indeed functional for displaying his conception of philosophical investigation as a shared, relentless and potentially never-ending research, in which intelligent questioning and educated contending play a major role. Furthermore, he often resorts to the technique of arguing *'pro et contra' (in utramque partem disputare*[90]); this is adopted not just in the Delphic dialogues, but also in other kinds of writings – such as *quaestiones*, scientific writings, polemical treatises. Following his master Plato, Plutarch frequently introduces myths and analogies, thus structuring his writings as a combination of logical argument (λόγος) and myth (μῦθος) – exactly like in *De defectu oraculorum*, where rational claims as well as mythical narratives are proposed in order to prove the existence and nature of the demons[91]. Several of the works of the Chaeronean are built on a complementarity or synergy between myth and rational enquiry: explanations result from an accurate blending of these two elements – which helps to provide a cautious and tentative, softened, imagistic and not-definitive account of the problems debated.

This is clearly manifest in those of his dialogues devoted to the topics of demonology, such as *De facie in orbe Lunae* and *De genio Socratis*. *De facie*, with its complex astronomical arguments[92], as well as with its concluding mythological narrative, shows the path leading from physics to metaphysics: the knowledge of earthly phenomena finds its completion in the apprehension of the divine. In other words, sensory knowledge is the necessary starting point for the knowledge of the highest being. In *De genio* the possibility of overcoming the limits imposed by suspension of judgement, thus approaching somehow a superior level knowledge, is

---

[88] Cf. *De def. or.* 430B.

[89] Cf. *ibid.* 431A.

[90] Cf. for instance *De Stoic. rep.* 1037B: πρὸς τὰ ἐναντία ἐπιχειρεῖν.

[91] Cf. *De def. or.* 421A: ἐπεὶ δὲ μύθων καὶ λόγων ἀναμεμιγμένων κρατὴρ ἐν μέσῳ πρόκειται.

[92] For an attentive analysis of the astronomical arguments in *De facie*, see Donini (1988).

explicitly stated: in their peculiar, veiled and allusive way, myths almost *touch* the truth (καὶ γὰρ εἰ μὴ λίαν ἀκριβῶς, ἀλλ᾽ ἔστιν ὅπῃ ψαύει τῆς ἀληθείας καὶ τὸ μυθῶδες)[93].

3.2. Some remarks on the practical dynamics of Delphic divination

The practical dynamics of divination, as described in the Delphic dialogues, present interesting points of contact with some concepts and passages of the *Timaeus*, especially considering its third part (69a-92c). The last section of the *Timaeus* is devoted to the description of complex natural structures, produced from the synergy of the divine-intelligent and the auxiliary-necessary cause. Intelligence defines the general purpose, while necessity determines the peculiar properties of the material elements involved. Necessity tends to exert its resistance against the action of the primary cause, and by so doing it impairs the level of perfection of the cosmos.

The relevant correspondences between the *Timaeus* and Plutarch that I have noted and intend to stress in the present section concern: (1) the analogy between vision and divination; (2) the mantic faculty; (3) the distinction between two kinds of divination; (4) the hypothesis of a plurality of worlds.

(1) With regard to divination, one of the clearest points of contact between Plato and Plutarch is the parallelism that can be established between the explanation of the physiology of vision in the *Timaeus*[94], and the psychology of divination in *De defectu oraculorum*[95]. The similarity between these accounts is two-folded. First, both phenomena are explained according to the principles 'like acts on like' and 'like is known by like' (based on the συγγένεια of the two components involved). As the sunlight acts on the light of the eye[96], in the same way the *pneûma* acts on the *irrational* part of the Pythia's soul – with which it has a special affinity – and stimulates its natural prophetic faculty[97]. Second, both phenomena are based on, and display with great evidence, the simultaneous presence of two different hierarchical causal levels: one material, the other transcendent.

In the *Timaeus*, sight and hearing are the two most fundamental senses that give us the capacity to contemplate the rationality of the universe, by also revealing the contrast between the purpose of reason and the

---

[93] Cf. *De genio Socr.* 589F-590A.
[94] Cf. Plato, *Ti.* 42e-47e.
[95] Cf. *De def. or.* 433D.
[96] Cf. Plato, *Ti.* 45c-d.
[97] Cf. Lamprias' intervention in *De def. or.* 433A-B.

limitations exerted by the natural power of necessity inherent in matter[98]. Similarly, in Plutarch's Delphic dialogues, the dynamics of divination – ultimately caused by the god – come to pass necessarily in the material world; this means that the correct functioning of prophecy depends on material factors and conditions, and is subject to failure and to decay.

Furthermore, Lamprias stresses that it is exactly according to the design of reason and providence (κατὰ λόγον καὶ πρόνοιαν) that we have been endowed with the senses of sight and hearing[99]. Vision indeed results from the combination (συγκεραννυμένη) of the light of the eye with the clearness of the sun; although the functioning of our sensory faculties responds to material factors and dynamics, it is fundamental to stress that the very senses of sight and hearing are bestowed on humankind according to a superior rational project[100].

If taken together, the two aspects of this parallelism (i.e., the similarity of the substance of the patient and agent, and the double causation theory) effectively highlight the innate (σύμφυτον[101]) character of the faculty of vision as well as of that of divination. Both sight and prophecy exploit innate human faculties, thus emerge as natural gifts bestowed on us according to an intelligent design and with a precise purpose: to enable us to appreciate the order and rationality of the universe, as well as the (at least partly predictable) providential plan underlying the earthly events.

(2) If we focus on the section of the *Timaeus* explicitly devoted to divination[102], we will find some notions that turn extremely useful in order to better understand Plutarch's own view. In both Timaeus' speech and Plutarch's dialogues, the presence of a cosmic plan underlying the divinatory activity is confirmed by the treatment of the notions of 'mantic faculty' (μαντικόν) and 'enthusiasm' (ἐνθουσιασμός).

In the *Timaeus*, the faculty of divination (τὸ μαντεῖον) is associated to a precise bodily organ: the liver[103]. This organ has two main functions. First, it creates a connection between the rational and the appetitive soul, and changes its physical status and shape according to the commands coming

---

[98] Cf. Brisson (1997).

[99] Cf. *De def. or.* 436C-D.

[100] Cf. Plato, *Resp.* 6,507c-508d.

[101] *De def. or.* 432C.

[102] Cf. Plato, *Ti.* 71a-72c. Peter Struck has written two interesting articles on the topic of divination in Plato: cf. Struck (2003), esp. 133-135, and Struck (2013). In the former, he investigates the connections between the material (signifier) and the immaterial (signified), especially in dream divination; in the latter, he presents Plato's use of the concept of 'divination' as a metaphor for a kind of intuitive and non-discursive knowledge, acquired in a state of consciousness – which is a topic that he has further developed and explored also in other authors, in his recent monographical work (Struck, 2016).

[103] Cf. Plato, *Ti.* 71a-b.

from the reason. Deaf to rational persuasion, it is rather moulded by reason, as it was clay. The liver was indeed made bright so that it could receive rational thoughts (διανοήματα, τύποι) and translate them, like a mirror (οἶον ἐν κατόπτρῳ), into 'images and phantasms' understandable by the lower part of the soul (such 'images and phantasms', εἴδωλα καὶ φαντάσματα, are images of εἰκόνες, so three times far from the truth). Second, when the liver does not share in reason and wisdom (ἐπειδὴ λόγου καὶ φρονήσεως οὐ μετεῖχε), it becomes calm and serene, and thus practices divination (μαντείᾳ χρωμένην). Divination was assigned to the appetitive part of the soul (ἐπιθυμητικόν), exactly in order to redeem and ennoble it, so that it could somehow grasp the truth (ἵνα ἀληθείας πῃ προσάπτοιτο)[104].

In the first place, it is important to note that, in this description, divination emerges as an irrational activity, appointed to the part of the soul devoid of reason (ἀφροσύνῃ [...] ἀνθρωπίνῃ). This model envisions rationality and divination as mutually exclusive – an opposition on which is grounded the distinction between inspired and technical prophecy. Divination is not practised when someone is in full possession of his faculties, but when his rational understanding is weakened by sleep, illness, prophetic enthusiasm. In these circumstances, one undergoes a radical change of status (παραλλάξας)[105].

The messages and contents received through divination and enthusiasm (ὑπὸ τῆς μαντικῆς τε καὶ ἐνθουσιαστικῆς φύσεως) can be recalled and interpreted only in a state of lucidity, by means of memory (ἀναμνησθέντα) and logical reasoning (λογισμῷ). This kind of hermeneutic activity is also performed by appointed professionals – namely, prophets (προφῆται), distinct from diviners (μάντεις) – who are the interpreters (ὑποκριταί) of the enigmatic messages and visions revealed through inspired divination[106]. In other words, while someone is in an altered state of mind, and directly receives prophetic words and images, he can neither judge nor understand what he is experiencing, since his intellectual capacity (φρόνησις) is diverted from its usual function. Instead, the authentic meaning of the revealed message can be decoded only through a rational process of interpretation. Revelation and interpretation are thus two clearly distinct activities.

As I think, although Plutarch does not inherit Plato's anatomical disposition of the parts of the soul, he seems to re-elaborate and introduce some aspects of Timaeus' description in his own theory of divination – in particular of Delphic oracular divination. In the first place Plutarch, although he does not connect the function of divination to any bodily location, similarly ascribes it to the irrational part of the soul and defines

---

[104] Cf. *ibid.* 71d-e.
[105] Cf. *ibid.* 71e.
[106] Cf. *ibid.* 72a-b.

the mantic faculty as an innate, irrational, indeterminate and receptive 'psychological engine'. Moreover, he reintroduces the reflective virtue of the liver in his description of the Pythia (especially in *De Pythiae oraculis*): similarly to what has been said about the liver, she works as a 'prophetic mirror', which needs to be bright and sharp in order to properly reflect Apollo's thoughts and instructions, and to correctly perform her mediating role – in the same way as the moon reflects the light of the sun[107].

Plutarch also employs the very word 'phantasms' (φαντασίαι) and its derivatives (φανταστικόν, φαντασίαι) – used by Plato to indicate the 'images' of the rational thoughts when reflected on the liver – in order to account for various aspects of the mantic activity[108]. The image-creating faculty of *phantasia* is a pivotal notion within the psychological dynamics underlying oracular prophecy, which is performed exactly in an enthusiastic and fantastic way (ἐνθουσιαστικῶς [...] καὶ φαντασιαστικῶς)[109]. Oracular prophecy involves representations – similar to images of dreams and memories –, intended as mental tokens that do not come from a current and concomitant sensory perception[110].

Plutarch explains this psychological process by stressing that an affection (πάθος) may also arise in our imaginative soul (τῷ φανταστικῷ τῆς ψυχῆς) independently from actual perception (αἴσθησις), thus giving us the impression of perceiving sounds and images, just like in dreams[111]. I would like to remind that Aristotle ascribes both memory and imagination to the same part of the soul[112] – distinct from perception, which by contrast is always true. Imagination encloses a repertoire of representations, which

---

[107] Cf. *De def. or.* 416E. The 'receptive' role of the Pythia and the similitude between her and the moon also recall the qualification of the moon in *De facie* 943F-944A, where it is characterised by a mixed substance (neither dense nor subtle) that makes it 'receptive of soul' (ψυχῆς δεκτικόν). These characteristics and analogies have been analysed in greater detail in the first chapter of the present book.

[108] Cf. *De def. or.* 432B-D.

[109] Cf. *ibid.* 433C.

[110] Cf. *ibid.* 438A. It is useful to remind that the word 'φαντασία' is not present in *De genio Socratis*. It is worth noting nevertheless that in *De genio* demonic communication employs an expressive mode that somehow *reveals* the importance of imagination. In this regard, as I believe, we should look at the use of 'δόξα' and its derivatives: Theanor *had the impression* to hear a voice (ἀκοῦσαι δὲ φωνῆς ἔδοξα, 585F); *impressions* or understandings (δόξας καὶ νοήσεις) of speeches in dream give us the *impression* of hearing someone talking (588D); Timarchus, as soon as he descended into Trophonius' cave, had the *impression* (δόξα) to be struck on his head (590B).

[111] Cf. *Cor.* 32, 3. The impression of having heard a voice is what held back Socrates, according to what he declares in Plato, *Phdr.* 242c: τινα φωνὴν ἔδοξα αὐτόθεν ἀκοῦσαι.

[112] Cf. Aristoteles, *Mem.* 450a22.

are recalled to perform cognitive and practical activities[113]. Plutarch may have endorsed a similar conception of imagination – declined in a sceptical, anti-Stoic sense – in order to reject the absolute epistemological certainty that the Stoics attributed to cataleptic impression (φαντασία καταληπτική)[114].

The notion of 'enthusiasm' corresponds to another important point of connection between Timaeus' account of divination and the conceptual structure emerging from Plutarch's Delphic dialogues: in both cases, enthusiasm is a radical switch from rationality to irrationality that corresponds with a complete psycho-physical overturn[115]. But while for Plato – at least if we rely on his notorious account in the *Phaedrus* – enthusiasm is a form of divine 'possession' (κατοκωχή)[116], Plutarch instead, radicalising Plato's ontological dualism between the human-material level and divine-transcendent level, rejects the idea that any god would ever enter into a human body, and posits some specific intermediary factors (such as the *pneûma* or the demons) to bridge the gap between the god and the prophet(ess).

(3) Plato and Plutarch also agree on the existence of two different kinds of divination: the one independent-individual, and the other oracular-institutional. Although the *Timaeus* does not deal with this latter kind of mantic, I think that the distinction that Plutarch posits between oracular and individual prophecy nevertheless receives the influence of that dialogue. As my analysis of *De genio Socratis* has helped to show, individual and oracular divination are intrinsically different, for their respective nature, aims, and especially for the psychic parts involved. In order to describe the Socratic, independent kind of mantic, Plutarch resumes the Platonic concept of individual demon (δαίμων) – which in the *Timaeus*, as already explained, is said to correspond to the supreme part of human soul[117] – and identifies it with intellect (νοῦς). Intellect in *De genio Socratis* is conceived as a divine element sharply distinct from the rest of the soul, which, if rendered pure through an authentic philosophical life and a proper education (παιδεία), will receive direct indications from superior powers. As I believe, the main discriminating factor between Socrates (or any other practitioner of 'individual divination') and the Pythia lies in the notion of παιδεία, which is fundamental in *De genio Socratis*[118]. Individual divination

---

[113] Cf. Aristoteles, *de An.* 3,3,428a16-b10; 429a4-7.

[114] For a comparison with the Stoic position on this theme, see Watson (1988). For an account of the scientific foundation of divination for the Stoics, see Hankinson (1988).

[115] Cf. *De def. or.* 432D: διαθέσει τοῦ σώματος ἐν μεταβολῇ γιγνόμενον, ὃν ἐνθουσιασμὸν καλοῦμεν; Plato, *Ti.* 71e: τινα ἐνθουσιασμὸν παραλλάξας.

[116] Cf. Plato, *Phdr.* 245a.

[117] Cf. Plato, *Ti.* 90a: περὶ τοῦ κυριωτάτου [...] ψυχῆς.

[118] In the speech of Theocritus the diviner, we can find a sort of distinction between what

is a form of 'direct education' that the gods reserve for the wisest and most virtuous of us; in this way, these privileged individuals will receive in the sublime part of their soul the messages coming from above, instructive also with regard to *practical* life. The sage, who has acquired this sublime knowledge, shares it with other humans – exactly like Socrates did – in order to improve their moral and intellectual status. Nevertheless, this divine 'superior educational program' directly addresses those who have *already* perfected their philosophical education and furthered their own intellectual development, which, according to Plutarch, goes hand in hand with moral improvement. This is the very pre-condition for receiving the divine *paideia*, through demonic words 'made of light'.

The requisites and goals of individual divination are hence different from those of oracular divination – which is especially clear if we focus on the Delphic prophetic human medium, who significantly works as the lively 'instrument' (ὄργανον) of divination: the Pythia. As remarked in my analysis of *De Pythiae oraculis*, the Delphic priestess is a simple peasant, inexperienced and uneducated when she first enters into the shrine, and devoid of any knowledge when she comes into conjunction with the god[119]. The ritual purity required from the prophetess, in order that she properly fulfils the prophetic function, simply involves no contact with strangers or other contaminating factors, and – at least according to what we can infer from Plutarch's Delphic dialogues – it lacks any

---

we might call a 'practical' and a 'theoretical' kind of wisdom. The former is embodied by Charon: he is not a *philosophos* and lacks a sophisticated *paideia*; nevertheless, he behaves heroically and displays a natural inclination to pursue the good, while also following the laws (576D). The latter is embodied by Epameinondas, who considers himself superior in virtue to all the others because of his *paideia* (ἁπάντων τῷ πεπαιδεῦσθαι πρὸς ἀρετὴν ἀξιῶν, 576E), and patiently waits for the right moment (καιρός) to intervene. As Simmias reminds, Plato – when he solved the 'strange, geometrical oracle' that Apollo gave to the Delians – explained that the god intended to scold the Greeks for their lack of education (παιδεία vs. ἀμαθία, 579C). Further, Simmias says that the life-guide that Socrates found in his own soul was superior to the teachings of many instructors and educators (μυρίων διδασκάλων καὶ παιδαγωγῶν, 589F). Galaxidorus defines Socrates the real philosopher, whose education (παιδεία) and reasoning (λόγος) were authentically philosophical in character. The demonic voice in the mythological narrative explains that the souls that in the afterlife move in an orderly manner have received in life a good philosophical education (διὰτροφὴν καὶ παίδευσιν ἀστείαν, 592A), which made them obedient to the 'bridle' (by contrast, those moving unevenly are characterised by ἀπαιδευσία, 592B). Finally, according to Theanor, the best among humans are defined as 'worthy of a superior kind of education' (ἰδίας τινὸς καὶ περιττῆς παιδαγωγίας ἀξιοῦσι, 593B) – which directly points to the kind of 'divine education' received by chosen, wise, 'educated' individuals from the intelligible realm through demonic signs.

[119] Cf. *De Pyth. or.* 408C: οὔτ'ἀπὸ τέχνης οὐδὲν οὔτ'ἀπ'ἄλλης τινὸς ἐμπειρίας καὶ δυνάμεως ἐπιφερομένη κάτεισιν εἰς τὸ χρηστήριον.

kind of more sophisticated philosophical-ethical implications. Suffice it to recall what Lamprias explains in *De defectu oraculorum* about the Pythia: her body must be chaste (ἁγνὸν τὸ σῶμα), and her life must exclude any external contact, mixture or influence (τὸν βίον ὅλως ἀνεπίμικτον ἀλλοδαπαῖς καὶ ἄθικτον ὁμιλίαις φυλάττουσι[120]). Ammonius also reminds that the Pythia is compelled to be 'pure and chaste' (ἁγνὴν διὰ βίου καὶ καθαρεύουσαν[121]) throughout her entire life[122].

(4) Finally, the topic of the plurality of worlds – which, following Lamprias' expression, Plato presents in an 'enigmatic way' (αἰνιγματώδη μετ'εὐλαβείας[123]) – is introduced in *De defectu oraculorum* as a possible proof for the existence of demons as non incarnated souls who, with their escape to other worlds, might have caused the oracular decline. The reference to the enigmatic character of Plato's hypothesis is highly significant, since in Plutarch's time the alleged obscurity of Plato's words was a primary trigger for the exegetical reading of his dialogues[124]. Employing the *Timaeus* hypothesis of a plurality of worlds helps Plutarch to acknowledge the fact that the action of god, together with divination and providence (θεός, μαντική, πρόνοια), could also extend to more than one world. This is mainly justified by the inter-relational and non self-reflective character of god's power, providence and virtues (such as δικαιοσύνη and φιλία[125]).

4. The 'matter' of divination

In order to reconstruct Plutarch's cosmological theory, and then to better understand the role of the material agents involved in divination (such as the Pythia, the sacrificial animals, the prophetic *pneûma*), I believe that it is fundamental to consider his original elaboration of the Platonic concept of 'receptacle' (χώρα).

Plutarch tends to assimilate together the notions of '*chóra*' and 'matter': in *De animae procreatione in Timaeo* he explains that Plato called matter 'mother', 'nurse' (ὁ γὰρ Πλάτων μητέρα μὲν καὶ τιθήνην καλεῖ τὴν ὕλην[126])

---

[120] *De def. or.* 438C.

[121] *Ibid.* 435C-D.

[122] Note that the word 'ἁγνός', which is used to express the *ritual* purity of the Pythia, occurs both in *De Pythiae* and *De defectu*, but is never employed in *De genio Socratis*, not even with regard to Socrates' characteristics. Other occurrences of the word in the Delphic dialogues are found in: *De Pyth. or.* 397B; 402C (twice, in two quotations from Skythinos and Simonides); *De def. or.* 417B; 417E; 421C; 431E.

[123] *De def. or.* 420E-F.

[124] Cf. *supra* 60. Konrat Ziegler indeed considers this discussion in *De defectu* (§§ 22-27: 421E-425B) as a sort of section of a commentary to the *Timaeus* – cf. Ziegler (1964) 112.

[125] Cf. *De def. or.* 423D and *supra* 80.

[126] *De an procr.* 1015D; cf. Plato, *Ti.* 50d-52d.

and also *chôra*, which is the seat and receptacle (χώραν τε γὰρ καλεῖ τὴν ὕλην ὥσπερ ἕδραν ἔστιν ὅτε καὶ ὑποδοχήν[127]). Another reference to this identification is found in *De Iside et Osiride*, in particular in the phrase '*chôra* and matter' (χώρα καὶ ὕλη[128]), where the conjunction 'and' clearly has an identification value.

In *De defectu oraculorum* Plutarch apparently employs the couple of terms 'matter and nature' (ὕλη καὶ φύσις) to refer to the *chôra*. At a closer look, the concept of matter in *De defectu* shows two different aspects: on the one hand it is a neutral substrate or 'receptacle' (ὑποκείμενον)[129]; on the other hand, it has an unusual *destructive* qualification, when associated with matter and necessity[130]. Accordingly, matter is there defined as an active principle of privation (στέρησις) and destruction (φθορά) that causes things to reverse to an earlier state or to dissolve: god, who is not omnipotent, can do nothing against the necessity (ἀνάγκη) inherent in matter, which is itself responsible for the oracular decline[131]. This interpretation constitutes a problem in Plutarch's account, since this is the only place where matter receives such an active-destructive characterization.

I nevertheless want to point out that the destructive power ascribed to matter in this passage closely recalls the character of Typho in *De Iside et Osiride*, identified with a material force that cyclically destroys the body of Osiris (while Isis reassembles it again). Indeed, while Osiris' immanent facet is subject to dismemberment, his soul, transcendent and unchangeable, remains always uncorrupted[132].

Following Lamprias' words, the substance (οὐσία) and power (δύναμις) of earthly and (necessarily) perishable goods that god bestows on humankind should be looked for (ζητεῖν) within the material world (ἐν τῇ φύσει καὶ τῇ ὕλη) – which is never exempt from change and destruction. Instead, the *origin* (ἀρχή) of these material gifts corresponds with the god, and is therefore immutable and divine. The same holds true when applied to divination. As Typho (i.e., the negative power inherent in matter) does not always overpower the principle of order and rationality, but periodically destroys the established harmony, and can be never removed

---

[127] *De an procr.* 1024C.

[128] *De Is. et Os.* 372E-F; see Ferrari (1996a). As it is known, the first explicit association between the notion of '*chôra*' and that of 'matter' is found in Aristoteles, *Ph.* 6,2,209; in Plutarch's era it was commonly adopted by Middle-Platonists (cf. Alcinous, 162, 29-31).

[129] Cf. *De def. or.* 414F-415A.

[130] Cf. *supra* 77-78.

[131] Cf. *De def. or.* 414D.

[132] Cf. *De Is. et Os.* 373A: τὸ γὰρ ὂν καὶ νοητὸν καὶ ἀγαθὸν φθορᾶς καὶ μεταβολῆς κρεῖττόν ἐστιν. Cf. *supra* 78: 'unqualified matter' (ἄποιος ὕλη).

completely[133], in the same way historical-material crises may recursively overwhelm the practice of divination, without nevertheless ever destroying its metaphysical foundation.

As the section of my work regarding the 'double causation theory' has shown[134], Plutarch firmly believes that a properly scientific understanding of natural phenomena requires to grasp both levels of causality that are simultaneously at work behind them: first, the divine-intelligible level – divided into a final (τὸ δι'ὅ) and an efficient cause (ὑφ'οὗ); second, the necessary-physical level – divided into a material (τὸ ἐξ'ὧν) and an instrumental cause (δι'ὧν)[135].

This model, applied to the mantic phenomenon, helps to justify the fluctuations that affect divination and modify the quality and quantity of the oracles[136]. Divination is indeed necessarily subject to change as every earthly thing, and its functioning depends on the complex net of material factors and agents that – by working in synergy – determine its development and outcomes. At the same time, this epistemic paradigm of double causation helps to ensure the divine origin of prophecy, since god's intervention – the admission of which, as Ammonius states in *De defectu oraculorum*, makes the prophetic art *really* rational and divine – provides its first principle (ἀρχή) and 'higher cause'[137].

The bifurcation of the first level of causality with regard to divination is neither made explicit in *De defectu*, nor in any other of the Delphic dialogues; while the god seems to correspond to the efficient cause, the final cause may correspond to his desire to sustain humankind through the oracle – while stimulating the intellectual curiosity of some of us[138]. The bifurcation of the second level of causality is instead clearly stated: the

---

[133] Cf. *De Is. et Os.* 368D.

[134] Cf. *supra* 98.

[135] For this division cf. *Quaest. conv.* 720E, where Plutarch distinguishes between two kinds of physical causes (δι'ἀνάγκης φύσει τῶν αἰτιῶν): 'ὑλικαί' and 'ὀργανικαί'. Michiel Meeusen has demonstrated that the scientific paradigm of the double causality also characterises the explanations proposed in Plutarch's *Quaestiones naturales*; he therefore re-evaluates this work and emphasises the soundness and coherence of Plutarch's scientific approach – cf. Meeusen (2013).

[136] I wish to remind in this regard that the word 'oracle' has both the meaning of 'prophetic utterance' and 'prophetic shrine'.

[137] Cf. *De def. or.* 436E-437A: οὐ γὰρ ἄθεον ποιοῦμεν οὐδ' ἄλογον τὴν μαντικήν, ὕλην μὲν αὐτῇ τὴν ψυχὴν τοῦ ἀνθρώπου τὸ δ' ἐνθουσιαστικὸν πνεῦμα καὶ τὴν ἀναθυμίασιν οἷον ὀργάνῳ [ἢ] πλῆκτρον ἀποδιδόντες.

[138] Cf. *De E* 384E-F. The presence of a final and an efficient cause might be connected with the *Timaeus*, where these two causes – if we accept Thomas Johansen's account developed in Johansen (2008) esp. 474-475 – can be expressed as follows: the first with the word 'αἰτία', as god's desire to make the world as good as possible; the second with the word 'αἴτιον', as god himself, the maker of the world.

priestess' soul, which is the matter (ὕλη) of divination, corresponds to the material cause; the prophetic *pneûma*, which is the plectrum (πλῆκτρον) hitting human soul as a musical instrument (οἷον ὀργάνῳ), corresponds to the instrumental cause.

In *De defectu oraculorum*[139], as I pointed out in my second chapter, the mantic practice is compared to the model of artistic creation. The prophetic episode represents a sort of divine work of art: the primary cause (κυριωτέρα ἀρχή, corresponding to τέχνη and λόγος) moves the inferior, necessary causes (ὑλικαὶ ἀρχαί) and operates through them. Exactly like an artistic production, the cosmopoietic process is articulated upon the following elements: the acting subject (ποιοῦντι καὶ κινοῦντι) and matter (ὑποκείμενον καὶ πάσχον)[140]. Although not explicitly stated, the paradigmatic-formal cause emerges from this relation, as the form or idea imposed by the demiurge on the priestess' soul. This 'moulding' action follows the laws of physical necessity that regulate bodily reactions (τὸ κατ' ἀνάγκην τοῖς τῶν σωμάτων ἀποτελούμενον πάθεσι), while always respecting the opportune time (καιρός) and right balance (μέτριον). Therefore, bearing in mind the paradigm of craftsmanship, the soul of the Pythia corresponds to the *matter* of divination; matter (in divination, as well as in the demiurgic act of the cosmogenesis) is indeed necessary for the manifestation of the divine project (ἔργον τοῦ νοήματος) – which otherwise would remain invisible (ἄδηλον), enclosed in the mind of the creator. In a way that is utterly similar to that of the cosmic material principle, the soul of the Pythia exerts its influence and contaminates the abstract model, thus introducing a variation (διαφορά) to the original plan[141].

4.1. The multiple characters of the Pythia

In order to prove the correspondences between Plutarch's cosmological and oracular-mantic conception – which is the main aim of the present chapter, as mentioned several times in the course of this book – it is essential to focus on the image of the Pythia, the protagonist of the divinatory session. In this paragraph, I intend to demonstrate that some typical features of the Delphic priestess directly recall precise metaphysical notions: first, the Platonic *chôra* – which, as we have seen, is assimilated by Plutarch to matter (ὕλη); second, the evil soul, unevenly moving matter, in *De animae procreatione*[142].

---

[139] Cf. *De def. or.* 435F-436A.

[140] Cf. the artistic production in Aristoteles, *Ph.* 2,3,195a6-34.

[141] Cf. *De Pyth. or.* 404C. Cf. also *supra* 41.

[142] Cf. *De an. procr.* 1016C: πλημμελῶς πάντα καὶ ἀτάκτως κινοῦσαν. For the *chôra* cf. Plato, *Ti.* 50d-52e; for the Pythia cf. *De def. or.* 430C; *De Pyth. or.* 404E. I anticipated this crucial parallelism in the first chapter of this work (cf. *supra* 46).

First, Plutarch's Pythia and the Platonic *chôra* share the feature of *neutrality*; they lack any inherent features (τῶν ἰδεῶν) and are ready to receive them from outside. This aspect is exemplified in the *Timaeus* by the metaphor of gold or other soft materials liable to be impressed and reshaped[143], or by that of the odourless base for perfumes[144]. Similarly to the Platonic receptacle, the soul of the Pythia needs to be characterless and pure in order to properly reflect the thoughts that Apollo wants to convey to humanity. Only if this condition is satisfied, she functions as an effective human intermediary, and the divine thoughts (νοήματα) that she conveys are contaminated to the least possible extent by her own nature and qualities.

I would like to point out that the Platonic receptacle can be also assimilated to a mirror, which remains unchanged by the different images that it reflects and mediates into the sensible world[145]. This aspect may also apply to the image and role of the Pythia, as a reliable mirror for the thoughts of god – a prerogative that, as we have seen, also characterises the organ of liver in Timaeus' account.

Second, the characteristics ascribed to the Pythia (especially considering *De Pythiae oraculis*) closely remind those of the precosmic soul in *De animae procreatione*. The erratic movements affecting the Pythia's soul (cf. σάλος[146]) recall the chaotic, irrational motions of the evil precosmic principle[147] – a parallelism reinforced by the analogy that Plutarch generally establishes between the human and the cosmic soul[148].

Plutarch describes the precosmic nature (φύσις) as an active disordered material principle (ψυχὴ γὰρ αἰτία κινήσεως καὶ ἀρχή), amorphous and incoherent, devoid of reason (νοῦς), animated by a senseless and disordered motion (ὑπὸ τῆς ἀνοήτου ταραττομένην αἰτίας), and characterized by manifold and changing passions (ἐν πάθεσι παντοδαποῖς καὶ μεταβολαῖς). It is brought to an ordered and a harmonic state (τάξεως καὶ συμφωνίας) by the demiurge, who mitigates its destructive power through rational persuasion (πειθώ)[149].

Similarly, relying on *De defectu oraculorum*[150], the Pythia appears to be affected by varying influences and disturbances, and to be at the

---

[143] Cf. Plato, *Ti.* 50a-b.

[144] Cf. *ibid.* 50e.

[145] Cf. Comford (1961); Mohr (2006).

[146] Cf. *De Pyth. or.* 404E; *De def. or.* 430C; 437C-D. Cf. also σάλος ψυχῆς in *Amatorius*. 758E; 763A.

[147] Cf. *De an. procr.* 1041B; 1014D-1015C; 1015E.

[148] Jan Opsomer has thoroughly analysed the complex implications of the analogy that Plutarch develops between the human and the cosmic psychical constitution in Opsomer (1994); cf. also Opsomer (2004).

[149] Cf. *De an. procr.* 1014B; 1015E-F.

[150] Cf. *De def. or.* 437C-D.

mercy of the irrational and passive part of her soul (παθητικόν) that is responsible for divination. She abdicates to her own rationality (λογιστικὸν καὶ φροντιστικόν[151]), while the *pneûma* paralyses her rational soul. The priestess is eventually brought from this state of disorder and a-rationality, to one of relative order, divinely created for the purpose of divination – a dynamics similar to the one according to which the evil world soul gets ordered by the demiurge[152]. She thus submits herself to the divine power of inspiration – an attitude that highlights a substantial difference between oracular divination and the controlled kind of individual (Socratic) mantic, which principally appeals, and resorts to, the most rational and divine part of human soul[153].

In oracular inspiration as well as in the creation of the cosmos, god exerts a non-constrictive, gentle action against the resistance of matter. As described in *De Pythiae oraculis*, enthusiasm is the combination (μεῖξις) of two distinct movements (κινήσεων δυοῖν): the external divine force and the intrinsic motions of the Pythia's *psychê*[154]. God inspires the prophetess indirectly, by creating representations (φαντασίαι) in her soul: she, as an active and non-indifferent material medium, reacts to this impulse according to her simple nature and limited knowledge[155]. In other words, in divination as well as in cosmogony, the design of god is not violently

---

[151] The apprehension of the future happens indeed in an irrational way (ἀσυλλογίστως, ἀλόγως, φαντασιαστικῶς); cf. *De def. or.* 432D; 433C.

[152] Cf. *De an. procr.* 1015E. Just like the precosmic soul, the Pythia has the inherent inclination – provided that the movements of her soul are not excessive nor vehemently contrary to it – of submitting herself to the 'ordering' action exerted by god, without nevertheless renouncing to her own intrinsic nature.

[153] Cf. *De Pyth. or.* 404E. In the *Timaeus*, an important reference to the concept of 'disorder' is found in a passage describing the agitation of the receptacle when it receives the forms impressed on it by the demiurge (cf. Plato, *Ti.* 52d-53a). According to the winnowing-basket analogy, the receptacle is described as unbalanced, oscillating (ταλαντουμένην) and agitated (σείεσθαι), by the traces of the elements, and shaking them in turn with its own movement. The similarity between this image and the psychic state of the Pythia has been pointed out by Frédirique Ildephonse in her excellent edition of the Pythian dialogues – cf. Ildefonse (2006) 47-48 of the *Introduction* and p. 297, n. 220.

I think it can be interesting to remind another crucial occurrence of the notion of 'disorder' in the *Timaeus*: when the inferior gods place the individual souls inside human bodies, the souls then start to move violently, shaking the entire body in an utterly disordered and irrational way (cf. Plato, *Ti.* 43a-b: βίᾳ δὲ ἐφέροντο καὶ ἔφερον, ὥστε τὸ μὲν ὅλον κινεῖσθαι ζῷον, ἀτάκτως μὴν ὅπῃ τύχοι προϊέναι καὶ ἀλόγως, τὰς ἐξ ἁπάσας κινήσεις ἔχον). The souls reach for their rational, mature state only when the interior revolutions become calm and controlled, and the mind aligns its spinning movement to that of the cosmos (cf. *ibid.* 44b: αἱ περίοδοι λαμβανόμεναι γαλήνης τὴν ἑαυτῶν ὁδὸν ἴωσι; [...] ἔμφρονα τὸν ἔχοντα αὐτὰς γιγνόμενον ἀποτελοῦσιν).

[154] Cf. *De Pyth. or.* 404F.

[155] Cf. *ibid.* 397C.

impressed, but is realized gently, through persuasion, while respecting the characters inherent to the 'raw material' involved[156].

Beside those of *'chôra'* and 'irrational soul', there is one ulterior image that I would like to signal, which could enhance our understanding of divination in Plutarch, in particular with regard to the notion of 'receptivity'. In *De Iside et Osiride*[157], Plutarch describes the lovely tension permanently moving Isis towards her spouse Osiris – who embodies the supreme principle of everything and the supreme good itself. Isis, as the feminine principle of nature and generation, is receptive, *dektikos* (τὸ τῆς φύσεως θῆλυ καὶ δεκτικὸν ἀπάσης γενέσεως) of shapes and forms (μορφὰς δέχεσθαι καὶ ἰδέας)[158]. Strikingly, in *De defectu oraculorum* the mantic faculty (μαντικόν) is equally defined 'receptive', *dektikon*, of phantasms and impressions (δεκτικὸν δὲ φαντασιῶν πάθεσι καὶ προαισθήσεων)[159].

Furthermore, Isis escapes from the evil power and tends towards the god Osiris, from which she receives 'effluxes and similarities' (ἀπορροὰς καὶ ὁμοιότητας); by these she is fecundated and thus engenders the earthly beings. In an utterly similar way, the Pythia gets out from a condition of irrationality and disorder, and tends towards the divine power of inspiration; she is 'fecundated' by divine thoughts, and accordingly 'gives birth' to the prophetic messages. This parallelism is reinforced by Plutarch's depiction of the Pythia as a simple, inexperienced bride, and by the hyerogamic character of her union with the god, to whom she surrenders her virginal soul[160].

5. Apollo and the oracle: from chaos to harmony

At this point, it can be fruitful to analyse the figure of the Pythia, who is the principal human agent of oracular divination, in connection with other material elements and conditions necessary for the prophetic inspiration to arise. The correct synergy of the accessory factors involved in Delphi

---

[156] As I have pointed out especially in my analysis of *De E apud Delphos*, Plutarch's god is transcendent, but can exert his influence within the material world. He is not omnipotent: every action that he performs in the contingent world must comply with the rules of physical necessity, while thus respecting the peculiarities (τέχνη καὶ δύναμις) of inanimate objects, as well as of human beings. This formulation – from Plutarch's perspective – helps to counteract the excesses of a complete mixing of the god within material reality (as in Stoicism), as well as his absolute withdrawal from the world (as in Epicureanism). By resorting to Plato's vision of the cosmos, Plutarch finds the *proper distance* between god and the sensible realm.

[157] Cf. *Is. et Os.* 372E-F.

[158] The reference here is again Plato's receptacle defined as a 'nurse' and 'all-receptive' (cf. Plato, *Ti.* 49a-51a).

[159] Cf. *De def. or.* 432D.

[160] Cf. *De Pyth. or.* 408C.

allows for the transmission of god's thoughts within the corruptible world: if these components are not properly harmonized among themselves, the divinatory act is subject to chaos and failure[161]. My analysis, aimed at understanding the broader significance and possible cosmological references of Delphic prophecy, will start from the consideration of animal sacrifice and will then take into account the notions of *pneûma*, *krâsis*, and *kairos*.

As Michiel Meuseen has very well shown in his recent contribution on Plutarch's physical problems[162], animals can work as "natural mediums": the correct understanding of their functions and properties contributes to our comprehension of the oblique messages that god wants to send us. Indeed, as he explains, "a deeper semantic is incorporated in natural phenomena" and the natural philosopher has the task of extrapolating the divine significance that they enclose[163].

We have seen in the previous chapters that all the phenomena connected to Delphic divination – with their puzzling character and intriguing appearance – manifest this principle to the highest degree. With specific regard to sacrificial animals, the trembling (σάλος, παλμός) affecting their whole body, accompanied by a quivering sound, and the exceptional agitated movement of the victim (cf. τὴν κίνησιν αὐτοῦ καὶ τὸν τρόμον[164]; σείσασθαι[165]) constitute an absolutely peculiar requisite, if compared to all other Greek sacrifices. This extraordinary event is a sure sign (βέβαιον σημεῖον) that the oracle is functioning correctly (χρηματίζειν[166]; θεμιστεύειν[167]).

Plutarch's reflection on animals and their psychology may help us to better understand the role that they play in Delphic divination[168]. He believes that the psychic constitutions of animals and humans are utterly similar – as shown by an important section of *De sollertia animalium*. There Autobulus, starting from the assumption that rationality goes together with sensation[169], explains that animals have sense-perception (αἴσθησις) and imagination (φαντασία) as well as some kind of opinion and

---

[161] From this, terrible outcomes can derive as shown in *De def. or.* 438A.
[162] Cf. Meeusen (2013).
[163] *Ibid.* 134.
[164] *De def. or.* 437A.
[165] *Ibid.* 437B.
[166] Cf. *ibid.* 435C: οὐ γὰρ ἀρκεῖ τὸ διασεῖσαι τὴν κεφαλὴν ὥσπερ ἐν ταῖς ἄλλαις θυσίαις, ἀλλὰ πᾶσι δεῖ τοῖς μέρεσι τὸν σάλον ὁμοῦ καὶ τὸν παλμὸν ἐγγενέσθαι μετὰ ψόφου τρομώδους.
[167] *Ibid.* 437B.
[168] Cf. *supra* 109-110. For the wider context of Plutarch's ethical reflection on animals, Barigazzi (1992) is very instructive.
[169] Cf. *De soll. an.* 960C-F.

reason (δόξα τις καὶ λογισμός)[170]. One supporting evidence that he provides for animal rationality is of extreme interest: precisely because animals have complex rational faculties (τὸ φρονεῖν καὶ διανοεῖσθαι καὶ λογίζεσθαι), they can be affected by madness. In a state of folly, the rational part is indeed confounded and agitated (ταραττομένης καὶ συγχεομένης[171]) and – similarly to what happens to human beings – their reflective, rational and mnemonic powers are out of place and damaged[172].

All this considered, I think we could hypothesise that the peculiar quivering motion experienced by animals in Delphi, when sprinkled with the holy water, might display a certain degree of similarity with the disturbances and the chaotic motions affecting the Pythia's soul, when uncontrolled and deprived of the rational ordering principle. Similarly to the priestess, indeed, animals need to be pure and sound in their body and soul. Under these condition, their 'vital principle' (ψυχή) can express its intrinsic kinetic power, and thus confer its uncontrolled motion to the whole body of the victim.

The special bodily reaction of animals signals that the proper time (καιρός) for consultation has come; this prerogative is in line with a general principle – fundamental in the Delphic dialogues – according to which every force expresses its natural effect in the appropriate moment (πᾶσα γὰρ δύναμις ὃ πέφυκε σὺν καιρῷ βέλτιον ἢ χεῖρον ἀποδίδωσι[173]). And only in the 'perfect moment', the *pneûma* fruitfully modifies the disposition (διάθεσις) of the Pythia's body and engenders a temperament (κρᾶσις) favourable for divination (provided that she is ready to prophesy)[174], by reawakening her prophetic faculty (φανταστικὴ καὶ μαντικὴ δύναμις) through the imaginative part of her soul (φανταστικὸν τῆς ψυχῆς)[175].

It is indeed extremely important to stress that both the imaginative part of the human and the world soul are in contact with the sensible substance. As for the human soul, in particular, Plutarch explains in *De virtute morali* that its irrational part (ἄλογον μέρος, τὸ παθητικόν, ταχαρῶδες) is responsible for the contact with the corporeal-sensible element and possesses kinetic, imaginative and perceptive faculties (κινητική, φανταστική, αἰσθητικὴ δύναμις). The irrational *psychê* arguably allows for the *pneûma*, as a *material* element engendered by the earth, to be transmitted from the body – with which it enters into direct contact – to the soul[176].

---

[170] Cf. *ibid.* 960D-E; cf. also *Gryllus* 987B.
[171] *De soll. an.* 963D-E.
[172] Cf. *ibid.* 963E.
[173] *De def. or.* 437B-C.
[174] Cf. *ibid.* 432C-D.
[175] Cf. *ibid.* 438A.
[176] Cf. *supra* 101 and 114.

The encounter and favourable mixture (κρᾶσις) between the *pneûma* and the soul also happens just in the 'appropriate time' (καιρός). In the framework of the complex set of meanings of *kairos* in ancient philosophical reflection, the acceptation that seems closer to Plutarch's use is to be found in Plato, where the notion of 'appropriate moment' is often linked to concepts conveying the sense of measure, balance, aptness (μέτριον, πρέπον, δέον). For the Chaeronean the notion of *kairos* also acquires a special importance with regard to moral virtue[177]. It may be interesting to remind that the concepts of 'enthusiasm' and 'decisive moment' appear together as strictly interconnected in a famous passage of Plutarch's *Life of Caesar*, when Cassius passes by the statue of Pompey and performs a superstitious gesture. Despite Cassius' Epicurean affiliation, that dramatic moment (ὁ καιρός) inspires in his heart enthusiasm and emotion, which suddenly come to replace his previous attitude, which was instead calm and reflective (ἐνθουσιασμὸν ἐνεποίει καὶ πάθος ἀντὶ τῶν προτέρων λογισμῶν)[178].

In oracular divination, when the balanced combination between the soul and the *pneûma* occurs at the right time, it gives rise to the prodigious phenomenon of divine inspiration. Demigods – similarly to the inferior gods in the creation of the cosmos – partake in this process, by facilitating the fruitful encounter between the prophetic *pneûma* and the Pythia's soul and by harmonizing their combination in order to produce a propitious mixture. The demons engender the harmonic combination by removing (ἀφαιροῦντας) all the excessive elements that are 'ecstatic', 'disturbing' and 'turbulent' (τὸ ἄγαν ἐκστατικόν [...] ταρακτικόν [...] κινητικόν). In this regard I would like to stress that this harmonizing process strictly resembles those performed at the universal level by the god, who incessantly presides over the cosmic *harmonia*, and at the individual level by us, who must regulate our psychic balance in order to realize the end of moral virtue. I also think that the terms employed to describe the excessive elements removed by the demons are now better understandable in the light of Plutarch's psychological account, reconstructed in the first paragraphs of the present chapter[179]: they indeed pertain to the disordered and unbalanced irrational psychic component and are opposed to the favourable and propitious ones that the demons introduce (καταμιγνύντας) in order to create the right temperament for prophetic enthusiasm[180].

---

[177] Cf. *De virt. mor.* 444B: τὴν δ᾽ ὁρμὴν τῷ πάθει ποιεῖ τὸ ἦθος, λόγου δεομένην ὁρίζοντος, ὅπως μετρία παρῇ καὶ μήθ᾽ ὑπερβάλλῃ μήτ᾽ ἐγκαταλείπῃ τὸν καιρόν.

[178] Cf. *Caes.* 6. Interestingly, Plutarch states that the murderous act was attracted to the place by some divine power (δαίμονός τινος).

[179] Cf. *supra* 180-182.

[180] Cf. *De def. or.* 437A-438A.

From the character and nature of the demons' action it is possible to infer that the mixture between the human soul and the *pneûma* in divination is a sort of 'harmonic and complete union' (δι' ὅλων κρᾶσις). This image can be fruitfully paralleled to other passages in Plutarch's works that involve the notion of '*krâsis*'. First of all, this notion is central in moral virtue, where it refers to the order that reason imposes on passions; other interesting fields of application range from the explanation of natural phenomena to the definition of marital union.

Jacques Boulogne, who has explored the homogeneity of the concept of '*krâsis*' in various fields of Plutarch's reflection[181], explains, with reference to the moral theory of *De virtute morali*, that "la crase implique des dosages calculés sur le modèle de l'harmonie musicale, qui réunit en un tout et sans discordance les notes situées aux deux extrémités de la gamme"[182]. According to this principle, the irrational element, contributing to the psychic harmony, is indispensable for moral virtue; reason does not abolish passions, but balances them with their opposites. Christian Froidefond has similarly stressed the musical character of the psychic harmony in Plutarch – an aspect that can be likely found in neo-Pythagorean treatises[183].

Similarly, in *De primo frigido* Plutarch, while discussing the balance between hot and cold in the world, underlines god's harmonic and musical action (ὁ θεὸς ἁρμονικὸς καλεῖται καὶ μουσικός), which he manifests in his act of creating and preserving the cosmic order. God does not merge the opposites into one same entity, but governs their association and dispersion (κοινωνίαν καὶ διαφοράν) and removes their excesses (τὸ ἄγαν ἑκατέρας ἀφαιρῶν εἰς τὸ δέον ἀμφοτέρας καθίστησι), thus establishing a 'correct proportion' between them[184].

A harmonic union also characterises the perfect couple of spouses (γαμικῆς κοινωνίας) united by Eros, who is bearer of, and contributes, a mild feeling of affection. The complete fusion that the spouses experience resembles a mixture of liquids (ὥσπερ ὑγρῶν πρὸς ἄλληλα συμπεσόντων): at first, when united, they create effervescence and confusion (ζέσιν ἐν ἀρχῇ καὶ τάραξιν – an expression that recalls the uncontrolled psychic motions of the Pythia), but a solid balance is eventually set (τὴν βεβαιοτάτην διάθεσιν)[185].

---

[181] Cf. Boulogne (2006/2007).

[182] *Ibid*. II. Boulogne in this article also makes two short remarks (cf. p. 9, nn. 20-21) concerning *De def. or*. 436F-437A, where he reminds that demons realize, indeed, a good *krâsis* out of the prophetic *pneûma*.

[183] Cf. Froidefond (1987) 202; Froidefond recalls in this regard *De an. procr*. §§21-33.

[184] Cf. *De prim. frig*. 946F.

[185] The same metaphor of the mixing of liquids is found in *Con. praec*. 142F-143A: ὥσπερ οἱ φυσικοὶ τῶν ὑγρῶν λέγουσι δι' ὅλων γενέσθαι τὴν κρᾶσιν. This image is apparently drawn from the Stoic philosopher Antipater of Tharsus, who talks about a 'complete union', and similarly assimilates the marital bound to the mixture of liquids, namely water and wine

All these examples therefore clarify and apparently confirm my previous assumption that the Pythia is not in a state of madness (μανία)[186]. She is neither completely frenzy and out of control, nor absolutely rational and lucid; instead, her body and soul are in a peculiar condition: a harmonic, propitious balance between external influences and their proper nature. As I believe, this seemingly oxymoronic solution displays Plutarch's profound theoretical originality, his innovative and creative reading of Plato's heritage, and his utterly personal way of coping with a long and revered philosophical-religious tradition.

6. The importance of studying the oracle

Plutarch, as his explanation of Delphic prophecy has helped us to understand, is convinced that natural investigation does not discard faith in gods, oracles and portents. Rather, scientific research, if conducted with caution (ἀσφάλεια), leads to correct and acceptable accounts of the sensible world, as well as to a noble kind of rational piety and respect towards the gods (εὐσέβεια). This conviction complies with the general theoretical scheme adopted by the Chaeronean, in which the physical world has a metaphysical foundation; accordingly, the knowledge of the sensible reality paves the way to transcendence.

Rainer Hirsch-Luipold has underlined how the material cosmos, according to Plutarch, is scattered of images of the intelligible realm, reflected in natural objects and artefacts, like in mirrors[187]. God is known through sensible objects (ὄργανα, or εἰκόνες, αἰνίγματα, σύμβολα) working as mediums for this purpose. Religion, aesthetics, ontology, epistemology and ethics in Plutarch are therefore unified under this gnoseological-metaphysical conception. In such a framework, as Hirsch-Luipold effectively explains, the material world works as a "hermeneutical key to god[188]" and to the intelligible realm as a whole. The contingent cosmos constitutes a repository of signs whose correct interpretation is endowed with a soteriological function and ultimate aim – that of the assimilation to god (ὁμοίωσις θεῷ). Plutarch's gnoseological approach hence stresses the value of bodily perception and enhances the epistemic relevance of the sensible realm.

(cf. SVF III 63: ἀνδρὸς καὶ γυναικὸς ταῖς δι᾽ ὅλων κράσεσιν, ὡς οἶνος ὕδατι καὶ τοῦτο ἐπιμέν<ων> μίσγεται δι᾽ ὅλων). For an analysis of the concept of κρᾶσις with reference to the marital union in Plutarch, see Scannapieco (2009); Boulogne (2009/2010) esp. 27-30. For the connections between love and moral philosophy in Plutarch, see Opsomer (2006b).

[186] Cf. *supra* 37. An authoritative confirmation of this is found in Van der Stockt (1999) esp. 520-521.

[187] Cf. Hirsch-Luipold (2005).

[188] *Ibid.* 209.

I believe that all these metaphysical and gnoseological prerogatives are masterfully displayed in Plutarch's Delphic dialogues: there, the explanations in order to account for oracular divination start from its *material* dynamics and the *sensible* appearance of the temple itself, but aim to overcome them, and to grasp the further meaning that they hide. Indeed, as I pointed out in the beginning of *De E apud Delphos*, the 'spirit' – i.e., the profound meaning of a text, object, myth, ritual custom, etc. – lies behind the 'body' – i.e., its formal, external aspect.

As a consequence, a satisfactory comprehension of the phenomenon of divination must necessarily explore its deeper significance and metaphysical foundation. For this reason Plutarch's investigation of the dynamics of the Delphic oracle directly recalls the cognitive path indicated in the *Timaeus*: accordingly, we should always look for both the material-necessary and the transcendent-divine cause (τὸ μὲν ἀναγκαῖον, τὸ δὲ θεῖον) – the latter being *essential* for achieving a happy life[189].

It is interesting to note that the same epistemological paradigm employed in the explanation of oracular prophecy characterises the famous episode of the unicorn ram in the *Life of Pericles*[190]. There, the account given by the philosopher Anaxagoras (a φυσικός, embodying the rational-scientific spirit) plus the one given by the seer Lampon (a μάντις, representing instead the religious world-view) concur to offer a comprehensive justification for that surprising phenomenon. The philosopher identifies the material cause (αἰτία) in the overgrown brain of the ram, which has engendered the strange protuberance on its forehead. The mantis, instead, identifies the final cause (τέλος) of that single horn that has appeared on the head of the animal: its function is to provide the 'sign' that either Thucydides or Pericles would have ruled the city, thus predicting the latter's prominence[191]. This episode intends to show that the philosopher investigates 'out of which' and 'how' one phenomenon is produced (ἐκ τίνων γέγονε καὶ πῶς πέφυκε), while the *mantis* has the equally important task of understanding its 'scope' and 'meaning' (πρὸς τί γέγονε καὶ τί σημαίνει).

Plutarch's scientific spirit displays a "simultaneity of skills[192]" typical of the perfect *pepaideumenos* and an authentically curious spirit, which has a sound humanistic foundation. He embodies the ideal man of knowledge, who has that widely comprehensive cultural preparation (ἐγκύκλιος παιδεία) of the major intellectuals of his time. This attitude is in line with the

---

[189] Cf. Plato, *Ti.* 68e-69a.

[190] Cf. *Per.* 6, 2-4.

[191] The real meaning of this prediction is disclosed only *a posteriori*.

[192] Cf. the expression "contemporaneità delle competenze" in Battegazzore (1992) 25-26 and 33-35. For Plutarch's approach to science, see Van der Stockt (2011) and (1992). For Plutarch and the arts see also fr. 147 from the unfortunately lost *On the Art of Prophecy*.

educational curriculum of the Imperial age, in which physical science was intended as part of the standard philosophical knowledge[193]. Accordingly, as Plutarch explains in a notorious and meaningful passage of *De primo frigido*[194], causal explanation (τῆς αἰτίας τὴν εὕρεσιν ἀναίρεσιν) alone is not sufficient to find the 'sign' (σημεῖον) and decode the hidden meaning of phenomena. Natural phenomena – including portents and *mirabilia* – and human artefacts hide, behind their physical appearance, an ulterior significance that awaits to be deciphered. When the physical philosopher wants to investigate the reality (θεωρίας ἕνεκα), while having 'truth' as his goal (τἀληθὲς), he does not stop at the knowledge of the last material causes (τῶν ἐσχάτων γνῶσις οὐ τέλος ἐστίν – to which the research of the mere 'technician' is instead limited). Rather, he tries to overcome the material entities and their reciprocal relations: this is only the first step of his ascending research path (ἀνωτάτω πορεία), ultimately leading towards the supreme intelligible causes (ἐπὶ τὰ πρῶτα).

The Delphic oracle is a place of *direct* investigation for the Chaeronean and, as I tried to demonstrate, the temple itself, with its oracular activities and ritual customs, comes to embody for Plutarch the 'concrete image' of the forces that are at work in the universe. The Delphic temple is the privileged, chosen, potentially 'perfect' place on earth – whose foundation seems to reveal an intelligent, divine plan[195] – where the two causal orders (the material-necessary and the divine-providential plan) jointly manifest themselves, thus realising the sublime end of making the presence and the thoughts of god manifest (so physically *felt* and *heard*) by humans. The ritual orthopraxis, as a kind of 'templar rationality', completes this image, by regulating and controlling the irrational elements of chaos and fortune that are constitutive of contingency. The ritual procedures enacted in Delphi, indeed, help to prepare and 'tune up' the material factors – ultimately unreliable and unpredictable, as any other earthly being – that are involved in divination, and to determine the appropriate time (καιρός) for the encounter between divine perfect knowledge and human desire to know.

According to Plutarch, natural research and philosophical investigation help humans to climb the ladder of virtue, based on the strong coincidence

---

[193] Cf. Donini (1984) 360: "[...] l'indagine del mondo naturale e sensibile è presupposta come il primo passo per la conoscenza dell'opera e delle figure divine; le scienze della natura e del vivente sono perciò ora divenute le ancelle più accreditate della teologia razionale". Donini effectively stresses that the philosophers of the first centuries "studiarono la natura essenzialmente per convincersi che Timeo aveva ragione", thus their scientific knowledge was deeply influenced by some elements (demons, portents, rites, religious beliefs) that we would tend to label (simplistically and anachronistically) as 'irrational'.

[194] Cf. *De prim. frig.* 948B-C; see also Meeusen (2013); (2014).

[195] Cf. *De def. or.* 435A-E.

established between intellectual and moral improvement. From the investigation that I have proposed in this book, I think it is possible to conclude that the case study of Delphic divination as a 'divine artefact' has, exactly like the broad-scale study of the cosmos in the *Timaeus*, a clear ennobling cognitive and ethical aim – all the more so as the oracle is a sort of microcosm, and a supreme, potentially perfect, communication bridge between the human and the divine.

Conclusion

Delphic divination is a valuable prism through which to observe and examine important aspects of Plutarch's thought. In the present study, the Delphic oracle, with its ritual practices and cultic traditions, has indeed emerged as an effective, although constitutionally imperfect, element of mediation between the absolute knowledge of the god (σοφία) and human quest for truth (φιλοσοφία), and has proven to embody the zetetic and provisional nature of human rational enquiry. At the centre of the earth, and at the core of a complex net of symbols endowed with a cosmic significance, it provides the words and inspires the concepts of Plutarch's philosophy, which, despite its Platonic roots, displays impressing and charming elements of novelty and is enriched by the harmonic conjunction of rational reflection with religious belief.

The epistemic model of explanation that Plutarch employs in the Delphic dialogues in order to provide an authentically rational and scientific account of divination, founded on the consideration of the material and the immaterial forces simultaneously at work behind particular phenomena, has revealed itself as a constitutive element of his philosophy, strongly connected to his cosmological conception.

Divination is at first sight an unexplainable and surprising phenomenon (θαυμαστόν), which attracts our intellectual curiosity with its startling appearance. Scientific analysis reveals its sound physical foundation, but has to stop where the causal chain surpasses our rational comprehension, and our cognitive capabilities show their intrinsic limits. Indeed, as explained in Plutarch's *Quaestiones convivales*[1], rationalistic explanations risk to destroy wonder (ἀναιρεῖ τὸ θαυμάσιον) in phenomena. This process recalls Ammonius' path of knowledge exposed in *De E apud Delphos*: wonder and uncertainty lead us to inquiry (ζητεῖν), which is the beginning of philosophy (φιλοσοφεῖν)[2]. And philosophy starts exactly where the higher principles escape our understanding.

Conceiving and analysing oracular divination in the same way as any other phenomenon, while preserving its wondrous character – which is the element that really spurs and stimulates human reflection – requires to respect the limits of rational-scientific investigation, founded on the awareness that truth exists but is fundamentally inaccessible for us. Rational inquiry according to Plutarch is guided by a reverential

---

[1] Cf. *Quaest. conv.* 680C-D.
[2] Cf. *De E* 385C.

respect towards the divine (εὐλάβεια πρὸς τὸ θεῖον) and the sceptical-Academic precept of suspension of judgement (ἐποχή), and is oriented by the maxims – endowed with both an epistemic and ethical value – 'never too much' (τὸ μηδὲν ἄγαν) and 'know yourself' (γνῶθι σαυτόν).

The analysis here proposed has proven the relevance of the topic of divination also for reconstructing Plutarch's position with respect to his polemical targets (Epicureanism and, to a lesser degree, Stoicism) as well as his search for a 'middle path' between atheism and superstition. His solution counteracts the excesses of a complete mixing of the divine with material reality (as in Stoicism) and its absolute withdrawal from the world (as in Epicureanism), and by resorting to Plato's metaphysics formulates the 'correct distance' between god and the cosmos. In this perspective, the oracle – as a valuable intermediate element between transcendence and immanence – comes to embody the (mediated) interaction between human freedom and self-determination on the one hand, and divine providence on the other.

Chapter 1 has displayed the connections between Plutarch's account of divination and his anthropology: the interaction of the god with the Pythia is analogous to that of the soul with the body – as a way of the interplay between the immaterial and the material substance. This section has shown that, in the dramatic time of the dialogue, the prophetic utterances of the Pythia are clear and comprehensible, therefore they do not need any hermeneutical decipherment. Instead, rational interpretation has to be applied on the temple *itself*, considered both in its riddling physical appearance and its ritual and divinatory dynamics. Moreover, it is not just the Delphic shrine to be endowed with a symbolic value; rather, all beings present in the material realm are intended as repositories of hidden meanings.

In Chapter 2 Delphi has emerged as a unique place on earth where the prodigious communication between mankind and the god takes place and as a sublime paradigm for all the cosmic phenomena. In this framework, the role of material factors involved in divination has proven its relevance. The Pythia, by virtue of her ritual purity and preparation, is the only human individual able to perform the extraordinary mediating function required, while a precise ritual orthopraxis helps to signal the correct time for consultation. The investigation into the notion of '*historia*' has defined the Delphic oracle as a place where historical testimonies and mythical narratives – *both* constituting *valuable* sources of knowledge – ideally merge together.

Chapter 3 has shown the tension between the essence of Apollo, simple, incorruptible and eternal on the one hand, and his manifold appearance and multiple earthly characterizations on the other – thus revealing Plutarch's idea of a god both transcendent and immanent in the cosmos. This analysis has helped to shed light on the concepts of 'henotheism' and 'syncretism' in Plutarch's thought, to understand his relations with foreign wisdom and traditions, and to explore his dualistic theory. The Delphic temple has finally appeared as the place of the (instantaneous and provisional) connection between the radically antithetical plans of becoming (τὸ γιγνόμενον) and being (τὸ ὄντως ὄν).

Chapter 4 has thematised Plutarch's analogy between the human and the cosmic soul – balanced and controlled by our rational power and by that of the demiurge, respectively. Socrates, by virtue of the purity of his inner demon (νοῦς), appears as the human, chosen medium, in which the sky and the earth ideally find a meeting point: the divine wisdom that he acquires through demonic illumination makes him the privileged addressee of a kind of divine education and a sublime *exemplum* of virtue for others. Direct prophetic revelations reach only exceptional individuals, loved by the gods, while all common mortals have to resort to the various tools offered by technical divination. In this perspective, the oracle itself works as a 'democratic' communicative means, at the service of the majority of us, while direct inspiration is reserved to some privileged men, who have a peaceful character and a pure soul. In contrast to the perfectly wise man who is a direct, selected recipient of the divine messages, the simple Delphic priestess (lacking any kind of intellectual and philosophical preparation) is apparently incapable of reaching *per se* demonic illumination – in fact, she needs the support of the institutional-ritual framework of the oracle. Differently from Socrates, she abdicates to her own rational capabilities (λογιστικὸν καὶ φροντιστικόν) and surrenders to the superior divine power of inspiration.

Plutarch's profoundly original and balanced view of divination, founded on the idea of the Pythia being neither rational nor completely irrational, has been emphasised in this study. The prophetic act clearly excludes any logical-dialectical means (indeed, the apprehension of the future is fantastic and imaginative in nature); nevertheless, Plutarch also evidently refutes the idea of a raving Pythia, captured in ecstatic madness. As the analysis of the psychic structure of the priestess has shown, her soul is shaped by the harmonic encounter with the prophetic *pneûma*, presided over by the demons, who create the balanced and fruitful composition between the apparently two incompatible elements of the material stream and the Pythia's soul. Concepts like temperament, mixture (κρᾶσις, μῖξις) and perfect time (καιρός) have proven to be relevant in this respect, especially in order to recognise the important role of the irrational psychic principle in divination (as well as in Plutarch's ethics and cosmology).

The analysis of Plutarch's view of the psychic status of the Delphic prophetess has clarified another pivotal aspect of his thought: his convic-tion that human *technai* are necessarily founded on the principles of 'right medium' and 'balance' (τὸ μέτριον). This also holds true for the oracular mantic, which, just like any other divine production (ἔργον), is intrinsically characterized by adequacy and measure.

In the framework of the correspondence between divination and Plutarch's cosmology, the parallelism connecting the Pythia and matter (based on the multiple determinations of this problematic concept in Plutarch's physics and metaphysics) has proven illuminating. In the first place, like the evil precosmic world soul of *De animae procreatione in Timaeo*, the soul of the priestess is subject to chaos and irrational motion. In the second place, according to an analogy with craftsman production, the Pythia's soul, as the raw material of the divinatory process, is the element necessary for the physical realization of the model that the demiurge has conceived. Similarly to the cosmic material principle, the prophetess – with her intrinsic psycho-physical qualities – exerts her resistance and 'contaminates' the ideal model.

According to Plutarch's literal reading of Plato's psychogonia developed in *De animae procreatione in Timaeo*, the creative action of the demiurge brings order into the precosmic chaos – as a *real* event performed in a *definite* time: god appeases the chaotic movement of matter, agitated by an irrational psychic principle[3], by turning it into an intelligent order and harmony[4]. Similarly, in divination, a divine principle of order (here embodied by Apollo) works upon irrational matter (the Pythia and her soul): the prophetess is modelled by the superior power of inspiration and thus reaches for a propitious balance that enables her to perform the prophetic act – provided that the required preliminary material conditions are respected.

Delphic divination therefore displays the same dynamics of cosmogony: that of a gentle and persuading ordering action of the superior, rational force of *logos* upon the irrational force of necessity. Plutarch employs this same theoretical standard of explanation – based on the opposition and interaction of a superior and an inferior level of causality – on problems concerning the physical world and moral psychology: as it is now evident, in divination this epistemic scheme finds another important and original field of application.

The oracle appears as the designated place and ideal location where the two causal orders at work in the cosmos cooperate and evidently manifest themselves: the divine-transcendent and the material-immanent principles, in a constant struggle according to the standard accounts found in *De virtute morali* and *De animae procreatione in Timaeo*, seem to find a meeting point thanks to the divinatory dynamics enacted at the Delphic temple. The established rites provide the necessary preconditions for the occurrence of this extraordinary event and dictate the modalities of the

---

[3] Cf. *De an procr.* 1015D-E.
[4] Cf. *ibid.* 1016C.

encounter between divine perfect wisdom and human thirst for knowledge. It can be affirmed that a sort of 'templar rationality', expressed by the 'collective attuning' of all the material factors involved in the process, replaces the 'philosophical rationality' of which the Pythia is defective.

With regard to the dichotomy between the visible-temporal and the intelligible-atemporal realm, the Delphic oracle provides the spiritual and material conditions for the occurrence of the 'perfect moment' (καιρός) favourable for the prodigious encounter between human time (χρόνος) and divine eternity (αἰών). This prerogative reflects the 'a-temporal' character of ancient Greek divination, as not limited to any precise temporal dimension, but aimed at embracing them all and at overcoming the limits of 'ordinary investigation'[5].

Indeed, as the consideration of Plutarch's moral philosophy in the beginning of Chapter 4 has helped to show, human decisions and actions (guided by practical wisdom, φρόνησις) pertain to the domain of fortune and chaos. Ritual orthopraxis intervenes to regulate the magmatic, unpredictable nature of earthly events, through codified acts and sacrifices: rite permeates and regulates the contingent reality – constitutively mutable and imperfect – while preparing and orienting it towards the (mediated) encounter with the divine.

In this framework, the activity of the Pythia appears as part of the cosmic order, which is implemented in a necessarily imperfect way, due to the constitutive fallibility of the sensible nature. Unavoidable failures do not undermine the fact that oracular divination belongs to an 'intelligent design' (as expressed by its practical procedures and metaphysical grounds), as well as to the god's provident plan to provide help and support to humankind. This recalls Plato's idea – as shown by the comparison with the *Timaeus* – of the material world as an 'image' (εἰκών) of its transcendent model, as well as his dichotomy between two ontological levels (becoming – being) and epistemological standards (opinion – science).

Imperfection marks the distance between the model and its material realization, while verisimilitude is the key criterion for the study of the world and indicates the level to which every discourse on the sensible reality has to arrest. The oracle, attesting to the variable character of the physical realm and its phenomena, is thus profoundly imperfect and fallible, liable to error and destruction.

---

[5] As Bouché-Leclercq points out in his pioneering work *Histoire de la divination dans l'antiquité*, the domain of divination includes the entire flow of time, inasmuch as rationality and 'ordinary investigation' are insufficient. Cf. Bouché-Leclercq (1975) I, §3, p. 7: "La divination a pour domaine tout ce que l'esprit humain ne peut connaître par ses seules forces: en premier lieu l'avenir, en tant qu'il échappe à la prévision rationnelle, puis le passé et le présent, dans ce qu'ils ont d'inaccessible à l'investigation ordinaire".

Additional research still needs to be done in order to explore extensively the philosophical reflection of the Chaeronean, and, in particular, to fully exploit the interpretative proposal advanced by the present research, which has attempted to define the Delphic oracle as one of the main theoretical cores of Plutarch's thought, as well as the 'imperfect' place where, according to his metaphysics, the cosmic forces of reason and necessity manifest themselves on a smaller scale.

Bibliography

Abbreviations

ANRW = *Aufstieg und Niedergang der römischen Welt*, Berlin-New York, 1972-.

DK = Diels, H., Kranz, K. (1966-1967), *Die Fragmente der Vorsokratiker*, Dublin-Zurich.

Merkelbach-Stauber = Merkelbach, R., Stauber, J. (1996), "Die Orakel des Apollon von Klaros", *EA* 27, 1-54.

PGM = Betz, H.D. (1986), *The Greek Magical Papyri in Translation. Including the Demotic Spells*, Chicago-London.

SVF = Arnim, J. von (1903-1924), *Stoicorum Veterum Fragmenta* [indices by M. Adler], Leipzig.

Dictionaries

LSJ = Liddell, G.H., Scott, R. (1996), *A Greek-English Lexicon*, 9th edition, rev. H.S. Jones, with a revised supplement, Oxford.

References

A

Addey, C. (2014), *Divination and Theurgy in Neoplatonism. Oracles of the Gods*, Farnham.

Algra, K. (2014), *Plutarch and the Stoic Theory of Providence*, in D'Hoine, P., Van Riel, G. (eds.), *Fate, Providence and Moral Responsibility in Ancient, Medieval and Early Modern Thought. Studies in Honour of Carlos Steel*, Leuven, 117-136.

Amandry, P. (1950), *La mantique apollinienne à Delphes. Essai sur le fonctionnement de l'oracle*, Paris.

Arnim, H. von (1921), *Plutarch über Dämonen und Mantik*, Amsterdam.

Athanassiadi, P. (1992), "Philosophers and Oracles: Shifts of Authority in Late Paganism", *Byzantion* 62, 45-62.

— (1993), "Dreams, Theurgy and Freelance Divination: The Testimony of Iamblichus", *JRS* 83, 115-130.

B

Babut, D. (1969), *Plutarque et le stoïcisme*, Paris.

— (1984), "La doctrine démonologique dans le *De genio Socratis* de Plutarque: cohérence et fonction", *L'Information Littéraire* 35, 201-205.

— (1992), "La composition des *Dialogues Pythiques* de Plutarque et le problème de leur unité", *JS* 27, 189-234.

— (1993), "Stoïciens et Stoïcisme dans les *Dialogues Pythiques* de Plutarque", *ICS* 18, 203-227.

— (1994a), *Le dialogue de Plutarque* Sur le démon de Socrate. *Essai d'interprétation*, in Id. (ed.), Parerga. *Choix d'articles de Daniel Babut (1974-1994)*, Lyon, 405-430.

— (1994b), *Le rôle de Cléombrote dans le* De defectu oraculorum *et le problème de la "démonologie" de Plutarque*, in Id. (ed.), Parerga. *Choix d'articles de Daniel Babut (1974-1994)*, Lyon, 531-548.

— (1996), *Plutarque, Aristote, et l'Aristotélisme*, in Van der Stockt, L. (ed.), *Plutarchea Lovaniensia*, Leuven.

— (2003), *Plutarco e lo stoicismo*, It. trans., Milano.

— (2007), *L'unité de l'Académie selon Plutarque*, in Bonazzi, M., Levy, C., Steel, C. (eds.), *A Platonic Pythagoras. Platonism and Pythagoreanism in the Imperial Age*, Turnhout, 63-98.

Baldassarri, M. (1976), *Plutarco. Gli opuscoli contro gli stoici. Traduzione, introduzione e commento con appendice critico-testuale*, 2 vols., Trento.

Baltes, M. (2000), "La dottrina dell'anima in Plutarco", *Elenchos* 21, 245-270.

Barigazzi, A. (1992), *Implicanze morali nella polemica plutarchea sulla psicologia degli animali*, in Gallo, I. (ed.), *Plutarco e le scienze. Atti del IV Convegno plutarcheo (Genova-Bocca di Magra, 22-25 aprile 1991)*, Genova, 297-315.

Battegazzore, M. (1992), *L'atteggiamento di Plutarco verso le scienze*, in Gallo, I. (ed.), *Plutarco e le scienze. Atti del IV Convegno plutarcheo (Genova-Bocca di Magra, 22-25 aprile 1991)*, Genova, 19-59.

Beaujeu, J. (1973), *Apulée. Opuscules philosophiques (Du dieu de Socrate, Platon et sa doctrine, Du monde) et Fragments*, Paris.

Beard, M. (1986), "Cicero and Divination: The Formation of a Latin Discourse", *JRS* 76, 33-46.

Becchi, F. (1981), "Platonismo medio ed etica plutarchea", *Prometheus* 7, 125-145.

— (1990), *Plutarco. La virtù etica. Introduzione, testo critico, traduzione e commento*, Napoli.

— (1995), *Plutarco e la dottrina dell'ὁμοίωσις θεῷ tra platonismo e aristotelismo*, in Gallo, I. (ed.), *Plutarco e la religione. Atti del sesto Convegno Plutarcheo (Ravello 29-31 maggio 1995)*, Napoli, 321-335.

— (2008), *Virtù e fortuna nelle* Vitae *e nei* Moralia *di Plutarco*, in Ribeiro Ferreira, J., Van Der Stockt, L., Do Céu Fialho, M. (eds.), *Philosophy in Society. Virtues and Values in Plutarch*, Coimbra, 39-52.

Beck, R. (1988), *Planetary Gods and Planetary Orders in the Mysteries of Mithras*, Leiden-New York.

Beck, M. (2014), *A Companion to Plutarch*, Malden.

Belayche, N. (2007), "Les dieux 'nomothètes'. Oracles et prescriptions religieuses à l'époque romaine impériale", *RHR* 2, 171-191.

Bellanti, A. (2003), "Aristotele pitagorico? La concezione della medietà nel *De virtute morali* di Plutarco", *RFN* 95, 3-36.

Bendlin, A. (2011), *On the Uses and Disadvantages of Divination. Oracles and their Literary Representations in the Time of the Second Sophistic*, in North, J.A., Price, S.R.F. (eds.), *The Religious History of the Roman Empire. Pagans, Jews, and Christians*, Oxford, 175-250.

Betegh, G. (2006), *Greek Philosophy and Religion*, in Gill, M.L., Pellegrin, P. (eds.), *A Companion to Ancient Philosophy*, Oxford, 625-639.

— (2010), *What Makes a Myth* eikôs? *Remarks Inspired by Myles Burnyeat's* EIKÔS MYTHOS, in Mohr, R.D., Sattler, B.M. (eds.), *One Book, the Whole Universe. Plato's «Timaeus» Today*, Las Vegas, 213-224.

Betz, H.D. (1970), "The Delphic Maxim ΓΝΩΘΙ ΣΑΥΤΟΝ in Hermetic Interpretation", *HThR* 63, 465-484.

Bianchi, U. (1971), "Seth, Osiris et l'ethnographie", *RHR* 179, 113-135.

— (1986), *Plutarco e il dualismo*, in Brenk, F.E., Gallo, I. (eds.), *Miscellanea plutarchea. Atti del I Convegno di studi su Plutarco (Roma, 23 novembre 1985)*, Ferrara, 111-120.

Bloch, R. (1984), *La divination dans l'antiquité*, Paris.

Bluck, R.S. (1964), *Plato. Meno. Edited with Introduction and Commentary*, London.

Boer, J.Z. de (2007), "Delphi's small 'Omphalos': an Enigma", *SyllClass* 18, 81-104.

Boer, J.Z. de, Hale, J.R. (2000), "The Geological Origins of the Oracle at Delphi", *Geological Society Special Publications* 171, 399-412.

Boer, J.Z. de, Hale, J.R., Chanton, J. (2001), "New Evidence for the Geological Origins of the Ancient Delphic Oracle (Greece)", *Geology* 29, 707-710.

Bonazzi, M. (2004), "Contro la rappresentazione sensibile: Plutarco tra l'academia e il platonismo", *Elenchos* 25, 41-71.

— (2008), "L'offerta di Plutarco. Teologia e filosofia nel *De E apud Delphos* (capp. I-II)", *Philologus* 152, 205-211.

— (2014), *Middle Platonists on Fate and Human Autonomy: A Confrontation with the Stoics*, in Destrée, P., Salles, R. (eds.), *What is Up to Us?: Studies on Agency and Responsibility in Ancient Philosophy*, Sankt Augustin, 283-294.

— (2015), *À la recherche des idées: platonisme et philosophie hellénistique d'Antiochus à Plotin*, Paris.

Bonazzi, M., Lévy, C., Steel, C. (eds.) (2007), *A Platonic Pythagoras. Platonism and Pythagoreanism in the Imperial Age Bonazzi*, Turnhout.

Bonazzi, M., Helmig, C. (eds.) (2008), *Platonic Stoicism – Stoic Platonism. The Dialogue between Platonism and Stoicism in Antiquity*, Leuven.

Bonazzi, M., Opsomer, J. (eds.) (2009), *The Origins of the Platonic System. Platonisms of the Early Empire and their Philosophical Contexts*, Leuven.

Bonnechere, P. (2007), *Divination*, in Ogden, D. (ed.), *A Companion to Greek Religion*, Malden, 145-160.

Borthwick, E.K. (2003), "Text and Interpretation of Plato *Philebus* 56a", *CPh* 98, 274-280.

Bouché-Leclercq, A. (1879-1882), *Histoire de la divination dans l'antiquité*, 4 vols., Paris.

Boulet, B. (2008), *Why does Plutarch's Apollo Have Many Faces?*, in Nikolaidis, A.G. (ed.), *The Unity of Plutarch's Work: Moralia Themes in the Lives, Features of the Lives in the Moralia. Proceedings of the Seventh International Congress of the International Plutarch Society (Rethymno, 4-8 May 2005)*, Berlin, 159-170.

Boulogne, J. (2003), *Plutarque dans le miroir d'Epicure. Analyse d'une critique systématique de l'épicureisme*, Villeneuve d'Ascq.

— (2004), "L'unité multiple de dieu chez Plutarque", *RPhA* 22, 95-106.

— (2006/2007), "Le paradigme de la crase dans la pensée de Plutarque", *Ploutarchos* 4, 3-17.

— (2008), *Plutarque et l'hermétisme*, in Ribeiro Ferreira, J., Van der Stockt, L., do Céu Fialho, M. (eds.), *Philosophy in Society: Virtues and Values in Plutarch*, Coimbra, 53-64.

— (2009/2010), "La philosophie du mariage chez Plutarque", *Ploutarchos* 7, 23-34.

Boulogne, J., Broze, M., Couloubaritsis, L. (éds.) (2006), *Les platonismes des premiers siècles de notre ère*, Bruxelles.

Boyancé, P. (1938), "Sur les oracles de la Pythie", *REA* 40, 305-316.

Boys-Stones, G. (1997), "Plutarch on the Probable Principle of Cold. Epistemology and *De primo frigido*", *CQ* 91, 227-238.

— (2007), *"Middle" Platonists on Fate and Human Autonomy*, in Sharples, R., Sorabji, R. (eds.), *Greek and Roman Philosophy 100 BC-200AD*, II, London, 431-447.

Bowden, H. (2005), *Classical Athens and the Delphic Oracle. Divination and Democracy*, Cambridge.

Bowersock, G.W. (1965), "Some Persons in Plutarch's *Moralia*", *CQ* 15, 267-270.

— (1969), *Greek Sophists in the Roman Empire*, Oxford.

Boyce, M. (ed.) (1991), *A history of Zoroastrianism*. Vol. 3: Boyce, M., Grenet, F., *Zoroastrianism under Macedonian and Roman Rule. With a contribution by Roger Beck*, Leiden.

Brenk, F.E. (1973), "'A most strange doctrine'. *Daimon* in Plutarch", *CJ* 69, 1-11.

— (1977), *In Mist Apparelled. Religious Themes in Plutarch's Moralia and Lives*, Leiden.

— (1987a), "In the Light of the Moon. Demonology in the Early Imperial Period", in ANRW 2.13.3, 2068-2145.

— (1987b), "An Imperial Heritage: The Religious Spirit of Plutarch of Chaironeia", in ANRW 2.36.1, 248-349.

— (1994), *The Origin and the Return of the Soul in Plutarch*, in Valdés, M.G. (ed.), *Studios sobre Plutarco: Ideas religiosas. Actas del III Simposio Internacional sobre Plutarco (Oviedo 30 de abril a 2 de mayo de 1992)*, Madrid, 3-24.

— (1996), *Time as Structure in Plutarch's* The daimonion of Socrates, in Van der Stockt, L. (ed.), *Plutarchea Lovaniensia*, Leuven, 29-51.

— (1998), *Genuine Greek Demons, "In Mist Apparelled"? Hesiod and Plutarch*, in Id., *Relighting the Souls: Studies in Plutarch, in Greek Literature, Religion, and Philosophy, and in the New Testament Background*, Stuttgart.

— (2005), *Plutarch's Middle-Platonic God: About to Enter (or Remake) the Academy*, in Hirsch-Luipold, R. (ed.), *Gott und die Götter bei Plutarch. Götterbilder – Gottesbilder – Weltbilder*, Berlin-New York, 27-49.

— (2007), *With Unperfumed Voice. Studies in Plutarch, in Greek Literature, Religion and Philosophy, and in the New Testament Background*, Stuttgart.

Brisson, L. (1974), *Le même et l'autre dans la structure ontologique du* Timée *de Platon: un commentaire systématique du* Timée *de Platon*, Paris.

— (1997), *Plato's Theory of Sense Perception in the* Timaeus: *How it Works and What it Means*, in Cleary, J.J., Gary, M., Gurtler S.J. (eds.). *Proceedings of the Boston Area Colloquium in Ancient Philosophy* 13, 147-176.

— (1999), "Qualche aspetto della storia del platonismo", *Elenchos* 20, 145-169.

Brouillette, X. (2010), *Apollon au-delà de tout ce qui est visible: Plutarque et* République *XI 509b*, in Brouillette, X., Giavatto, A. (eds.), *Les dialogues platoniciens chez Plutarque. Stratégies et méthodes exégétiques*, 2010, 29-46.

— (2014), *La Philosophie delphique de Plutarque. L'itinéraire des* Dialogues pythiques, Paris.

Brouillette, X., Giavatto, A. (eds.) (2010), *Les dialogues platoniciens chez Plutarque. Stratégies et méthodes exégétiques*, Leuven.

Brout, N. (2004), "Au carrefour entre la philosophie grecque et les religions barbares: Typhon dans le *De Iside* de Plutarque", *RPhA* 22, 71-106.

Brown, P. (1971), "The Rise and Function of the Holy Man in Late Antiquity", *JRS* 61, 80-101.

— (1997), *The Making of Late Antiquity*, Harvard.

Bryan, J. (2012), *Likeness and Likelihood in the Presocratics and Plato*, Cambridge.

Burkert, W. (1985), *Greek Religion. Archaic and Classical*, Eng. trans., Oxford.

— (1992), *The Orientalizing Revolution*, Harvard.

— (1996), *Plutarco: religiosità personale e teologia filosofica*, in Gallo, I. (ed.), *Plutarco e la religione. Atti del VI Convegno plutarcheo (Ravello, 29-31 maggio 1995)*, Napoli, 11-28.

Burnyeat, M., "*Eikōs Muthos*", *Rhizai* 2, 143-165.

Busine, A. (2005), *Paroles d'Apollon. Pratiques et traditions oraculaires dans l'Antiquité tardive (IIe - VIe siècles)*, Leiden-Boston.

C

Calabi, F. (1977/1978), "Il Signore il cui oracolo è a Delfi non dice né nasconde, ma indica (Eraclito B93)", *Bollettino dell'Istituto di Filologia Greca dell'Università di Padova* 4, 14-34.

Casanova, A. (2012), *Plutarch as Apollo's Priest at Delphi*, in Roig Lanzillotta, R., Muñoz Gallarte, I. (eds.), *Plutarch in the Religious and Philosophical Discourse of Late Antiquity*, Leiden, 151-157.

Casevitz, M. (1992), "Mantis: le vrai sens", *REG* 105, 1-18.

Cavalli, M. (1991), *Modelli stilistici oracolari nei* Dialoghi delfici *di Plutarco*, in D'Ippolito, G., Gallo, I. (eds.), *Strutture formali dei "Moralia" di Plutarco. Atti del III Convegno plutarcheo (Palermo, 3-5 maggio 1989)*, Napoli, 83-89.

Celia, F., Ulacco, A. (eds.) (2012), *Il* Timeo. *Esegesi greche, arabe, latine*, Pisa.

Centrone, B. (2000), *Cosa significa essere pitagorico in età imperiale. Per una riconsiderazione della categoria storiografica del neopitagorismo*, in Brancacci, A. (ed.), *La filosofia in età imperiale*, Napoli, 137-168.

— (2011), *Note sull'etimologia di* eudaimonia, in Amoroso, L., Ferrarin, A., La Rocca, C. (eds.), *Critica della ragione e forme dell'esperienza. Studi in onore di Massimo Barale*, Pisa, 117-126.

Cherniss, H. (1976), *Plutarch's Moralia in Fifteen Volumes*, XIII, part I, *1012B-1032F, with an English Translation*, London-Cambridge MA.

Chiaradonna, R. (2007), *Platonismo e teoria della conoscenza stoica tra II e III secolo d. C.*, in Bonazzi, M., Helmig, C. (eds.), *Platonic Stoicism-Stoic Platonism: The Dialogue Between Platonism and Stoicism in Antiquity*, Leuven, 209-242.

Chiodi, S.M. (1986), *La tematica ierogamica nel* De Iside, in Brenk, F.E., Gallo, I. (eds.), *Miscellanea plutarchea*, Ferrara, 121-126.

Chirassi Colombo, I. (1991a), *Dionysus Bakhos e la città estatica: immagini, messaggi e modelli di buon disordine*, in Berti, F. (ed.), *Dionysus. Mito e Mistero*, Ferrara, 337-360.

— (1991b), "Le Dionysos oraculaire", *Kernos* 4, 205-217.

Chlup, R. (2000), "Plutarch's Dualism and the Delphic Cult", *Phronesis* 45, 138-158.

Cilento, V. (2008), *Plutarco. Diatriba isiaca e dialoghi delfici*, Milano.

Cornford, F.M. (1937), *Plato's Cosmology. The Timaeus of Plato. Translated with a Running Commentary*, London.

Couloubaritsis, L. (1990), "L'art divinatoire et la question de la vérité", *Kernos* 3, 113-122.

Crepaldi, M.G. (1985), *La concezione del tempo tra pensiero biblico e filosofia greca: saggio su Filone di Alessandria*, Brugine.

Crepaldi, M.G. (2009), *Farsi Dio, farsi uomo. La salvezza tra filosofia e rivelazione nel pensiero tardo-antico*, in Prinzivalli, E., *Questioni di storia nel cristianesimo antico I-IV sec.*, Roma, 113-151.

Cumont, F. (1896-1899), *Textes et monuments figurés relatifs aux mystères de Mithra*, 2 vols., Brussels.

Cumont, F. (1966), *Recherches sur le symbolisme funéraire des Romains*, Paris.

D

Defradas, J. (1954), *Les thèmes de la propagande delphique*, Paris.

Delcourt, M. (1955), *L'oracle de Delphes*, Paris.

Del Re, R. (1934), *Il dialogo sull'estinzione degli oracoli di Plutarco da Cheronea*, Napoli.

Demulder, B. (2015), *From Chaos to Cosmos (and Back Again): Plato's* Timaeus *and the Composition of* De animae procreatione *and* De facie in orbe lunae, in Meeusen, M., Van der Stockt, L., (eds.), *Natural Spectaculars. Aspects of Plutarch's Philosophy of Nature*, Leuven, 199-214.

Desideri, P. (1996), *Il* De Defectu oraculorum *e la crisi della religione antica in Plutarco*, in Gabba, E., Desideri, P., Roda, S. (eds.), *Italia sul Baetis. Studi di storia romana in memoria di Fernando Gascó*, Torino, 91-102.

— (2012), *Plutarco e la storia: una lettura obliqua dei Dialoghi Delfici*, in Id., *Saggi su Plutarco e la sua fortuna*, a cura di A. Casanova, Firenze, 355-366.

— *La città di Pericle*, in Casanova, A. (ed.) (2013), *Figure d'Atene nelle opere di Plutarco*, Firenze, 19-30.

De Simone, P. (2016), *Mito e verità. Uno studio sul "De Iside et Osiride" di Plutarco*, Milano.

Deonna, W. (1939), *Εὐωδία. Croyances antiques et modernes: l'odeur suave des dieux et des élus. Introduction et épilogue par Carlo Ossola*, Torino.

Detienne, M. (2001), "Forgetting Delphi between Apollo and Dionysus", *CPh* 96, 147-158.

Deuse, W. (1983), *Untersuchungen zur mittelplatonischen und neuplatonischen Seelenlehre*, Wiesbaden.

Dietrich, B.C. (1978), "Reflections on the Origins of the Oracular Apollo", *BICS* 25, 1-18.

— (1992), "Divine Madness and Conflict at Delphi", *Kernos* 5, 41-58.

Dillery, J. (2005), *Chresmologues and Manteis: Independent Diviners and the Problem of Authority*, in Johnston, S.I., Struck, P.T. (eds.), *Mantikê. Studies in Ancient Divination*, Leiden, 167-232.

Dillon, J.M. (1977), *The Middle Platonists: A Study of Platonism, 80 B.C. to A.D. 220*, London.

— (1988), "Plutarch and Platonist Orthodoxy", *ICS* 13, 357-364.

— (1993), *Alcinous. The Handbook of Platonism*, Oxford.

— (1996), *Middle Platonists: 80 B.C. to A.D. 220*, Ithaca.

— (2001a), *Plutarch and the Separable Intellect*, in Pérez Jiménez, A., Casadesús Bordoy, F. (eds.), *Estudios Sobre Plutarco. Misticismo y Religiones Mistéricas en la Obra de Plutarco. Actas del VII Simposio Español Sobre Plutarco (Palma de Mallorca, 2-4 de Noviembre de 2000)*, Málaga, 35-44.

— (2001b), *Seres intermedios en la tradición platónica tardía*, in Pérez Jiménez, A., Cruz Andreotti, G. (eds.), *Seres intermedios. Angeles, demonios y genios en el mundo mediterráneo*, Madrid, 179-215.

— (2002), *Plutarch and God. Theodicy and Cosmogony in the Thought of Plutarch*, in Frede, D., Laks, A. (eds.), *Traditions of Theology. Studies in Hellenistic Theology, its Background and Aftermath*, Boston, 223-237.

Dillon, J.M., Long, A.A. (eds.) (1988), *The Question of "Eclecticism". Studies in Later Greek Philosophy*, Berkeley-Los Angeles, 208-233.

Dodds, E.R. (1984), *The Greeks and the Irrational*, Berkeley.

Donini, P. (1984), *Problemi del pensiero scientifico a Roma: II primo e il secondo secolo d.C.*, in Giannantoni, G., Vegetti, M. (eds.), *La scienza ellenistica. Atti delle tre giornate di studio (Pavia, 14-16 aprile 1982)*, Napoli, 353-374.

— (1986a), *Plutarco, Ammonio e l'Academia*, in Brenk, F.E., Gallo, I. (eds.), *Miscellanea Plutarchea*, Ferrara, 97-110.

— (1986b), *Lo scetticismo accademico, Aristotele e l'unità della tradizione platonica secondo Plutarco*, in Cambiano, A. (ed.), *Storiografia e dossografia nella filosofia antica*, 203-226.

— (1987), "Testi e commenti, manuali e insegnamento: la forma sistematica e i metodi della filosofia in età postellenistica", in ANRW 2.36.7, 5027-5100.

— (1988), *Science and Metaphysics. Platonism, Aristotelianism, and Stoicism in Plutarch's On the Face in the Moon*, in Dillon, J.M., Long, A.A. (eds.), *The Question of "Eclecticism". Studies in Later Greek Philosophy*, Berkeley, 126-144.

— (1992), *I fondamenti della fisica e la teoria delle cause in Plutarco*, in Gallo, I. (ed.), *Plutarco e le scienze. Atti del IV Convegno Plutarcheo (Genova-Bocca di Magra, 22-25 aprile 1991)*, Genova, 99-120.

— (1994), *Plutarco e la rinascita del Platonismo*, in Cambiano, G., Canfora, L., Lanza, D. (eds.), *Lo spazio letterario della Grecia antica*, I, tomo 3, Roma, 35-60.

— (1999), *Platone e Aristotele nella tradizione pitagorica secondo Plutarco*, in Perez Jiménez, A., Garcia Lopez, J., Maria Aguilar, R. (eds.), *Plutarco, Platon y Aristóteles. Actas del 5. Congreso Internacional de la I.P.S. (Madrid-Cuenca, 4-7 de Mayo de 1999)*, Madrid, 359-374.

— (2002), *L'eredità academica e i fondamenti del platonismo in Plutarco*, in Barbanti, M., Giardina, G.R., Manganaro, P. (eds.), *Unione e amicizia. Omaggio a Francesco Romano*, Catania, 247-273.

— (2003), "Socrate 'pitagorico' e medioplatonico", *Elenchos* 24, 333-359.

— (2007), *Tra academia e pitagorismo. Il platonismo nel* De genio Socratis *di Plutarco*, in Bonazzi, M., Levy, C., Steel, C. (eds.), *A Platonic Pythagoras. Platonism and Pythagoreanism in the Imperial Age*, Turnhout, 99-125.

— (2009), *Il silenzio di Epaminonda, i demoni e il mito: il platonismo di Plutarco nel* De genio Socratis, in Bonazzi, M., Opsomer, J. (eds.), *The Origins of the Platonic System. Platonisms of the Early Empire and Their Philosophical Contexts*, Paris, 187-214.

— (2011), *Plutarco. Il volto della luna. Introduzione, testo critico, traduzione e commento*, Napoli.

Döring, K. (1979), *Exemplum Socratis: Studien zur Sokratesnachwirkung in der kynish-stoischen Popularphilosophie der fruhen Kaiserzeit und im fruhen Christentum*, Wiesbaden.

Dörrie, H. (1983), *Der "Weise vom Roten Meer". Eine okkulte Offenbarung durch Plutarch als Plagiat entlarvt*, in Händel, P., Meid, W. (Hg.), *Festschrift für Robert Muth Zum 65. Geburtstag am 1. Januar 1981*, Innsbruck, 95-101.

Doyle, J. (2004), "Socrates and the Oracle", *AncPhil* 24, 19-36.

Dušanić, S. (1996), "Plato and Plutarch's Fictional Techniques: the Death of the Great Pan", *RhM* 139, 276-294.

E
Eliasson, E. (2008), *The Notion of* That Which Depends on Us *in Plotinus and Its Background*, Leiden-Boston.

F
Faraone, C. (1992), *Talismans and Trojan Horses. Guardian Statues in Ancient Greek Myth and Ritual*, New York.

Ferrari, F. (1996a), *Dio, idee e materia: la struttura del cosmo in Plutarco di Cheronea*, Napoli.

— (1996b), "La generazione precosmica e la struttura della materia in Plutarco", *MH* 53, 44-55.

— (1996c), "Il problema della trascendenza nell'ontologia di Plutarco", *Rivista di filosofia neoscolastica* 88, 363-389.

— (1996d), "La teoria delle idee in Plutarco", *Elenchos* 17, 121-142.

— (1996e), *Dio: padre e artefice. La teologia di Plutarco in* Plat. Quaest. *2*, in Gallo, I. (ed.), *Plutarco e la religione*, Napoli, 395-409.

— (1999), Πρόνοια *platonica e* νόησις νοήσεως *aristotelica: Plutarco e l'imposibilità di una sintesi*, in Jiménez, A.P., García López, J., Aguilar, R.M. (eds.), *Plutarco, Platón y Aristóteles. Actas del V Congreso Internacional de la I.P.S. (Madrid-Cuenca, 4-7 de Mayo de 1999)*, Madrid, 63-77.

— (2000), *La falsità delle asserzioni relative futuro: un argomento epicureo contro la mantica in* Plut. Pyth. Orac. *10*, in Erler, M., Bees, R. (eds.), *Epikureismus in der späten*

Republik und der Kaiserzeit, (Akten der 2. Tagung der Karl-und-Gertrud-Abel-Stiftung vom 30.September-3. Oktober 1998 in Würzburg), Stuttgart, 149-163.

— (2001), "La letteratura filosofica di carattere esegetico in Plutarco", *Orpheus* 22, 77-108.

— (2002), *La trascendenza razionale: il principio secondo Plutarco*, in Calabi, F. (ed.), *Arrhetos Theos. L'ineffabilità del primo principio nel medioplatonismo*, Pisa, 77-91.

— (2004), *Dottrina delle idee nel medioplatonismo*, in Fronterotta, F., Leszl, W. (eds.), *Eidos-Idea. Platone, Aristotele e la tradizione platonica*, Sankt Augustin, 233-246.

— (2005), *Der Gott Plutarchs und der Gott Platons*, in Hirsch-Luipold, R. (ed.), *Gott und die Göttern bei Plutarch. Götterbilder – Gottesbilder – Weltbilder*, Berlin-New York, 13-25.

— (2010), "La costruzione del Platonismo nel *De E apud Delphos* di Plutarco", *Athenaeum* 98, 71-87.

— (2011/2012), "La psichicità dell'anima del mondo e il divenire precosmico secondo Plutarco", *Ploutarchos* 8, 15-36.

Ferrari, F., Baldi, L. (2004), *Plutarco. La generazione dell'anima nel Timeo. Introduzione, testo critico, traduzione e commento*, Napoli.

Festugière, A.-J. (1944-1954), *La Révélation d'Hermès Trismégiste*, 4 vols., Paris.

Filoramo, G. (2005), *Profeti falsi e profeti veri da Plutarco a Celso*, in Volpe Cacciatore, P., Ferrari, F. (eds.), *Plutarco e la cultura della sua età. Atti del X Convegno plutarcheo, (Fisciano, Paestum, 27-29 ottobre 2005)*, Napoli, 41-56.

Flacelière, R. (1938), "Le fonctionnement de l'oracle de Delphes au temps de Plutarque", *Annales de l'École des hautes études de Gand* 2, 69-107.

— (1943), *Plutarque et la Pythie*, *REG* 56, 72-111.

— (1959), *Plutarque et l'épicureisme*, in *Epicurea in memoriam Hectoris Bignone. Miscellanea philologica*, Genova, 197-216.

— (1964), *Sagesse du Plutarque*, Paris.

— (1974), *Plutarque. Œuvres morales*. Tome VI: *Dialogues pythiques*, Paris.

— (1976), *Greek Oracles*, London.

Fontenrose, J. (1978), *The Delphic Oracle: Its Responses and Operations with a Catalogue of Responses*, Berkeley.

Fox, R.L. (1995), *Pagans and Christians. In the Mediterranean World from the Second Century AD to the Conversion of Constantine*, San Francisco.

Franke, W.A., Mircea, M. (2005), "Plutarch's Report on the Blue Patina of Bronze Statues at Delphi. A Scientific Explanation", *Journal of the American Institute for Conservation* 44, 103-116.

Frazier, F. (2000), *L'ame ensorceleé. Magie des Muses et magie de l'amour selon Plutarque*, in Moreau, A., Turpin, J.-C. (éds.), *La magie. Actes du Colloque International de Montpelier (25-27 mars 1999)*, II: *La magie dans l'antiquité grecque tardive. Les mythes*, Montpellier, 37-58.

— (2010), *Le* De sera, *dialogue pythique: hasard et providence, philosophie et religion dans la pensée de Plutarque*, in Frazier, F., Leão, D.F. (eds.), *Tychè et Pronoia. La marche du monde selon Plutarque*, Coimbra, 69-92.

Frazier, F., Leão, D.F. (eds.), *Tychè et Pronoia. La marche du monde selon Plutarque*, Coimbra.

Fritsche, J. (2006), *Aristotle on χώρα in Plato's* Timaeus. *(*Physics *IV:2, 209 b 6-17)*, ABG 48, 27-44.

Froidefond, C. (1987), "Plutarque et le platonisme", in ANRW 2.36.1, 184-233.

— (1988), *Plutarque. Œuvres morales.* Tome V, 2e partie: *Isis et Osiris*, Paris.

Fronterotta, F. (2003), *Platone. Timeo*, Milano.

G

Gabrielli, F. (2004), *Platone. La repubblica*, Milano.

Gallo, I. (2003), *Funzione e significato dei miti nei dialoghi "morali" di Plutarco*, in Lopez, J.A. (ed.), *Mitos en la literatura griega helenistica e imperial*, Madrid, 197-208.

— (ed.) (1988), *Aspetti dello stoicismo e dell'epicureismo in Plutarco. Atti del II Convegno di studi su Plutarco, (Ferrara 2-3 aprile 1987)*, Ferrara 1988.

— (ed.) (1996), *Plutarco e la religione. Atti del IV Convegno Plutarcheo, (Ravello 29-31 maggio 1995)*, Napoli.

Gerson, L.P. (2005), "What is Platonism?", *JHPh* 43, 253-276.

Gill, C. (2003), *The School in the Roman Imperial Period*, in Inwood, B. (ed.), *Cambridge Companion to the Stoics*, Cambridge 2003, 33-58.

Graf, F. (2009a), *Apollo*, London.

— (2009b), *Apollo, Possession and Prophecy*, in Athanassaki, L., Martin, R.P., Miller, J.F. (eds.), *Apolline Politics and Poetics*, Athens, 587-605.

Green, P. (2009), "Possession and Pneuma: the Essential Nature of the Delphic Oracle", *Arion* 17, 27-47.

H

Haake, M. (2008), *Philosopher and Priest. The Image of the Intellectual and the Social Practice of the Elites in the Eastern Roman Empire (First-Third Centuries AD)*, in Dignas, B., Trampedach, K. (eds.), *Practitioners of the Divine. Greek Priests and Religious Officials from Homer to Heliodorus*, Cambridge-London, 145-165.

Hamilton, W. (1934), "The Myth in Plutarch's *De genio* (589F-592E)", *CQ* 28, 175-182.

Hani, J. (1964), "Plutarque en face du dualisme iranien", *REG* 77, 489-525.

— (1976), *La religion Égyptienne dans la pensée de Plutarque*, Paris.

— (1980), *Plutarque. Œuvres morales.* Tome VIII: *Du destin. Le démon de Socrate. De l'exil. Consolation à sa femme*, Paris.

Hankinson, R.J. (1988), "Stoicism, Science and Divination", *Apeiron* 21, 123-160.

Hardie, Ph. R. (1992), "Plutarch and the Interpretation of Myth", ANRW 2.33.6, 4743-4787.

Hardie, Ph. R., Gaye, R.K. (1991), *Aristotle. Physics*, in Barnes, J. (ed.), *The Complete Works of Aristotle*, vol. 1, Princeton.

Hawes, G. (2014), *Rationalizing Myth in Antiquity*, Oxford.

Hershbell, J.P. (1984), "Plutarch's Pythagorean Friends", *CB* 60, 73-79.

— (1987), "*De animae procreatione in Timaeo*: An Analysis of Structure and Content", in ANRW 2.36.1, 234-247.

— (1988), "Plutarch's Portrait of Socrates", *ICS* 13, 365-382.

Hirsch-Luipold, R. (2002), *Plutarchs Denken in Bildern. Studien zur literarischen, philosophischen und religiösen Funktio des Bildhaften*, Tübingen.

— (2005a), *Aesthetics as Religious Hermeneutics in Plutarch*, in Pérez Jímenez, A., Titchener, F. (eds.), *Valori letterari delle Opere di Plutarco. Studi offerti al Professore Italo Gallo dall'International Plutarch Society*, Malaga-Logan, 207-213.

— (Hrsg.) (2005b), *Gott und Götter bei Plutarch. Götterbilder – Gottesbilder – Weltbilder*, Berlin.

— (2005c), *Der eine Gott bei Philon von Alexandrien und Plutarch*, in Id. (ed.), *Gott und Götter bei Plutarch. Götterbilder – Gottesbilder – Weltbilder*, Berlin, 141-168.

Holzhausen, J. (1993), "Zur Inspirationslehre Plutarchs in *De Pythiae oraculis*", *Philologus* 137, 72-91.

Hunt, E.D. (1984), "Travel, Tourism, and Piety in the Roman Empire. A Context for the Beginning of Christian Pilgrimage", *EMC* 28, 391-417.

I

Ildefonse, F. (2006), *Plutarque. Dialogues pythiques. L'E de Delphes, Pourquoi la Pythie ne rend plus ses oracles en vers, La disparition des oracles*, Paris.

Indelli, G. (1996), *Plutarco. Le bestie sono esseri razionali. Introduzione, testo critico, traduzione e commento*, Napoli.

Ingenkamp, H.-G. (1985), "Luciano e Plutarco: due incontri con il divino", *AFLS* 6, 29-45.

Ioppolo, A.M. (2004), "Il dibattito antico sullo scetticismo di Platone", *Elenchos* 25, 413-446.

J

Jagoda Luzzatto, M. (1988), "Plutarco, Socrate e l'Esopo di Delfi", *ICS* 13, 427-445.

Jaillard, D. (2007), "Plutarque et la divination: la piété d'un prêtre philosophe", *RHR* 224, 149-169.

Jiménez, A.P. (1992), "Religión y Política en Grecia: Temístocles y el Oráculo de Delfos", *Minerva* 6, 61-82.

Johansen, T.K. (2008), *The* Timaeus *on the Principles of Cosmology*, in Fine, G. (ed.), *The Oxford Handbook of Plato*, Oxford, 463-483.

Johnston, S.I. (2008), *Ancient Greek Divination*, Oxford.

Jones, C.P. (1966), "Towards a Chronology of Plutarch's Works", *JRS* 56, 61-74.

— (1967), "The Teacher of Plutarch", *HSPh* 71, 205-213.

— (1971), *Plutarch and Rome*, Oxford.

— (1978), "Three Foreigners in Attica", *Phoenix* 32, 222-234.

— (2004), *Multiple Identities in the Age of the Second Sophistic*, in Borg, B.E. (ed.), *Paideia: the World of Second Sophistic*, Berlin, 13-21.

Jones, R.M. (1980), *The Platonism of Plutarch and Selected Papers*, New York-London.

Jones, W.H.S. (1933), *Pausanias. Description of Greece*. Volume III: *Books 6-8.21 (Elis 2, Achaia, Arcadia)*, London-Cambridge MA.

— (1935), *Pausanias. Description of Greece*. Volume IV: *Books 8.22-10 (Arcadia, Boeotia, Phocis and Ozolian Locri)*, London-Cambridge MA.

Jouanna, J. (1975), "Plutarque et la patine des statues à Delphes (*Sur les oracles de la Pythie*, 395b-396c)", *RPh* 49, 67-71.

Jourdan, F. (2015), "Plutarque développe-t-il réellement une pensée dualistique?", *Χώρα. REAM Dualismes*, 185-223.

Jürgen, H. (1988), *Die Orakelkritik des Kynikers Oenomaus*, Frankfurt am Main.

K

Karamanolis, G.E. (2006), *Plato and Aristotle in Agreement? Platonists on Aristotle from Antiochus to Porphyry*, Oxford.

— (2014), *s.v.* "Plutarch", in *The Stanford Encyclopedia of Philosophy* (Winter 2014 Edition), edited by Zalta, E.N., URL = <http://plato.stanford.edu/archives/win2014/entries/plutarch/>.

Ker, J. (2000), "Solon's θεωρία and the End of the City", *CA* 19, 304-329.

Keyt, D. (1961), "Aristotle on Plato's Receptacle", *AJPh* 82, 291-300.

Kung, J. (1988), "Why the Receptacle is not a Mirror", *AGPh* 70, 167-178.

L

Lamberton, R. (2002), *Plutarch*, New Heaven-London.

Latte, K. (1940), "The Coming of the Pythia", *HThR* 33, 9-18.

Laurenti, R. (1966), *Il Filebo in Plutarco*, in Cosenza, P. (ed.), *Il Filebo di Platone e la sua fortuna, (Atti del convegno di Napoli 4-6 novembre 1993)*, Napoli, 53-71.

Lernould, A. (2000), "*E de Delphes* 387 d2-9. Une interprétation philosophique de l'épisode de l'enlèvement du trépied par Héraclès: une erreur de jeunesse", *REG* 113, 147-171.

Levin, S. (1989), "The Old Greek Oracles in Decline", in ANRW 2.18.2, 1599-1649.

Loraux, N. (1995), *The Experiences of Tiresias: The Feminine and the Greek Man*, Princeton.

Lévêque, P. (1973), "Continuité et innovations dans la religion grecque de la première moitié du I millénaire", *PP* I, 36-37.

Lincoln, K. (1998), *La morte della sibilla e le origini mitiche delle pratiche divinatorie*, in Chirassi Colombo, I., Spinelli, T. (eds.), *Sibille e linguaggi oracolari: mito, storia, tradizione. Atti del Convegno (Macerata-Norcia, Settembre 1994)*, Pisa, 209-223.

Lozza, G. (1983), *Plutarco. Dialoghi delfici*, Milano.

M

Manetti, G. (1993), *Theories of the Sign in Classical Antiquity*, Indiana.

Maurizio, L. (1995), "Anthropology and Spirit Possession: A Reconsideration of the Pythia's Role at Delphi", *JHS* 115, 69-86.

Meeusen, M. (2013), "How to Treat a Bee-Sting? On the Higher Cause in Plutarch's *Causes of Natural Phenomena*: the Case of *Quaest. Nat.* 35-36", *QUCC* 105, 131-157.

— (2014), "Plutarch and the Wonder of Nature. Preliminaries to Plutarch's Science of Physical Problems", *Apeiron* 47, 310-341.

— (2017), *Plutarch's Science of Natural Problems. A Study with Commentary on Quaestiones Naturales*, Leuven.

Merker, A. (2006), "Miroir et *chôra* dans le *Timée* de Platon", *EPlaton* 2, 79-92.

Miller, A.M. (1986), *From Delos to Delphi. A Literary Study of the Homeric Hymn to Apollo*, 1986.

Miller, D.R. (1997), "Plutarch's argument for a plurality of worlds in *De defectu oraculorum* 424c10-425e7", *AP* 17, 375-395.

Miller, D.R. (2003), *The Third Kind in Plato's Timaeus*, Göttingen.

Mohr, R.D. (1985), *The Platonic Cosmology*, Leiden.

Moreschini, C. (1969), "Atteggiamenti scettici ed atteggiamenti dogmatici nella filosofia accademica", *PP* 24, 426-436.

— (1989), "Divinazione e demonologia in Plutarco e Apuleio", *Augustinianum* 29, 269-280.

— (1996), "Religione e filosofia in Plutarco", in Gallo, I. (ed.), *Plutarco e la religione. Atti del Sesto Convegno plutarcheo (Ravello, 29-31 maggio 1995)*, Napoli, 29-48.

— (2013), *Storia del pensiero cristiano tardo-antico*, Roma.

Morrow, G.R. (1950), "Necessity and Persuasion in Plato's *Timaeus*", *PhR* 59, 147-163.

N

Naiden, F.S., (2007), "The Fallacy of the Willing Victim", *JHS* 127, 61-73.

Napolitano Valditara, L. (1988), *Le idee, i numeri, l'ordine. La dottrina della "mathesis universalis" dall'Accademia antica al neoplatonismo*, Napoli.

Natali, C. (2009), *Aristotele. Etica Nicomachea*, Roma-Bari 2009.

Natoli, S., Sini, C., Vegetti, M. (1995), *Pensiero e parola: dialogo sul* Cratilo, *con traduzione e testo a fronte*, Milano.

Nikolaïdis, A.G. (ed.) (2008), *The unity of Plutarch's work:* Moralia *themes in the* Lives, *features of the* Lives *in the* Moralia, Berlin-New York.

Nilsson, M.P. (1949), *A History of Greek Religion*, Oxford.

O

Obsieger, H. (2013), *Plutarch:* De E apud Delphos. *Über das Epsilon am Apolltempel in Delphi: Einführung, Ausgabe und Kommentar*, Stuttgart.

Ogilvie, R.M. (1967), "The Date of *De Defectu Oraculorum*", *Phoenix* 21, 108-119.

Olster, D. (2004/2005), "Why the Oracles do not Speak (like before): Plutarch and the Riddle of Second-Century Religion", *Ploutarchos* 2, 55-70.

Oppé, A.P. (1904), The Chasm at Delphi, *JHS* 24, 214-240.

Opsomer, J. (1994), *L'âme du monde et l'âme de l'homme chez Plutarque*, in Valdés, M.G. (ed.), *Estudios sobre Plutarco: Ideas religiosas. Actas del III Simposio Internacional sobre Plutarco (Oviedo 30 de abril a 2 de mayo de 1992)*, Madrid, 33-49.

— (1996), *Divination and Academic "Scepticism" according to Plutarch*, in Van der Stockt, L. (ed.), *Plutarchea Lovaniensia: A Miscellany of Essays on Plutarch*, Leuven, 164-194.

— (1997), *Quelques réflexions sur la notion de Providence chez Plutarque*, in Schrader, C., Ramón, V., Vela, J. (eds.), *Plutarco y la Historia. Actas del V Simposio Español sobre Plutarco (Zaragoza, 20-22 de Junio de 1996)*, Zaragoza, 343-356.

— (1998), *In Search of the Truth. Academic Tendencies in Middle Platonism*, Turnhout.

— (2001), *Neoplatonist Criticisms of Plutarch*, in Pérez Jiménez, A., Casadesús Bordoy, F. (eds.), *Estudios Sobre Plutarco. Misticismo y Religiones Mistéricas en la Obra de Plutarco. Actas del VII Simposio Español Sobre Plutarco (Palma de Mallorca, 2-4 de Noviembre de 2000)*, Madrid, 187-199.

— (2002), *Is a Planet Happier than a Star? Cosmopolitanism in Plutarch's* On Exile, in Stadter, P., Van der Stockt, L. (eds.), *Sage and Emperor. Plutarch, Greek Intellectuals, and Roman Power in the Time of Trajan (98-117 A.D.)*, Leuven, 281-295.

— (2004), *Plutarch's* De animae procreatione in Timaeo. *Manipulation or Search for Consistency?*, in Adamson, P. (ed.), *Philosophy, Science, and Exegesis in Greek, Arabic and Latin Commentaries*, London 2004, I, 137-162.

— (2005a), *Plutarch's Platonism Revisited*, in Bonazzi, M., Celluprica, V. (eds.), *L'eredità platonica. Studi sul platonismo da Arcesilao a Proclo*, Milano, 161-200.

— (2005b), *Demiurges in Early Imperial Platonism*, in Hirsch-Luipold, R. (ed.), *Gott und Götter bei Plutarch. Götterbilder – Gottesbilder – Weltbilder*, Berlin, 51-99

— (2006a), *Éléments stoïciens dans le De E apud Delphos de Plutarque*, in Boulogne, J., Broze, M., Couloubaritsis, L. (eds.), *Les platonismes des premiers siècles de notre ère. Plutarque, L'E de Delphes*, Bruxelles, 147-170.

— (2006b), *Eros in Plutarchs moralischer Psychologie*, in Görgemanns, H. (ed.), *Plutarch. Dialog über die Liebe*, Tubingen, 208-235.

— (2007), *The place of Plutarch in the history of Platonism*, in Volpe Cacciatore, P., Ferrari, F. (eds.), *Plutarco e la cultura della sua età*, Napoli, 281-310.

— (2009), *M. Annius Ammonius, a Philosophical Profile*, in Bonazzi, M., Opsomer, J. (eds.), *The Origins of the Platonic System. Platonisms of the Early Empire and their Philosophical Context*, Leuven, 123-186.

— (2011), *Virtue, Fortune and Happiness in Theory and Practice*, in Roskam, G., Van der Stockt, L. (eds.), *Virtues for the People. Aspects of Plutarchan Ethics*, Leuven, 151-173.

— (2012), *Plutarch on the Division of the Soul*, in Barney, R., Brennan, T., Brittain, C. (eds.), *Plato and the Divided Self*, Cambridge, 311-330.

— (2014a), *Plutarch and the Stoics*, in Beck, M. (ed.), *A Companion to Plutarch*, Oxford, 88-103.

— (2014b), *Plutarch on the One and the Dyad*, in Sharples, R., Sorabji, R. (eds.), *Greek and Roman Philosophy 100 BC - 200 AD*, London, 379-395.

— (2014c), *The Middle Platonic Doctrine of Conditional Fate*, in d'Hoine, P., Van Riel, G. (eds.), *Fate, Providence and Moral Responsibility in Ancient, Medieval and Early Modern Thought: Studies in Honour of Carlos Steel*, Leuven, 137-167.

Opsomer, J., Steel, C. (1999), *Evil without a Cause: Proclus' Doctrine on the Origin of Evil, and its Antecedents in Hellenistic Philosophy*, in Fuhrer, T., Erler, M., Schlapbach, K. (eds.), *Zur Rezeption der hellenistischen Philosophie in der Spätantike, Akten der 1. Tagung der Karl-und-Gertrud-Abel-Stiftung, (Trier, 22-25 September 1997)*, Stuttgart, 229-260.

P

Parke, H.W. (1939), *A History of the Delphic Oracle*, Oxford.

— (1943), "The Days for Consulting the Delphic Oracle", *CQ* 37, 19-22.

— (1967), *Greek Oracles*, London.

— (1985), *The Oracles of Apollo in Asia Minor*, London.

Parke, H.W., Wormell, W. (1956), *The Delphic Oracle*, 2 vols., Oxford.

Parker, R. (1983), *Miasma. Pollution and Purification in Early Greek Religion*, Oxford.

Pelling, C.B.R. (1997), "Tragical Dreamer: Some Dreams in the Roman Historians", *G&R* 44, 197-213.

— (2005), "Plutarch's Socrates", *Hermathena* 179, 105-139.

Pépin, J. (1958), *Mythe et allégorie. Les origines grecques et les contestations judéo-chrétiennes*, Paris.

Phillips, J. (2002), "Plato's Psychogonia in Later Platonism", *CQ* 52, 231-247.

Piccardi, L. (2000), "Active Faulting at Delphi, Greece: Seismotechnic Remarks and a Hypothesis for the Geologic Environment of a Myth", *Geology* 28, 651-654.

Pleše, Z. (2010), *Plato and Parmenides in Agreement: Ammonius's Praise of God as One-Being in Plutarch's* The E at Delphi, in Turner, J.D., Corrigan, K. (eds.), *Plato's Parmenides and Its Heritage*. Volume 1: *History and Interpretation from the Old Academy to Later Platonism and Gnosticism*, Atlanta, 93-114.

Poilloux, J. (1986), *L'air de Delphes et la patine du bronze*, in Id. (éd), *D'Archiloque à Plutarque. Littérature et réalité. Choix d'articles de Jean Pouilloux*, Lyon, 267-279.

Préaux, C. (1973), *La lune dans la pensée grecque*, Bruxelles.

Price, S. (1985), *Delphi and Divination*, in Easterling, P., Muir, J. (eds.), *Greek Religion and Society*, Cambridge, 128-154.

Puech, B. (1992), "Prosopographie des amis de Plutarque", in ANRW 2.33.6, 4831-4893.

R

Ramelli, I., Lucchetta, G.A. (2004), *Allegoria.* I: *L'età classica*, Milano.

Reibnitz, B. von (1992), *Ein Kommentar zu Friedrich Nietzsche, "Die Geburt der Tragodie aus dem Geiste der Musik": Kap. 1-12*, Stuttgart.

Rescigno, A. (1995), *Plutarco. L'eclissi degli oracoli. Introduzione, testo critico, traduzione e commento*, Napoli.

Reydams-Schils, G. (1999), *Demiurge and Providence. Stoic and Platonic Readings of Plato's* Timaeus, Turnhout.

Richter, D.S. (2001), "Plutarch on Isis and Osiris: Text, Cult, and Cultural Appropriation", *TAPhA* 131, 191-216.

Ries, J. (1982), *Plutarque historien et theologien des doctrines dualistes*, in Ries, J., Janssens, Y., Sevrin, J. (eds.), *Gnosticisme et monde hellenistique. Actes du Colloque de Louvain-la-Neuve (11-14 mars 1980)*, Louvain, 146-163.

Rist, J.M. (2001), "Plutarch's *Amatorius*: A Commentary on Plato's Theories of Love?", *CQ* 51, 557-575.

Robbins, F.E. (1916), "The Lot Oracle at Delphi", *CPh* 11, 278-292.

Rohde, E. (1925), *Psyche. The Cult of Souls and Belief in Immortality among the Greeks*, Eng. trans., London.

Roig Lanzillotta, L., Muñoz Gallarte, I. (eds.) (2012), *Plutarch in the Religious and Philosophical Discourse of Late Antiquity*, Leiden-Boston.

Romeo, L. (1977), "Heraclitus and the Foundations of Semiotics", *Versus* 15, 73-90.

Romilly, J. de (1979), *La douceur dans la pensée grecque*, Paris.

Rosenberger, V. (ed.) (2013), *Divination in the Ancient World: Religious Options and the Individual*, Stuttgart.

Roskam, G. (1999), *Dionysius Sublimated. Plutarch's Thinking and Rethinking of the Traditional Dionysiac*, in Montes, C., Sanchez, O., Gallé, C. (eds.), *Plutarco, Dioniso y el vino. Actas del VI Simposio Español sobre Plutarco (Cádiz, 14-16 de mayo de 1998)*, Madrid, 433-445.

— (2001), *"And a great Silence filled the Temple..."*. *Plutarch on the Connections between Mystery Cults and Philosophy*, in Pérez Jiménez, A., Casadesús Bordoy, F. (eds.), *Estudios sobre Plutarco. Misticismo y religiones mistéricas en la obra de Plutarco. Actas del VII Simposio Español sobre Plutarco (Palma de Mallorca, 2-4 de noviembre de 2000)*, Madrid, 221-232.

— (2005), *On the Path to Virtue. The Stoic Doctrine of Moral Progress and its Reception in (Middle-) Platonism*, Leuven.

— (2006), *Apollon est-il vraiment le dieu du Soleil? La théorie plutarquéenne des symboles, appliquée à un cas concret*, in Boulogne, J., Broze, M., Couloubaritsis, L. (eds.), *Les platonismes des premiers siècles de notre ère: Plutarque, L'E de Delphes*, Bruxelles, 171-210.

— (2007), *A Commentary on Plutarch's De latenter vivendo*, Leuven 2007.

— (2010), *Socrates' daimonion in Maximus of Tyre, Apuleius, and Plutarch*, in Frazier, F., Leão, D. F. (eds.), *Tychè et Pronoia. La marche du monde selon Plutarque*, Coimbra, 93-108.

Roux, G. (1976), *Delphes: son oracle et ses dieux*, Paris.

Russell, D.A. (1973), *Plutarch*, London.

S

Sabbatucci, D. (1989), *Divinazione e cosmologia*, Milano.

— (1992), *Rito e sacrificio*, in Vegetti, M. (ed.), *L'esperienza religiosa antica*, Torino, 14-28.

Scannapieco, R. (2010), *I doni di Zeus, il dono di Prometeo. Strutture retoriche ed istanze etico-politiche nella riflessione plutarchea sulla τύχη*, in Frazier, F., Leão, D.F. (eds.), *Tychè et Pronoia. La marche du monde selon Plutarque*, Coimbra, 207-238.

— (2009), *Krasis oinou diken: amore coniugale e linguaggio del simposio nell'Amatorius di Plutarco*, in Ferreira, J.R., Leão, D.F., Troster, M., Dias, P.B. (eds.), *Symposion and Philanthropia in Plutarch*, Coimbra, 313-332.

Scarpi, P. (ed.) (2009-2011), *La rivelazione segreta di Ermete Trismegisto*, 2 vols., Milano.

Schachter, A. (2005), *Egyptian Cults and Local Elites in Boiotia*, in Bricault, L., Versluys, M.J., Meyboom, P.G.P. (eds.), *Nile into Tiber. Egypt in the Roman World. Proceedings of the III International Conference of Isis studies (Faculty of Archaeology, Leiden University, May 11-14 2005)*, Leiden-Boston, 364-391.

Schmidt, T.S. (2002), *Plutarch's Timeless Barbarians and the Age of Trajan*, in Stadter,

P.A., Van der Stockt, L. (eds.), *Sage and Emperor. Plutarch, Greek Intellectuals and Roman Power in the Time of Trajan, 98-117 A.D.*, Leuven, 57-71.

Schofield, M. (1986), "Cicero for and against Divination", *JRS* 76, 47-65.

Scott, M. (2014), *Delphi: A History of the Center of the Ancient World*, Princeton.

Settembrini, L. (2007), *Luciano di Samosata. Tutti gli scritti*, Milano 2007.

Sfameni Gasparro, G. (1993), "Oracolo, divinazione e profetismo nel mondo greco-romano da Augusto alla fine del II secolo", *RSB* 5, 11-42.

— (2002), *Oracoli, profeti e sibille: rivelazione e saggezza nel mondo antico*, Roma.

— (ed.) (2005), *Modi di comunicazione tra il divino e l'umano: tradizioni profetiche, divinazione, astrologia e magia del mondo mediterraneo antico. Atti del II seminario internazionale (Messina 21-22 marzo 2003), con la collaborazione di A. Cosentino, M. Monaca e E. Sanzi*, Cosenza.

Sharples, R.W. (2003), *Threefold Providence: the History and Background of a Doctrine*, in Sharples, R.W., Sheppard, A. (eds.), *Ancient Approaches to Plato's Timaeus*, London, 107-127.

— (2007), *The Stoic Background to the Middle Platonist Discussion of Fate*, in Bonazzi, M., Helmig, C. (eds.), *Platonic Stoicism – Stoic Platonism*, Leuven, 169-188.

Sieveking, W. (1972), *Plutarchi Moralia*, vol. III, editionem correctiorem curavit H. Gärtner, Lipsiae.

Sissa, G. (1990), *Greek Virginity*, Eng. trans., London.

Sorabji, R. (1993), *Animal Minds and Human Morals. The Origins of the Western Debate*, London.

— (2004), *The Philosophy of the Commentators, 200-600 AD: a Sourcebook*. I: *Psychology (with Ethics and Religion)*, London.

Sourvinou-Inwood, C. (1987), *Myth as History: The Previous Owners of the Delphic Oracle*, in Bremmer, J. (ed.), *Interpretations of Greek Mythology*, London, 215-241.

Soury, G. (1942a), "Plutarque, prêtre de Delphes. L'inspiration poétique", *REG* 55, 50-69.

— (1942b), *La démonologie de Plutarque. Essai sur les idées religieuses et les mythes d'un platonicien éclectique*, Paris.

— (1945), "Le problème de la Providence et le *De sera numinis vindicta* de Plutarque", *REG* 58, 163-179.

Struck, P.T. (2003), *Viscera and the Divine: Dreams as the Divinatory Bridge between the Corporeal and the Incorporeal*, in Noegel, S., Walker, J., Wheeler, B. (eds.), *Prayer, Magic, and the Stars in the Ancient and Late Antique World*, Pennsylvania, 125-136.

— (2004), *Birth of the Symbol. Ancient Readers at the Limits of Their Texts*, Princeton.

— (2013), "Plato and Divination", *ARG* 5, 17-34.

— (2016), *Divination and Human Nature. A Cognitive History of Intuition in Classical Antiquity*, Princeton-Oxford.

Stadter, P.A. (2004), *Plutarch: Diplomat for Delphi?*, in Bons, J., Kessels, T., Schenkeveld, D., de Blois, L. (eds.), *The Statesman in Plutarch's Works*. Volume I: *Plutarch's Statesman and his Aftermath: Political, Philosophical and Literary Aspects*, Leiden-Boston, 19-31.

— (2005), *Plutarch and Apollo of Delphi*, in Hirsch-Luipold, R. (Hrsg.), *Gott und die Götter bei Plutarch. Götterbilder – Gottesbilder – Weltbilder*, Berlin, 197-214.

Strobach, A. (1997), *Plutarch und die Sprachen. Ein Beitrag zur Fremdsprachenproblematik in der Antike*, Stuttgart.

Swain, S. (1989), "Plutarch: Chance, Providence, and History", *AJPh* 110, 272-302.

— (1991), "Plutarch, Hadrian, and Delphi", *Historia* 40, 318-330.

T

Tarrant, H. (2000), "Reason, Faith and Authority: some Platonist Debates about the Authority of the Teacher", *Sophia* 39, 46-63.

Tarrant, H., Baltzly, D. (eds.) (2006), *Reading Plato in Antiquity*, London.

— (2010), *Platonism before Plotinus*, in Gerson, L.P. (ed.), *The Cambridge History of Philosophy in Late Antiquity*, I, Cambridge, 63-99.

Teodorsson, S.T. (2010), *Plutarch's Interpretation of Plato's Cosmology: Plausible Exegesis or Misrepresentation?*, in Van der Stockt, L., Brenk, F.E. (eds.), *Gods, Daimones, Rituals, Myths and History of Religions in Plutarch's Works: Studies Devoted to Professor Frederick E. Brenk by the International Plutarch Society*, Utah, 419-435.

Thévenaz, P. (1938), *L'âme du monde: le devenir et la matière chez Plutarque, avec une traduction du traité "De la genèse de l'âme dans le Timée" (1re partie)*, Paris.

Thum, T. (2013), *Plutarchs Dialog* De E apud Delphos: *eine Studie*, Tübingen.

Timotin, A. (2012), *La démonologie platonicienne: histoire de la notion de* daimōn *de Platon aux derniers néoplatoniciens*, Leiden-Boston.

Tirelli, A. (2005), *Plutarco. Ad un governante incolto. Introduzione, testo critico, traduzione e commento*, Napoli.

Torraca, L. (1991), *Linguaggio del reale e linguaggio dell'immaginario nel* De sera numinis vindicta, in D'Ippolito, G., Gallo, I. (eds.), *Strutture formali dei Moralia di Plutarco. Atti del terzo convegno plutarcheo (Palermo, 3-5 maggio 1989)*, Napoli, 91-120.

Toye, D.L. (2000), "Plutarch on Poetry, Prose, and Politeia", *AncW* 31, 173-181.

Tredennick, H. (1933-1935), *Aristotle. Metaphysics*, 2 vols., London-Cambridge MA.

Turcan, R. (1975), *Mithras Platonicus: recherches sur l'hellénisation philosophique de Mithra*, Leiden.

— (1989), *Les cultes orientaux dans le monde romain*, Paris.

— (2003), "Les démons et la crise du paganisme gréco-romain", *RPhA* 21, 33-54.

Tusa Massaro, L. (2005), Εὐωδία. *La sintassi della "fraganza" in Plutarco*, in Pérez

Jiménez, A., Titchener, F.B. (eds.), *Valori letterari delle opere di Plutarco. Studi offerti al professore Italo Gallo dall'International Plutarch Society*, Malaga-Logan, 437-454.

V

Valgiglio, E. (1988a), *Divinità e religione in Plutarco*, Genova.

— (1988b), "La teologia in Plutarco", *Prometheus* 14, 253-265.

— (1991), *Dall ἵστωρ omerico al βίος plutarcheo, I*, in *Studi di filologia classica in onore di Giusto Monaco*, Palermo, 17-35.

— (1992), *Plutarco. Gli oracoli della Pizia. Introduzione, testo critico, traduzione e commento*, Napoli.

Van der Stockt, L. (1992), *Plutarch on τέχνη*, in Gallo, I. (ed.), *Plutarco e le scienze. Atti del IV Convegno plutarcheo (Genova-Bocca di Magra, 22-25 aprile 1991)*, Genova, 287-295.

— (1999), *Plutarch on* mania *and its therapy*, in Montes, C., Sanchez, O., Gallé, C. (eds.), *Plutarco, Dioniso y el vino. Actas del VI Simposio Español sobre Plutarco (Cádiz, 14-16 de mayo de 1998)*, Madrid, 517-526.

— (2011), *Some Aspects of Plutarch's View of the Physical World. Interpreting Causes of Natural Phenomena*, Candau Morón, J.M., González Ponce, F.J., Chávez Reino, A.L. (eds.), *Plutarco transmisor. Actas del X Simposio Internacional de la Sociedad Española de Plutarquistas (Sevilla, 12-14 de noviembre de 2009)*, Sevilla, 447-456.

Van Liefferinge, C. (1998), "Jamblique, lecteur de Plutarque?", *RPhA* 16, 37-53.

Vasiliu, A. (2009), *La contemplation selon Plutarque et Plotin (retour su le lien invisible)*, in Trottmann, C. (éd.), *Vie active et vie contemplative au Moyen Age et au seuil de la Renaissance*, Roma, 43-65.

Velde, H. te (1967), *Seth God of Confusion. A Study of his Role in Egyptian Mythology and Religion*, Leiden.

Verbeke, G. (1945), *L'Evolution de la doctrine du pneuma du stoicisme à Saint Augustin*, Paris-Louvain.

Vernant, J.-P., Vandermeersch, L., Gernet, J. (eds.) (1974), *Divination et rationalité*, Paris.

Vernière, Y. (1977), *Symboles et mythes dans la pensée de Plutarque. Essai d'interprétation philosophique et religieuse des Moralia*, Paris.

— (1990), "La théorie de l'inspiration prophétique dans les dialogues pythiques de Plutarque", *Kernos* 3, 359-366.

Veyne, P. (1986), "Une évolution du paganisme gréco-romain: injustice et piété des dieux, leurs ordres ou 'oracles'", *Latomus* 45, 259-283.

— (1999), "Prodiges, divination et peur des dieux chez Plutarque", *RHR* 216, 387-442.

Vlastos, G. (1939), "The Disorderly Motion in the *Timaios*", *CQ* 33, 71-83.

Vogel, C.J. de (1953), "On the Neoplatonic Character of Platonism and the Platonic Character of Neoplatonism", *Mind* 245, 43-64.

— (1954), "À la recherche des étapes précises entre Platon et le néoplatonisme", *Mnemosyne* 4, 111-122.

W

Wardle, D. (2006), *Cicero. On divination: Book 1*, Oxford.

Waterfield, R. (2008), *Plato. Timaeus and Critias*, Oxford 2008.

Watson, G. (1988), *Discovering the Imagination. Platonists and Stoics on* phantasia, in Dillon, J.M., Long, A.A. (eds.), *The Question of "Eclecticism". Studies in Later Greek Philosophy*, Berkeley-Los Angeles, 208-233.

West, M.L. (2003), *Homeric Hymns. Homeric Apocrypha. Lives of Homer, with an English Translation*, London-Cambridge MA.

Whittaker, C.R. (1965), "The Delphic Oracle: Belief and Behaviour in Ancient Greece – And Africa", *HThR* 58, 21-47.

Whittaker, J. (1969), "Ammonius on the Delphic E", *CQ* 19, 185-192.

Will, E. (1942), "Sur la nature du *pneuma* delphique", *BCH* 66-67, 161-175.

Z

Zagdoun, M.A. (1995), "Plutarque à Delphes", *REG* 108, 586-592.

Zambon, M. (2002), *Porphyre et le Moyen-Platonisme*, Paris.

— (2006), *Middle Platonism*, in Gill, M.L., Pellegrin, P. (eds.), *A Companion to Ancient Philosophy*, Oxford, 561-576.

Ziegler, K. (1964), *Plutarchos von Chaironeia*, Stuttgart.

Index Locorum